Philosophy and Its History

Philosophy and Its History

Aims and Methods in the Study of Early Modern Philosophy

Edited by

MOGENS LÆRKE,

JUSTIN E.H. SMITH,

and

ERIC SCHLIESSER

OXFORD
UNIVERSITY PRESS

OXFORD
UNIVERSITY PRESS

Oxford University Press is a department of the University of Oxford.
It furthers the University's objective of excellence in research, scholarship,
and education by publishing worldwide.

Oxford New York
Auckland Cape Town Dar es Salaam Hong Kong Karachi
Kuala Lumpur Madrid Melbourne Mexico City Nairobi
New Delhi Shanghai Taipei Toronto

With offices in
Argentina Austria Brazil Chile Czech Republic France Greece
Guatemala Hungary Italy Japan Poland Portugal Singapore
South Korea Switzerland Thailand Turkey Ukraine Vietnam

Published in the United States of America by
Oxford University Press
198 Madison Avenue, New York, NY 10016

Library of Congress Cataloging-in-Publication Data
Philosophy and its history : aims and methods in the study of early
modern philosophy / edited by Mogens Lærke, Justin E.H. Smith, and
Eric Schliesser.
pages cm
Includes bibliographical references.
ISBN 978–0–19–985714–2 (alk. paper) – ISBN 978–0–19–985716–6 (pbk. : alk. paper)
1. Philosophy, Modern–History. I. Lærke, Mogens, 1971- editor of compilation.
II. Smith, Justin E. H., editor of compilation. III. Schliesser, Eric,
1971- editor of compilation.
B791.P435 2013
190.9'03–dc23

1 3 5 7 9 8 6 4 2
Printed in the United States of America
on acid-free paper

Contents

Contributors

Roger Ariew is Professor and chair, Department of Philosophy, University of South Florida. Ariew is the author of *Descartes and the Last Scholastics* (Cornell University Press, 1999; 2nd edition, *Descartes among the Scholastics*, Brill, 2011)—co-author of *Historical Dictionary of Descartes and Cartesian Philosophy* (Scarecrow Press, 2003; 2nd edition forthcoming), editor and translator of such works as *Descartes, Philosophical Essays* (Hackett, 2000) and *Pascal, Pensées* (Hackett, 2005), and editor of the quarterly journal *Perspectives on Science: Historical, Philosophical, Social* (MIT Press).

Leo Catana is associate professor at the Division of Philosophy at the University of Copenhagen, and director of the Centre for Neoplatonic Virtue Ethics. Author of *The Historiographical Concept "System of Philosophy": Its Origin, Nature, Influence, and Legitimacy* (E.J. Brill, 2008); *The Concept of Contraction in Giordano Bruno's Philosophy* (Ashgate, 2005), and of numerous articles on Renaissance philosophy and Platonism in the Enlightenment period.

Michael Della Rocca is Andrew Downey Orrick Professor of Philosophy at Yale University. He is the author of two books, *Representation and the Mind–Body Problem in Spinoza* (Oxford University Press, 1996) and *Spinoza* (Routledge, 2008), and numerous articles in early modern philosophy and in contemporary metaphysics.

Mary Domski is associate professor of philosophy, University of New Mexico. She is the co-editor of *Discourse on a New Method: Reinvigorating the Marriage of History and Philosophy of Science* (Open Court, 2010), and has published a number of articles on Descartes, Locke, Newton, and Kant with special interest in the relationship between mathematics and philosophy.

Ursula Goldenbaum is associate professor of philosophy, Emory University. She is the author of *Appell an das Publikum. Die öffentliche Debatte in der* *deutschen Aufklärung 1687–1796*. 2 vols. (Akademie Verlag, 2004), *Einführung in die Philosophie Spinozas* (Hagen, 1993), co-editor of *Infinitesimal Differences: Controversies between Leibniz and His Contemporaries* (de Gruyter, 2008), and author of numerous articles on a wide variety of topics in early modern philosophy.

Julie R. Klein is associate professor of philosophy, Villanova University. She has published numerous articles on Medieval Jewish philosophy and Early Modern philosophy as well as in contemporary French reception of Spinoza.

Delphine Kolesnik-Antoine is associate professor of philosophy at the École Normale Supérieure de Lyon. Member of the *Centre d'Études en Rhétorique, Philosophie et Histoire des idées* (CERPHI, UMR 5037). Author of *L'Homme cartésien. La "force qu'a lame de mouvoir le corps." Descartes, Malebranche* (Presses Universitaires de Rennes, 2009), *Descartes. Une politique des passions* (Presses Universitaires de France, 2011), and of numerous articles on Cartesian philosophy.

Mogens Lærke is Senior Research Fellow, CNRS, France, and professor of philosophy, University of Aberdeen, Scotland. Member of the *Centre d'Études en Rhétorique, Philosophie et Histoire des idées* (CERPHI, UMR 5037) at the Ecole Normale Supérieure de Lyon. Author of *Leibniz lecteur de Spinoza. La genèse d'une opposition complexe* (Champion, 2008) and of some fifty articles, mainly on early modern philosophy. Editor of *The Use of Censorship in the Enlightenment* (Brill, 2009) and co-editor of *The Philosophy of the Young Leibniz* (Franz Steiner, 2009).

Yitzhak Y. Melamed is associate professor of philosophy at Johns Hopkins University. He is the author of *Spinoza's Metaphysics of Substance and Thought* (Oxford, 2012) and of several articles on Spinoza and Descartes. He is the co-editor of *Spinoza's Theological-Political Treatise* (with Michael Rosenthal: Cambridge, 2010) and *Spinoza and German Idealism* (with Eckart Förster: Cambridge 2012), and the editor of *The Young Spinoza* (Oxford: Forthcoming).

Alan Nelson is professor of philosophy, University of North Carolina at Chapel Hill. He is the author of a large number of influential articles in Early Modern philosophy, especially the Rationalists, and philosophy of economics.

Eric Schliesser is BOF Research Professor, philosophy and moral sciences, Ghent University. Co-editor of *New Voices on Adam Smith* (Routledge, 2006) and *Interpreting Newton* (Cambridge, 2012) as well as the author of *Adam Smith* (Forthcoming). He has published widely in philosophy of economics and early modern philosophy, including papers on Hume, Spinoza, Newton, Berkeley, Adam Smith, Sophie de Grouchy, and Huygens.

Tad M. Schmaltz is professor of philosophy at the University of Michigan, Ann Arbor. He has published articles and book chapters on various topics in early modern philosophy, and is the author of *Malebranche's Theory of the Soul* (Oxford, 1996), *Radical Cartesianism* (Cambridge, 2002), and *Descartes on Causation* (Oxford, 2008). He is a co-editor of the *Historical Dictionary of Descartes and Cartesian Philosophy* (Scarecrow, 2003), and is the editor of *Receptions of Descartes* (Routledge, 2005). Most recently he and the historian of science Seymour Mauskopf have co-edited the collection, *Integrating History and Philosophy of Science: Problems and Prospects* (Springer, 2012).

Justin E. H. Smith is professor of philosophy at Concordia University. He is the author of *Divine Machines: Leibniz and the Sciences of Life* (Princeton University Press, 2011), as well as the forthcoming *Nature, Human Nature, and Human Difference: Early Modern Philosophy and the Invention of Race*, also with Princeton University Press. He has edited or co-edited a number of volumes on the history of early modern philosophy.

Koen Vermeir is Senior Research Fellow, UMR 7219, CNRS, Paris. His most recent publications include the co-edited volumes *The Science of Sensibility. Reading Edmund Burke's Philosophical Enquiry* (Springer, 2012), *States of Secrecy. From Alchemy to the Atomic Bomb* (Special Issue of *British Journal for the History of Science*, 2012), and *Malebranche et l'imagination puissante* (Special Issue of *Rivista di Storia della Filosofia*, 2012). He also recently published a number of articles on early modern philosophy, science and technology, as well as on science policy.

Joanne Waugh is American Foundation for Greek Language and professor of Greek culture at the University of South Florida. She also serves as director of Graduate Studies and associate chair for the Department of Philosophy. She has published articles and book chapters on topics in ancient Greek philosophy, as well as aesthetics and art criticism, the philosophy of language, the history and philosophy of science, and feminist philosophy. She served as co-editor of *Hypatia* from 1995 to 1998, and of *Feminists Doing Ethics* (2002) and *Philosophical Feminism and Popular Culture* (forthcoming). She is currently working on a book on Plato's *Sokratikoi Logoi* in their historical context.

Introduction

ALMOST ALL PHILOSOPHERS agree that one cannot be properly trained in current philosophy without knowing something of either the historical development of the discipline or without some familiarity with the writings of certain canonical figures. Beyond acknowledging this requirement, however, there is very little agreement as to what relationship, exactly, the study of the history of philosophy should have to contemporary philosophy. Moreover, given that there is little consensus about the purpose that the historiography of philosophy should serve within philosophy as a whole, there is also little consensus about how historians of philosophy should go about their work, that is to say, about what kind of methodology to follow when approaching past philosophical texts. This volume takes a measure of the current range of views on this complicated issue and aims to show a way forward, for specialists in the history of philosophy as well as for philosophers with a theoretical interest in the question of the relationship of philosophy to its history and histories.

While there are many further, finer-grained distinctions to make, it seems that in the English-speaking world of philosophy at present there are two principal ways of thinking about this relationship. First, the history of philosophy is held to be a source of ideas and arguments that may be of use in current philosophy, and it is to be studied as a way of advancing in the resolution of problems of current interest. Second, it is supposed that the history of philosophy is to be studied and understood for its own sake and on its own terms, even when the problems of interest to the figures in this history have since fallen off the philosophical agenda. Representatives of the first line of thinking, who might be called "appropriationist," criticize defenders of the second approach, who might in turn be dubbed "contextualists," for abandoning the aim of making a positive contribution to current philosophy and instead engaging in "mere history."

Representatives of the contextualist approach criticize the appropriationists for sacrificing the original, intended meaning of historical doctrines on the altar of current philosophical fashion, and thus being culpable of a certain species of revisionism. The appropriationists can return the allegations made against them by arguing that there just is no way to really engage with the thoughts of a past philosopher other than by confronting his or her arguments with our own. Learning from past philosophers, and thus also paying tribute to their greatness, is necessarily to pull historical arguments out of the storehouse of history, dusting them off, and reactivating them in our own contemporary context. Consequently, the use of the history of philosophy for philosophy does not lie in the correct historical account of what the intentions of some past philosopher were but instead in the possible solutions that can be extracted from these texts to perennial problems of philosophy. In this fashion, it is simply not philosophically relevant whether the rational reconstructions of past philosophers one develops correspond to the intentions of that philosopher, as long as these reconstructions yield conceptual results and address contemporary concerns in an interesting way.

The contextualists, in turn, defend the principle laid down by Quentin Skinner that "[n]o agent can eventually be said to have meant or done something which he could never be brought to accept as a correct description of what he had meant or done." But to place Plato or Descartes or Hume in conversation with our own intellectual community, the contextualists worry, is inevitably to impute such unacceptable meanings or actions to past philosophers. It may be true that there is some set of problems that all of these thinkers were focused upon, and that continues to interest us today. But the problem with the "conversational" approach to the history of philosophy is that it is necessarily a one-way conversation: the long-dead figures from the past cannot respond with any more than what they have already said, whereas the living can continue adding and revising and advancing. The contextualist believes that the most urgent thing to do for the scholar of the history of philosophy is to make sure that we have properly understood the full set of reasons a historical figure had for addressing a certain philosophical problem and for attempting a certain solution to it.

It appears, then, that historians of philosophy are caught between their own Scylla and Charybdis, between either being untrue to the aims and intentions of the historical figures or abandoning the project of philosophy altogether in order to engage in social and cultural history, paleography, or the minute forensic work of the archival researcher. Meanwhile, a non-negligible part of the readership of the scholarly output of historians of, for example, early modern philosophy is instructors and students in introductory courses on the so-called Empiricists and Rationalists; these readers seek illumination of and background material to the canonical figures they teach and study. The potential tensions between the needs of scholarship and service to the discipline have barely been theorized.

In addition to the contextualist and appropriationist approaches practiced in Anglo-American philosophy, there is a third approach more familiar from Continental philosophy, in which one's philosophical position is developed dialectically with a tradition that is often simultaneously constructed for that purpose. Sometimes work done in this mode sets the agenda for renewed detailed engagement with the history of philosophy. Scholars working in this tradition tend not to agree with the contextualists that the best thing to do is to let past figures "speak for themselves" and even tend to doubt that we can know what they were saying independent of our own interest in using them for some end or another of our own. But they also often disagree with the appropriationists, who tend to mine past philosophy for timelessly good arguments; for Continental historians, philosophy, as a dialectical activity, tends to be understood as a fundamentally historical process rather than a timeless source of truths. Thus, a Continental historian will not mine the past for usable nuggets, but will rather attempt to build on the past in a way that is both attentive to it and, at the same time, seeking to overcome its historically conditioned limitations. A scholar in this tradition is, like the appropriationist, eminently a philosopher rather than a historian, to the extent that she rejects the task of recovering the past figure's world, and instead prefers to use the past figure to make sense of her own world. As with the appropriationist, though, there is the lingering danger that this sort of scholarship does not do justice to the actual concerns of the historical figure whose work has selectively been called into service.

What, then, is to be done? Most significantly, the once widespread view of history as strictly irrelevant to the current practice of philosophy, warranted by a certain interpretation of logical positivism, has by now gone almost completely extinct. As a result, in most philosophical circles one no longer needs to expend any effort justifying an interest in Descartes, say, as such. One needs only to give an account of how Descartes relates to one's philosophical interests. Another significant development in the English-speaking world has been an increase in attention to original-language texts, to the less familiar or unpublished works of philosophers, to the so-called minor figures with whom the major thinkers were in contact, and to the development of ideas and arguments over the course of a philosopher's life. Thirty years ago, among

English-speaking philosophers the names "Descartes" and "Kant" were taken to stand for fixed sets of views, and ones that could be expressed in English just as well as in German, French, or Latin. Today, as a result of the work of Daniel Garber and many others, this once common approach to historical figures now seems to most researchers far too simplistic, and today almost everyone at least strives for a somewhat higher-resolution picture of the actual historical person who stands behind the familiar arguments. There has also been, in recent years, a growing interest in questions of methodology in the history of philosophy.

This volume aims to create an inclusive discussion such that a range of different methodological approaches from different traditions of philosophy can be read alongside each other and be seen in sometimes very critical conversation with each other. In order to achieve this we invited leading specialists in what is known as "early modern" philosophy (roughly the period between Descartes and Kant) to address the methodology of the history of philosophy.

The present collection reflects the rapid internationalization of research that has opened up the field to a wide range of approaches much less (if at all) present on the horizon of Anglo-American scholarship, say, thirty years ago. This increase in exchange between various national traditions has heightened the sensitivity among scholars to methodological issues. Moreover, it has given rise to a sort of second-order, metaphilosophical problem. For the historian of philosophy trying to address these different approaches in a balanced fashion, and extracting something useful and coherent from them, questioning the role of her discipline within philosophy as a whole is no longer just a question of how philosophy relates to itself and its history. It is also a question of how various traditions for thinking about such meta-philosophical issues relate *to each other*, and of reflecting on the conditions under which these traditions may inform each other in a productive way.

We have assembled prominent and upcoming scholars, with a wide range of philosophical orientations, to contribute new essays on the subject of the relationship between philosophy and the history of philosophy. The contributors include both specialists in the history of philosophy as well as philosophers who work primarily on current problems in systematic philosophy but who have a pronounced interest in history. The contributors have been chosen among specialists working in the area of early modern philosophy, broadly defined. This choice does of course to some extent reflect the areas of specialization of the editors. There are, however, also good, intrinsic reasons for focusing on this period. Ancient philosophy, and to some extent medieval philosophy, are areas in the history of philosophy that are already and necessarily very much informed by historical considerations. It is generally recognized that any philosophical exchange between contemporary philosophers and ancient philosophy requires the historical work of philologists and historians in order to be possible at all. Not so with early modern philosophy. Early modern philosophers are often taken to be those who are "closest" to ourselves in terms of basic problems, concerns, and approaches. They often write in the vernacular rather than Latin, thus reducing the need for translations. For these reasons, it is with the early modern philosophers that basic questions of how to approach them—as if they were colleagues with whom you discuss philosophy in the hallway of the department, or rather as if they were historical aliens speaking a different philosophical tongue—come up with the greatest urgency. From the point of view of practical methodology, the relation between early modern philosophy and philosophy is the most problematic, and therefore also the most interesting, interface between the history of philosophy and contemporary philosophy. The volume will, however, be of interest to a wide variety of specialists, teachers, and reflective students of other periods as well.

The contributions to the volume all seek to go beyond the standard ways of doing history of philosophy sketched here. The chapters can be roughly divided into four general orientations. First, the largest group of chapters (Lærke, Smith, Vermeir, Goldenbaum, and Waugh and Ariew) advocate methods that promote history of philosophy as an unapologetic, autonomous enterprise with its own criteria within philosophy. Within this group, Lærke, Smith, Vermeir, and Goldenbaum offer competing ways to professionalize the history of philosophy by focusing on its proper method. They offer exemplars from a wide variety of disciplinary practices: Lærke turns to anthropology to conceptualize a notion of historical truth embedded in a controversy; Smith turns to archaeology as a model for an interdisciplinary approach to the history of philosophy; Vermeir explores the merits of genealogical approaches; and Goldenbaum models the historian of philosophy on the careful detective who seeks out clues. The first three chapters also include trenchant criticism of Skinner's influential methodological writings. Ariew and Waugh make the case for the benefits of a contextual approach to history of philosophy and remind us of the days when factually accurate history of philosophy could not be taken for granted.

Second, three chapters (Catana, Klein, and Kolesnik-Antoine) can be seen as historicizing the history of philosophy from within. They argue that history of philosophy without historiography is blind to highly relevant features of its past. Catana focuses his account on the development of the very idea of a "systematic philosophy." Kolesnik-Antoine explores how an image of what Cartesian philosophy essentially is was constructed by nineteenth-century scholars. Klein explores the methodological lessons that can drawn from within the past philosophical texts we study, focusing in particular on Spinoza's conception of philosophical and non-philosophical readers in order to discuss what kinds of readers of philosophical text *we* are, and *must* be, from a Spinozist perspective.

Third, four chapters (Della Rocca, Schliesser, Nelson, and Melamed) argue for history of philosophy as a means toward making contributions to contemporary philosophy. In particular, they agree that the history of philosophy plays a crucial role in overcoming the confines of present philosophy. Drawing on the principle of sufficient reason, Della Rocca takes aim at what he calls the "method of intuition," which he claims privileges common sense. Nelson also expresses reservations about the role of common sense in the way the contemporary emphasis on enduring problems in philosophy blinds us to the systematic nature of significant (and often incompatible) philosophical projects of the past and present. Yet another attack on common sense is mounted by Melamed, who argues against the principle of charity, which he claims prevents us from using the history of philosophy as a way to improve our philosophical understanding. Schliesser advocates creating new concepts through which past and present philosophy can be fused. Della Rocca and Schliesser argue their case by re-telling the history of the origins of analytic philosophy. Representative of all four chapters is Nelson's insistence that there is a crucial difference between an analytical presentation, which he embraces, and substantive analytical philosophical commitments, which he rejects for the historian of philosophy.

Finally, two chapters (Domski, Schmaltz) explore the relationship between the history of philosophy and the history of science. They both do so by deploying the resources of a classic (1992) article by Margaret Wilson. Against the hopes of the generation following Thomas Kuhn, Schmaltz argues that history of philosophy and history of science are distinct approaches that can sometimes learn from each other but should remain separate. By contrast, Domski argues that a more integrated approach is possible, but only if we abandon the idea that the past is a reservoir of conceptual resources. Rather she insists that philosophical reflection on the past can enrich the foundations of present debates.

1

The Anthropological Analogy and the Constitution of Historical Perspectivism

Mogens Lærke

1. Introduction

IT IS A noteworthy fact that among historians of early modern philosophy the question of methodology, i.e., of *how* it should be done, often tends to be swallowed up by worries about *why* it should be done. To some extent, it is also an unsurprising fact. To be sure, Gary Hatfield is right to say that "there is little reason for today's contextually oriented historians to consider themselves lonely revolutionaries. Nor should they bemoan a lack of appreciation from ahistorical colleagues."[1] Nonetheless, the history of philosophy remains a subordinate topic in most Anglo-Saxon philosophy departments. Moreover, framing the question in this fashion has become somewhat of a standard approach. Hence, even if their philosophical colleagues may no longer scoff (so much) at the history of philosophy and no longer ask (as much) for justification as previously for the peculiar activity historians of philosophy are engaged in, the latter largely continue to behave as if it was the case.

It must however be possible to study the history of philosophy in a way that is both methodologically conscious and does not sound like a perpetual excuse. Why that is desirable is not only a question of institutional self-vindication. The apologetic mode of methodological discourse has done much damage in creating considerable confusion about the kind of truth historians of philosophy are supposed to dislodge from past philosophical texts. In this chapter, I say something about what is required for the establishment

1. Hatfield (2005), 88–89.

of a historiography of philosophy overcoming this problem, i.e., what I call an unapologetic historiography of philosophy. Next, and more important, I discuss one way of studying the history of philosophy that satisfies those requirements. I argue how an oft-repeated comparison between the historiography of philosophy and contemporary cultural anthropology, habitually invoked in order to support arguments in favor of relativist if not outright skeptical arguments about historical truth, can be put to a more constructive use. First, by spelling out the epistemological implications of some methodological intuitions most acutely formulated by anthropologists, I sketch out a method for the historiography of philosophy dubbed *historical perspectivism*. This method stresses the role that contextually internal perspectives play in the constitution of the true historical meaning of past philosophical texts. By such internal perspectives, I understand interpretations of texts developed by agents moving within the relevant historical context, i.e., agents who took an active part in the historical debates to which the text is a contribution. Finally, I discuss how historical perspectivism is also a form of *historical actualism*, in that it excludes from the horizon of correct historical reconstruction perspectives or interpretations that are merely contextually *possible*, including only those that are actually deployed within the relevant context.

2. *Requirements for an Unapologetic Historiography of Philosophy*

I believe that an unapologetic historiography of philosophy requires that we respect the following three points.

First, one must do away with the misconception that the historiography of philosophy will *ever* manage to justify itself vis-à-vis other sub-disciplines by posing as philosophy *simpliciter*. Requiring that historians of philosophy should simultaneously "do philosophy" puts them in the impossible position of having to cater for historical exactitude and philosophical truth at the same time, constantly running from one camp to the other. One readily available issue from this exhausting exercise is to mediate between these two poles by means of a philosophy of history, defending the idea that there is something inherently historical about the philosophical enterprise as such. Hegel's history of philosophy is the most famous variant of such a strategy. Charles Taylor is a more recent example of a historian of philosophy taking that route.[2] While often ingenious,

---

2. Taylor (1984), 17–30.

solutions of this kind, however, suffer from one fatal strategic flaw. They require that our philosophical colleagues be converted to the philosophy of history proposed before they are properly conditioned to see the value of the history of philosophy. But most of them are as unlikely to do that as they are to recognize the value of the history of philosophy in the first place.[3] Justifying the historiography of philosophy requires that the discipline be defined in such a way that it caters *equally* for a wide range of possible philosophical positions and not only for positions that fall within the category of philosophy of history. However, the most straightforward option for doing that is equally desisting from catering for them at all. Historians of philosophy would then simply behave toward their colleagues in other branches of philosophy as the latter already behave toward each other, including toward historians of philosophy. It would be perceived as unreasonable if historians of philosophy demanded that contemporary epistemologists should conduct their research in such a way that it would be helpful for the historiography of philosophy. So why should the reverse be the case?

Next, it should be emphasized that the historiography of philosophy deals with the interpretation of past philosophical texts.[4] Whatever counts as "philosophical" is a matter of discussion and subject to considerable historical variation. One may also wonder when exactly it is that a philosophical text becomes part of the "past." However, it is uncontroversial that the interpretation of past philosophical texts is indeed what the historian of philosophy is concerned with. This does not imply that traces of historical practices other than writing, such as, for example, scientific measurement and experimentation, are irrelevant for the study of the history of philosophy.[5] It does not mean either that what counts as past philosophical text should necessarily be narrowly defined as words written on pages.[6] It simply means that the study of whatever counts as non-textual traces by definition only is relevant for the historian of philosophy to the extent that they are conducive for understanding the meaning of primary texts. Now, it is a radically different question to ask about the correct interpretation of a text than to ask why we should take an interest in or adopt the position it propounds. The historian of philosophy must then, qua historian, emphatically distinguish the levels of *meaning* and *truth* of historical texts and restrict his professional business

3. For a reaction of this kind, see Graham (1982), 37–52.

4. See Garber (2001), 235; Kenny (2005), 22.

5. See Vermeir, this volume.

6. See Smith, this volume.

to the reconstruction of the former. In other words, he must from the outset be emphatically indifferent to the philosophical merits of the doctrine under scrutiny and focus exclusively on the historical meaning of the texts. Such unapologetic antiquarianism is not valuable for philosophy *in spite of* its disregard for the concerns of "real" philosophers.[7] In fact, being unapologetically antiquarian is a necessary condition for having any such value. For, as Michael Ayers and Daniel Garber note, "we must certainly understand past philosophies before we can learn either from their insights or from their mistakes."[8]

Finally, the historian of philosophy cannot do without a principled conception of what *true historical meaning* of past texts *is*, i.e., about what it *means* to have acquired a correct historical interpretation of a past philosophy. Indeed, the question concerning the nature of true historical meaning, or of what will count as a correct historical interpretation and why, is the one genuine philosophical question—and a meta-philosophical question at it—with which the historian of philosophy should be concerned, much in the same way as a moral philosopher is concerned with what morality is, an epistemologist with what truth is, and a metaphysician with what being is. Moreover, the historiography of philosophy cannot do without a corresponding method for accessing this true historical meaning. This requirement should, however, by no means be taken as a rejection of methodological pluralism. There still can be, indeed are, different types of historiography of philosophy with different assumptions about the nature of true historical meaning.

Hence, to summarize: (i) the historiography of philosophy is an independent sub-discipline of philosophy and is not accountable to any other sub-discipline; (ii) it is concerned with the correct historical interpretation of past philosophical texts, not with the philosophical merits of the doctrines it reconstructs; and (iii) it cannot do without some notion about the nature of true historical meaning, including a corresponding method for dislodging it from the texts. These three points summarize the fundamental requirements for an unapologetic historiography of philosophy.

In the following sections, I turn to the second and more substantial part of this chapter. It concerns *one* way in which I believe it is possible to satisfy these requirements. It is a methodology that I have dubbed "historical perspectivism." In order to preempt fatal misunderstanding, it should be noted that other theories labeled "historical perspectivism" already exist, but that

7. See Garber (2005), 145.

8. See Garber and Ayers (1998), 4.

these homonymous theories have little in common with what I propose. Among philosophers, "historical perspectivism" evokes the theses developed by Friedrich Nietzsche in *On the Use and Abuse of History for Life*, where he complained that the writing of history should be put in the service of "life" and that nineteenth-century German history writing failed to do that. It is not a moustache I have any intention of growing. For a Nietzschean, the very ambition of writing unapologetic history of philosophy would undoubtedly seem like yet another fiction about writing a *history* which is not already a *use* of history, and dismiss it as an "antiquarian" historiography of the kind denounced by Nietzsche as "a repulsive rage for blind for collecting, a restless raking together of everything that ever existed."[9] For those better acquainted with literary theory, "historical perspectivism" is also associated with a particular type of approach to literary works from about half a century ago, mainly represented by Erich Auerbach. Auerbach himself thought of his historical perspectivism in terms of a "historical relativism," although he denied that any skeptical conclusions should be drawn from it.[10] Like it is for Nietzsche, "historical perspectivism" is for Auerbach a theory according to which the historian necessarily is involved in the constitution of the historical truth he discovers. It thus turns on the idea that *contextually external* perspectives, and in particular our own, necessarily determine how we construct the meaning of historical texts. These brands of "historical perspectivism" are unlikely to have much appeal to contemporary historians of philosophy. Fortunately, they have little in common with the position I advocate in the following, namely, that *contextually internal* perspectives on past philosophical texts are constitutive of the true historical meaning of those texts.

3. The Anthropological Analogy

When reading various methodological pieces written by historians of philosophy over the last fifty years, one cannot help being struck by how often past philosophical texts are conveyed as products of some alien culture and the historian of philosophy correspondingly described as a sort of intellectual time-traveler. The image, of course, has a distinguished pedigree. Descartes famously writes in *Discours de la méthode* that "conversing with those of past centuries is much the same as traveling," explaining that "it is good to know

9. See Nietzsche (1983), 75.

10. See Auerbach (1967), 262.

something of the customs of various peoples, so that we may judge our own more soundly and not think that everything contrary to our own ways is irrational, as those who have seen nothing of the world ordinarily do."[11] In his contribution to Peter Hare's *Doing Philosophy Historically*, Daniel Garber quotes Descartes's text when accounting for his own practice of "disinterested history."[12] By traveling foreign intellectual lands, he argues, we will be rewarded with a "certain perspective on our own lives."[13] Along similar lines, Quentin Skinner argues that doing intellectual history may teach us how "those features of our own arrangements which we may be disposed to accept as traditional or even 'timeless' truths may in fact be the merest contingencies of our peculiar history and social structure."[14] To a great many historians of philosophy, the value of studying past philosophical texts is directly proportional to the extent to which grasping their meaning forces us to challenge our own basic epistemic assumptions.[15] It is, however, far from clear that there is any point in traveling into the lands of past philosophy if we do this only to behave like tourists strolling through the historical texts like freshly disembarked cruise guests pouring into the local market, hunting for exotic souvenirs vaguely reminding us of other worlds than our own. We need a clearly formulated notion of how to go about grasping the truth of a foreign philosophy steeped in a historically distant intellectual culture.

In this context an oft-repeated and yet underexploited analogy between the historiography of philosophy and cultural anthropology can be of some help. The analogy is often invoked by historians of philosophy when stressing the difficulty of gaining access to the meaning of past philosophy, arguing that understanding, say, Francis Bacon, is just as difficult as decoding the culture of pygmies in Cameroon. Alasdair MacIntyre, for example, points out that the study of "culturally and intellectually alien periods in the history of philosophy may make us aware of modes of philosophical thought and enquiry whose forms and presuppositions are so different from ours that we are unable to discover sufficient agreement in concepts and standards to provide grounds for deciding between the rival and incompatible claims embodied in such modes without begging the question," and he adds: "that precisely

11. Descartes (1984–1991), I, 113.

12. Garber (1988a), 34–37.

13. Ibid., 35.

14. Skinner (1969), 52.

15. See, for example, Williams (2006), 258–59, 263–64, or Rorty (1984), 51.

the same type of issue could obviously arise in defining our relationship to the mode of philosophical activity carried on within some alien cultural tradition has of course been noticed on occasion by anthropologists."[16] Here, the anthropological analogy serves to illustrate a somewhat negative claim and supports, willingly or not, historical relativism or even skepticism.[17] In what follows, however, I recycle the analogy in a more affirmative mode. Rather than invoking the methodological tribulations of cultural anthropologists in order to lament the difficulties of reconstructing the "alien" intentions underlying historical utterances, I prefer turning to cultural anthropologists to see what methodological tools they have in fact developed in order perform the seemingly impossible task of decoding alien utterances; how, against all odds, they have in fact managed to grasp at least some of the things that Cameroonian pygmies "are up to," as Clifford Geertz would put it.

4. Fieldwork in the History of Philosophy

Let me first anticipate an obvious objection. According to Bronislaw Malinowski's original formulation, the proper conditions for ethnographic fieldwork "consist mainly in cutting oneself off from the company of other white men, and remaining in as close contact with the natives as possible, which really can only be achieved by camping right in their villages."[18] In other words, the cultural anthropologist must make an active effort to immerse himself deeply in the culture he studies. An historian of philosophy, however, cannot aspire to such immersion, because the intellectual culture he studies no longer exists. Thus inescapably confined to the proverbial armchair, barred by time itself from that authentic world of the great cultural outdoors that the anthropologist prides himself in taking part in, the historian of philosophy has no use for hiking boots.

The dilemma is of course well known to "real" historians, i.e., those historians who write about the Thirty Years War, sixteenth-century trading routes, or the intricate politics of Cardinal Richelieu. They can never go back and verify whether the information they obtain from the texts handed over from the past provide an accurate account of that past, i.e., whether the sources provide reliable representations of the experienced, historical reality of warfare,

16. MacIntyre (1984), 34.

17. For a good example, incidentally appealing to Descartes's travel metaphor, see Lepenies (1984), 146–47.

18. Malinowski (1922), 6.

trading, or politics. I am, however, unconvinced that this is an adequate description of the situation for the historian of philosophy whose relation to "historical reality" is different. The written material the historian of philosophy works on simply cannot be considered "sources to" historical reality in the sense that seventeenth-century documents on Richelieu's premiership are considered sources to the political reality of early modern France. It is a trademark of intellectual cultures that they *happen* in writing, i.e., their being written is to a large extent how they *occur* and not just how they are *registered*. For the historian of philosophy, the texts he studies just *are* the historical reality under scrutiny, not a *representation* of it. In that respect, the work of the historian of philosophy is closer to that of an archaeologist excavating past monuments than to that of a "regular" historian studying historical sources: he works with texts as if they were ruins, vestiges, or monuments of philosophical meaning to be excavated, dusted off, and rebuilt.[19]

There is however an even better analogy available. In an insightful reflection on Wilhelm Dilthey, Lepenies evokes a certain family resemblance between the archival work of the historian of philosophy and the cultural anthropologist's work in the field:

> Listening to Dilthey as he talks about the necessity to reconstruct the context and to retrace the development of philosophical systems not just from published books but from the philosophers' original manuscripts, he resembles a field-worker more than an armchair-philologist. Dilthey's history of philosophy is an anthropology carried out in the archive.[20]

There is much truth to this account. Historically at least, the birth of modern historiography in mid-nineteenth-century Germany—beginning with Leopold Ranke—was characterized by an approach to archival work in many ways similar to anthropological fieldwork.[21] But there is more than just historical truth to this when it comes to the history of philosophy, given its particular focus on *texts*. If, here putting to one side the question of participation, anthropological fieldwork essentially consists in prolonged immersion in the culture in question and the refusal to rely on non-native informants, then spending long periods of time reading the texts of Leibniz, Bayle, etc. just *is*

19. See Smith, this volume.

20. Lepenies (1984), 149–50.

21. See Eskildsen (2008), 430–33.

doing fieldwork in seventeenth-century intellectual culture. In fact, the historian of philosophy moves from the armchair to the great outdoors as easily as he shifts from reading a commentary to opening a volume containing his primary text.

Now, importantly, if the field of investigation is the past philosophical *texts* on the library shelves, then this also implies that *philosophers* are *not* the object under investigation. Let me linger a bit on that point by considering a fatally careless account of the intellectual historian's task by Richard Rorty. According to Rorty, the intellectual historian should proceed like the anthropologist "who wants to know how primitives talk to fellow-primitives as well as how they react to instructions from missionaries. For this purpose he tries to get inside their heads, to think in terms which he would never dream of employing at home."[22] The passage is a good example of the ubiquity of the anthropological analogy in the methodological literature. The formulation is, however, unfortunate on several accounts. First, cultural anthropologists take no interest in the inside of people's heads. As Geertz writes: "The trick is not to get yourself into some inner correspondence of spirit with your informant. Preferring, like the rest of us, to call their souls their own, they are not going to be altogether keen about such an effort anyway. The trick is to figure out what the devil they think they are up to."[23] Next, for analogous reasons, historians of philosophy have no interest either in what the texts may tell him about the inside of past philosophers' heads.[24] On pains of violating the maxim that the historiography of philosophy aims at understanding the meaning of past philosophical texts, one cannot slide toward the standpoint that this meaning is reducible to the representation of original authorial intentions. The relation of representation is exactly the reverse. Studying the biography of an author, for example, helps the historian of philosophy reconstruct one representation among others of the philosophical text, i.e., namely, the particular understanding of the text that is the author's own. Now, there may still be good reasons for privileging the author's own representation/interpretation of his text. But there is no good reason for doing *more* than that and grant the author complete authority over it.[25]

22. Rorty (1984), 50.

23. Geertz (1983), 58.

24. Ibid. 9–10. To be fair, Rorty gets it right when writing that "intellectual history consists of descriptions of what the intellectuals were up to at a given time, and of their interaction with the rest of society" (op. cit., 68; see also Rorty, Schneewind, Skinner (1984), 12).

25. See Hatfield (2005), 97; Skinner (1972), 405.

Cutting in this way the umbilical cord from textual meaning to authorial intention gives rise to concerns about how to situate philosophical texts in history. For, if it is not by reference to an author writing at a specific place at a specific time, how is a text qualified as "historical" to receive a meaning in any essential way related to some specific point in history justifying that qualification? If the historical meaning of Spinoza's *Tractatus theologico-politicus*, for example, cannot be reduced to what Spinoza had in mind when he wrote it, then what prevents the text from floating freely in history, the true historical meaning being whatever the text has meant at any given time in history, including today? In a certain way I believe philosophical texts do float in that way. The historian of philosophy should not necessarily focus narrowly on the time when a text was written, but can also focus on the subsequent history of the text, its transmission and reception. It seems reductive to think that the history of reception cannot *add* anything to the meaning of the text, but only either *repeat* or *misrepresent* the original meaning intended by the author. For example, when John Toland in the fourth and fifth *Letters to Serena* criticizes Spinoza for "having given no account of how matter comes to be mov'd" and having ignored that option that "motion is essential to matter," it is no rare occurrence among commentators to simply interpret this as a clumsy misreading of Spinoza. Such interpretations, however, overlook the crucial fact that Toland's text is a contribution to an early eighteenth-century debate between Toland, Leibniz, and Johann Georg Wachter. Hence, as Tristan Dagron has shown, even though Toland refers directly to Spinoza's texts in the *Letters*, he is not so much discussing Spinoza as he is refuting Wachter's interpretation of Spinoza in *Elucidarius Cabalisticus* in an attempt to show how his own brand of pantheism might prove as efficient a solution to certain constitutive problems with traditional Cartesian mechanism as Leibniz's rehabilitation of substantial forms.[26] Spinoza himself, it seems, has simply spiraled out of the zone of contextual relevance for the simple reason that in the four decades that separate the publication of the *Opera posthuma* in 1677 and Toland's *Letters* from 1704, the intellectual context for the discussion of Spinoza's text has changed to such a degree that Spinoza arguably would not recognize himself in it at all. Hence, the Spinozism we encounter in the *Letters to Serena* is, as Pierre-François Moreau would put it, a "Spinozism without Spinoza."[27] Nonetheless, we would still want to be able to say that Spinoza's *texts* play an

26. See Dagron (2009), 167–259.

27. See Moreau (2007), 289–97.

important role in the constitution of this "Spinozism without Spinoza" and, conversely, that this "Spinozism without Spinoza" *in this context* contributes to the true historical meaning of Spinoza's texts.

So how are we to proceed if we want to maintain that the history of reception can teach us something essential about the true historical meaning of a text, but without ending up completely uprooting the text from history as such? I believe that Skinner is right in stressing that past philosophical texts must be studied as concrete interventions in concrete historical debates that have been produced in response to other such interventions and that in turn will provoke the production of yet other interventions.[28] The meaning of a past philosophical text is in an essential way determined by the historical debate that the text is considered a contribution to by those who write or read it.[29] The interpretation of a past philosophical text, then, should take the form of a study of the relations that the text entertains with other philosophical or non-philosophical texts that contribute to the same historical debate as it does. Thus, in summary, what the historian of philosophy should be interested in is not so much isolated individual texts as it is texts insofar as they are precisely situated in larger *clusters of texts* all historically placed around a given *controversy*, be it local (e.g., the 1697 controversy in the *Journal des Sçavans* between Leibniz and Régis on the relations between Descartes and Spinoza) or more global (e.g., the controversies on *jus circa sacra* in Holland from Grotius to Spinoza). Determining the meaning of some text is then nothing but determining the role the text plays as a concrete intervention in some historical debate and situating the text in a complex network of intellectual positions actually in play at the time.

A single text may be an element in a multitude of such clusters. It is up to the historian of philosophy interested in the past philosophical text to pick the controversy he will study and to identify the exact cluster of texts he will pitch his tent next to. Exactly how such clusters are to be circumscribed is, I suspect, a somewhat pragmatic process involving some initial provisional determination of the field, followed by interrogations put to the intellectual agents within that field about the exactitude of the initial circumscription. In any case, I would resist providing a priori conceptual principles for the circumscription of such clusters, because this would be yielding to the temptation of proposing yet another rudimentary philosophy of history. What is, however, more important at present is to realize that while the initial determination of

28. Skinner (1969), 45–46.

29. Ibid., 37.

a given cluster may have, indeed should have, something empirical, pragmatic, or even intuitive to it, it is still the case—as I argue in the following section—that once a cluster *is* determined, the restrictions upon what will count as historically true interpretation of the texts taking part in it is given by exact principles that have nothing empirical, pragmatic, or intuitive about them.

Hence, to summarize, the relevant intellectual context for establishing the true historical meaning of a given past philosophical text is circumscribed by the totality of other texts contributing to the historically determined controversy to which the text in question is also a contribution, the "controversy" being here defined as a given cluster of texts that historically "gathers" around the text in question and that, as it were, constitute a historical commentary on that text. This determination will be important since it allows for a principled distinction between interpretive perspectives on a given text that are contextually internal or external, and thus provides a criterion for what I in the following will term *historical immanence*.

5. Historical Perspectivism

It is a truism among contextually inclined historians of philosophy that the philosophies of dead philosophers should be reconstructed "on their own terms," meaning by this that we are bound to misrepresent their views if we employ the conceptual categories of contemporary philosophy as an interpretive grid for reading their texts. Gary Hatfield, for example, while expounding the merits of his "historically oriented philosophical methodology," invokes the importance of "taking past texts seriously on their own terms, seeking to understand the problems and projects of past philosophy as they were, instead of only seeking a reading that solves a current philosophical problem."[30] The view is often associated with the fundamental rule of historical reconstruction stated by Skinner, namely, that "no agent can eventually be said to have meant or done something which he could never have been brought to accept as a correct description of what he had meant or done."[31] Hence Rorty explains that "when we respect Skinner's maxim we shall give an account of the dead thinker 'in his own terms,' ignoring the fact that we should think ill of anyone who still used those terms today."[32] I have some misgivings about

30. Hatfield (2005), 91, 97.

31. Skinner (1969), 28.

32. Rorty (1984), 54.

Skinner's formula that I return to later, but I remain sympathetic to its main point, which is to stress that "the perpetual danger, in our attempts to enlarge our historical understanding, is... that our expectation about what someone must be saying or doing will themselves determine that we understand the agent to be doing something he would not—or even could not—himself have accepted as an account of what he *was* doing."[33]

This said, it is far from clear exactly how we are to go about doing what Skinner recommends us to do, i.e., how we shall manage to determine in a precise fashion and according to certain principles what some agent could possibly have accepted as a correct description of what he meant. In fact, browsing through the methodological texts propounding this or similar views, I have been struck by the fact that most of them are surprisingly unhelpful on the matter, but generally just seem to invoke, explicitly or implicitly, some kind of sensitivity to the wording of the texts and to the general contextual framework, both intellectual and non-intellectual.[34] We are also presented with a host of good examples that convincingly illustrate how such sensitivity comes in handy when reading the texts. An example, however, is no demonstration and will not tell us how to acquire the requisite historical sensitivity, what exactly it consists in, and how it translates into concrete methodological rules to follow in the interpretation of past philosophical texts.

Let us take yet another educational visit to the department of cultural anthropology. When justifying his contextualist rule, Skinner denounces a "conceptual parochialism," where an observer "may unconsciously misuse his vantage-point in describing the *sense* of a given work" and "the danger ... that the historian may conceptualize an argument in such a way that its alien elements are dissolved into an apparent but misleading familiarity."[35] There is nothing coincidental about Skinner's appeal to the anthropological dichotomy of the "alien" and the "familiar" in this formulation. That the historian of philosophy must account for a past philosophy "on its own terms" conveys essentially the same intuition as that of an anti-ethnocentric cultural anthropologist committed to depicting a primitive society without evaluating it according to criteria belonging to his own worldview. In this context, anthropologists are particularly aware of the epistemological disaster lurking behind the appeal to some unspecified cultural *Einfühlung* such as Malinowski's

---

33. Skinner (1969), 6.

34. For a strong version of this approach, see Goldenbaum, this volume.

35. Ibid., 27.

claims that he "acquired 'the feeling' for native good and bad manners" or "began to feel that [he] was indeed in touch with the natives."[36] Indeed, after the publication of Malinowski's *Diary in the Strict Sense of Term* in 1967, brutally extinguishing whatever romanticism was still left in the discipline, much methodological work in cultural anthropology has consisted in searching for a more trustworthy replacement for their forefather's now tainted cultural sensitivity.[37] They realized that they could not do without a clear, meta-epistemological criterion allowing determining whether or not they had "accessed" a native mind-set, grounded in a concept of what such access even *means.*

Now, this criterion is not easily satisfied, but very easily formulated. As Malinowski already put it himself, it is "to grasp the native's point of view, his relation to life, to realize *his* vision of *his* world."[38] Franz Boas also formulated it when writing in 1943 that "if it is our serious purpose to understand the thoughts of a people, the whole analysis of experience must be based on their concepts, not ours."[39] The notion that one should thus describe "from the native's point of view," later transformed by Geertz into a kind of catchphrase,[40] corresponds to a requirement of *cultural immanence* of correct anthropological interpretation. The anthropologists' attempts to develop the adequate tools for such culturally immanent interpretation have been prominently displayed in the 1970s for example in the discussions concerning so-called *emic* analysis (as opposed to *etic*). Hence, the "emicists" insisted on describing cultures according to distinctions formulated within that culture itself and undertook, on the basis of a model originally conceived by linguists, the construction of a "method of finding where something makes a difference for one's informants," as Ward H. Goodenough put it in his *Description and Comparison in Cultural Anthropology* from 1970.[41]

This brief visit to the anthropology department equips us with an additional insight about what it *means* to account for some past philosophy "on

36. Malinowski (1922), 8.

37. See Geertz (1983), 56.

38. Malinowski (1922), 25.

39. Boas (1943), 314.

40. Cf. Geertz (1974), reprinted in Geertz (1983), 55–70.

41. Goodenough (1970), cit. in Olivier de Sardan (1998), 155. The distinction between "emic" and "etic" is derived from the linguistic distinction between phonetic and phonemic differences, i.e., between acoustic differences considered significant independently from the language user and acoustic differences perceived as significant by the language user. Transferring the distinction to cultural analysis was first proposed in Pike (1954). The distinction emic/etic was intensely debated throughout the 1960s and 1970s.

its own terms"—an insight that is not captured well at all by the habitual reference to Skinner's rule. This insight is that we are fundamentally dealing with a *perspectivist* requirement. Developing the meaning of some philosophy "on its own terms" simply *means* taking departure from an *internal perspective*. The requirement of understanding past philosophies "on their own terms," or what we can call the requirement of *historically immanent reconstruction*, implies then that the parameters and guiding principles of the reconstruction must have been formulated from *a perspective situated within the historical context* of these past philosophies.

Importantly, the formulation here determines interpretive perspective as "internal" or "external" in terms of a specified *context* rather than the *text itself* or a *text corpus* associated with the *author*. In contrast, another much narrower formulation of interpretive immanence would be to maintain that "internal perspective" and "immanence" should refer *exclusively* to the author's authority over his own text, so that only interpretations developed by the author himself, or which follow principles of interpretation explicitly indicated by the author himself, will eventually count as interpretations having a genuine claim on the true meaning of the text. This is the approach taken by Martial Gueroult when he writes that "the study of a philosophical enterprise ... must, when it has at its disposal documents that allows for it, take its point of departure in the methodological teaching of the author."[42] Gueroult narrows down the range of legitimate interpretive perspectives to include only perspectives expressed in texts belonging to the text corpus of the *author*. This is indeed the fundamental axiom of his "structuralist" method. As has been noted often enough, however, the approach is fatally insensitive to the relation between historical context and meaning. Gueroult's method is incapable, for example, of accommodating the intuition that Lambert Van Velthuysen's elaborate reading of Spinoza's *Tractatus Theologico-Politicus* in a letter to Jacob Ostens from 1671 has some claim on the historical truth about what Spinoza's treatise *actually meant*, simply *because* Velthuysen was a liberal Dutch philosopher who wrote his assessment within a year of the publication of the *Tractatus*. If we are to respect this intuition, close contexts must be included into the sphere of interpretive immanence.

In order, however, to provide a more principled and less intuitive formulation of the point and get a better grasp of how exactly to set up the boundaries of contextual immanence, we should return to the notion that a past philosophical text is a concrete intervention or contribution to a determined past philosophical controversy. From this, one may conclude that the relevant

42. Gueroult (1962), 172–84.

context for the determination of the true historical meaning of a text is limited to the set of texts that are actual contributions to that same controversy. Hence, the criterion of contextual immanence is something one can term *contextual agency*, which, in short, may be formulated as the idea that only those who contribute to the controversy have a word to say in the interpretation of the true meaning of the text or texts that the controversy is about. Moreover, the determination of a given perspective as contextually internal or external turns on the determination of the debate or controversy to which the text was considered a contribution by those involved in the controversy, whether that be the author or some other participant in the controversy (as already seen, in some cases, the author may even *not* have any such contextual agency—it was the case in relation to Toland's refutation of Wachter's Spinoza-reading, the latter being a "Spinozism without Spinoza.")

The importance of the study of controversies for the determination of contextual agency has been intuitively grasped in recent scholarship insisting on the study of close intellectual contexts. Jonathan Israel, for example, has recently stressed the importance of controversies in intellectual history in his *Enlightenment Contested*.[43] Skinner has also come a long way in formulating historical principles of this kind. It is however necessary to signal a significant difference between historical perspectivism and Skinner's brand of contextualism. As we have seen, according to Skinner, the historical plausibility of a given interpretation of a past philosophical text hinges on the acceptability of that text for the author, i.e., whether the interpretation states the meaning of the text in terms that would be recognizable for the author. One must thus avoid "crediting a writer with a meaning he could not have intended to convey, since that meaning was not available to him."[44] Contrary to what Skinner suggests, however, acceptability for the author cannot to my mind count as the sole criterion for inclusion of a given interpretation into the constitution of the true historical meaning of a text. Rather, it is the acceptance (or actual statement) of an interpretation in the relevant historical context that warrants such inclusion. For example, republican reinterpretations of Hobbes written in the seventeenth-century Dutch Republic, such as those by Pieter de la Court and Lucius Antistius Constans, have their share in the true historical meaning of *De Cive* in the second half of the seventeenth century regardless of whether Hobbes was inclined to republicanism or not. In this

---

43. See Israel (2006), 23–25.

44. Skinner (1969), 9; cf. Skinner (1972), 393–408, esp. 406.

case, inclusion into the range of contextual immanence is warranted by the fact that these interpretations contribute to the same controversy about the conditions and limits of Sovereignty prompted by Hobbes's political texts in seventeenth-century Holland. Whether a given interpretation of past philosophical text should be included as a part of the authentic meaning of that text thus is no way hinges on the acceptability of the interpretation from the point of view of the author, i.e., of whether this would be an interpretation that Hobbes could possibly have endorsed, but exclusively on how the relevant historical controversy has been circumscribed.

Granting methodological privilege to contextually internal perspectives turns on the conviction that essential information about the true meaning of some past philosopher's text can be obtained by interrogating the interlocutors of that past philosopher. There is, however, more to historical perspectivism than an intuition about what one should understand by gaining access to the true historical meaning of a text. What is at play concerns the very definition and constitution of such true historical meaning, and is thus closely related to the third requirement for an unapologetic historiography of philosophy described earlier in section 2. Hence, according to historical perspectivism, any reading of a past philosophical text that is not contextually internal cannot, because of this very fact and regardless of its content, lay any claim on the true historical meaning of that past philosophical text. Any interpretation making claims about true historical meaning *must* be either explicitly grounded in some actually deployed internal perspective or be shown to have a direct equivalent in some such perspective. Indeed, the true historical meaning of a past philosophical text should be defined as *the sum of actual historically immanent or contextually internal perspectives on that past philosophical text*. On this definition, the complete historical truth about some utterance or set of utterances under investigation—a philosophical statement, passage, book, work—may defined as the sum of accounts, i.e., perspectives or interpretations, actually developed by the totality of agents moving within the contextual field constituted around that utterance or utterances. To state the principle somewhat crudely, the "objective" or "complete" account just is the sum of subjective accounts given by the agents within that field.

6. Historical Actualism

I have argued that the true historical meaning of a past philosophical text must be understood in terms of the contextually internal interpretations of that text. Now, this could seem to simply reiterate a widespread contextualist insight.

For example, fifteen years ago, in the introduction to their *Cambridge History of Seventeenth-Century Philosophy,* Daniel Garber and Michael Ayers present this *opus Herculeum* among edited volumes on Early Modern Philosophy as conveying "one way, at any rate, in which an educated European of the seventeenth century might have organized the domain of philosophy."[45] This reflects an ambition that corresponds to the requirement of contextual immanence. Nonetheless, to my mind, Garber and Ayers's formulation remains problematic because it fails to address the question of *which* educated European's perspective they adopt. The internal perspective from which they aim at contemplating the terrain is that of some unspecified, generic seventeenth-century intellectual, whose equally generic level of information and sensitivity are then taken as a parameter for understanding the actual structure of the intellectual landscape under scrutiny. The problem, of course, is that no such generic intellectual ever existed, and that the very construction of such an abstract figure inevitably imports quite a bit of externality into a vantage point the main virtue of which was exactly to be internal. Moreover, it is epistemologically problematic to think that an actual and concrete historical meaning should have its unique source in a perspective that is non-actual and abstract. For this reason, historical perspectivism requires that the internal perspective adopted be *identifiable, specific,* and *actual.* In short, one must know *whose* perspective one assumes, i.e., be able to put a *name* on it (and, in some cases, even a *date*). This requirement is what I formulate in terms of a commitment to *historical actualism.*

I here finally arrive at the role that historical perspectivism reserves for past *philosophers*, i.e., the role that one should assign to past authors and readers in the constitution of the true historical meaning of past philosophical texts. They provide subjective perspectives, and these perspectives taken together make up the complex true historical meaning about the text. These actual and concrete subjective perspectives of various intellectuals cannot and should not be reduced to a generic but non-actual and abstract "seventeenth-century philosopher" of the kind evoked by Ayers and Garber. Indeed, I believe the true historical meaning of past philosophical texts is irreducibly "thick," as it were, i.e., constituted by a multitude of perspectives that in the vast majority of cases do *not* converge toward a single unified interpretation. It comprises interpretations that are sometimes contradictory and incompatible, but also sometimes converging and mutually supportive. Moreover, it is constituted by historical meanings the truth of which does not reach further than the

45. Garber and Ayers (1998), 4; Garber (2001), 236–38.

specific controversy to which the text is considered a contribution, i.e., it is constituted only internally among contextual agents and has no direct truth value outside this specific sphere of contextual agency. It would not occur to an anthropologist to ask whether the true meaning of, say, the belief system of the tribe of pygmies he describes is the true meaning of that belief system for anyone else than those pygmies. Similarly, for the historian of philosophy, the true historical meaning of, say, Malebranche's doctrine of vision in God in the controversy between Arnauld, Malebranche, and Leibniz is nothing but the sum of perspectives on the doctrine of vision in God actually developed by Arnauld, Malebranche, and Leibniz.

When studying a past historical text, then, one must first identify the historical debates to which the text under scrutiny contributes in order to determine the range of the historically immanent context. Next, one must pick out from within this context one or several internal perspectives on the text and reconstruct the interpretations deployed from this or these specific perspectives, each of them representing their part or aspect of the full historical meaning about the text. The historian himself here has a role to play in the choice of internal perspectives that he will privilege, since clearly, in most cases, he will not be able to reconstruct all perspectives actually deployed and, in some cases, must even limit his account to *one* such perspective, thus narrowing his ambition down to reconstructing only one aspect or specific part of the historical truth about a past philosophical text or cluster of texts.

For the historian of philosophy, thus picking out a specific internal perspective resembles in important respects the anthropologist's field practice of picking out a "key informant." Understandably—and I apologize in advance to the anthropologists for the caricature—a cultural anthropologist messing about in some village trying to figure out what the natives are up to would rather have as his key informant the local witch doctor than the village idiot, regardless of the many and varied practical and theoretical problems that may also arise from taking this approach.[46] The choice of key informants follows fairly pragmatic criteria relating to the role of the candidate in the community, his knowledge, willingness, and ability to communicate. Similarly, the historian of philosophy working on Descartes's texts might want to privilege the sophisticated and methodologically thought-out perspectives on the Cartesian philosophy worked out by Gottfried Wilhelm Leibniz or Pierre-Daniel Huet rather than go ask, say, Jean-Baptiste Morin about his thoughts on the topic. This, of

46. See Tremblay (1991), 98–106.

course, does not mean that Morin does not have his say in the constitution of the true historical meaning of Descartes's texts, or that studying Morin's texts may not yield interesting results. Morin is representative of a broadly accepted position among minor seventeenth-century philosophers. So whereas studying Descartes from Morin's perspective may not get us very deep into Descartes's text, the "Morin perspective" still has some claim on the true historical meaning of Descartes's work in that his interpretation resonates with a multitude of other "minor" interpretations in the period. Moreover, studying Morin's perspective can help the historian of philosophy in establishing a sort of contextual baseline for the study of the other more interesting and comprehensive stories about Descartes's philosophical texts he is likely to get out of Leibniz or Huet. Picking out informants and ranking them, however, does remain largely dependent on what aspect of the true historical meaning one is looking for. Working out the details of such qualitative "ranking" of internal perspectives in terms of their importance and weight is a complex matter and cannot be worked out within the scope of this paper. In this context, I simply wanted to point to *the necessity of picking one*, and of picking one that is both *identifiable* (i.e., associated with a name) and *actual* (i.e., actually deployed).

The requirement that the internal perspectives adopted be both identifiable and actual leads me finally to formulate an important difference to Skinner's brand of contextualist history, namely, that it is committed to *historical actualism*. If we look closely at Skinner's rule—i.e., that we should never attribute to an author something which he could never have been brought to accept as a correct description of what he had meant or done—it is clear that the hypothetical "could have" formally allows for the inclusion within the scope of historical interpretation of past utterances meanings that were in fact never actually put forward, neither by the author himself nor by intellectual interlocutors in the immediate context. Skinner's approach thus leaves the domain of historical truth wide open to a broad field of acceptable but essentially hypothetical interpretations. Thus, according to Skinner:

> ... the appropriate methodology for the history of ideas must be concerned, first of all, *to delineate the whole range of communications which could have been conventionally performed on the given occasion by the utterance of a given utterance*, and, next, to trace the relations between the given utterance and this wider *linguistic* context as a means of decoding the actual intention of the given writer.[47]

47. Skinner (1969), 48; my italics; cf. Skinner (1972), 406.

I find the italicized bit of this passage very problematic. First, clearly, one cannot convincingly include all historically acceptable but merely hypothetical interpretations in the constitution of true historical meaning. No hypothetical claim about the past can be formally included in the notion of what was actually the case, which arguably is the sole object of historical study. In that respect, I accept Leopold Ranke's famous conception of historical truth in *Geschichten der romanischen und germanischen Völker* from 1824 as the reconstruction of "how it actually [*eigenlich*] was." Skinner does, of course, also acknowledge this when insisting on eventually "decoding the *actual* intention of the writer." But I fail to see how, in principle, his method can achieve this. By "delineating the whole range of communications which could have been conventionally performed" we exclude a number of contextually or historically *impossible* interpretations, e.g., that Marsilius of Padua meant to contribute to a discussion about the separation of powers in *Defensor pacis*.[48] Certainly, it is an important step toward historically correct interpretations to have determined which interpretations *can* be true. But from there on, we are left with very little in terms of help in picking out the interpretation corresponding to the *actual* intention among the remaining possible, i.e., acceptable, interpretations. And I simply do not see how "tracing the relations to a wider linguistic context" will ever help us in achieving this task, exactly because doing so only amounts to placing the utterance within a general framework of (linguistically) possible significations, without in any way narrowing down the available possible options to a particular, actual one. In principle, then, Skinner's method abandons true historical meaning to the hypothetical space delineated by the reference to what the "author could have been brought to accept." However, the domain of meaning occupied by "true historical meaning" is not and cannot be a logical or hypothetical one. It is by definition actual (otherwise it would not be "historical"). We thus require a firmer procedure allowing us to move from the hypothetical space of the merely acceptable to that which was indeed accepted.

For this reason, the definition of true historical meaning of texts that I have provided earlier does not leave room for any such *merely possible* perspectives, i.e., it does not include perspectives on those texts that *could have* been internally formulated but which were in fact *not* formulated. This puts some important restrictions on what can count as a legitimate interpretation in the history of philosophy and rules out a series of hypothetical methodological procedures that otherwise present themselves as a temptation. One can, in

48. See Skinner (1969), 8.

the analysis of some past philosophical text, imagine a hypothetical contextual space where one perspective on that text is deployed differently from it actually was or a situation where more perspectives are deployed than there actually were. For example, when discovering the glaring misconstrual of Spinoza's notion of substance pervading Leibniz's critical comments on *Ethics* from 1678, one could be tempted to ask what Leibniz would have thought of Spinoza's metaphysics had he, contrary to what is in fact the case, grasped that for Spinoza himself substance is nothing like a logical subject. Arguably, this would provide us with something like a *conceptually* meaningful comparison between Leibniz's and Spinoza's respective conceptions of substance and give us some valuable information about the philosophical resources that Leibniz's philosophy has for generating a viable criticism of Spinoza's Spinozism, since the criticism he *actually* provides is in many ways just beside the point. Another example: Malebranche considers Spinoza to be a monster. Nonetheless, Dortous de Mairan claimed that Malebranche's own theory of intelligible extension ultimately led the Oratorian straight to Spinozism. Leibniz, in turn, claimed that the doctrine of occasional causes could only gain consistency by either developing into Leibnizianism or into Spinozism. Since the history of the immediate reception of Malebranchism is thus full of accusations of Spinozism that Malebranche would reject, it could be tempting, in order to arbitrate between Malebranche and his adversaries, to propose a conjecture about what *Spinoza* might have thought of Malebranche's theory *if* he had had the opportunity to read the relevant works. I grant that such hypothetical exercises can be quite fun. But they tell us nothing about the true historical meaning of Malebranche's text. Indeed, it seems hard to defend the view that true historical meaning as such includes un-actualized possibilities unless one is willing to abandon any meaningful distinction between history and fiction.[49] I have, at the outset of this chapter, somewhat axiomatically declared that I do not see how contextual history of philosophy can exist without a viable notion of historical truth. To this I will now add that I do not see how it is possible to establish any such notion if there is no clear boundary between historical truth and fiction. This boundary is determined by the set of historically immanent perspectives actually deployed as opposed to those that were not, but could have been.

49. By adopting this actualist position, I have no intention of banning counterfactual propositions from the writing of the history of philosophy. They are absolutely necessary for any historical account. I am grateful to Daniel Garber and Eric Schliesser for prompting me to insist on this point.

7. Conclusion

When Daniel Garber develops his own brand of unapologetic antiquarianism, he calls out for a "disinterested" historiography of philosophy. This however requires some principled interpretive technique allowing us to assume such a disinterested stance, i.e., an interpretive vantage point from which the interpreter can be said to have bracketed his own interests. Historical perspectivism is one such technique. According to historical perspectivism, the true historical meaning of a past philosophical text can be defined as the sum of the internal perspectives on that philosophy deployed within the relevant context, i.e., the set of historically immanent interpretations of it actually developed. Relevant context is here circumscribed by a sphere of contextual agents contributing to a determined historical controversy about that text and the corresponding cluster of texts that constitute their contributions to that controversy. In a great many respects, historical perspectivism resembles Quentin Skinner's conception of intellectual history. I would however also stress the ways in which it differs from it. First, the definition of true historical meaning in terms of context-immanent perspectives includes a wider range of interpretations than is allowed for by Skinner's requirement of the *author's* possible acceptance. Second, and conversely, the definition also includes a narrower range of interpretations than is allowed for by Skinner's requirement of the author's *possible* acceptance. Historical perspectivism includes perspectives that surely were *not* acceptable to its *author*, but only those that were *actually* propounded in the relevant historical *context*. Hence, in opposition to Skinner's rule, I reject the idea that hypothetical acceptability for the author can serve as a touchstone for the inclusion of some interpretation as part of the true historical meaning of a text. For the historian of philosophy should primarily be interested in past texts and their meaning, not dead authors and their intentions, and there is no good reason to think that these two domains should be identical.

Acknowledgment

This text was written with support of the Marie Curie Foundation (Intra-European Fellowship for Career Development, Project LEIBENLIG) at the ENS de Lyon (CERPHI, UMR 5037) in 2011–2012. I have benefited hugely from the comments of participants in the Montréal Workshop and a session of the Philosophy Society at the University of Edinburgh. I am grateful to Bob Plant and Catherine Wilson who both commented extensively on an early version of this chapter.

2

The History of Philosophy as Past and as Process

Justin E. H. Smith

1. Introduction

MICHEL FOUCAULT WROTE a book called *The Archaeology of Knowledge*,[1] which as far as I can tell has nothing to do with the topic implied in its title. The title alone, however, is already enough to inspire an intriguing question: what would a study of the history of knowledge—of which the history of philosophy is a part—look like if it were to adopt the aims and methods of archaeology, that is, the project of comprehensively reconstructing the human historical past through the totality of its material traces?

Current history-of-philosophy scholarship, in whatever tradition, is for the most part as far away from pursuing this project, indeed from recognizing the value of pursuing this project, as Foucault himself appears to have been. Historians of philosophy are generally content to take the written traces of the ideas of a handful of thinkers—or, more usually, the published editions or even translations of these written traces—as granting them adequate access to as much of the past as they are going to have to consider in order to do what they aim to do as historians of philosophy. But it is at least a bit ironic that in the discipline that proposes to question everything—including the very reality of the past[2]—the specialists who deal in particular with the discipline's past should take it for granted that they are dealing with an immediately accessible storehouse of ideas, preserved in texts that directly reveal the intended meanings of their authors, and that, while dealing with philosophical problems, do not, in their transmission, give rise to any philosophical

1. See Foucault (1969).

2. See, e.g., Dummett (2004).

problems of their own. If I do not cite any examples of this taking-for-granted here, it is not because there are none, but only because scholarship that takes this approach is to such an extent the normal science of the day[3] that scholars do not feel compelled to make their assumptions about the accessibility of the past explicit.

While philosophers of science and metaphysicians have pursued interesting questions about the reality and knowability of the past, these questions seem so far to have remained entirely off the radar of historians of philosophy. How could this be? Even if we are not paying attention to what is going on in archaeology departments, surely we should be aware of what our metaphysician colleagues are doing? I believe the answer to this question is that, as already suggested, for the most part we do not think about the history of philosophy as essentially involving pastness at all. Instead, we generally think of philosophy's past as a timeless repository, and this excuses us, we tend to suppose, from asking questions as to how, for example, we can come to know the past at all; what the proper methods of coming to know it are; what special epistemological problems emerge in the sciences of the past that do not emerge in the sciences of the present; and in what way these special problems arise not only in, say, evolutionary biology or paleontology, but in the very study of philosophy's past as well.

The problem of knowing the past has not been totally ignored in some of the more specialized areas of philosophy that are focused upon the actual historical past. It has been impressively treated by philosophers of evolutionary biology such as Elliott Sober,[4] and by the handful of Anglo-American philosophers of archaeology, such as Alison Wylie in her excellent work *Thinking from Things*.[5] But it has not generally been noticed that the *general* problems about the past with which philosophers such as Sober and Wylie are engaging in their respective domains are problems that apply just as much to philosophy's past as to that of paleontology or to archaeology. This failure of recognition, I believe, stems from two errors in the way we tend to conceive the history of philosophy: first, as already mentioned, the belief that it is a timeless repository of ideas and arguments rather than a *history* properly speaking; second, and closely related to the preceding, the belief that insofar as history-of-philosophy scholarship deals with a repository of texts, that is, of

3. See Kuhn (1962).

4. See Sober (1991).

5. See Wylie (2002); see also Salmon (1982), Krieger (2006).

ideas frozen in time through linguistic inscription, it is fundamentally a different sort of study from that of the disciplines, such as evolutionary biology, paleontology, or archaeology, that are explicitly concerned with reconstructing the past. In this essay I will attempt to bring us some way toward a correction of this pair of misconceptions.

2. *The Real Archaeology of Knowledge*

Interestingly, the scholarly field that has contributed most to the epistemological problems involved in coming to know the past is one that does not deal with texts at all but rather with non-textual traces of past material cultures. While philosophers of archaeology are few, they have plenty of colleagues in archaeology to speak with who can hold their own philosophically. The so-called New Archaeology, sometimes also called "processualism," emerged in fact out of a direct engagement with twentieth-century philosophy of science.[6]

The New Archaeology was built upon two cornerstones of twentieth-century philosophy of science, even if these were somewhat transformed to suit the needs of the discipline. First of all, it openly adhered to logical positivism, which it took to be the doctrine that all human intention and culture is discernible in its material manifestations. Second, it adopted the hypothetico-deductive model of scientific reasoning, and in particular a version of the model developed by Carl Hempel, who, in opposition to many of his positivist colleagues, saw history as potentially a scientific discipline. In these two respects, it rejected the basic tenets of traditional archaeology, according to which material traces from the past could at most be collected and catalogued, while the intentions behind their production and the cultural-evolutionary path that brought them into being would have to remain forever matters of speculation. Of course, people felt free to speculate, to write odes on Grecian urns, to make judgments as to which ancient civilizations were the

6. As John Sutton rightly points out (in personal correspondence), more recent archaeological theory, influenced by the notions of extended and distributed cognition as developed in cognitive science and in cognitively oriented philosophy, tends to take a critical stance toward the overwrought positivism of the New Archaeology, while nonetheless steering clear of thedefeatism of the post-processualists who believe that accounts of the past built upon past cultures' material traces can at most have the status of narratives. For recent work that takes this promising middle path, see Knappett (2005), Boivin (2008), Jones (2007). If however the study of material culture has over the past few decades come to find a moderate path between positivism and storytelling, it may be that in this early round of reflection on the historiography of ideas, a case needs to be made for something like what the processualists initially advocated in archaeology, even if in its pure formulation it proves unsustainable in the long run.

most refined, and so on. But the thought of applying anything like the scientific method to the reconstruction of the past was out of the question.

According to the New Archaeologists, as Wylie explains, earlier archaeologists adopted a strictly inductive approach in their methods; they "made it their first priority to assemble and systematize the observable facts of the archaeological record on the principle that conclusions about past lifeways could be drawn when all the relevant facts were in." Wylie maintains that this put them in an impossible position. "Given the limitations of archaeological data, they were forced… to defer interpretation and explanation indefinitely." The New Archaeologists, by contrast, insisted that their objective should be to produce not just richer, more accurate *descriptions* of culture history and past lifeways but rather an *explanatory* understanding of the underlying structure and dynamics of cultural systems—the cultural processes—that are responsible for the forms of life and trajectories of development documented by cultural historians.[7]

Historians, and a fortiori historians of philosophy, have in some sense been approaching the sliver of the past that is of interest to them from precisely the opposite direction: they start out with an assumption of the resistance-free accessibility of explanatory understandings of the object of their study. They don't think of the object of their study as consisting in past objects that might be assembled and systematized at all. Perhaps more significantly, they tend not to think of this object as part of the dynamics of a cultural system but rather as a more or less context-independent ideal thread that spans the ages and unites philosophers (or at least those who can trace their heritage back to Greece) across the centuries. Thus, if there is any possibility or desirablity of a *rapprochement* between history of philosophy and archaeological processualism, it would be a matter of meeting halfway, having arrived from opposite directions. But once on this common ground the conception of the task of the historian would be greatly transformed: it would now be a matter of seeing ideas and arguments, conserved in texts, as products of the underlying structure and dynamics of cultural systems, and of seeing our work as discerning what these processes were.

In order then for such a *rapprochement* to make sense—in order for the textual traces of the history of philosophy to be seen as part of a cultural system which includes a great many other aspects, most of which are not textual traces—it must be agreed that there is nothing special about the category of

7. Wylie (2002), 3.

written texts among the material traces left by past cultures. This is a suggestion that prehistorians, at least, are increasingly taking seriously. Colin Renfrew,[8] for example, has compellingly argued that *all* material culture is symbolically dense, and that, in this respect, in the broad sweep of human history writing may be seen as a relatively recent species appearing in an already densely populated sea of symbols. From a very different starting point, the medieval historian Daniel Lord Smail[9] has argued that the very idea of prehistory, the study of the pretextual human past, has been contrived as a sort of buffer zone between the human science of history and the natural science of paleo-anthropology. Lord Smail maintains that the distinction is ultimately untenable: there is no categorical distinction between written traces and other traces of the human cultural past; indeed as scholars such as Jack Goody[10] have vividly shown, it is often not at all clear whether we are dealing with a bit of writing or not. The past yields up all sorts of cases of semi-writing; if we include the extra-European cultural sphere, moreover, such cases are not only found in deep antiquity but indeed co-exist alongside the great efflorescence of European modernity. Once we accept this as historians—that is, as people who deal with the textual traces of the past—we are in a better position to learn from debates in a seemingly distant field, such as archaeology, that deal with, as Henry Glassie put it, "the endless silent majority who did not leave us written projections of their minds."[11]

Renfrew, developing certain elements of the processualist understanding of the study of the past, has also adopted the extended-mind conception of material culture defended recently by philosophers such as Andy Clark.[12] On this view, all material traces of past human activity may be "read" as manifestations of intentions and even of beliefs. But if a stone tool is a bit of exosomatic mind from which we may reconstruct the past, then a fortiori this must be the case for a papyrus or a manuscript. It may be that the marking up of paper with symbols explicitly intended to convey thoughts has the effect of causing us to think of these objects from the past as categorically different, as the special object of study of the historian, who need not get her hands dirty, so to speak, with all the artifacts that were produced by human intentional activity, but that, unlike writing, were produced without the explicit purpose of

8. See Renfrew (2008).

9. See Lord Smail (2008).

10. See Goody (1986).

11. Glassie (1977), 29.

12. See Clark (2008).

conveying intentions: texts are written to be read by *others*, while stone tools are just made to break stuff. Yet there is a good deal of overlap between the two sorts of material manifestations of extended mind. Consider a cross inscribed on an early medieval marking stone, or for that matter an illuminated manuscript, which contains text but is obviously meant to be doing a lot more than transmitting the ideas expressed in the text. All the traces of human ingenuity we have from the past are symbolically dense, and it is an artificial division to think of the texts we have as being the objects of an entirely different sort of study than all the other things left behind.

Given that we are not just historians but historians of philosophy, this tends to mean that we are dealing with a very special and rare variety of material trace from the past: not projections of minds dealing with the sale of grain or the transfer of title, but projections of mental activity in what we take to be its purest expression. Because of the nature of this special sub-domain of traces, it easily happens that those who study it lose sight of the textual, inscriptional basis of the object of their study altogether. It is, fairly enough, not what interests most of us most of the time. And yet the absence of interest in it does not make us any the less dependent on it: if there were no material traces of ideas from the past, we would not be studying these ideas. The more we learn about the material traces, moreover, the more we learn that our eventual conception of what ideas from the past *are* is often, and often significantly, conditioned by the circumstances of their material transmission. And, finally, their initial expression is often no less conditioned by the totality of social and historical circumstances in which the thinker found himself or herself. This means that if we insist that we are only idea people and not engaged in a common project with all the other human and even natural sciences that are engaged in reconstructing the past, we run the risk of mistaking an accident of a text's reception history for a sort of message in a bottle that a past philosopher threw out toward an unknown future in the hope that it would be received. One way to avoid this historiographical mistake is to try to think of textual traces from the past as somewhat more like stone tools: the traces of human intention, through which, along with a great many other such traces, we may reconstruct what it was people in the past—be they hunter-gatherers or philosophers—were in fact trying to do.

3. *A Wissenschaft der Neuzeit?*

Curiously, the proximity to the present of a trace of an idea from the past seems to have an impact on our ability or inability to see it as simply one exosomatic trace of mind among others. The nearer to us it is, the less we seem to believe we are required to take a paleographical, let alone an "archaeological," interest in its first expression. Thus historians of ancient philosophy are much more likely to be skilled in paleography and to be familiar with the scholarship on the material culture of antiquity than scholars of early modern philosophy are to be with respect to the era of interest to them.

The rigorous study of ancient philosophy emerged within the context of *Altertumswissenschaft* as developed by Friedrich August Wolf in the early nineteenth century,[13] in which the study of Greek philosophy was held to be only one component, alongside the study of other features of Greek culture. There has never been a comparable development of, so to speak, *Neuzeitwissenschaft*. In large part this is precisely because it is the *Neuzeit* that is in question, the "new era," and we naturally suppose in view of this periodization that we and the moderns inhabit one single epoch. The past of the early moderns might have some, as it were, regional peculiarities, but the past of the ancients really is a foreign country. Or so it is often thought, even if the presumption of shared citizenship threatens to cause us to overlook real differences. To some extent this danger arises in the study of the ancients as well; scholars such as Walter Burkert, for example, have done much to show the various respects in which the "Greek miracle" has been exaggerated, placing the Athenians back into a shared world with the Mesopotamians and Egyptians, rather than with, say, nineteenth-century Europe.[14]

The idea of doing for seventeenth-century Europe what Wolf initiated for classical antiquity might seem strange. After all, what makes the seventeenth century "modern" is its recognition of its own distance from antiquity, which means that it is already beginning to take a sort of removed or objective stance vis-à-vis that particular foreign country of the past, and in this respect it is initiating the process that will two centuries later lead to the proper emergence of *Altertumswissenschaft*. So if we are to treat the *Neuzeit* scientifically on the model of what has already been done for *Altertum*, taking it as a truly foreign land whose disparate elements must be pieced together into a whole by anyone seeking to understand any part of it, then who is to say where to draw the line? Without taking a stand on this difficult question, we may yet recognize that much recent scholarship has been painting for us a picture of the concerns of early modern thinkers that places them very much in a different country with respect to their aims and their background motivations in taking on this or that philosophical problem, and we misunderstand what they were doing

13. See Wolf (1807).

14. See, e.g., Burkert (1977, 2004).

if we presume at the outset that these were the same as ours. Early modern Europe might be a neighboring country, but it is still in many respects quite foreign. It is, so to speak, the present's Canada (at least from a US perspective): close by, but nonetheless deserving of attention on its own terms.

Yet, without wishing to idealize overmuch the integration of the different disciplines dedicated to the study of antiquity, it is hard to imagine a general reaction among historians of early modern philosophy to, say, what Shapin and Schaffer[15] had to say about Hobbes that would be as receptive as that of historians of ancient philosophy to, say, Burkert's treatment of Pythagoras.[16] Now this may be simply because Burkert produced a better work of scholarship, one that specialists in ancient philosophy could recognize as getting to the heart of their own concerns. But one also suspects that at least some of the resistance in this case had to do with a jealousy about disciplinary boundaries and a sense that a thinker such as Hobbes, to the extent that he was a philosopher, ought to remain off limits to the sort of approach Shapin and Schaffer undertook.

In general, of course, the past is not just a foreign country. It is also a ghost town, abandoned by its citizens, who leave nothing but scattered material traces, generally quite haphazardly, without any anticipation of their eventual reception by us. This might appear to mean that if there is going to be a model from among the other human sciences for how to approach this new *Neuzeitwissenschaft*, it will not be cultural anthropology, as many contextualizing historians of philosophy have suggested.[17] We cannot do any fieldwork at a meeting of the original members of the Royal Society. But to suppose that this temporal obstacle precludes any possibility of a sort of anthropological turn in history-of-philosophy scholarship is to preserve a conception of anthropology that is at least a half-century out of date. By the 1960s the eminent anthropologist E. E. Evans-Pritchard had come to the conclusion that anthropology has no option but to take a historical turn,[18] thus in effect meeting the French *Annales* school of Fernand Braudel,[19] Marc Bloch,[20] and others halfway, who all along had supposed that history is through and through an anthropological matter. For Evans-Pritchard, there was a future to the study

15. See Shapin and Schaffer (1985).

16. See Burkert (1972).

17. See Lærke (this volume), Lepenies (1984), MacIntyre (1984).

18. See Evans-Pritchard (1962).

19. See Braudel (1969).

20. See Bloch (1941).

of human culture that consisted not in ethnographic fieldwork but in the examination of the written record of the human cultural past. At the same time, the New Archaeology, or the processualist school, was converging on the view that, as Willey and Phillips put it in 1958, "archaeology is anthropology or it is nothing,"[21] which is to say that for them the study of material traces of the past has as its aim an "explanatory understanding of the underlying structure and dynamics of cultural systems."[22]

So archaeology has blended into anthropology, while anthropology meanwhile has increasingly come to overlap with history. If we take the history of philosophy to be part of history proper, then, we might now be able to see how these developments together might serve to make possible an approach to the history of philosophy that may rightly be called an "archaeology of knowledge."

4. Holding Water

A processual approach to the history of philosophy obviously cannot subordinate itself to the agenda set by contemporary, non-historical philosophy. Arguably, however, to do so makes no more sense than for, say, cladistics to subordinate itself to molecular biology. To paraphrase Evans-Pritchard, history of philosophy is history, or it is nothing; it must, for reasons that will become fully clear by the end of section 6, be fundamentally oriented toward the real, historical past. And here we may understand "real" not in any excessively robust sense of the sort that would have troubled an anti-realist such as Dummett, but simply as designating whatever it is that in fact happened in the past, quite apart from any question of whether the past is, now, real.

What historians of philosophy *can* contribute to the present, like archaeologists or big-bang cosmologists, is an ever more fine-grained and vivid picture of, as Leopold Ranke first put it, *wie es eigentlich gewesen ist:* of how it actually was. Now, of course, Rankean historiography was widely criticized from its original appearance in the nineteenth century. Walter Benjamin would call Ranke's historical empiricism "the strongest narcotic" of that century.[23] As an actual project, seeking to give an exhaustive account of how it actually was is indeed a grandiose one and may without much straining be

21. Willey and Phillips (1958), 2.

22. Wylie (2002), 3.

23. See Benjamin (1999), Oo 71, 863; for a clear account of some of the specific criticisms of Ranke's methodology, see Lærke, this volume.

seen as connected with a number of that century's other excesses, all variously motivated by the idea of total control of uncontrollable domains of conquest (colonies, nature, the past, etc.). But as a transcendent aim, it is rather less noxious, and perhaps it would be useful to distinguish between the belief that we can get the past *exhaustively* right (something which as far as I can tell Ranke never claims) and the idea that we should seek to get whatever we can about the past right.

Even the latter, more modest goal is a difficult one to attain, and the path is riddled with all sorts of hermeneutical dangers. But the goal of gaining an accurate picture of the past is not intrinsically any more unrealistic than the goal of arriving at scientific truth in any domain. As the New Archaeologists have compellingly shown, there is nothing in principle about the pastness of an object of scientific study that makes it any more scientifically out of reach, even by the most rigorous Hempelian standards of what is to count as science, than any present object of scientific study. As in archaeology and evolutionary biology with their unique objectives, what the slow, massive project of piecing together the totality of philosophy's past could eventually yield is a convergence on the truth about the range and bounds of human philosophical reflection; and this, surely, must be considered a desideratum of the present day. So one need not believe that direct engagement with non-historical philosophy should be a requirement of employment in a philosophy department, in order to believe that historians of philosophy can play a vital role in, let us say, the ecosystem of contemporary philosophy. Historians of philosophy can help current philosophers to gain perspective on their projects by showing them the scope and range of what has been able to pass as an important philosophical question in different times and places, thereby providing a picture of the flexibility and contingency of what ought to count as a philosophical question.

This sort of contribution might have the effect of changing contemporary debates by showing that some resolution to them was already proposed long ago in an unfamiliar idiom (which often happens, for example, in the study of ancient Indian epistemology: we find the answers to contemporary questions, but we often don't even realize it because the style of argumentation is so unfamiliar). Or this sort of contribution might simply help current philosophers to bear in mind the extent to which what we call "philosophy" today really is a mixed bag of leftover questions from various historical legacies. This flexibility inevitably leads the historian of philosophy down paths that cannot easily be connected up with current philosophical concerns. But it is up to the current philosophers themselves, if they wish to go through the intellectual exercise and thereby to be edified, to take an interest in the findings of the historians of philosophy—the findings that are often so far from current concerns—and to allow these findings to serve as fuel for reflection on what this project we call "philosophy" is in fact all about.

If there had been some sudden and total semantic shift at some point in the past in the meaning of the term "philosophy," after which what they called "philosophy" no longer overlapped at all with what we call "philosophy" (say, like the shift from Thomas Aquinas's use of "metaphysics" to Shirley MacLaine's use), then there really would be no value to current philosophy in studying everything that has ever been called "philosophy." But what we see instead is a gradual and continuous transformation, with one fairly abrupt and large transformation occurring over the course of the eighteenth century, when the particular natural sciences come to be parted out from what was until then known as "natural philosophy."

There are at least a few ways in which studying these transformations as a historian of philosophy may be fruitful, rather than simply zeroing in on those elements of past philosophy that remain of clear relevance to us. First of all, we might find that when someone in the past was doing something that he thought of as philosophy but that we do not think of as philosophy, he might nonetheless have been making observations that we can recognize as philosophical; e.g., Galen on the function of the pancreas can tell us something about teleology; Daniel Sennert's alchemy/chemistry can tell us something about the range of possible theories of compound bodies, which should be of interest not only to, say, those who might also be working on Democritean atomism or Descartes's corpuscularianism, but also to readers of, e.g., Van Inwagen's *Material Beings*.[24]

Yet again, while this sort of payoff is nice, there is no clear reason it must be a condition of considering some research on some past work to be research in the history of philosophy. For one thing, at the outset, the historian of philosophy is not going to know where these "... still-philosophically relevant nuggets might be hidden within some vast treatise on calendrical astrology or some such no-longer-legitimate thing." Second, in taking, say, Libavius's claim seriously that in trying to transmute base metal into gold he is doing "philosophy," or Joachim Becher's claim that he has invented a *perpetuum mobile*, sometimes described as the ultimate *machina philosophica*, we might be forced to reflect on forgotten (but still perhaps latent) elements of the philosophical project: in fact, these two examples are not so different from

24. See Van Inwagen (1995).

at least one of the two accusations, made justly or not, against Socrates at his trial: that of looking into what goes on in the heavens above and in the earth below.

Historians of philosophy, on the view I am elaborating, should differ from their non-historian colleagues on this crucial point, that they do not take the strength or weakness of a historical figure's ideas as the sole or even the principal criterion for taking an interest in them. Rather, we take an interest in them in order to gain a clearer picture of how, to speak with Rorty, things once hung together. So we take an interest in false ideas, stupid ideas, crackpot ideas. But this does not mean that we are "relativists" or that we have an "anything goes" approach to the search after philosophical truth. It is simply that we have bitten off a different part of the vast and necessarily shared philosophical project: one that aims at a different register of truths. One does not reject the truth in studying, say, Kenelm Digby's false theory of the weapon salve, for it is among the truths in this world that there once was a man named Digby who believed this false theory. This is a truth, among very many other such truths, in the history of ideas.

And these are not just curious truths. In fact, often, they are revealing truths: truths that reveal to us important aspects of debates in history, aspects that might not be noticed if we did not aspire to gain a maximally rich and vivid picture of the period, and aspects, moreover, that might contain philosophical lessons. To return once more to the archaeological parallel, imagine a team of archaeologists coming across a trove of Mesopotamian pottery from the sixth millennium BCE. Many of the specimens have been damaged over the course of time; they have gaping holes in them; some are entirely shattered. Now suppose the archaeologists attempted to fill these pots with water and proceeded to judge the significance of their find on the ability of the containers to hold it. This would of course be preposterous. They judge the find's significance based on what it can tell them about the material culture of the period and region; any damage the containers might have undergone as the centuries passed might create a challenge to reconstructing what the vessels were like in their pristine state, but this is not a count against the vessels themselves; it's only an incitement to double up the dedication and sophistication of the methods of study.

It is revealing that we often speak of arguments as "holding water": historians of philosophy, to follow this example through to the end, often seek to do something much like the clueless archaeologists who judge the vessels they've found based on their ability to hold water. What if, instead of taking the measure of the current usefulness of the old vessels we find, that is, of the old texts we read, we were instead to think of them as artifacts, of interest whether they hold water or not, to the extent that they help us to fill out our picture of the period in question? Let me now provide a few examples of how, in the specific context of the study of early modern philosophy, we might start thinking about texts not as a special class of objects that are to be studied according to totally different rules by a totally separate science, but instead might start studying them in connection with the study of all the other exosomatic mentral traces from a given region and period.

5. Case Studies

(i) *Microscopy: Paying Attention to the History of Technology.* Some authors have rejected as prima facie implausible the view that microscopy may have been part of the initial inspiration for Leibniz's model of organic bodies for the simple reason that Leibniz, as a philosopher, had to have been drawing his inspiration from, as Leibniz himself puts it, "higher principles." This conviction can at its worst lead commentators to muddle the historical facts about Leibniz's philosophical development and his knowledge of empirical science. Hans Poser, for example, correctly discerns evidence of the doctrine as early as the *De conditionibus* of 1665, and, more clearly, in the *De arte combinatoria* of 1666, "thus long before the discovery of microorganisms by Antoni van Leeuwenhoek in 1672."[25] From this, Poser concludes that when Leibniz finally looked through a microscope in 1676, "it was for him a matter of empirical corroboration of a principle, which for him had to be true on primarily metaphysical grounds."[26] But microorganisms were not unknown in 1665; it was only a particular kind of microorganism, the spermatozoon, that was discovered in 1672, seven years after Leibniz first considered some version of the worlds-within-worlds doctrine. As Robert Hooke's 1665 *Micrographia* clearly reveals, the microworld was already at the center of scientific attention by the time of Leibniz's first formulation of the doctrine in 1665. Indeed, Balthasar de Monconys reports of the presence of "an infinity of minute invisible insects" in the human body as early as 1647.[27] One of the people known to have influenced Leibniz very early on, Athanasius Kircher, had already

25. Poser (1978), 141.

26. Ibid., 142.

27. Wilson (1995), 173.

conducted decades of microscopic research and developed a theory of putrefaction involving invisible insects by 1658. In 1669, Leibniz expresses agreement with this theory, as well as indicating familiarity with Hooke's work. To suggest that Leibniz could have had no idea of the existence of microorganisms earlier than 1672 is simply wrong.

This is just one instance of the sort of reasoning we see very frequently in history-of-philosophy scholarship: that insofar as it is the work of a *philosopher* we are studying, the ideas in question could only flow from "higher principles," and any apparent connection they might have to contemporaneous developments in a technology-dependent field such as microscopy must be merely coincidental, and at most a convenient support for a philosophical idea, rather than being directly constitutive of that idea.

(ii) *Chemistry: Reconstructing Experiments.* In an impressive series of scholarly studies, William R. Newman has shown that there was a long medieval tradition of distinguishing between mixtures, in which initial ingredients come to form a perfectly homogeneous mass, and compositions, which were considered as something intermediate between the purely homogeneous and the mere juxtaposition. According to Newman, the medieval alchemists who argued for such an intermediary, sometimes called a *fortissima compositio*, were intuiting something like a molecular bond in today's sense: something that would permit all the properties of an ingredient added to the composition to disappear while still permitting this ingredient, with its initial properties, to be reestablished through the alchemical method. The medieval alchemists who argued along these lines, Newman maintains, set themselves up starkly against the Scholastics who argued, in contrast, that any given body can have only one substantial form. In this way they significantly anticipated the early modern rejection of the doctrine of substantial forms in favor of a view of the qualitative diversity of bodies as arising from variations in the arrangements of corpuscles.

Newman has compellingly argued that it was principally the Thomist strain of Aristotelianism that held that any given substance must have one, and only one, substantial form. But there were many opponents of this view, identified by Newman as "pluralists" (in opposition to Thomas's "unitism"), who held that there could be a plurality of substances within matter, and that we must posit such a plurality if we are to account for a vast array of chemical operations. For Thomas, a given body—for example, that of a human—contains the substantial forms of the four elements only potentially: these will come to actuality only after the body dies and the elements separate out from it in the decomposition of the cadaver. For a pluralist such as Paul of Taranto, in contrast, the endurance of the wood after the tree is chopped down and killed shows that the substantial form of wood was there all along, and, similarly, mercury and sulfur are always there in a certain fashion in any complete metal. Since fused metals can be made to return through laboratory operations, Paul believes, "it is manifest that they were only resolved to certain components of theirs and not to the simple elements or to the prime matter."[28]

An important part of Newman's revisionist account of the secret prehistory of early modern corpuscularianism has consisted in his elaborate repetitions of early modern experiments on the mixture of silver into compounds and subsequent separation out from them. This has required not just difficult laboratory work and a significant grasp of modern chemistry but also the hard work of translating the idiom of early modern "chymistry" into terms that would make it possible at all to repeat the experiments. But Newman's laboratory confirmation centuries later of an early modern experiment has served as important corroboration of his revisionist account of the origins of corpuscularianism: the pluralists knew what they were talking about; their theory was based on sound practice. They were doing something other than writing, which we can rediscover today, and which helps us to reconstruct the history of natural philosophy.

(iii) *Botany: Reading beyond Texts.* In a thoroughly researched 2006 article, Peter Anstey and Stephen Harris make a compelling case that John Locke was in fact a very serious and dedicated botanist, and that, moreover, his work as a botanist should cause us to understand his discussion of the nature of species in the *Essay concerning Human Understanding* in a new way. Anstey and Harris base their case for Locke's contribution to botany on his manuscript notes and correspondences, but also, significantly, on his personal herbarium. The authors note that "it is somewhat ironic that Locke himself actually contributed to the herbaria which were predicated on an essentialist view of species and which, being the definitive repositories of type-specimens, became the basis for establishing the credibility of claims for the discovery of new species."[29] In other words, they conclude, scholars who take the *Essay* as their point of entry into Locke's views on

28. Newman (2006), 41.

29. Anstey and Harris (2006), 167.

species will come to a rather different conclusion from those who study his well-preserved collections of pressed plants.

Here we have a particularly vivid case of the utility of going beyond the textual. Type-specimens pressed into the pages of books are virtually textual themselves: they are both things from the world and signs standing for and referring to the things in the world of which they are the type-specimen. The practice of collecting type-specimens presupposes the existence of types. In this way, Locke's compilation of this special sort of book, a book with things squeezed directly into it rather than with words about things, tells us something very different about the mental activity of which these transformed things become traces than do the traces in his more conventional books, such as the *Essay*. But there is simply no good reason to acknowledge the one sort of trace while ignoring the other.

(iv) *Calendry: Friedman's Dynamics of Reason*. Michael Friedman has developed an approach[30] to the history and philosophy of science that he calls "the dynamics of reason," which in broad outline is very much in line with the processualist account we are beginning to sketch here. Friedman has argued that in order to understand Kant's conception of a priori scientific principles, this conception must be relativized to a particular theory in a given historical context. He accordingly lays out an ambitious project in which ultimately this relativization leads to historicizing the notion of scientific objectivity itself. His approach seems altogether compelling to me, but rather than defend it here I only wish to discuss the particular instance of the unlikely path down which Friedman's relativization of modern philosophy leads him.

Friedman believes that the philosophical debates arising in the early modern period around the nature of space and time and culminating in Kant's conception of these as the a priori forms of pure intuition arise in no small measure from the project of making the measurement more precise, relatively speaking, of solar, lunar, and astral motion. He believes that this project, in turn,

> was inextricably entangled, from the very beginning, with a fundamental human interest in keeping track of the progression of the seasons.... The calendar, we might say, represents our fundamental material technology for regulating both the practice of agriculture

30. See Friedman (2001) and (2010).

and associated religious rituals.[31]

Accurate calendrical measurement had always been a technological challenge since a solar year does not contain an integral number of solar days. This led different time-keeping civilizations in different periods to decree various means of, so to speak, making the calendar whole. In 45 BCE Julius Caesar introduced the leap year by adding one quarter of a day to the 365-day calendar, which yielded a 366-day year once every four years. But as Friedman notes, "the seasonal year is actually 11 minutes and 14 seconds shorter than 365 and one quarter days, so that, by the time of the publication of Copernicus's *De revolutionibus* in 1543, the vernal equinox had moved backwards from March 21st to March 11th." This lag created the need for a new calendar reform, which took the shape of the Gregorian calendar adopted in 1582.

Drawing on the work of John Heilbron,[32] Friedman argues that many of the precise measurements that were made from the late sixteenth century into the mid-seventeenth century, and that eventually consolidated the preference for Copernican measurement over Ptolemaic, were in fact made by mathematical astronomers who were taking advantage of the church's interest in precisely pinpointing the vernal equinox. They did this by having the equipment for astronomical observation built directly into the architecture of cathedrals: the cathedrals themselves were made to function as gnomons for accurately charting the solar orbit. Heilbron argues on the basis of this example that the church had a much more nuanced relationship to the new astronomy than has generally been noticed. "During the same period in which Galileo was very publicly condemned for defending the Copernican system," Friedman writes, "the Church itself—because of its overriding interest in precisely fixing the date of Easter once and for all—was providing the new astronomy with important observational support."[33] Friedman believes that the entanglement of the new astronomy with wider cultural struggles "emerging from the aftermath of the Reformation and the scientific revolution"[34] were still very much present, in Leibniz's mind in developing a Keplerian alternative

31. Friedman (2010), 504.

32. See Heilbron (1999).

33. Friedman (2010), 507.

34. Ibid., 508.

to Newton's orbital theory spelled out in the *Principia*. And the disagreement between Leibniz and Newton of course, would define much of the trajectory of eighteenth-century reflection on the nature of space and time, whose culmination is Kant's own "Copernican" transformation of these concepts.

Now we've left out almost all of the details of Friedman's account, but we have enough to be prepared to ask: what, in the end, is the use of tracing early modern debates about the nature of space and time back to the agrarian cycles of premodern Europe? As Friedman notes, the fact that we are dealing with "mutual interactions among quasi-autonomous cultural processes" gives rise to "the emergent appearance of unpredictable novelty."[35] Friedman himself does not stress this point, but it seems evident that this appearance is reduced by the very method he proposes, namely, refusing to treat cultural processes as autonomous. What happens when we do this is that new innovations, including innovations in the history of philosophy, come to look, if not entirely predictable, at least like the results of events rather less mysterious, and rather more tractable, than the internal workings of individual geniuses' minds. In other words, we root philosophy in cathedral architecture, and that in turn in calendry, and that in turn in agriculture because this is what enables us to make the past make sense.

6. History, Philosophy, and Myth

The broad resistance to the approach taken in the examples of the previous section shows not so much a total rejection of the past on the part of philosophers as it does a desire to conceptualize the past in a way that minimizes or denies altogether its essential pastness. One common name for the conceptualization of the past that treats it as eternal—and as so to speak the transcendental condition of the present—is "myth." One version of philosophical myth-making is the crude Straussian conception of a thread that runs across the centuries and ties an enlightened few together in the same continuous conversation. It recognizes history, but in a sense detemporalizes history by positing a hidden continuity. Inadvertently, analytic history of philosophy takes this detemporalization even further: it seeks to flatten history out, to eternalize it, not in a Straussian manner, but at its extreme, in the manner of Jonathan Bennett, making all of the history of philosophy into a contemporary

35. Ibid., 512.

conversation. It is acknowledged that a historical Plato existed at some point in the past, exactly how long ago is not so important, but the Plato, or let us call him "Plato*" who is of interest to philosophy exists eternally in the literal sense of being outside of historical time.

Historians of philosophy might think that what they are doing is simply bracketing the pastness of Plato, because it is not qua past thinker, but qua thinker, that Plato interests them. But there may be an unintended distortion of the thinker when his pastness is bracketed in this way and he is set up as representative of or standing for an eternal set of ideas. A comparative-religionist would tell you that this conception of Plato*, of Plato-who-just-always-exists, is not at all far from what in other cultures might be said to be conceptualized in terms of "mythological time" as contrasted with "historical time."[36] So it is not that Plato is really being removed altogether from the temporal, but only that he is being placed in a conceptually very different temporal category. If you were to ask a Greek mythologer when exactly Zeus appeared to Leda as a swan, or if you were to ask a Cree elder when exactly bears and humans shared a common language, the response would probably be something like: well, never really; these are things that never happened but in some sense are always happening. They are conditions of reality, lenses through which reality can always be filtered, rather than being so to speak the property of the past, present, or future.

So in bracketing Plato's historical existence, we are not so much taking him out of time as we are unwittingly placing him in mythological time, or, to put it more succinctly, we are turning philosophy's past into myth. The only way to avoid doing this, I think, is to call the history of philosophy down from the clouds and to inaugurate a sort of processualist turn in history-of-philosophy scholarship. If this reeks of positivism, the idea that what we are after is nothing short of *wie es eigentlich gewesen ist*, then we might do better to reopen the question of what is really wrong with positivism anyway, rather than to take the faint scent of it as a reason for immediate dismissal of this approach.

It might seem that we are faced with a Scylla-and-Charybdis situation, between myth on the one hand, and, on the other hand, a sort of detective work that many philosophers would consider tedious. But in the end this is a false dichotomy, as the real resolution is much more moderate: it simply requires history of philosophy as a discipline to reconceive its project; rather than mining a timeless trove for arguments that might be of interest to current philosophy—arguments that probably do not end up impressing

36. See, e.g., Durkheim (1915), Harkin (1988).

non-historian philosophers as much as historians like to imagine—history of philosophy must instead come to see itself as embedded within a vastly larger historical project, one that includes the history of material culture, and the history of climate, and the history of everything else, along with the history of that very special thing historians of philosophy focus on: the textual traces of the past's exceptional minds, or at least those of them who happened to leave such traces.

3

Philosophy and Genealogy: Ways of Writing History of Philosophy

Koen Vermeir

1. Appropriationists versus Contextualists

IT IS COMMON to distinguish between "appropriationist" and "contextualist" versions of the history of philosophy.[1] These would constitute two distinct ways of doing history of philosophy. "Appropriationist" appropriate classical texts for current philosophical needs and interests. "Contextualists" try to understand past philosophers by placing them in their historical context. This distinction is often framed in terms of anachronism, presentism, or historical revisionism. In the first part of this chapter, I will criticize these characterizations of appropriationist and contextualist history of philosophy and I will propose and defend an alternative distinction.

The term "revisionism" has been used to refer to a methodological reform in intellectual history, spearheaded by Quentin Skinner, J. G. A. Pocock, and John Dunn in the 1960s and 1970s.[2] Skinner's principle is taken as the centerpiece of the contextualist point of view: "No agent can eventually be said to have meant or done something which he could never be brought to accept as a

1. See the introduction to this volume. Dan Garber (2005) makes a more fine-grained distinction between his "antiquarian" approach, John McDowell's "historical mythology" in philosophy, and Jonathan Bennett's "collegial approach to the history of philosophy."

2. For the term "revisionism" in this sense, see Tarlton (1973) and Femia (1981). This is different from recent uses of "revision" (and "revisionism") in historiography, denoting the view that historiography will keep changing over time, depending on changing historians interests, and approaches, which are in their turn embedded in broader cultural, intellectual and social changes (see the December 2007 theme issue of *History and Theory*). The main colloquial use of "revisionism" is of course to refer to those who deny that the Holocaust actually happened.

correct description of what he had meant or done."[3] I find Skinner's principle rather unintelligible (indeed, it escapes me how I would ever convince a long dead philosopher to accept any statement I make).[4] Even a generous interpretation of the principle, assuming an imaginary debate between the historian and the historical actor, seems to presuppose what it tries to achieve. In order to decide whether the historian presents a good interpretation of a historical statement, he or she already needs to know what the historical agent would have accepted as a correct description of what he had meant, but this is exactly what Skinner would like to find out in the first place. Furthermore, it does not strike me as the right way to distinguish between "appropriationists" and "contextualists." The main aim of Skinner's method as described in his 1969 paper was to recover the intention of the author, an aim that is not necessarily shared by many contextualist historians today.[5]

Anachronism does not seem to be a promising way to distinguish "appropriationists" and "contextualists" either. The use of anachronism, the use of categories or explanatory models alien to the period in question, is not altogether inappropriate in "contextualist" history after all. Nick Jardine argues convincingly that anachronism "is often entirely in order precisely when our interest is, like Skinner's, in the 'historical identity' of deeds and works. Their original historical significances, their meanings in their own times and places, are not confined to the significances that were (or could have been) attached to them at those times and places."[6] Jardine works out a series of theoretical and practical guidelines for distinguishing vicious from legitimate anachronism. Richard Evans, for his part, has argued that we often need to use questions and tools from the historian's present perspective, because this often allows us to read a given source against the grain.[7] The problem is subtle, and there might well be a distinct difference in degree in the use "appropriationists" and

3. Cf. note 1. For the quotation, see Skinner (1969), 28. Note that Skinner in this classic paper criticizes contextualists as misguided ("social" contextualists, that is, but Skinner does not always make a clear distinction in this paper). See also Boucher (1985) and Tully (1988).

4. This is not meant as a pun, but the "imaginary conversation" approach seems problematic to me. It is also hard to imagine, as Rorty does, that Aquinas would change his mind after reading Newton or Hume. (Rorty 1984), 51. I do not think such imaginations lead to good historiography.

5. For an overview, see Mulligan et al. (1979) and Jardine (2000), 246–53. For Skinner as a contextualist, see, e.g., Diggins (1984), 157. For other detailed criticisms of Skinner's 1969 paper, see Tarlton (1973) and Femia (1981).

6. Jardine (2000), 252. See also Evans (2000), 92.

7. Evans (2000), 83.

"contextualists" make of anachronism or "vicious anachronism," yet it is clear that this difference is not absolute.[8] There is nothing in principle wrong with the use of our concepts and methodologies in the description of the past.[9]

This problem can be taken one step further, to a general problem of understanding, translation, and interpretation of historical material. Philosophers have wondered if it is possible to "understand" a culture or a period in its own terms. Jonathan Bennett has claimed, for instance, that we can only understand past philosophers if "we can say, clearly and in contemporary terms, what his problems were, which of them are still problems, and what contribution they have made towards their solution."[10] Bennett thus defends the need to translate past statements in contemporary terms and the existence of enduring problems and solutions. Postmodernist philosophers of history have given this view another twist: they would agree with the need to translate past statements, but instead of discovering or interpreting their real meaning, they claim that historians create their own meanings. According to these philosophers, we have no objective access to history. Historiography is only one discourse among many that constructs the past.[11] The weaker view, that historiography is more like an art than a science, and that it necessarily involves an imaginative process of re-creating the past, is less controversial. Such views were already central in debates at the start of the twentieth century. Yet the extent of the historians' involvement in re-creating the past is contentious, and many consider the postmodern stance as too extreme. Again, this might be an issue of degree, but it seems clear that both the so-called appropriationist and contextualist historians of philosophy re-create the past to some extent, and in this process they bring their current concepts to bear on their scholarship.

A similar argument can be made for presentism. Presentism, the interest in the past that stems from contemporary questions and concerns, is perfectly compatible with a contextualist approach. J. G. A. Pocock, together with Skinner at the origin of the "Cambridge school" of "contextualist intellectual history," studied the history of renaissance republicanism guided by a deep

8. For one, Jardine accuses "contextualist" historians who apply interest theory or Latour's Actor Network Theory for the early modern period of vicious anachronism.

9. In the introduction to *Philosophy in History*, Rorty, Schneewind, and Skinner construct ideal types of historians of philosophy versus intellectual historians but in the end admit that "we might do well to forget the bugbears of 'anachronism' and 'antiquarianism'" (Rorty, Schneewind, and Skinner (1984), 10), because no one would fit in the most extreme versions of these positions anyway.

10. See Rorty (1984) 52, n.1.

11. Cf. White (1973), White (1978), Ankersmit (1994).

engagement in and concern for contemporary politics. For those interested in tracing back current political constellations, in order to better understand them, it is not necessary to give up a rigorous contextualist approach. Furthermore, to a certain extent, presentism is unavoidable. If one reads past histories of philosophy or the history of historiography, it quickly becomes clear that these past historians had different focuses, ideologies, concerns, etc., partly due to the times in which they were living and the fashions in which they took part, which played out in the way these historians have written history.[12] In *What Is History?* (1961), E. H. Carr already maintained that history books are products of their own times, and he urged students to study the historians before studying the histories they wrote. Again, therefore, almost all history has a tinge of presentism, and it will be difficult to make clear distinctions between "appropriationist" and "contextualist" history of philosophy in these terms. In all these cases, a "puritan" approach, in which all anachronism and presentism is banned, is impossible. It is also unnecessary and it would probably be uninteresting anyway. What is important is to have criteria that can help historians of philosophy to distinguish in practice between better and worse historical interpretations.

2. *History of Philosophy versus Philosophical Uses of History*

I would like to introduce the distinction I am aiming at by making a comparison with the role of history in the sciences. Alasdair MacIntyre has made the interesting argument that theories in the natural sciences have an essential historical existence. He did not only mean that a scientific theory at time t_1 and at time t_2 are not identical, but also that a scientific theory can only be judged in comparison with its predecessors. "No natural scientific theory is ever vindicated as such; it is vindicated or fails to be vindicated only relative to those of its predecessors with whom it has competed so far."[13] This installs an essential historical aspect at the core of scientific development. My point here will be different but related: it is based on the observation that scientists often use history in their pedagogical practices and even in their research.

Apart from the usual short historical accounts that are supposed to enliven science course books, the coursework in many disciplines is structured according to the historical evolution of the discipline. This is partly for institutional

12. Cf. Kelley (1998).

13. MacIntyre (1984), 44.

reasons (educational structures adapt rather slowly to changes in the discipline) but also for pedagogical reasons. This might be most clearly the case in theoretical physics, where students specializing in high energy physics are usually first introduced to classical Newtonian mechanics, then to electromagnetism and Lagrangian and Hamiltonian mechanics, and later, more or less in sequence, to statistical mechanics, quantum mechanics, special relativity, general relativity, particle physics, quantum field theory, and superstring theory. Note that this succession corresponds to an actual historical succession of different "paradigms" in high energy physics. In many other disciplines, the teaching of topics also follows the chronological succession of their discovery to some extent, but on a smaller scale (e.g., within molecular biology, rather than biology as a whole). The point is that it is difficult to understand the basic presuppositions of an advanced theory without a historical narrative that refers to predecessor theories. One of the reasons is that the recent theories are so far removed from everyday experience that it is difficult to make sense of their basic axioms without historical knowledge of why (and in contrast to which theory) these new axioms were proposed. Relativity theory makes little sense without reference to the Michelson-Morley experiment, which itself was inspired by (problems with) theories in electromagnetism and classical mechanics. The idea that the basic constituents of the world are strings in ten or eleven dimensions comes across as unintelligible if one has no prior knowledge about the history of physics.

The way in which scientists use and present history is not professional historiography, of course. Nevertheless, there is an often explicit non-trivial use of history in the sciences. Such uses seem to corroborate MacIntyre's claim that a successor theory only makes sense in light of predecessor theories, i.e., in a historical perspective. I think we can see the same in philosophy, where certain problems and theories can only be understood in light of a historical lineage. Even analytic philosophy, which presumes a break with the past, often needs its *own* history, referring back to formulations by, e.g., Frege, Gettier, or Tarski, to make the latest philosophical presuppositions, problems, and answers intelligible, and to determine what counts as interesting problems and solutions. What is important here are structural relationships between theories, not the actual histories as they came about. Rational reconstructions therefore suffice, and these sometimes even degenerate in mythological history.[14] MacIntyre sees writing such histories as a desideratum, even for historians of philosophy, it seems.[15] The authors of such histories often care little

---

14. Cf. the case studied by Waugh and Ariew in this volume.

15. MacIntyre (1984), 47.

whether their historical account is correct, as long as it clarifies their current theoretical positions. Even if the authors do not care much, such myths should be debunked if false, because they are still presented as history (and not as myth). As such, they abuse and pervert the intuition that historical insight contributes to the understanding of contemporary problems. Furthermore, such myths can lead to a mistaken view of current problems (philosophical and other) because history can shed light on current problems if applied correctly. Even if some philosophers only "use" history, they should be careful to use it correctly, if they present it as "history". The histories MacIntyre desires to be written are the mythological and potted histories constructed by the scientists or philosophers themselves, and they have little *historical* interest.

Science, it is often assumed, does not have a historical consciousness. Previous theories that are rejected are quickly forgotten. Yet sometimes false old theories retain certain relevance. As a typical example, classical mechanics is still useful, especially in applied science and engineering (where the utilitarian aspect prevails over the truth aspect). It is less well known that there are still many unresolved problems in classical mechanics, and some professional scientists today spend their careers researching these. Even if classical mechanics is technically speaking "false," this does not mean it is irrelevant or uninteresting, even for a current day theoretical physicist. Again, I think this compares to the use of history in philosophy. Many of Descartes's propositions are superseded, but some of the problems he raised are still relevant (within certain constraints or with some adaptations) and pose still interesting problems for philosophers today. Maybe this is more the case in philosophy than in the sciences, but I do not think that they are essentially different in this respect. Both philosophy and the sciences have problems that seem superseded (e.g., about substantial form or occult qualities)[16] and others (about the mind-body problem, or the passions) that are still relevant.[17]

What these uses of history in philosophy or in the sciences have in common is that they are not about how (past) philosophy or science really worked. The subject matter under investigation remains "being" or "knowledge" in

16. Of course, these judgments are always open to reassessment. Aristotelian views on organisms have recently been resurrected by philosophers of biology, for instance.

17. It is true that Newton is less read by scientists than Descartes is by philosophers (although most philosophers still encounter Descartes only through rational reconstructions, like scientists get to know Newton mechanics). This may be due to a difference in reception of technical notation (Newton's way of writing is less well preserved than Descartes's way of writing), as well as a difference in the history of the historiography of philosophy as compared to the history of the historiography of science (they had a different institutional embedding and were used differently in pedagogical practice).

the case of metaphysics and epistemology, for instance, and "nature" in the case of the sciences. The interest is in the object of science or philosophy, not in science or philosophy *in se*. It is clear therefore that the use of history in science or philosophy remains firmly embedded in the practice of science or philosophy. In contrast, the history of science has science itself as its object, and I think it is fair to say that, similarly, the history of philosophy should have philosophy itself as its object. The history of philosophy is a historical inquiry into *philosophy*, not into "being" or "knowledge." Traditionally, the focus of the history of philosophy has been on philosophical texts, but this seems a rather limited interpretation of "philosophy." I think it is an evident and fruitful challenge for the history of philosophy, in analogy to the history of science, to take the full richness of the practice of philosophy as a subject matter, including practices of philosophizing (writing, reading, acting, philosophical engagement in the world), institutions, social structures, material culture, and, of course, the resulting philosophical texts.[18]

The difference between the use of history in philosophy and the history of philosophy is thus not a question of anachronism or presentism; rather, they have a different object that is of interest, and their practice is adapted to this interest.[19] The practices of the former are philosophical, while the practices of the latter are historical. This does not preclude the possibility that the latter involves philosophical practices as well, of course, and in order to do good history of philosophy (e.g., interpreting past philosophical texts), the historian of philosophy needs considerable philosophical skill. Furthermore, I think these two approaches are in general characterized by a different way of understanding: while the first is more systematic in orientation, the second is more characterized by what I would call a "genealogical" understanding.[20] In trying to understand why things are as they are, both ask different questions. The philosopher wonders how phenomena or concepts are interrelated with other phenomena and concepts. The historian, in contrast, asks how these phenomena or concepts have come into being. It has been common to frame this distinction as the difference between looking for "reasons" and looking for "causes." I think this dichotomy is not very useful, as historians are interested in more than just causes. What is also important to note in this respect,

18. For importing methods from the history of science into the history of philosophy, see also Justin E. H. Smith in this volume.

19. Of course, there are more interesting philosophical uses of history than the one I mentioned above. See, e.g., Williams (2002) and even Craig (1999).

20. I will not go into a comparison with the "genealogical" project of Foucault and Nietzsche.

however, is that reasons can be causes. A past philosopher might have had many reasons to perform certain acts (including writing or defending a certain position) but these reasons are only effective when they become causes. What interests the historian are those reasons that caused the past philosopher to act, insofar as a historian is interested in actuality (in what actually happened) and not so much in possibility (what would have happened if . . .). Indeed, it is with such reasons that the historian of philosophy will usually be confronted, looking at how different reasons (understood in their historical context) have caused philosophers to develop and change their theories.

In the second part of this chapter, I will address the interest or relevance of this kind of history of philosophy. Is it "mere history" and does it necessarily abandon the aim of making a positive contribution to current philosophy?[21]

3. Genealogies and Sameness

To start with, I would like to stress that there is an intrinsic irreducible and autonomous *historical* interest. There is no need to be apologetic about doing history. History does not have to serve any utilitarian goal; it is legitimate to be interested in history as such.[22] (The same is true for philosophy, of course). I therefore see no reason to subordinate a historical interest to a philosophical one in the history of philosophy.[23] To the contrary, in the light of the distinction I argued for earlier, the "use of history in philosophy" is subordinate to a philosophical interest, but "history of philosophy" is mainly driven by a historical interest. The main aim for a historian of philosophy is to get the historical story (in which philosophers as well as philosophical texts figure prominently) right. This, however, does not mean that history of philosophy should be uninteresting for philosophers. Even if history of philosophy is not done mainly for philosophical purposes, it does not mean that it cannot be relevant for current philosophical concerns. It is such kind of supplementary relevance that I will explore in what follows.

---

21. See the introduction to this volume.

22. For a spirited defense, see, e.g., Tollebeek and Verschaffel (1992); but see Henkes (1993) for a criticism of their position.

23. One could argue that in contrast to the history of science, the history of philosophy is still insufficiently professionalized, in that it has not been able to separate itself enough from its object of study, philosophy. The history of science used to be practiced in science departments, but this has now become the exception. Historians of science now work in independent departments (sometimes in alliance with philosophers or sociologists of science) or belong to history departments. This institutional (in)dependence also has consequences for the dominance of historical versus philosophical/scientific interests.

In the remainder of this chapter, I will address the specific question of what kind of history of philosophy is *philosophically* relevant, without it jeopardizing its historical accuracy.[24] My answer neither precludes that other kinds of history can be interesting nor does it rule out that other kinds of philosophy are valuable. Nevertheless, I will restrict myself here to the theme of the volume, and I will argue that a genealogical approach is the most promising methodology for the history of philosophy if the historian of philosophy wants it to be relevant for current day philosophers. Indeed, genealogy shows that there is no gap between the present and the past. We are all part of history, and therefore, philosophers today are part of the history of philosophy (whether they want it or not). A genealogical study aims at showing this and at drawing consequences from it. In particular, a genealogical history of philosophy, in showing how current philosophical concepts, theories, and practices actually come into being, will be the most interesting for present day philosophers.

The questions asked and the way of understanding proposed in a genealogical approach are different from the way this is done in systematic philosophy, but nevertheless, the answers this approach can deliver may be very useful for philosophy. A historical account may shed new light on current concepts, theories, and problems and may even show alternatives.[25] It is not about a "comparison" between, e.g., early modern and twenty-first-century problems or theories (such a comparison might be more a projection of the historian than a real relation between the two periods), but a genealogical account that traces the actual evolution of concepts and theories and makes clear how the current conceptual schemes came about. Of course, this does not deliver the philosopher a straightforward philosophical justification or rejection of these schemes, but it gives us a causal story that sheds a different kind of light on the problem, which a contemporary philosopher might find useful. This approach comprises one way of heeding Wittgenstein's advice that philosophy should be therapeutic and should solve problems of language. Since language is historical, and since concepts have been developed for particular reasons in specific contexts, these past uses will still affect our current uses.[26] It is through

24. One could of course also ask the question which kinds of history of philosophy are interesting for *historians*, but this would be a different topic.

25. Cf. Taylor (1984).

26. Even if one accepts the existence of some instances of "total discontinuity" in the way a concept is deployed at different points in history, it is important to identify these historical moments and to trace the genealogical development from there. But it is equally important to understand how and why these discontinuities occurred, and in order to do that, one will

a genealogical study that these relations can be brought to light. A historical account therefore seems essential to such a therapeutic enterprise.

One example of such a genealogy of concepts and practices up till today is Lorraine Daston and Peter Galison's recent study of "objectivity," which deals in particular with how objectivity is represented in scientific atlases. They express the force of the genealogical approach as follows: "A study like this one should ultimately shed light on the grand epistemological visions and moral anxieties now associated with scientific objectivity.... It may also be possible to unravel the conceptual tangle of the current meanings of objectivity. If the concept grew historically, by gradual accretion and extension from practices, it is not so surprising that its structure is confused rather than crystalline."[27] They stress the importance of practices, but the same could be said about concepts and ideas, of course, and the result would not necessarily be more "crystalline." As a project in history of philosophy, instead of scientific atlases, one could study how objectivity was conceptualized by philosophers through the ages, as part of broader knowledge practices. One could then also inquire into how this genealogy still affects current philosophical debates on objectivity (something Daston and Galison do not address).[28]

It is still rare to explore the history of philosophy by treating philosophy as a practice. I think philosophers could be more open to this approach. The object of the history of philosophy is past philosophy as a whole. Crucial questions therefore are: What is past philosophy? How did it work? The history of philosophy should inform us about the practices of past philosophy, and even if "philosophy" is not a natural kind or does not have an essence, past philosophy is still relevant for philosophy today. Because, again, philosophy today is part of a genealogy and is linked to past philosophy, studying the history of philosophy will make philosophy more self-reflexive.[29] Someone trained in analytic epistemology might think philosophy is preeminently concerned with truth and follows a clearly delineated method in this pursuit;

---

have to understand the earlier genealogy of the concept, historical conditions, and the historical contexts at the time, and how all these interacted to generate this putative discontinuity. Discontinuities do not come out of nowhere and are not necessarily unintelligible. They too should be understood and analyzed by means of a historiographical methodology.

27. Daston and Galison (2007), 53.

28. Early modern philosophy does not just consist of different theories but also of different practices (e.g., disputation), different aims (e.g., the good life), etc. One could (and should) incorporate these practices as well as the material culture, interactions with the sciences and wider culture, etc.

29. Garber (2005) explores one kind of such reflexivity.

a confrontation with the history of philosophy might make him aware of other aims and other methods (e.g., the good life versus conceptual analysis or the method of intuitions).[30] Furthermore, a genealogical story might make the student understand why analytic philosophy took a different approach, for intrinsic as well as contextual factors. It might make him wonder if the same contextual conditions are still valid, and if current analytic philosophy has succeeded in its aims.[31]

In contrast to Daston and Galison, authors such as Jonathan Israel mainly focus on ideas, an approach closer to the stock-in-trade of the philosopher. Israel starts from a strong political engagement and belief in the values of the Enlightenment, but he is absolutely convinced that genealogy—how the Enlightenment came into being—is crucial for understanding what it is and how the project of the Enlightenment can be advanced today. This does not necessarily lead him to do bad history (although a "genealogy" of such a complex phenomenon comes across as somewhat naive, despite the almost 3,000 pages Israel devotes in his trilogy to the genealogy of the Enlightenment).[32] It is commonly accepted that current views of modernity and Enlightenment are tributary to the French Revolution, but Israel aims to show that the genealogy runs further back, to Spinoza and to what he calls the "Radical Enlightenment." He also thinks that we can draw lessons from this genealogy that can help us to address contemporary problems. Israel presents an interesting approach, but this does not mean that everyone should start doing such *longue durée* studies, of course. Israel's work clearly shows the possibilities but also the limits of what one can achieve with these kinds of genealogy.[33] Nevertheless, the writings of an individual historian fit in a broader discipline, which as a whole spans all of history, and the individual historian's work therefore contributes to and belongs to a genealogical project.

Several contributions to this volume also use a genealogical approach to describe the historical development of philosophical ideas and practices. Eric Schliesser and Michael Della Rocca, for instance, follow similar genealogical

30. E.g., Hadot (1995).

31. See, e.g., Della Rocca and Schliesser in this volume.

32. Israel (2001); Israel (2006); Israel (2011). I am here not entering into particular criticisms against Israel's work.

33. Israel's aim was very ambitious, especially because the enlightenment is such a complex phenomenon, and a genealogy of one problem or concept, for instance, seems a more manageable enterprise.

strategies in looking for the origins of analytic philosophy. Schliesser goes back to Ernest Nagel, analyzing the problems of this original position and offering a "counter-history of analytic philosophy" embodied in the work of Schlick as a possible genealogical therapy. Della Rocca similarly goes back to the origins of analytic philosophy—in his case, the discussion between Russell, Moore, and Bradley, as a result of which the method of intuition came to dominate the field. When we revisit this original moment, we can find a diagnostic of the current ills of philosophy, or so they claim. We are still part of a long story, in which central decisions and directions were chosen a long time ago, and we can revisit these basic choices in order to renew current philosophical practice. The article in this volume written by Delphine Kolesnik-Antoine shows the importance of studying the genealogy of the historiography of philosophy, a historiography that is institutionalized in the teaching curricula, and of which we are the direct inheritors. The history of the reception and interpretation of past philosophers still affects current schools or traditions in philosophy, as well as our personal understanding of these philosophers.

Even if the possibility of writing a full-fledged genealogy might be an illusion, I do think most historians and especially historians of philosophy assume that there is such a genealogical connection to the past they study. It is usually because of this genealogical connection (or by a reconstruction of this genealogical lineage) that philosophers got interested in the work of a past philosopher in the first place.[34] Philosophers are part of a community of scholars and their work is part of larger historiographical framework within which it gets its meaning. Is this genealogical approach a kind of appropriation of history? Not really. History does not have to be written with a utilitarian purpose in

34. This argument seems to render world history problematic. It seems that the past of alien cultures can only be approached through some knowledge and interaction with the contemporary alien culture. The "western" orientation of history of philosophy seems to confirm the interest in one's "own" genealogy, especially if one wants to draw conclusions from it relevant for current philosophy. This is changing now that our knowledge of intercultural contacts and circulation of knowledge becomes more detailed, and we learn that our "own" past has never been as isolated as we might think. Indeed, the history of historiography shows how the interest of historians has long been guided by an ethnocentric genealogy. Evans (2000), 178, cites a number of historians who until the 1990s claimed that Africa had no history and that writing the history of Asia was impossible. John Vincent wrote "We do not understand Asia and will not need to" (ibid.). Evans correctly remarks that the changing balance of global economic power will quickly make such views obsolete, again indicating the importance of changes in the present for the changing evaluations by historians of what counts as interesting (or even possible) research topics.

mind in order to be interesting and useful (often in for the author unexpected ways). Genealogical history can be executed out of a purely historical interest; it can be historically accurate and of philosophical relevance.

On the one hand, genealogical writing might lead to historiographical pitfalls. In particular, one should avoid a teleological historiography of precursors and anticipations. Also, the vague notion of influence should be shunned, as it makes historians postulate relations without good grounds. Indeed, all these concepts represent a historiography based on dubious notions of historical causality. The aim of looking for origins can be similarly flawed, if executed uncritically. Usually only a few origins or a few founding figures are identified, which results in a reductive historical picture that denies the richness of historical causation. The search for origins often gives a distorted view of the past, if one selects just a few elements as relevant for the later historical developments one is interested in, ignoring the rich historical context that would help us to better understand the past.[35] Genealogical histories tend to fit everything in a rather linear narrative, and also this should be avoided.[36]

Finally, the metaphor of "genealogy" should not be taken too strictly. Even if we can talk about a relationship that binds two historical events, there are many possibly relevant lineages. Drawings of the genealogy of species show an origin and lines that are branching out. The genealogical figures that trace back a person's forefathers show a similar network that extends in the other direction. Both representations are of course partial (and depend on the point of interest). A historical genealogy is also infinitely more complex. Unlike offspring (of sexual reproduction), which has only two parents, historical events can have many relevant causes, substantially complicating the picture. Genealogies do not need to fall into these pitfalls. Furthermore, even if historians are motivated to study a certain period because of its genealogical relevance, they should still explore this past era in a wider perspective, bringing in different contemporary contexts, in order to arrive at a better understanding of crucial past moments.

On the other hand, genealogies have a very important function in historical research. They are very helpful, even necessary, to make historical

35. The precursor approach is very much present in the history of technology. In my own work on the magic lantern, which is generally conceived of as the origin of the movie projector, I have argued that such an approach misses the richness of instruments, their aims and variations at the time. Of course, when Christiaan Huygens first conceived of the magic lantern in 1662, he did not envision it as the forerunner of the movie projector. See Vermeir (2005), 128.

36. Daston and Galison (2007) have tried to avoid this, but have only partly succeeded. See also Daston and Park (1998), 10–11, and the difference with Park and Daston (1981).

interpretation possible. The existence of a genealogical connection is the main methodological difference between anthropology and history. This indicates that the problem of interpretation and the kind of relevance of historical work is different from that of anthropology. An anthropologist can interact with the culture under study, creating shared practices (or "trading zones"), which is crucial for his interpretative efforts. This, of course, is impossible for historians. (The "conversation" imagined by Rorty and others only goes one way. Even if you recognize some kind of "resistance" in the text, this is still not a conversation.) Historians are, however, in contact with their past in virtue of a genealogical connection. Their past is not entirely alien for them, because they know that they are historically connected to it. This is a crucial advantage for historical interpretation, and it is one of the main tools for avoiding vicious anachronisms. As Jardine puts it: "When seeking entry points for interpretation of bafflingly alien works and deeds, [we should] look for specific traditions of practices linking them to us, rather than postulating common ground at the level of supposed human universals,"[37] or, as I would put it more generally, rather than postulating unfounded similarities.

4. Genealogies and Difference

The true-blue historian is interested in the strangeness of history. It is exactly in this "strangeness" that history shows itself irreducible to current concerns. By studying the strange aspects of history, the historian can display his disciplinary autonomy. In contrast, the historian of philosophy (and philosophers even more) seems more interested in sameness, i.e. in problems in the past that resemble current problems, or that at least are at the origin of current problems. A little strangeness can be interesting, because it confronts the historian of philosophy with something unexpected, with historical resistance, from which he can learn. Too much strangeness is unwelcome, however (historians of philosophy are usually not interested in the history of witchcraft or vampirism). Strange are those things that were not handed on, what fell out of the canon, the dead branches in the genealogy that cannot be traced to the present day and therefore seem of little interest.

In what follows, I want to indicate that even the strangeness of history can be interesting and relevant to philosophers today. A first thing that the strangeness of history can show us is that the perceived "sameness" of history is often a construction. (Of course, strangeness can also be a construction,

37. Jardine (2000), 266.

especially in romantic accounts of history, similar to orientalism, which stressed the strangeness in other cultures, but, as already indicated, this is usually not the problem in history of philosophy.)[38] Recently, a philosopher colleague expressed his conviction that past philosophers, such as Aristotle, were much more intelligible than other past writers. Hacking too writes about the immediate intelligibility of Descartes for his students and his own shared sensibilities with Leibniz.[39] The past *is* different, however, and the strangeness of history shows this. Aristotle, Descartes, and Leibniz are not our contemporaries. A genealogical study of the *reception* of Aristotle, Descartes, and Leibniz will show that a lot of effort went into keeping or making these philosophers intelligible. Would Aristotle be intelligible were it not for long-lasting and strong traditions, continuing over centuries, interpreting and reinterpreting Aristotle? The latest commentaries, such as the work by John Cooper, make Aristotle more familiar for us, but Cooper too is the heir of a long tradition of reinterpretation.[40] Furthermore, the prominence of some of these schools (in certain historical periods) have diffused their reinterpretations of Aristotle's ideas into general intellectual culture, making it into a more general cultural heritage.[41] It is this continuous reinterpretation by historians of philosophy, different ways of reading, the changing curricula and textbooks that expounded canons of past philosophers, the methods and institutions that standardized questions, answers, and meanings (e.g., the sophismata), as well as a (relative) omnipresence in general cultural life, that should be studied. Such a study of reception will show that all these efforts have kept the thought of past philosophers more accessible and familiar to us than other ideas from the past. The modernity of Descartes is the result of a lot of work by generations of philosophers and historians of philosophy.[42]

There are more benefits to studying the strangeness of history. The strangeness of the past also creates wonder (the basic passion of philosophy, according to Aristotle!). This alienation prompts us to put into question a number

38. E.g., Said (1978).

39. Hacking (1984).

40. See Kolesnik-Antoine, this volume.

41. Even if it might seem that Avicenna does not make Aristotle much more familiar for us today, Avicenna played a crucial role in the medieval reception of Aristotle in the West. He is therefore a central figure in the genealogical reception story, and our current interpretations might still owe a lot to him, even if mediated through centuries of other reinterpretations.

42. See also the chapter by Kolesnik-Antoine, where she shows how historians of philosophy fit in past philosophers into the general background beliefs of dominant contemporary schools (e.g., spiritualism in the case of Cousin).

of basic attitudes, presuppositions, and concepts. Furthermore, the fact that something comes across as strange today does not mean that it did not have a crucial role in the past. It might have affected in an important way the course of history, and therefore the genealogy of our ideas and concepts. Charles Taylor has argued for studying origins of philosophical problems in order to open the black box.[43] Studying origins (but keeping in mind the possible pitfalls described earlier) allows us to see how these problems came into being, why they were formulated as they were, and what alternatives there may be that are not immediately available to us today. Nothing guarantees that these alternatives can be easily assimilated in our own conceptual schemes, however. As a matter of fact, because these are the "lost" options in history, which fell out of the genealogy, they might come across as rather strange, but that does not mean that they are therefore less important to understand.

Finally, I would like to argue not only for the importance of history of philosophy but for a broader vision of history with a philosophical sensibility and relevance (this could include crossovers between history of philosophy and other kinds of histories, or even history that uses philosophy).[44] I think protracted debates about the identity of history of philosophy are not very interesting or fruitful (usually, they are performed rather for institutional reasons than for intrinsic reasons). Furthermore, the idea of philosophy as an unworldly and isolated enterprise is itself only a rather recent historical construction.[45] We should instead be open to other approaches to the history of intellectual life, culture, and philosophical practice. One version of such a way of writing history with crossover potential and with a philosophical sensibility is historical epistemology. I already mentioned *Objectivity* by Daston and Galison, but there are many different *currents* in historical epistemology.[46] At a conference in Berlin, Lorraine Daston has attempted to characterize the difference between (her kind of) historical epistemology and the history of epistemology as follows.[47] Historical epistemology is the emergence and articulation of new epistemological categories and problems

43. Taylor (1984).

44. Cf. Chartier (2009), chapter 10, for some possible interactions between history and philosophy.

45. Something similar holds for natural philosophers; see, e.g., Schaffer (2009).

46. See, e.g., the recent conferences at the Max Planck Institute for the History of Science, Columbia University, and Leuven University, as well as symposia and seminar series in Nancy and Paris, exploring the different strands in historical epistemology.

47. For other policing and demarcation attempts by Daston, however, see Daston (2009).

out of knowledge practices. She opposes this to the history of epistemology, which is the history of philosophical theories, or more generally, the history of reflections, both philosophical and scientific, on the ways of acquiring and justifying knowledge.[48] As I have argued, history of philosophy can (and should) incorporate this focus on practices (although it would be a stretch to ask it to incorporate all kinds of scientific practices). Ideally, I think historical epistemology and the history of epistemology would in practice have large areas of overlap and collaboration. Indeed, there might remain some difference of focus, because of the different objects under study, but more interaction seems to be a desideratum.

I now want to take up a very different example, a more extreme case, because it shows more clearly the limits of interpretation and historiography. In his magisterial *Thinking with Demons*, Stuart Clark has applied "postmodern" philosophy to the history of witchcraft and demonology.[49] Maybe surprisingly for some, the result is interesting and successful.[50] Clark's problem was how to write the history of witchcraft or demonology if you do not want to simply reject the ideas of the people you study as false or even as nonsensical? Taking recourse to the "linguistic turn" popular in the 1990s (without desiring to take sides in the philosophical controversy), he took the work on "discourse" as a tool for his own historical aims. In this case, he applied the idea that signifiers did not need to refer to any real signified to make sense, but that only its differences with other signifiers were relevant.[51] He decided to treat all beliefs on the same par with this methodology, and the difference between what he considered physical possibilities and impossibilities became irrelevant. I find Clark's philosophical struggle with his recalcitrant historical material enlightening and the resulting book is highly readable and interesting. One striking result: it turns out that witchcraft discourse was very much preoccupied with issues of language and signs, which makes

48. Lorraine Daston's comment at the conference *What (Good) Is Historical Epistemology*?, Max Planck Institute for the History of Science, Berlin, July 24–26, 2008.

49. See Clark (1997).

50. In particular, Clark stresses the importance of the "linguistic turn" as well as an anti-realist approach for his work in the preface and chapter 1 of his book. Evans (2000), 307, calls Clark's approach "explicitly postmodernist." The Lévi-Straussian title refers to his (post-) structuralist interests and in particular to his treatment of demonology as an intellectual resource. Clark (1997), viii.

51. For a more extreme application of these ideas to witchcraft, see Maggi (2001), 226, who uses de Certeau and Lacan as points of departure, focusing on "discourse" (quoting Vattimo: "there are no facts, only interpretations") and mingling history, psychoanalysis, anthropology, and philosophy.

his approach even more appropriate. In fact, the concern with language at the time of the witch craze was not rivaled until the linguistic turn in the twentieth century.

It is part of the cultural historian's sensibility not to take sides too easily (and it is maybe an inheritance of postmodernism that some historians prefer to take sides with marginalized groups or beliefs rather than with the mainstream). Historians usually try to judge the beliefs and actions of the actors according to their context. Even if some contemporaries denounced witchcraft beliefs as nonsense, this does not mean that these beliefs were unreasonable in the context of the time. We know that witchcraft beliefs are not alien to early modern philosophers (e.g., Henry More and Robert Boyle, to name only two), something historians of philosophy will have to learn to deal with. Furthermore, some early modern philosophical views may be considered even more outlandish than witchcraft beliefs (and they certainly were for contemporaries; e.g., Spinoza comes in mind). A historical sensibility urges philosophers to come to terms with this strangeness of the past.

To conclude this section, I also want to raise the issue of the strangeness of the present. Not only early modern philosophical views can be compared with witchcraft beliefs, but also some current philosophical views fall for some of us in the same category of "strangeness." In contrast to the sciences, where there is widespread consensus over many issues, this is a far cry from the situation in philosophy. Many philosophical debates, often originating in the early modern period or even earlier, are not yet closed. This poses specific problems for the history of philosophy. Rorty dismissed such concerns as unfounded:

> We take the pardonable ignorance of great dead scientists for granted. We should be equally willing to say that Aristotle was unfortunately ignorant that there are no such things as real essences, or Leibniz that God does not exist, or Descartes that the mind is just the central nervous system under an alternative description. We hesitate merely because we have colleagues who are themselves ignorant of such facts, and whom we courteously describe not as "ignorant," but as "holding different philosophical views." Historians of science have no colleagues who believe in crystalline spheres, or who doubt Harvey's account of circulation, and they are thus free from such constraints. There is nothing wrong with self-consciously letting our own philosophical views dictate terms in which to describe the dead.[52]

52. Rorty (1984), 49–50.

History of science has changed since Rorty wrote this article. It is not common practice anymore to call Galen "ignorant" and to let our own views dictate the terms in which to describe past scientists. Especially in the case of philosophy, where the current perspective is dispersed rather than being in consensus, it would be inappropriate for the historian of philosophy to impose one's own perspective not only on the historical actors but also on one's readers.[53]

The question is, however, whether we can really avoid imposing our perspective. Can we really write a history in which possibilities and impossibilities are irrelevant? If we want to go beyond just describing discourses, can we describe a witch flying to the Sabbath as an action that happened in the past? A recent trend in the history of science has replicated experiments from the past, in order to learn more about the practices of experimentation, the materials alchemists, natural philosophers and scientists used, the problems they encountered (but did not write down).[54] This approach has been very successful, sometimes with remarkable results. Larry Principe has replicated alchemical experiments on the transmutation of gold, for instance, and was able to show that the procedures jotted down by the alchemists were not merely symbolic, religious, or psychological expressions, but represented real chemical reactions.[55] In these cases, however, we assume that we have a non-textual access to these past practices and that we share to a large extent the same world and experiences. This approach, which seems promising, is opposite to the discourse analysis proposed by Clark, because it is very much concerned about "real" possibilities and impossibilities. Principe was careful, however, not to go to the end of the experiment. The procedures became vaguer and could not be interpreted so easily anymore. If he had been able to push the experiments to the end, would he have arrived at the transmutation of gold (which would have put him in an awkward spot with his chemist colleagues) or should he have concluded that the procedures in the end were nonsense or fraud (something he wants to avoid as a historian sensitive to the worldview of

53. Historical difference also shows the limits of the dialogical approach, or the idea of a conversation with the past. Of course, a lot of wisdom can be gained by such imaginary conversations. But such approaches belong rather to the philosophical *use* of history than to the history of philosophy proper.

54. See Sibum (1995).

55. See Principe (2000).

the actors he studies)? Principe's *own* position on alchemy would become important in his historical analysis, something he has so far avoided doing as a historian.[56]

One can wonder if not only this specific method used in the history of science, but all historical writing, is in the end not anchored in the life world and the beliefs of the historian, how much he might try to erase them, and that in some cases, these will come to the fore. A contemporary witch or astrologer writing the history of witchcraft or astrology does this in a very different fashion from that used by academic historians. Would it be so different for different kinds of philosophers?[57] We should be clear that our basic presuppositions about the world are not necessarily shared with the historical actors, and maybe not even with our contemporary colleagues and readers. For taking into account all these sensibilities, reflection on *ways of writing* the history of philosophy becomes important.[58]

5. Conclusion

The question I have tried to answer in this chapter is how history of philosophy can still be relevant for philosophy, after giving up the timelessness of philosophical problems and truths as well as the ideal of a conversation with the past. After the necessary caveats (that there can be other fruitful ways of doing history of philosophy, which do not necessarily answer to historical accuracy or philosophical relevance) I have argued that for an authentic history of philosophy, which takes the demands of both history and philosophy seriously, a genealogical approach seems to be the most fruitful way to go. Such a genealogy, if it avoids a number of typical pitfalls, is historically accurate, ambitious, and challenging, and is at the same time relevant for the present. Everything is in history, and the present will be history in an instant. Even the future can only be thought of in terms of the present and the past. It seems therefore inconceivable that history would not be relevant to philosophy.

56. I explored these themes in the workshop *Questioning "Occult Sciences,"* June 16, 2010, in Paris and a talk "Reconstruction and Re-enactment in the History of Science and Technology" on October 14, 2011, in Brussels.

57. See Luhrman (1989) for an interesting sociology of contemporary witchcraft. She showed that many contemporary witches are actually highly educated professionals, including engineers, physicians, and (who knows?) maybe even some professional philosophers.

58. For some reflections on narrativity, writing, and history, see Chartier (2009).

There are two different ways of understanding events (and under events I include here also texts as well as ideas), which we could call systematic and genealogical. Why is something the way it is? What is the meaning of something? One answer will look into the relation with other objects, concepts, practices, or uses that exist at the same time. A second approach is to look into how things came into being. Both methods of answering this basic question lead to different accounts, but these do not have to be in conflict with each other. Why is there a political left and right? What does "left" mean? A systematic answer will detail the general opposition between two political worldviews, each of which might have some kind of general coherence. A genealogical answer will go back to specific historical circumstances, among others, the historical event of two French political factions sitting at opposite sides of the isle, as part of a specific political system, and would trace the vicissitudes of these political views till today. This complex historical story has also a critical potential: given that political, social, and other circumstances have changed, one can wonder whether such a division in "left" and "right" still makes sense.

In order to acquire certain historiographical sensibilities, it is important to practice the research and writing of history. It is fruitful and enriching to practice different methodologies and not to focus exclusively on one kind (even if this is genealogy).[59] On an individual level, practicing a plurality of historiographical methodologies broadens one's interests; one learns a diversity of skills, and one becomes more tolerant for other ways of doing history. On a disciplinary level, however, different kinds of practicing the history of philosophy still fit into a larger genealogical framework. As a discipline, ideally, the entire history of philosophy will be covered. Therefore, systematic studies of Descartes, sociological studies of Hume, or intellectual histories of the German Enlightenment can all contribute to an overarching genealogical project. Even the strangeness of the past, typically seen as the domain of "historians proper," as well as the "broken-off branches" belong to genealogy, and the study of them is necessary for a correct understanding of the development of history in general and the history of philosophy in particular.

59. I have been arguing against views such as that of Martial Gueroult (1979, 49) who wrote that the "philosophical spirit" gives historical objects their *value as objects of history*, and it is therefore the philosophical side of the historian of philosophy that matters most. Historiography does not need a philosophical spirit to select its relevant objects, and this spirit is generally rather narrow minded.

4

Understanding the Argument through Then-Current Public Debates or My Detective Method of History of Philosophy

Ursula Goldenbaum

You did not know where to look, and so you missed all that was important.

SHERLOCK HOLMES[1]

"HISTORY OF PHILOSOPHY simply is philosophy, period! Philosophy of any time, if it is any good, can be understood by reading the text, checking the argument, and evaluating the suggested solutions by our professional standards."[2] That is what I get to hear since I began working in my field of early modern philosophy. I am perfectly fine with the claim that history of philosophy is philosophy and thus under its rules. I agree that we have to look at the argument and check whether the solutions of the discussed problems hold water by professional standards. I cannot accept though the "period!" The somewhat naive recommendation "Look at their texts and see if they got it right!" takes as granted what should be shown first—that we were able to understand these texts without historical knowledge about their intellectual environment. But how can we know what their problems were? How do we even know the meaning of their words? Do the words *they used* and *we still use*

1. Doyle (1976), 66.

2. This is the summary of what I got to hear over decades, not a quote of anybody in particular, although Thomas Williams describes it pretty well as a position he almost shares: "The point is always to understand what's at issue philosophically, not to understand how what's at issue came to be at issue" (Williams 2008).

refer to the same things?[3] How anachronistic the outcome of this assumption can become is evident from the long-lasting misunderstanding of "constitutionalism" as originating from the *Magna Carta* of England in 1225 creating a whole school in the Anglo-American literature.[4] Unfortunately, the term "the people" in this medieval contract does not refer to all the citizens of a state. In 1225, it meant a handful of barons.[5]

I share the suspicion against historical explanations that remain a mere addition to the actual philosophical discussion, without explanatory power. I am tired as well of hagiographic appraisals of past philosophers' achievements just because their outcome happens to fit our own results. Neither did Kant anticipate non-Euclidean geometries when talking about more than three dimensions in his first book[6] nor did Althusius ask for popular sovereignty in any modern sense.[7] Above all, I oppose *Ideengeschichte*,—as if ideas had a coherent history on their own. Ideas are found or created by human beings when they are needed, just as tools are invented or produced when needed.[8] Also, once found and then forgotten in the storage of the history of ideas, they can be rediscovered after long periods if people are looking for them when grappling with new problems—as we remember a tool that might be helpful to solve a problem when it had rested unused somewhere in the garage for years. Such a rediscovery happened, e.g., in the thirteenth century to the ancient idea of political liberty when the rising power of cities and city-states made their leaders want to justify their independence from the Holy Roman Empire, after hundreds of years without references throughout

3. Richard Kraut suggested in a recent lecture titled *An Esthetic Reading of Aristotle's Nicomachean Ethics* to translate the Greek word *kalon* no longer as "fine" or "noble" but as "beautiful"—because it often means that too and even just that. True, but will this solve the problem that the Greek word involved both, and even more meanings which we now distinguish? While we separate beauty from virtue, for the Greeks a man could not be beautiful without being good and noble.

4. For a critique of the anachronistic idea of the concept of "Constitutionalism," see Goldenbaum (2011a), 501–2.

5. Ibid., 505–6. See also Skinner (2002), 262.

6. Martin Schönfeld's article for the *Stanford Encyclopedia* is certainly hard to top—he seriously believes Kant's first book would show "the mark of genius" (Schönfeld 2012) in spite of the young Kant's violation of the principle of inertia or the law of conservation.

7. See Gierke (1966), 160–61; Hueglin (1999), 182–83. Again, who are "the people"? Do we speak of the leaders of the guilds and magistrates or of all individuals of a state? Althusius's concept of the people is still premodern, separating the people in about six ranks of social strata with different extension of rights and participation, the lowest being actors and executers.

8. With Hobbes I take *need* to be "the mother of all inventions" (Hobbes (1994), 16, chapter 4: "On Speech").

medieval times.[9] However, as soon as it was recycled it had also to be adapted to the new peculiar needs.

Thus, although we have a long tradition of philosophical texts, dealing with problems, and a big tool box of rules and concepts to solve them, acquired over the last 2,500 years, new philosophies originated because of new problems that had come up or because the old solutions were no longer sufficient. That is why there cannot be a *historia perennis* in any strict way. It was only with Galileo's *Assayer* that we understood the "properties of things", e.g. colors, as produced in our senses, i.e., as subjective.[10] Only then the question for the possible access to the external world arose and thereby epistemology as a discipline. In the same way, there was no need for "the sublime" before the seventeenth century and it did not exist. It became an issue only in 1674 when Boileau pointed to the sublime language of the Old Testament thereby causing a wave of theologically inspired esthetics throughout Europe.[11] There was no free will before Augustine understood it as a way to unburden the Christian God from our sins by ascribing to us a special faculty to will freely.[12] Greek philosophy was fine without as was again Spinoza in the seventeenth century in light of modern science. And, it has finally been "discovered shockingly" that the *Magna Carta* "merely sprang up from the private ambition of a few selfish barons"[13] and had nothing to do with *individual* human rights being an idea of modern time alone. Thus if we want to understand a past philosophy we have first to identify its problem and the possible and available options for its solution at the time. Only then we can discuss the suggested solution and judge its validity. To do this we need to grasp the *meaning* of a text before we can check its *truth*. Spinoza, in his rules of text interpretation, carefully distinguished these two different tasks to understand any past text. Thus—judging a text by our professional standards is absolutely fine with me—once the text's meaning, and the problem that is solved or pretended to be solved in that text, has been figured out. This latter task, I think, is the specific task of *history* of philosophy and it is for this task that I suggest the detective method.

---

9. For the republican recycling of Aristotle in earliest modern Italian city republics, see Skinner (1990), 121–22.

10. See Galilei (1957), 273–78.

11. See Boileau (1682), 16–17. For the theological implications of the origin of esthetics as a "new science," see Goldenbaum (2011b), 305–15.

12. See Augustine (1993), in particular 29–31, 57, 64–83.

13. Skinner (2002), 262.

The programmatic article of a new analytical journal on history of philosophy may serve as a perfect example for the spectacular failure of a mere "logical analysis" of a philosophical text of the past, due to its author's ignoring of the historical intellectual context.[14] The author chose the example of Kant's famous *Answer to the Question: What Is Enlightenment* as his subject to show the power of his method of mere "logical analysis." As a result, he criticized Kant for confusing the terms "immaturity" (*Unmündigkeit*) and "tutelage" (*Vormundschaft*).[15] Because the people in Prussia were ruled by an absolute monarch and lacked freedom of speech they "obviously" could not be blamed for bearing with their not "self-incurred" but "imposed tutelage." Kant, thus the author, simply chose the false categories. Not that I am bothered by the author's criticism of the great Kant; neither do I disagree with his statement about Prussia's political system. I simply wonder how a philosopher who pretends to understand Kant's text better by mere "logical analysis" can so completely miss the point of the famous opening sentence of that essay! As if Kant could have ignored the fact of political absolutism in Prussia! His declared subject in the essay is just about the possibility of enlightenment under the condition of absolute monarchy. Moreover, Kant's meticulous wording is notorious and he definitely *meant* to say that the people "incurred" their "immaturity" themselves. The famous first sentence of the *Essay*, so often quoted, offers in a nutshell the absolutely central idea of Kant's practical philosophy that everybody has the duty to choose the right maxim herself to become a moral being (or not), *no matter what circumstances* she is in. We have after all free will.[16] If one wants to criticize the opening sentence of Kant's *Essay on Enlightenment* by this suggested "logical analysis"—and still wants to be logically coherent—one has to abandon Kant's practical philosophy altogether. But I seriously doubt this to be the author's intention.

Thus history of philosophy is obviously needed, if only to clarify terminology. The meaning of the used terms can only be understood in the way they were used at the time.[17] But we further need to understand the *intention* of the past philosopher in order to get what he meant to say. I am aware that I am stirring up a hornet's nest—intentions are considered psychological, something beyond philosophy and argument. But I don't talk about psychological states of past authors. Neither will I go into the deep water of hermeneutics.

---

14. Newen (1998), 23–29.

15. Ibid., 26–27.

16. While this view prevails all of Kant's moral writing, see for a focused formulation in Kant (1996a), 65.

17. Admirers of Wittgenstein should know this. See *Philosophical Investigations*, § 43.

I simply ask for the intention of an author in the sense a detective asks for the motives of a wrongdoer. A detective's search for a motive for a crime leads her investigation as much as a scientist is led by his hypothesis. She will not close her case before she finds a convincing motive of the wrongdoer, just as a scientist will not stop before the phenomena fit a coherent hypothesis.[18] As soon as it is found, all pieces fall into their places, in both cases. For me, when I turn to a new philosophical text from the past, I feel and proceed like a detective, collecting data and looking for a hypothesis to make sense of them.

Of course, I begin by carefully reading the texts of the author under investigation, together with texts of related authors. But I do not trust their statements about their intentions. I suspend my judgment and compare the texts in what they suggest or argue against. Like a detective, I have to make sure that I understand their statements correctly, i.e., in the sense they were meant at that time, which does not only cause special problems in case of foreign languages but also when technical terms occur in these texts as it is pretty common in philosophy. Thus I need to learn about the use of these terms at the time. I try to figure out whether or in what sense the authors of the texts under my investigation were sincere in their mutual arguments: what they said in public and what in their letters, what was their explicit statement and what was said implicitly.[19] Also, I try to look for alternative options they could have chosen to solve their problem (in a mere philosophical way). Last but not least, as a detective I also look to "the facts" or the surrounding reality of my authors, the rules of discourse at the time, opportunities for publication, censorship, prevailing theological demands, political conditions, etc. in order to discover their options.

Thus, as a detective would look for "good reasons" some of the suspects might have had for committing the crime, I look for the "good reasons" a philosopher might have had to take a particular stance in a controversy. While a detective may search for last wills, bank accounts, love stories, and jealousy, I will ask for possible philosophical intentions to solve a particular problem in such a way that it can secure a certain intended outcome and will exclude those competing positions that could hinder that intended outcome—through argument. All human actions are driven by intentions. Aren't philosophical texts actions as well?

---

18. Einstein/Infeld (1971), 4–5 and 75–76.

19. To be sure, I am not favoring the often crazily arbitrary reading "between the lines" of Strauss (1989), 25. His naive suggestions for reading a text lack any consistent criteria to distinguish between what he calls esoteric and exoteric meaning as is clear from his practical results in using his method. He simply ascribes these attributes according to his own likings or dislikings, in case of the less-liked Mendelssohn even violating his duties as an editor.

A detective takes the statements of witnesses and involved agents and then checks them against each other by further interrogation. But I can't ask past philosophers anymore. However, we still have the philosophical controversies of their time. Since the late seventeenth century we even have public debates, which can provide the material and statements that allow me to search for the "good reasons" of past philosophers.[20] The way in which philosophers argue with their opponents during such philosophical controversies is far more illuminating in respect to their intentions as well as their logical strengths than any preface of their works could ever be. Moreover, nobody can see the weakness of a philosophical argument as clearly as a contemporary opponent who will also provide hints to see what is at stake in their mutual exchange of arguments. I see philosophical controversies and, even more, public debates as accelerated and dense periods of the discourse in a society, when philosophers, scientists, and theologians of a country discussed, simultaneously and intensively, one and the same particular subject, often referring directly to each other. Thus, the investigation of such public debates appears to me a perfect tool for the investigation of past philosophies, to understand why a problem was a problem for these philosophers and what kind of philosophical ammunition was needed to get them solved or to fight opposed positions.[21]

In addition, the rich material of public debates since early modern times provides us with different layers of the contemporary audience, from other philosophers or philosophical experts to theologians, politicians, newspaper-journalists, and court administrators in regard to censorship cases. The public debates, going on not only in books and philosophical journals, dissertation defenses and university programs, but in newspapers and flyers, sermons, and caricatures, enable us to trace the effect of philosophical statements on the audience for even periods as small as months. Thus we can see to what extent a book, an article, a public statement, or a measure of censorship

20. It was my interest in the *reasons* that would bring about new ideas, especially new philosophical ideas, that led me to my research project on public debates in eighteenth-century Germany. Together with my colleagues, we reconstructed seven such debates (see Goldenbaum 2004).

21. While Eric Watkins is perfectly right to state that quite a few Wolffians changed their position from preestablished harmony toward *influxus physicus*, his assumption that this was simply due to the convincing power of the latter position is bluntly wrong. In fact, it was the result of the extreme theologico-political pressure to not to teach preestablished harmony at all (if one wanted to keep or get an academic position). The example of Gottsched is striking. See Watkins (1995), 295–339, especially his introduction, 295–300; Watkins (1998), 136–203; for a critique, see Goldenbaum (2012b, forthcoming).

became the buzz of the city. But it is not only interesting with regard to the reception of a philosophy but also for the origin of new philosophical ideas, because philosophers were provoked and inspired by public debates or controversies to find and promote new arguments in order to counter their opponents and hinder their success. Investigating public debates is hard work and extremely time-consuming. However, as a result of the research into public debates and controversies, we can not only reconstruct the general intellectual conditions of philosophical work for one philosopher of that period but for all of them. Admittedly, the rich material of these public debates is a particular advantage of early modern philosophy and is lacked by ancient or medieval philosophy. Nevertheless, I would still consider investigating controversies in a broader context as an appropriate detective tool as often as we can find these controversies.

Thus what I see as the specific task of the *historian* of philosophy and what I am trying to do in my own work is to reconstruct the problems and the intention of a past philosopher as well as to explain his terminology. In this way, the *historian* has to explore the meaning that the text had for the author and his audience. Only then I can read the text as I read a contemporary philosophical text whose problem I can understand much more easily due to my familiarity with the current intellectual discourse and the ongoing controversies as well as the facts the text touches on. Only then the *philosopher* in the historian of philosophy can check the validity of the argument and its truth. In the following section, I will use Kant's *Essay on Enlightenment* to illustrate my suggested detective method for the *historical* task of a historian of philosophy in a short case study—i.e., I will try to find the *meaning* of Kant's *Essay* so that I can then judge the validity of his argument by the standards of philosophy.

2. *The Meaning of Kant's* Answer to the Question: What Is Enlightenment?

I chose this text because it is short, it is well known to a broader audience, and the contrast between my approach to it and the one criticized above may more easily illustrate my point. Thus what is Kant's *Essay* about? In addition to the often quoted opening sentence, providing Kant's famous definition of enlightenment, the essay suggests a way in which the enlightenment of a people is possible in whatever political circumstances. Such enlightenment can occur if and only if a free public discourse is allowed, among learned men on the one hand and between these learned men and the authorities of the church and state on the other.[22] This view of the text is generally accepted. I will begin my investigation by taking a closer look at the often noticed peculiar formulation of the first sentence, taking into account that Kant carefully chose his wording. Then I will discuss his suggested model for enlightenment—the public discourse—and situate it within the spectrum of then-current alternative models.

The term "self-incurred immaturity" (*selbstverschuldete Unmündigkeit*) has drawn quite some attention in Kant scholarship. Of course, its meaning has been discussed especially when it had to be translated. In English, "minority" or "immaturity" are used for "*Unmündigkeit.*"[23] Some authors suggested "tutelage," which does not seem right because it is imposed and cannot be self-incurred.[24] However, even "immaturity" or "minority" can hardly be regarded as self-incurred when they refer to age or mental health as the legal origin of these terms would suggest. Because of the origin of the term "*Unmündigkeit*" (and its English correspondents) in legal language there has been a long-lasting general agreement that Kant borrowed this term from jurisprudence. But while this understanding fits "immaturity" it does not go well with "self-incurred," or even worse, with the original German "*selbstverschuldet*," literally meaning being guilty of having caused something. While the refusal to get out of immaturity might be considered culpable, legal immaturity can hardly be thought of as self-caused.

However, the legal origin of Kant's term "immaturity" has been questioned in recent decades, though without great impact yet. First, the German theologian Frieder Lötzsch pointed to the use of the term by the enlightened theologian Johann Joachim Spalding in his Berlin *Inaugural Sermon* of 1764.[25] We know that Kant held Spalding's sermons in high regard[26] and that he sent

---

22. Habermas's *The Structural Transformation of the Public Sphere* (in German 1962) caused an entire historical literature about the public discourse in German Enlightenment, driven by literary critics, about journals, literary societies, salons, etc. (without ever looking at enlightened theology or at the long tradition of public debates in German Enlightenment since the seventeenth century) that is still lasting in the United States where the book has been translated in 1989. While its blunt historical shortcomings are usually excused by its systematic goals, these mistakes still shape historical research as well as systematic discussions of the public sphere.

23. Beck translated the term as "tutelage" (Beck (1995), 83), Mary Gregor as "minority" (Kant (1996b), 17), James Schmidt and others as "immaturity" (Schmidt (1996), 58).

24. In German, "Vormundschaft" is imposed by law in case of "Unmündigkeit" while "Unmündigkeit" is a matter of fact.

25. Lötzsch (1973), 320.

26. "Beobachtungen aus dem gemeinen Leben, wozu in Spaldings Predigten gute Anleitung gegeben wird," in Kant (1910-ongoing), *Gesammelte Schriften*, ed. by Academy of Prussia, vol. 24, 808 (this edition henceforth abbreviated KAA, followed by the volume number). This is also confirmed by Kant's biographer Borowski.

Spalding his *Dreams of a Spirit Seer* in 1766.[27] Spalding used the term "immaturity" when speaking of the process of our own education from immature to true Christians by following Jesus Christ and embracing the moral law.[28] Norbert Hinske, the well-known German Kant scholar, noticed that Kant had never used the term in any publication before the *Essay*.[29] Thus he dug deeper, following the hint of Lötzsch, and traced back the theological use of "immaturity" to the then common German Lutheran translation of the Bible (since 1704), and more specifically, to *Paul's Letter to the Galatians*.[30] Paul, in this translation, speaks of the "Unmündigkeit" of those who have not yet embraced Christian faith.[31] Thus Spalding's use of the term "Unmündigkeit" was in precise agreement with Paul's *Letter*. However, the original Lutheran translation of the Greek word was "Knechtschaft" and the respective English word "bondage" is still used in current English Bibles. Thus the use of the term "Unmündigkeit" in the revised German Lutheran Bible, and as a result, in German Lutheran theological literature of the eighteenth century, could hardly be discovered by a foreign or Catholic Kant scholar nor could it be seen by "logical analysis."

Once the theological origin of the term "immaturity" is clear, its striking combination with the adjective "self-incurred" becomes natural. This adjective obviously points to the fall of man—original sin. And if we look at Kant's *Religion in the Limits of Reason Alone* (nine years ahead) his statement there confirms such a reading. There he claims that the "promulgation of [the Christian doctrine of faith] can well be called the revelation of something which had hitherto remained a mystery for human beings through *their own guilt*."[32] Thus, the message of Christian faith ought to have been known by human individuals before its promulgation through Jesus Christ, but it was not—due to their original sin. Taking this together with the first sentence of the *Essay*, it says quite clearly and simply that we need to overcome our

27. Kant sent it via Mendelssohn to Spalding and Sack on February 7, 1766, in: KAA 10, 67–68.

28. See Spalding (1764), 19.

29. Hinske (1977), 545.

30. Ibid., 547.

31. What is striking when looking at this passage of Paul's *Letter* are the several occurrences not only of the term "*Unmündigkeit*" but also of the other term used by Kant in his essay, namely, "*Vormund*," respectively, "*Vormünder*."

32. Kant (2009), 142–43 (emphasis mine). The words in italics deviate slightly from the translation of Alan Wood and George di Giovanni who have "fault," which seems to address the sinner's guilt less pointed than the German "*eigene Schuld*."

failure to use the freedom we were given by Jesus Christ, to think on our own and embrace the moral law given by Jesus Christ. This would then be what Kant means by enlightenment and it is very much in agreement not only with Spalding's view of enlightenment but also with Kant's mature moral philosophy.

Paul's *Letter to the Galatians* is an extremely polemical text. Written to attack the then recent influence of Judaeo-Christian apostles under whose influence Galatians aimed to hold onto the Jewish law while becoming Christians (Judaeo-Christians), Paul is eager to draw a sharp line between Jews and Christians, and he does not shy away from abusing Jewish religion and law as incompatible with Christian faith. He calls the Jews "immature"—in obeying their law they were immature children and indistinguishable from servants; in contrast, Christians were led into freedom by Jesus Christ. The law is considered to have served as the "pedagogue," keeping us in line until the appearance of Jesus Christ, but no longer needed once the savior had come and set us free. The most aggressive passage, twisting even the textual evidence of the *Old Testament*, is Paul's juxtaposition of Abraham's two sons, one the legal son of his free wife (Sarah), being related to Jerusalem in heaven (meaning the Christian community), the other the son of the maid Hagar, being sent to the desert, related to the earthly Jerusalem on the hill (meaning the city of the Jews). Nothing could be more anachronistic if Paul were judged according to rules of textual interpretation. Today, especially in German Protestant systematic theology, this *Letter* is heavily under suspicion of being anti-Judaic[33] but current theological literature mostly focuses on the time of Paul and early Christianity and not on the *Letter*'s use in eighteenth-century Lutheran theology.[34]

To see how much Kant, picking "immaturity" from Paul's *Letter to the Galatians*, was simply in agreement with the mainstream of Lutheran theological enlightenment or perhaps in a greater distance to it, I checked the writings of his contemporaries. I found clear evidence for the use of Paul's *Letter* in the writings of Johann Georg Hamann, a rather close acquaintance of Kant. He discussed it not only in his London writings documenting his awakening as a "new Christian"[35] but also in the pamphlet (*Golgatha and Scheblimini*) that he wrote against Moses Mendelssohn's *Jerusalem*, published in the same

33. See Bachmann (1999), 127–58.

34. See the recent comprehensive study of Anders Gerdmar (2009). Unfortunately, Gerdmar does not explain the anti-Semitic positions from a theological standpoint but simply presents them as anti-Semitic.

35. See Hamann (1993), 415.

year as Kant's essay.[36] Hamann talks of the Jews as being immature and unable to act according to the moral law and thus needing to obey their external law as servants. In contrast, Christians had been set free by Jesus Christ in order to begin the process of education to leave such an immaturity. As a result, Hamann denies the Jews civil rights.

Although much less aggressive in style than Hamann, the leading enlightened theologians in Prussia and in Hannover, also called neologians, saw the process of enlightenment as identical with the education of true Christians, from immaturity to true morality—Spalding's *Inaugural Sermon* being exemplary in this respect. The enlightened Lutheran theologian Johann Friedrich Wilhelm Jerusalem shared this position, as did the Reformed theologian Sack at Berlin. But the one theologian who most obviously dwelled on "immaturity" and its overcoming through Jesus Christ, who indeed unfolded the educational potential of that notion into an entire *philosophy of history*, was Johann Salomo Semler, praised as *the* theologian of enlightenment.[37] When Spalding and Sack met with Jerusalem in 1770 to discuss the educational improvement of the Prussian College Kloster Bergen—and indeed education in general[38]—they invited the famous Semler to their meeting. This meeting of the four most influential German enlightened Protestant theologians even raised conspiracy rumors in the newspapers and caused resistance among conservatives.[39]

Semler started his theological project in the early 1770s due to the crisis of Protestant theology resulting from the continuous historical research about the origins of Christianity. He contrasted Christian religion, which he saw as universal and moral, with Jewish religion, seen as particular and political with hardly any morals. Being bound by the Jewish statutory law, Jewish religion could not develop any further and thus remained essentially static. In contrast, Christian religion was dynamic, constantly pushed forward by a discourse between "more able Christians," in particular the "more learned theologians," and the official church authorities. Christian religion had changed from its early beginning until the present time and it would further change in infinity, becoming less and less dogmatic and more and more pure in terms of morals. Interestingly, with respect to Kant, Semler saw the driving engine of this dynamic process of Christianity's development, from

---

36. Hamann (1825), 47–48, 50–51, 65.

37. See Hornig (1996).

38. They met at the behest of the Prussian enlightened state secretary for education, Karl Abraham von Zedlitz, a figure well known to Kant scholars.

39. See Hornig (1996), 41–44.

the early Judaeo-Christians via Catholic strengthening of church authorities toward Protestant freedom of faith and further to pure morality, in the *public discourse* and the struggle of learned theologians with church authorities. He called the former "private theology" (*Privattheologie*) and the latter "public theology" (*öffentliche Theologie*)[40]—which should ring a bell with Kant scholars, pointing us to the second important issue in Kant's *Essay*.[41]

According to Semler's eschatological understanding of Christianity, no particular Christian dogma could be taken as its essential religious truth. Its true and pure message lay rather hidden in all parts of its doctrine and emerged with increasing clarity throughout history. Only at the end of the world, pure morality would appear as its actual message. By turning the contingent history of Christianity with its dogmatic inconsistencies between various periods and various denominations into a theology of history, Semler made a virtue out of necessity. The continuous progress in historical and hermeneutical work by Lutheran and other Christian theologians since the seventeenth century had made it increasingly clear that, shockingly, Jesus Christ was not a Christian but a Jew; although he held beliefs, he kept the Jewish law. Simultaneously, the traditionally clear separation of Jews and Christians became unclear given the close relation of the Jew Jesus and his Jewish disciples, Christian Jews, and gentile Christians. What has traditionally been considered Christian religion had actually been taught only later—by Paul.

Semler's view reducing Christian religion to pure morality looks progressive—like a project of enlightenment. It stays away from dogmatic controversies and tries to see all disagreements as steps on the way to the true moral teachings of Christianity. However, while this new philosophy of history gives credit to all historical states of Christianity, it denies such historical consideration to all other religions. Moreover, by identifying morality with the inmost teaching of Christianity, Semler denies morality to all other religions and especially to Jews (being the only significant group of non-Christians in Prussia). According to Semler, to become a moral being one would necessarily have to become a Christian. Because the historical process would lead to more and more morality, it would create finally one universal religion of humankind, making all human beings Christians. Accordingly, the subject of Semler's philosophy of history was humankind, not only Christians, who would move to Christianity. As a result, Semler's theology or Christian philosophy of history is extremely intolerant,

40. See Semler (1777), 181–82.

41. Hornig states that he did not find any other distinction between "public" and "private religion" before Semler's introduction of these terms in the mid-1770s (Hornig (1996), 186, footnote 15). He uses the latter term when promoting the freedom of a public discourse on private religion, i.e., individual views in contrast to official church opinions.

which made him the particular target of Gotthold Ephraim Lessing's critique. Lessing wrote his *Education of Humankind*—often misunderstood as another version of Semler's philosophy of history—precisely to dispute Semler's project. Lessing attacked "enlightened" theologians for being even more intolerant than Lutheran orthodoxy.[42] Of course, the Jewish philosopher Moses Mendelssohn noticed Semler's anti-Judaic move as well and recognized such a "historical turn" also in other Christian theologians. That was the reason for his objections against the philosophy of history in *Jerusalem* in 1783.[43]

In contrast to Lessing and Mendelssohn, Kant in his *Essay on Enlightenment*, seems to be quite comfortable with Semler's philosophy of history. He makes it the courageous decision of the *single individual* to overcome his "self-incurred immaturity"—as do Semler and Spalding.[44] In addition, looking at Semler's driving engine of the suggested dynamic development of Christianity to morality, Kant did not have to change much to arrive at his own model of enlightenment of a people through *public discourse* of the *learned*. In fact, he had only to switch "public" into "private." As is well known, he explains how such a public discourse and struggle, given freedom, could allow for a slow but continuous process of enlightenment of a people and even of the authorities. Kant's surprising switch of "public" and "private," noticed by his contemporaries,[45] is simply due to the increasingly ambiguous use of the term "public" (*öffentlich*) in German during the second half of the eighteenth century. While it unequivocally referred to an office or authority in the past (from the Latin word "*officium*"), it had been increasingly used for the actual public discourse since the middle of the century—due to its frequent use in the journals. Of course, Kant also extended Semler's model of public discourse to other areas than theology, such as law and medicine. Notwithstanding, his own emphasis is clearly on religion and he explicitly calls religion "the main point of enlightenment."[46]

---

42. Lessing began the publication of the fragments of Reimarus's *Apology* in the third "*Beytrag*" of his series *Zur Geschichte und Litteratur. Aus den Schätzen der Herzoglichen Bibliothek zu Wolfenbüttel*, with the first fragment, and continued with five more fragments in the fourth "*Beytrag*" in 1777. See Lessing (1968), 12, 254–90, and 303–450. About the *Fragmentenstreit*, see Kröger (1979).

43. Mendelssohn (1971-ongoing), *Gesammelte Schriften. Jubiläumsausgabe*, vol. 8, 162–64 (this edition henceforth abbreviated JubA, followed by the volume number). Mendelssohn clearly had in mind philosophies of history like that of Semler (1771–1775), and (1777) or of Herder (1774). The title of Herder's work should be carefully read in relation to Semler and other theological authors producing philosophy of history as education of humankind.

44. These are the learned theologians Kant refers to in his *Essay* (see Kant (1996b), 17–18).

45. See Hinske (1977), 1st Einleitung, S. LVII.

46. Kant (1996b), 21.

Given the close agreement of Kant with Semler in their use of "immaturity" as well as in their model of enlightenment, the question arises of how the philosopher Kant could have been "influenced" by the earlier theological program of Semler? I am rather suspicious about "influences" and doubt that one can ever get influenced by simply reading a book if one is not already looking for a suggestion that it could provide. Although in this case the congruence is striking—almost literal—Kant is not particularly known for studying theological books. However, in the case of Semler's project it would have been rather hard for Kant as for any other intellectual in Prussia to ignore Semler's ideas—because of the many public debates that had flooded Prussia and the Protestant area of the Empire since the 1770s—with Semler heavily involved. I will not mention the discussion of his writings by his theological colleagues, although they often published their critiques in non-professional journals as well. But I have to point to the *Fragmentenstreit*,[47] initiated by Lessing when he published the *Reimarus Fragments*. These *Fragments* raised questions about the connection between the Old and the New Testament and about Jesus as the source for Christian moral religion. (The publication included Lessing's objections to the *Fragments* (1778)). Semler reacted vehemently.[48] Lessing's *Education of Humankind* was published in 1780,[49] though it was already circulating. In this work Lessing directly challenged Semler and his theology of history as the education of humankind. By suggesting the possibility of overcoming Christianity by an eternal "Gospel of Reason," Lessing raised doubts about the "infinite dynamic development" of Christianity and asked whether other than Christians could not as well embrace the "Gospel of Reason." In addition, he suggested that people other than learned men could contribute their thoughts about Christianity as well, thus also pushing authorities forward. Above all, Lessing criticized Semler for the striking intolerance of his *theology of history*, with its denial of morals to other religions.[50] Other important public debates taking place at that time concerned (1) the vow of clerics on the Symbolic Books of the churches—a vow that caused conflicts

47. See Kröger (1979).

48. Semler even included a satire in his reply to Lessing, although he denied being its author. For Lessing's reaction to Semler, see Lessing (1968) 16, 492.

49. See Lessing (2005), 217–40. See Kröger (1979) and Goldenbaum (2012c, forthcoming).

50. See Lessing to his brother Karl on April 8, 1773, in Lessing (1968) 18, 83: "*Was gehen mich die Orthodoxen an? Ich verachte sie eben so sehr, als Du; nur verachte ich unsere neumodischen Geistlichen noch mehr, die Theologen viel zu wenig, und Philosophen lange nicht genug sind. Ich bin von solchen schalen Köpfen auch sehr überzeugt, daß, wenn man sie aufkommen läßt, sie mit der Zeit mehr tyrannisiern werden, als es die Orthodoxen jemals getan haben.*" See also his better known letter to his brother on February 2, 1774 (in ibid. 101).

of conscience for many pastors—and (2) the Prussian Law. Kant refers to both public debates in his *Essay*.[51]

But above all—there was the other public debate on Jewish emancipation, going on in the very year of Kant's *Essay*. While most public debates concerned exclusively Christians, this one touched on the interests of both Jews and Christians. It began in 1781 with Christian Wilhelm Dohm's *On Civil Improvement of the Jews*.[52] This book came out just before the first *Tolerance Edicts* of Joseph II in Austria in 1782.[53] One year later, Moses Mendelssohn's *Jerusalem* appeared, providing a profound legal justification for the separation of state and church, thus allowing for a secular state, and presenting the Jews as capable of morals, and thus ready to become citizens.[54] Semler had been part of this debate too, if only because of the challenge presented by Mendelssohn's talk of morals in the Jewish law. In his book, Mendelssohn had implicitly criticized Semler and other Protestant theologians for their defense of the vow on the Symbolic Books by pastors when taking office because this vow perpetuated the traditional connection of state and church and was an obstacle to Jewish civil rights. In contrast, Mendelssohn defined churches (meaning all religious communities) as simply spiritual and voluntary communities, without any authoritarian power, allowing their members to develop their insights and their faith without restrictions by church authorities. In a way, Mendelssohn asked his Christian contemporaries to give up the statutory vows of clerics made on the *Symbolic Books* and to become free in their thinking and belief.[55] He was attacked immediately in a quite demagogic way by the Pietist theologian Johann David Michaelis. Mendelssohn had used the example of the English high clerics and members of the House of Lords (avoiding mention of the theologians next door) to raise his question about whether they all could still possibly believe precisely what they had made their vow on in their youth. Michaelis attacked the Jewish philosopher for allegedly accusing the English high clerics of being hypocrites.[56] This alone caused a controversy again. But of course, all influential enlightened theologians defended the vows as a legitimate practice of Christian churches.

51. Kant (1996b), 19 and 21.

52. Dohm (1781); for the public debate initiated by this book, see Heinrich (2004).

53. About the readiness of the Prussian administration for such reforms in Prussia, see Heinrich (2004), 827–32.

54. JubA 8, 109–31, 164–70, and especially 169.

55. JubA 8, 131–42.

56. See Löwenbrück (1994), 324–32.

All these public debates were very well known to Kant when he was writing his *Essay*. He closely followed the journals and newspapers and knew the positions of Semler, Spalding, Herder, Lessing, and Mendelssohn, all of whom published intensively in these years. Hamann also trumpeted the news to him. Kant's *Essay* is written in full awareness of all these positions and thus his own stake has to be situated in this field of alternatives. While I take it to be evident that Kant uses the term "immaturity" in the sense of Semler, Spalding, Herder, and Hamann—i.e., picking up on Paul's *Letter*—I think there is sufficient evidence as well that Kant found his model for enlightenment in Semler's theology of history. Obviously, he extended Semler's model beyond theology but he did not allow other than learned individuals to participate in the public discourse to pursue enlightenment (as had been suggested by Lessing and others). Also, Kant (as much as Semler, Spalding, and Herder) sees the development of pure morality as a progress *within* the history of Christianity, thus excluding Jews qua Jews from this process of enlightenment.[57] These findings about Kant's *Essay* are in precise agreement with what he explicitly states in his *Religion in the Limits of Reason alone*, published in 1793.

That this is the meaning of Kant's *Essay* is further confirmed by the specific statement in this text that the state is not supposed to do *anything* other than allow the public discourse. Rather, the state would endanger the process of enlightenment if it intervened in the slow course of enlightenment through public discourse. Finally, Kant explicitly praises the "enlightened" king Frederick for his *contempt of tolerance* which—at the peak of the hot discussion of Joseph's ongoing *Tolerance Edicts* for Jews in Austria—could not be misunderstood by his contemporaries. It was known that Friedrich stubbornly resisted the demands of his own administration (including Dohm) that he should follow Joseph's example. Kant, without using any invectives (as his friend Hamann preferred), unequivocally rejects Mendelssohn's and Dohm's political demand that the Prussian state give civil rights to Jews, e.g., allow them to buy their houses and stay without the constant threat of being expelled by state authorities. Thus Kant's *Essay* has to be read as his answer, not to Mendelssohn's essay on enlightenment, but to Mendelssohn's *Jerusalem* from the year before. Kant considers Jews qua Jews as "immature" due to their lack of courage to make a decision by means of their free will and to embrace

---

57. For the close relation of Spalding to Lavater, see the instructive introduction of Simon Ravidowicz to JubA 7, involving the material of the Lavater affair, xi-cv. That also Herder expected a positive philosophical proof of Mendelssohn in favor of his Jewishness is clear from his letter to Hartknoch; see ibid., lxxvii.

the moral law, taught exclusively by Jesus Christ, instead of their statutory Jewish law—the law that makes them servants, unable to become moral beings. From there he can "conclude correctly" they could not be accepted as equal citizens. That this was indeed Kant's view can be seen in his *Religion in the Limits of Reason Alone* where it is fully fleshed out.[58]

Finally, Kant also answers the question of religious vows on the *Symbolic Books*, agreeing again with the above-mentioned Lutheran theologians that the church has the right to ask its employed pastors to take the vow to teach their communities only what is in agreement with the *Symbolic Books* (as private officeholders, in Kant's wording). If they do not hold these opinions any more, they still have to teach them or, if their conscience does not allow this any more, they have to lay down their office. Kant justifies this policy by arguing that doctors, judges, and military officers also had to obey the authority as private men, while having the liberty to publish as learned men. He neglects to mention, though, that their obedience was mostly about action while pastors had to teach beliefs to their communities. For many Prussian pastors, the vow was felt as a burden and a hindrance to freedom of conscience. That is why Mendelssohn had addressed the vows as conflicting with the freedom of thought.

After this investigation of Kant's *Essay*, I wonder how I had never seen these specific statements, which I see now as clear as day as his specific answers to the then open specific questions under public debate. The reason for my blindness is obviously the same that Sherlock Holmes provided for the embarrassed police inspector who had overlooked an important trace in the mud. He comforted the police inspector: "It was invisible, buried in the mud. I only saw it because I was looking for it.'"[59] Do my findings mean that Kant did not ask for independent thinking in his *Essay*? Not at all; of course he did. Kant as much as Semler was an enlightener, and their writings presented huge challenges to their church authorities. Nevertheless, both men delivered another intolerant message as well, which got lost too easily in the course of the centuries since, or worse, which had never been noticed by Christian readers because they shared that part of the message with these authors.

At this point, my specific work as a *historian* of philosophy is done and it is now up to the *philosopher* in the historian of *philosophy* to judge the validity of Kant's argument and conclusion and to ask how these statements are grounded in his philosophical system—or how they shaped it. As a philosopher, I can see the validity of his argument once one accepts the following of

58. See Kant (2009), 71, 129–32, 113–16, 142–43.

59. Doyle (1976), 319.

his presuppositions: First, that the Jewish law is a statutory law that does not include moral teachings and thus does not allow a Jew qua Jew to be a moral being; second, that Christianity alone includes the moral law, third, that we have free will and can decide to become moral beings if we are courageous, fourth, that only learned men can make meaningful contributions to promote enlightenment, fifth, that the state must not intervene in any way in enlightenment. If I accept these assumptions, I can see Kant's point. However, I do not share any of these assumptions and do not see Kant giving evidence for any of them. He could simply rely on the agreement of most of his Christian contemporaries, with the exception of Lessing.

Seeing now the unjustified assumptions in Kant's *Essay*, I become curious to investigate Kant's obvious shift to the philosophy of history in 1784—a shift that might be informed by the very same theological project he follows in the *Essay.* I want to check whether his peculiar and extremely strict separation of morals from law might be informed by his strict division between Christian morals and Jewish law. To be sure, Kant expresses his opinion that Christian religion alone teaches the moral law not only in the *Essay* and the *Religion within the Boundaries of Reason Alone* but also in his *Critique of Practical Reason*—as I see now. His separation of morals and law is very close to that of Pufendorf and in open opposition to the view Mendelssohn takes in *Jerusalem,* as he follows Leibniz and Wolff in their *continuous* view of legal law and morals. These opposed positions should not easily be decided in Kant's favor; they are still under discussion today, as positivism versus natural right theories.

I would like to raise one more question in the end of my case study, although I have no space to pursue it. How can we criticize a past philosopher for violating those insights we now believe in but that we arrived at on the basis of argument? Can I criticize Kant for excluding Jews from morals or should I excuse him due to historical circumstances? While I don't see a way to find an absolute measure for such criticism I would consider critical alternatives and arguments available to Kant in his day that raised questions about his positions. In the case of Kant, this could be his younger fellow Christian Lessing who had published the plays *The Jews* in 1754 and *Nathan the Wise* in 1779 precisely to dispute the general prejudice of the "immaturity" of the Jews.[60] Kant did not like these plays.[61] Kant had also studied carefully

60. Lessing published his blunt reply to the critical review of his play *Die Juden* by Michaelis in his journal *Theatralische Bibliothek* in 1754 (see Lessing (1968) 6, 159–66).

61. According to Hamann, Kant considered *Nathan the Wise* as simply the other part of Lessing's *The Jews* and would not like any hero from this [Jewish] people anyway. See Hamann to Herder on May 6, 1779, in Hamann (1959), 77.

Mendelssohn's *Jerusalem* when he wrote his *Essay* but did not learn anything about the morals of the Jewish law from it. To me, this seems to be an ignorant attitude for a philosopher and shows him rather to be a "stubborn" Christian. And in case somebody would point me to Kant's well-known positive letter to Mendelssohn about *Jerusalem*,[62] look at it again. It finishes with the idea of the development of all religions toward *one universal religion*,[63] thus denying the main thesis of Mendelssohn's book as well as that of Lessing's *Nathan the Wise*—the view that God's house has *many mansions*.

3. Method

I can hear the protest that I have not used any "theory" for my method of history of philosophy[64] and I admit my reluctance to engage in "theory." I have simply learned how my growing historical (and philosophical) knowledge has helped me to "see" what is said in a philosophical argument—besides that which is obvious. I do not favor arbitrary readings between the lines. Rather, I have made historical discoveries while following the philosophical argument and found arguments while paying attention to the history. When I discovered Leibniz's marginalia in Spinoza's *Theologico-political Treatise* in 1994 it was not by luck. Rather, like a detective, I had "seen" Spinoza everywhere in the printed text of Leibniz's *Commentatiuncula de judice controversiarum*, although the name was not mentioned. I figured out the library Leibniz would have used in 1670 and went there in order to find the copy of the *Theologico-political Treatise* to show that Leibniz could have read it. I found indeed the copy Leibniz read—and I found Leibniz's marginalia as an extra proof.[65] In contrast, a careful study of Leibniz's marginalia in various Hobbes volumes in the same library allowed me to see precisely when and moreover why Leibniz actually picked up Hobbes's concept of the conatus, namely, for his philosophy of mind.[66] Up to then, we only knew *that* he adopted and adapted this Hobbesian concept. I felt again like a detective when I studied the history of

62. Kant to Mendelssohn on August 16, 1783, in KAA 10, 344–47.

63. Ibid., 347.

64. One review of my book (Goldenbaum, 2004) was titled "Fröhlicher Positivismus," thus presenting me and my colleagues as piling up facts and lacking (Foucault's ?) "theory." I am perfectly fine with this kind of criticism as long as even this reviewer admitted that in light of our great many new findings the understanding of German intellectual history changed. See Till (2006).

65. See Goldenbaum (2008a). For an earlier explanatory discussion of this finding, see Goldenbaum (1999).

66. See Goldenbaum (2008b).

the public debate on the Wolffian *Wertheim Bible* 1735–39 and was surprised to find quotes of Longinus's text on the sublime used against this translation of the Bible. Seeing that the theologian Alexander Baumgarten published his declaration for the new science of esthetics at the very moment of the general attack of Pietists against the *Wertheim Bible* in September 1735, I followed my suspicion, my hypothesis, and tried hard to get all the pieces together to give evidence for it.[67] I did not find them in the history of esthetics but I suddenly knew where to look. I was "sure" which correspondences would include such evidence. Since then, esthetics no longer seems to me a project encouraging our sense perception and the arts. Rather, I see it as theology changing horses. The way of my proof though was as much about philosophical arguments as about historical circumstances because I had to show how esthetic arguments could serve the theological project of saving the prophecies of Jesus Christ in the *Old Testament*.

Concerning "theory," I am content with Spinoza's advice that we approach a past text like any other natural phenomenon we want to understand—by means of science, i.e., checking the meaning of the words as they are used at the time, stating the used arguments, collecting the facts about their origin, searching for the authors and their intentions, and looking for the *one* hypothesis that could bring all the pieces together. Einstein and Infeld describe science in a similar way—as collecting facts and looking for the coherent hypothesis that can put them all into one story. Interestingly, they compare scientific method with that of a detective who after collecting a great many facts sits quietly in his armchair and thinks about a coherent explanation. "Suddenly, by Jove, he has it!"[68] He knows not only the explanation but also other things that must have happened as well. "Since he knows exactly where to look for it he may go out, if he likes, to collect further confirmation for his theory."[69] I find this a pretty good description of what I experience when doing history of philosophy.

67. See Goldenbaum (2011b), 305–15.

68. Einstein/Infeld (1971), 4.

69. Ibid., 4–5.

5

The Contingency of Philosophical Problems

Joanne Waugh and Roger Ariew

1. Introduction

OUR CHAPTER HAS two parts. In the first part we cite two discussions about two major figures from the history of philosophy, Descartes and Leibniz, written by two major twentieth-century professional philosophers, Gilbert Ryle and Benson Mates. Although Mates wrote a book about Leibniz, neither he nor Ryle worked exclusively—or primarily—in the history of early modern philosophy.[1] Indeed, we have chosen them precisely for this reason, for their work reflects two of the central myths of philosophy: first, that the problems of philosophy are perennial, not contingent; and second, that in light of this fact, we need not read philosophical texts in their historical contexts. Such philosophers read philosophical texts from the past and locate what they see as philosophical problems, formulate arguments for the texts' authors in the language of present day philosophers, and evaluate these arguments in light of contemporary standards of philosophy, rationality, and argumentation. The arguments are then assigned to their authors as solutions to one or more of the "problems of philosophy." This approach to studying the history of philosophy gained widespread acceptance in the English-speaking philosophical world in the decades after Ryle's and Mates's work, as is evident

1. Mates (1986). Mates began and ended his career working on logic and Greek philosophy—Stoicism in his early years and Skepticism in his later years. Ryle worked primarily in the philosophy of mind and the philosophy of language. He did write a highly speculative book about Plato that attempted to place Plato in his historical context. Such considerations of context do not loom large—or loom at all—in Ryle's discussion of other historical figures.

from the editorial statement of the inaugural issue of the *History of Philosophy Quarterly* (*HPQ*) in 1984:

> The HPQ plans to focus on papers that cultivate philosophical history in the spirit of *philosophia perennis*. Ideally its contributions will regard work in the history of philosophy and in philosophy itself as parts of a seamless whole. They will treat the works of past philosophers not only in terms of historical inquiry, but also as a means of dealing with issues of ongoing philosophical interest. The HPQ plans to specialize in papers of a particular sort, those manifesting a strong interaction between contemporary and historical concerns. Either historical matters should be exploited to deal with matters on the agenda of current discussion or present day concepts, methods, distinctions, arguments, etc. should be used to illuminate historical questions. The journal will accordingly dedicate itself to that approach to philosophical history increasingly prominent in recent years that refuses to see the boundary between philosophy and its history as an impassable barrier, but regards historical studies as a means of dealing with problems of continued interest and importance.[2]

Although the expression *philosophia perennis* seems to have fallen out of fashion, the approach to studying the history of philosophy sanctioned by the assumption of "perennial philosophical problems" persists. Indeed, as recently as the June 2011 volume of *HPQ* its editorial statement contains nearly identical wording as that found in its inaugural issue.[3]

In the second part of our chapter, we offer an explanation of how studying perennial philosophical problems came to be accepted as a substitute for the history of philosophy. Our explanation turns on the failure among many twentieth-century philosophers to distinguish the characteristics of formal languages from those of natural languages, and to attribute the characteristics

2. Editors (1984), 2.

3. "HPQ specializes in papers that cultivate philosophical history with a strong interaction between historical and contemporary concerns. Contributors regard work in the history of philosophy and in philosophy itself as parts of a seamless whole, treating the works of past philosophers not only in terms of historical inquiry, but also as a means of dealing with issues of ongoing philosophical concern. The journal favors the approach to the history of philosophy, increasingly prominent in recent years, that refuses to see the boundary between philosophy and its history as a impassable barrier" (Editors (2011)). There remain, of course, journals devoted to the study of the history of philosophy that advocate a more contextual approach to its study, and publish the work of scholars with acknowledged expertise in a specific historical period in philosophy.

of one to the other. This is often accompanied by a tendency to treat texts and speech acts indiscriminately, again ascribing the characteristics of one to the other, and reversing the relation between them. Since embodied speech acts are prior to texts, both in the history of a language and in the lives of its speakers, our suggestion is that we see a text as standing in for a speaker.[4] Like embodied speech acts and other cultural artifacts, a text is meaningful in its material and cultural context.[5] This includes philosophical texts and the "problems" their authors share with their contemporaries.

2. *Mythic Tales of "Philosophical History"*

At the end of *The Concept of Mind*, Ryle wonders whether some behaviorists he is considering "were espousing a not very sophisticated mechanistic doctrine, like that of Hobbes and Gassendi, or whether they were still cleaving to the Cartesian para-mechanical theory"[6]—whether they held that thinking consists in making some complex noises and movements or whether those

4. The priority of speech over writing prompts two questions: first, whether and how theories of language depend on the notions of language written and read; and second how we should conceive of speech in traditional, that is, nonliterate or preliterate, societies. Studies of orality and literacy in ancient Greece give us reason to question accounts of language that take "texts"—rather than Homer's "winged words," say—as their primary trope. It is a matter of argument as to when something like a modern notion of philosophical or theoretical discourse as a distinct genre of writing emerged; neither writing nor philosophy has always been a human activity (see later in the chapter). It is another matter to ask, as does Derrida, how philosophical writing, as a genre, disguises that it is a genre of writing (Derrida (1981) and (1974)). Derrida's point that for those who are the products of the "logocentric" tradition the notion of speech is parasitic on the notion of inscription is borne out by early studies of Greek literacy such as Havelock's, whose major trope in discussing the oral technology of oral communication is "storage" or "inscription" in the memory (Havelock (1981)). For further discussion of these points, see Waugh (1991). Later studies of oral, traditional literature emphasize that we should not see oral poetry simply as poetry that is not written; rather, we should see written poetry as poetry without voice. Cf. Zumthor (1990), 24.

5. The modifier "embodied" is applied to "speech acts" here to suggest a different emphasis from that of Quentin Skinner and other contextualist historians who talk about speech acts. Granted, history relies on texts, and composing texts is linguistic behavior; as historians we need to ask not only what their authors were saying, the locutionary force of speech acts, but also what they were doing by saying what they said, the illocutionary force. But in interpreting these texts in context, the historian needs to look beyond linguistic behavior to questions of material culture, e.g., is there evidence that a society was literate, or that philosophers were part of a logocentric tradition? This is especially true if with Haakonssen, one takes ideas as the purported objects of reference in linguistic behavior, especially since "a speaker's choice of words may be inadequate to the formulation of the ideas that he or she is trying to express" (Haakonssen (1996) 10). This emphasis on embodiment and material is one way of erasing "the boundary between knowing a language and knowing our way around in the world generally," to echo Davidson (1986) 446.

6. Ryle (1949), 327.

noises and movements were connected with "inner life" processes. Ryle continues his comparisons with Hobbes and Gassendi on one side of these issues and Descartes on the other, asking about "the theoretical fruitfulness of the Hobbes-Gassendi story of the mind" against "that of the Cartesians."[7] This line of inquiry persists into Ryle's discussions of his book. The film, *The Concept of Mind*, coordinated with readings and assignments for an Open University course, features a conversation between Ryle and Susan Haack. Godfrey Vesey introduces the film, characterizing Ryle's book as attacking the "official doctrine" about mind, coming chiefly from Descartes: "people like Gassendi and Hobbes had reduced man to the states of something to be explained by the principles of mechanical causation. Descartes couldn't accept that." Ryle speaks about the disagreement between Descartes and "contemporary reductionists, as we call them, people like Hobbes and Gassendi." For Ryle, Descartes's view is "a piece of inflationism to repair a piece of unwanted deflationism."[8]

Ryle recognizes a difference between his approach to Descartes and that adopted by those working in the historical mode. He characterizes his "official theory" as mostly ahistorical. He asserts, in what he thinks of as the "historical" mode,

> it would not be true to say that the official theory derives solely from Descartes' theories, or even from a more widespread anxiety about the implications of seventeenth century mechanics. Scholastic and Reformation theology had schooled the intellects of scientists as well as of the laymen, philosophers and clerics of that age. Stoic-Augustinian theories of the will were imbedded in the Calvinist doctrines of sin and grace; Platonic and Aristotelian theories of the intellect shaped the orthodox doctrines of the immortality of the soul. Descartes was reformulating already prevalent theological doctrines of the soul in the new syntax of Galileo.[9]

Were these pronouncements true, they still would not be an excuse for Ryle's "official theory." Others have shown that Descartes does not subscribe to Ryle's "official theory."[10] One not need much of Gassendi to realize that he is

7. Ibid., 329.

8. Ryle's statements come from the film, *The Concept of Mind*, which was coordinated with readings assignments in an Open University course in the UK.

9. Ryle (1949), 23.

10. Our favorite is Curley (1986), esp. 39–43.

not a materialist, like Hobbes, but a dualist, like Descartes—Gassendi accepts an incorporeal soul (*animus*) above and beyond a corporeal soul (*anima*), and for him, the possession of an *animus* plays a role in human cognition. The *animus* is distinct from corporeal imagination and allows us to know things of which we cannot form images. "Unlike corporeal things, the rational soul is capable of reflecting on itself. It is also able to reflect on the nature of universality in contrast to animals, which possess only the corporeal *anima*."[11]

Although Gassendi published a few works before 1641, the date of the publication of Descartes's *Meditations*, none of these contained any neo-Epicureanism. They included the first volume of his anti-Aristotelian skeptical program; another, documenting his controversy with Robert Fludd; some works on astronomical topics; and a biography of Fabri de Pereisc, his patron.[12] Gassendi first published an account of his neo-Epicurean philosophy in 1649, in his *Commentary on Diogenes Laertius*, expanding it into his major work, the *Syntagma Philosophicum*, issued in his posthumous *Opera Omnia,* in 1658.[13] Hobbes's main work before 1641 was his translation of Thucydides's *History of the Peloponnesian War*. His first notable philosophical treatises, the various parts of *Elements of Philosophy*, were issued from 1642 to 1658. *De cive* was first issued in 1642, then *De corpore* in 1655, and *De homine*, in 1658. Most important for our purposes is *De corpore,* which dealt with logic, physics, and some metaphysical elements. Hobbes's *De homine* may be also be important, covering other physical topics such as human nutrition, generation, optics, and such issues as speech, appetite, emotions, and dispositions. Hobbes's 1642 *De cive* was concerned mostly with political philosophy.[14] His most famous work, *Leviathan*, was published in 1651, with a Latin edition in 1668. In sum, Hobbes and Gassendi published almost all of their major metaphysical-epistemological works in the 1650s, *after* Descartes's death. Asking why Descartes rejected Hobbes's and Gassendi's mechanism and inflated their deflationary accounts is rather like asking why Descartes would reject Freud's and Skinner's accounts of the mind.

Ryle's "official doctrine" is complex, with many epistemological and metaphysical aspects, and he is probably right in thinking that this theory does not

11. Osler (2002), 88. This is just one, from hundreds of essays, describing Gassendi's dualism. One can find these views of Gassendi described as early as 1908 in Brett (1908), well before the publication of Ryle's book.

12. Gassendi (1624) for Book I and (1658) for Book II; Gassendi (1630a), (1630b), (1632), and (1641).

13. Gassendi (1649) and (1658).

14. Hobbes issued *De cive* in an English version (1651), and *De corpore* in1656.

derive solely from Descartes's theories, or those of anyone in the early modern period. We are unlikely to find any early modern holding the complete "official doctrine" before Descartes. Ryle's defenders may search for unsophisticated pure mechanists in the early modern period before Descartes, thinkers with a deflationary account that Descartes would want to inflate. There were, in fact, early seventeenth-century atomists, neo-Epicureans or neo-Democriteans such as Nicholas Hill and Sebastien Basso, offering alternatives to the predominant Aristotelianism.[15]

Neither Hill nor Basso can be considered pure Rylean mechanists. Hill fiercely attacked certain scholastic uses of forms and developed a view of natural objects composed of conglomerations of solid, indivisible, and variously shaped particles in his *Philosophia Epicurea*. Generation, qualitative alteration, corruption, and local motion are all explained in terms of changing atomic composition, not by an appeal to forms. A form becomes the mere "state and condition of things, resulting from the connection of material principles."[16] Unlike classical atomists, and some of his contemporaries for whom ultimate causal explanation is given in terms of primitive motion directed by God, for Hill, God acts directly on the atoms through a force: "The prime force, the efficient, active, universal cause, the simple, absolute essence, the foundation and root of all material power is God."[17] Physical processes are seen as a product of innumerable acts of immediate divine intervention and the universe thus is considered as animate, to some extent. Thus Hill was more of an eclectic than a systematic philosopher; ultimately, he retained elements of Aristotelian psychology and argued that his principles were in accordance with Catholic beliefs.

Basso, in humanist fashion, tried to recover the philosophy of the ancients before Aristotle, especially Democritus's atomism. Rejecting the matter-form debates altogether, he proposed that matter makes up its own natural *minima* by arrangement of homogeneous and incorruptible atoms; these "retain their differences when conjoined."[18] But, unlike ancient atomists, he posited in addition a *pneuma,* ether, world soul, or "spirit of the universe." For Basso, all natural change is explained in terms of the arrangement of atoms in the ether. Basso's ether allowed him to explain condensation and rarefaction and the motions of

15. There were, of course, also ancient atomists, such as Democritus, Epicurus, and Lucretius. Descartes refers to them as a group, usually in a dismissive fashion. See Descartes (1964–1975), I, 416, V, 241 and 271.

16. Hill (1619), 13–14, aphorism 35.

17. Ibid., 28, aphorism 110.

18. Basso (1621), 14.

atoms. Atoms also compose the ether, but these atoms, as a conglomerate, permeate the pores and gaps of all objects causing the motion of the other atoms and, consequently, all mutations of objects. Since the ether fills all space, an object becomes more rarefied because the ether interposes itself to a greater degree in the pores of the object, increasing its size and decreasing its density. All motions of objects occur within the ether and as a result of the ether's motion. The ether does not combine with the other four elemental atoms. Though the ether (a kind of world soul) is the cause of motion, it is in constant need of being kept in motion by a higher cause. For Basso, God is the higher cause on which the ether depends for its motion, and for directing the motion of the elementary atoms according to their aptitude. The ether or spirit is always dependent on God's continually infusing motive force: "By means of this spirit God moves the single elements not differently than they would move if this motive power were innate in them."[19] Basso, like Hill, is some kind of atomist, but not a pure mechanist, if mechanist at all. Basso may have been a proponent of mechanizing the mind and not advocating a "ghost in the machine," but he still should be thought of as having a ghost in the machinery.

There are also early seventeenth-century atomist alchemists who attacked scholastic matter theory—prime matter and substantial forms. On August 24 and 25, 1624, three alchemists, Etienne de Clave, Jean Bitault, and Antoine Villon, scheduled a disputation by posting a broadsheet containing fourteen anti-Aristotelian theses on the streets of Paris. The disputation did not take place. The president of the Parlement saw copies of the theses and prohibited the disputants from sustaining them on pain of death. Parlement then sent the theses to the Faculty of Theology of the University of Paris (the Sorbonne) to be examined. A few days later, the Sorbonne replied with a censure of some of the theses and, through an *arrêt* of September 4, 1624, Parlement ordered Villon, de Clave, and Bitaud to leave Paris, never to teach again within their jurisdiction, on pain of corporal punishment.[20] Among the prohibited theses were propositions concerning matter and form, one in particular denying all substantial forms, *except for rational soul*, along with prime matter; its official condemnation is that "this proposition is overly bold, erroneous, and close to heresy."[21]

There are many extant reports about the event of 1624, including some by Descartes's correspondents, Marin Mersenne and Jean-Baptiste Morin, as well

---

19. Ibid., 341.

20. See Garber (1988b).

21. Launoy (1653), 310–21. This prohibition was renewed in 1671 and became the basis for condemnations of Cartesianism.

as by others such as Jean-Cécile Frey, professor of philosophy at Paris. These reports have little favorable to say about the theses of de Clave, Bitaud, and Villon. Mersenne goes through all fourteen posted theses, expressing general disapproval. His main argument is that "if there is no form and no matter, then man has neither body nor soul, something contrary to the belief of the Catholic faith; if there are no other genera and no other species, except for the various mixture of the five substances established by them, man is of the same species as stones, plants, and animals, which is most false."[22] Morin seems to take as basic and beyond question the Aristotelian view that matter and form united is the essence of body as such. He argues that without matter and form, there can be no bodies—not even a human body for a soul to inform, since the body without its own form is nothing. In a similar vein, working on the lack of parallelism between humans and other animals (humans having rational souls, but animals lacking any substantial form), Frey asks rhetorically: if a donkey is a donkey without the substantial form for being a donkey, then why would a human not be human without the substantial form for humanity? And if a human is formally a human by its substantial form, why would a donkey not be a donkey by its own substantial form?[23] So the atomist alchemists were found foolish and erroneous in philosophy, and proximately heretical, even though they were at best Rylean para-mechanists. These judgments were made not just by the Sorbonne and Parlement, but by some people closest to Descartes, including his most frequent correspondent Mersenne.

Because of their views, Mersenne ranks all atomists—Hill, Basso, de Claves, and others—as atheists. In *L'impiété des Deistes,* after having discussed such "despicable" authors as Charron, Cardano, Machiavelli, Bruno, the "accursed" Vanini, "and similar rogues," Mersenne asserts: "I expect to refute everything these authors stated so inappropriately in the Encyclopedia I am preparing in the defense of all truths and against all sorts of lies, in which I will examine more diligently what has been advanced by Gorlaeus, Charpentier, Basso, Hill, Campanella, Bruno, Vanini, and a few others." Mersenne proceeds to gives examples of the "impertinence" of these authors. He complains specifically about the adherence of Gorlaeus and Hill to atomism, and to the doctrine "that inside bodies there are atoms which have quantity and figure." According to Mersenne, "ultimately, they are all heretics, which is why we should not be surprised that they agree, being all as thick as thieves."[24]

---

22. Mersenne (1625), 81–82.

23. Frey (1628), chap. 27. See Garber (2002).

24. Mersenne (1624), 237–38. See Mersenne (1625), 109–10.

There were indeed some atomists at the start of the seventeenth century, but they were not exactly mechanists and they were condemned as heretics even by Descartes's closest friends. There were also atomists who denied Aristotelian matter-form talk but made an exception for humans and their rational soul, something like Ryle's para-mechanists and like Descartes. Even they were condemned as near heretics by various authorities and by Descartes's closest friends. The philosophical horizon before 1640 does not provide much evidence for pure deflationary mechanists that Descartes would want to reject and inflate. So why would one think that Descartes was inflating Hobbes's and Gassendi's deflationary accounts? Perhaps, for the reason that having received Descartes's manuscript of the *Meditations*, Mersenne circulated it to others for comments, including Hobbes and Gassendi. They provided sets of *Objections*, to which Descartes replied. Still Descartes did not take anything Hobbes said very seriously; he even decided to respond to Hobbes point by point, as an insult. The exchange between Hobbes and Descartes leads to this wonderful tit-for-tat. Hobbes: "If there is no idea of God (and it has not been proved that there is one), this entire inquiry falls apart." Descartes: "If there is an idea of God (and it is obvious that there is), this entire objection falls apart."[25]

The exchange between Descartes and Gassendi leads to other burlesque moments, Gassendi referring to Descartes as "o Mens (O Mind)" and Descartes replying to Gassendi as "o caro (O flesh)." Gassendi can be considered a materialist, if one reads only his *Objections* to Descartes's *Meditations*. Although a dualist, Gassendi could adopt the persona of a materialist in his objections to Descartes. And Descartes, knowing of no early modern materialists and already propounding a highly rarefied metaphysics, one deemed almost heretical, cannot take seriously someone allegedly propounding a more parsimonious metaphysics than his, certainly not a Catholic priest, a friend of Mersenne, who had not yet published anything remotely like a materialist—and thus heretical—point of view. Descartes takes Gassendi about as seriously as he does Hobbes, which is why he ultimately decides to remove Gassendi's set of objections from the French translation of the *Meditations*. As Descartes states:

> I shall from now on gladly … relieve this volume of their presence. This was the reason why, on learning that Clerselier was taking the trouble to translate the other objections, I asked him to omit these. And in order that he may have no cause to regret their absence, I should inform the

25. Descartes (1964–1975), VII, 184.

> reader here that I have lately read them a second time and also read all the new counter-objections in the large volume containing them, with the purpose of extracting from them all the points I should judge to stand in need of reply; but I have been unable to discover a single one, to which, in my opinion, those who understand at all the meaning of my *Meditations* would not be able to reply without my help.[26]

Descartes added later:

> The brightest of my friends who read [Gassendi's] book [of objections and counter-objections] declared to me that they have found nothing in it to capture their attention; and they are the only people I desire to satisfy.... I believe that ... all the objections this book contains are based solely on some terms being misunderstood or some assumptions that are false.[27]

To hold as Ryle does, that Descartes inflates the Hobbes-Gassendi deflationary account is to misread Gassendi, to pay no attention as to when Hobbes and Gassendi issued their philosophies, to misunderstand the context in which Descartes was writing, the practice of objections and replies, and the audience for whom Descartes was writing.

In *The Philosophy of Leibniz,* Mates is not eschewing the historical mode in discussing figures from three or more centuries in the history of philosophy. Rather, Mates is doing the history of philosophy writ small, distinguishing studies of a single figure in the history of philosophy that exhibit his intellectual "development" from those studies that produce a "syncretic" picture of their thoughts.[28] Acknowledging the excellent work done in dating "the thousand of items that constitute Leibniz's *Nachlass,*" Mates asserts:

> [W]hen the materials are put into order as well as can be, it becomes obvious that Leibniz did change his mind on many topics, as would be expected. Indeed, he himself tells us about some of these changes, mostly having to do with his views on matters of physical science.

---

26. Descartes (1964–1975), IXa, 199.

27. Ibid., IXa, 203.

28. Mates (1986), 7–8.

And he continues:

> But on the fundamentals points of his philosophy, his constancy over the years is little short of astonishing. From the first of his publications, at age seventeen, to the end of his life he never wavered in holding to the rather unusual and implausible doctrine that things are individuated by their "whole being"; that is, every property of a thing is essential to its identity.

And Mates concludes:

> [I]n general, if one compares the doctrines of the *Discourse on Metaphysics* (1686) with those of the *Monadology* (1714), one sees that during the last thirty years there was almost no change in any of them.... . Consequently, in this account of the elements of Leibnizian philosophy I have felt free, on the whole to cite him without paying much attention to the date of the passage cited.[29]

This syncretic picture of Leibniz's thought about the individuation of things by their whole being can only be maintained if one puts aside contextual considerations and contingent circumstances. Leibniz's 1663 *Metaphysical Disputation on the Principle of the Individual* was a youthful scholastic exercise, with all that that implies.[30] The thesis begins with a preface to the *Metaphysical Disputation* written by Jakob Thomasius, Leibniz's professor at Leipzig. In the preface Thomasius discusses Aquinas and his followers on individuation, indicating that they hold a principle of individuation for simple creatures, such as angels, different from the one they hold for corporeal creatures.[31] For Thomas, spiritual creatures are altogether simple in their essence but have a dual composition of essence with existence and of substance with accidents. Corporeal creatures are additionally composed of potency and act, that is, of matter and

29. We leave it to Dan Garber to dispute the statement about alleged lack of changes between the *Discourse on Metaphysics* and the *Monadology;* see Garber (2009). It would be astonishing, of course, if Leibniz could change his views on matters of physical science and remain constant on the fundamental points of his philosophy.

30. The full title is *Disputatio Metaphysica/ De/ Principio Individvi,/ Quam/ Deo O. M. Annuente/ Et/ Indultu Inclytæ Philosoph. Facultatis/ In Illustri Academiâ Lipsiensi/ Præside/ Viro Excellentissimo et Clarissimo/ Dn. M. Jacobo Thomasio/ Eloqvent. P. P. Min. Princ. Colleg./ Collegiato/ Præceptore et Fautore suo Maximo/ Publicè ventilandam proponit/ Gottfredus Guilielmus/ Leibnuzius,/ Lips. Philos. et B. A. Baccal./ Aut. et Resp./ 30. Maji Anni MDCLXIII.* Thomasius is given "top billing" (in the largest font); Leibniz's name comes in second (and in smaller font).

31. Leibniz (1923–), VI.1, 6 and note.

form. Thus the principle of individuation for corporeal creatures, namely, *signate* or quantified matter, relies on something that angels do not possess. As a result, each angel constitutes its own species. Thomasius prefers Scotus's *haecceity*, but concludes that the "Nominalist Entity" is ultimately to be preferred as the simplest and truest view that resolves such thorny problems.[32]

In the *Metaphysical Disputation*, Leibniz follows the path traced out by his teacher. He dutifully sets aside Thomas's solution as not furnishing a single principle of individuation for both material and immaterial substances.[33] He discusses four other possible solutions to the problem, rejecting three, including the Scotist answer, and defends the "whole entity" principle of the nominalists as best. The positions and arguments discussed by Leibniz are all documented in great detail. In this way he demonstrates the breadth of his familiarity with the relevant sources. Perhaps the one novel element in Leibniz's discussion of individuation is the taxonomy he provides. A single general principle of individuation for all individuals can be given or, because different principles for material and immaterial individuals must be provided, a single principle cannot be given. Apropos the general principles, the whole entity can be proposed as a principle or something less than the whole entity can be proposed. Within the category of "something less," the principle can be expressed by negation or by something positive added to the essence. Two views have been proffered for the positive principle, existence and *haecceity*, depending upon whether a physical part or a metaphysical part is added. Since Leibniz rejects non-general principles (one of which he identifies as Thomas's), he discusses four primary options: (1) whole entity; (2) negation; (3) existence; and (4) *haecceity*.

The young Leibniz attributes the first principle he discusses, "whole entity," to some older and some recent scholastics: Aureol, Hervaeus, Gregory of Rimini and Biel, Durandus, Murcia, Suárez, Zimara, Calov, and Stahl. Further, he classifies the principle as that of the terminists or nominalists and defends it against the attacks of the "Scotists." There is no mystery about this principle of individuation. Leibniz claims that the whole entity of a composite being is simply its matter and form. He uses "whole entity" rather than "matter and form" because he wants the principle to be general and to cover immaterial substances.[34] Moreover, by "matter and form" he does not include accidents, which he specifically omits from the discussion.[35] (In this kind of

32. Ibid., VI.1, 8.

33. Ibid., VI.1, 11.3.

34. Ibid., VI.1, 12.4.

35. Ibid., VI.1, 14.10.

discourse, accidents are traditionally one of the rejected options for principle of individuation, apart from matter or form.) Leibniz specifically formulates one of the Scotist arguments as "species is not brought about through form or matter, or accidents, etc. Therefore, there remains *haecceity*."[36] Leibniz and Thomasius say that the view to be defended is the same as the nominalist view, by which they mean Suárez's. In the *Metaphysical Disputations* Suárez explains that prime matter is individuated by "its whole entity" and not by quantity or other accidents. Quantity would be separable from matter, at least by God's power. It is therefore extrinsic to and thus presupposes the entity of matter. The same argument holds for all the other accidents. Accidents cannot be the principles that individuate substantial forms. The principle of individuation for a composite creature therefore consists of a particular matter and a particular substantial form united to one another.[37]

Leibniz seemingly discusses the second and third principles simply for the sake of the schema. He attributes the fourth principle, *haecceity*, to Scotus and his followers, John of Bassols, Pereira, Mercenarius, Zabarella, Fonseca, and Eustachius a Sancto Paulo. He adopts the role of the nominalist and asserts that there are no species outside the mind, that genus and difference are distinguished only rationally, that there is no universal before the operation of the mind, and finally that things are distinguished only by a real distinction or by a distinction of reason. Since the *haecceity* was intended to be formally distinct from the common nature by virtue of being based on a third distinction between real and rational, it fails. (Leibniz's overall strategy in the *Metaphysical Disputation* is to use the Scotists against everybody except Suárez and the nominalists and then to use Suárez's rejection of the formal distinction against the Scotists.)

In 1668 Leibniz was in the service of Baron Johann Christian von Boinebourg who was interested in the reconciliation of the Catholic and Lutheran churches in Germany. The Lutheran Leibniz wrote some conciliatory essays on various theological topics for the Catholic convert Boinebourg including the mystery of the Eucharist. The sacrament of the Eucharist requires that the bread and wine of communion be transformed into the body and blood of Christ while still tasting and looking like bread and wine. The metaphysics of substance, matter, and form was thought to be suitable for explaining the miracle, despite difficulties regarding what supported the accidents of bread and wine after transubstantiation. There was general agreement that, by natural means, a body could not be simultaneously in two places and two bodies could not be

36. Ibid., VI.1, 16.20.

37. Suarez (1998), disp. 5, §6. 180–88.

simultaneously in the same place. Hence the difficulty of saying how Christ could be present as the subject of the accidents, with the change having taken place such that Christ would be present with those accidents. Leibniz indicated what he thought the Catholic Church's doctrine of "real presence" required, which he thought might have been acceptable to Protestants as well:

> Bread and wine, losing their own substance, acquire the substance of Christ's body and become everywhere numerically identical with it, only their species or accidents remaining, the substance of Christ's body being present in all places where the species of consecrated bread and wine exist.[38]

His suggestion was that bodies were not substances apart from a concurring mind because a substance is a being that subsists in itself; such a being "has a principle of action in itself," and "actions pertain to supposita—*actiones sunt suppositorum.*" As Leibniz said, "substance is union with a mind." Thus, bodies that lack reason are substances through a union with universal mind, or God.[39] Transubstantiation occurs simply when the body's union with the concurring mind is changed. The bread and wine of the sacrament are transubstantiated when the mind of Christ takes them on and substitutes its special concourse for the general concourse of the universal or divine mind. Using such propositions, Leibniz then proved that those bodies would have numerically the same substantial form as Christ's body and that a body transubstantiated in this way would not be changed except in the substantial form of the concurring mind. It would retain all its accidents or species. Since minds lack extension, are not in space, can act upon bodies in space, and can think many things at the same time, Christ's mind can be present everywhere in the species of consecrated bread and wine. Given that Christ's mind is his substance, Christ's substance can be present everywhere.

Leibniz recognized that his explanation of transubstantiation requires a particular principle of individuation, namely, substantial form alone, and not matter or accidents. He asserted in the scholium:

> These theorems of ours differ very little from the accepted philosophy. In Aristotle, nature is the principle of motion and rest. But substantial form is properly nature in the same philosopher. Hence Averroes,

---

38. Leibniz (1923–), VI.1, 508; translation in Leibniz (1969), 115 (modified).

39. There is a further complication I will disregard, in that Leibniz, trying to avoid the doctrine that God is the soul of the universe, states that "The idea is the union of God with creature" (Leibniz (1923–), VI.1: 509; translation in Leibniz (1969), 116).

> Angelus Mercenarius, and Jacob Zabarella also assert that substantial form is the principle of individuation.[40]

In the 1663 thesis, Mercenarius and Zabarella are cited as supporters of the Scotist view. Now they are among those who agree with Leibniz. In case the point is not fully understood, Leibniz also referred to "those who locate the nature of subsistence in the union of matter and form, like Murcia,"[41] thereby distancing himself from that earlier position. In 1663 Murcia was among those who agreed with Leibniz in holding the "whole entity" principle of individuation, which for composite beings is matter and substantial form. Leibniz emphasized that he was using the terms "substance," "transubstantiation," "accident," "species," and "identity" in the sense which the Council of Trent favored, that none of his conceptions were innovations, and that he demonstrated "the numerical identity of substance from the numerical identity of the substantial form, in conformity with the principle of the noblest scholastic and Aristotelian philosophers, for whom substantial form is the principle of individuation."[42] The inescapable conclusion is that Leibniz wrote a bachelor's thesis in 1663 in which he affirmed his teacher's position that the principle of individuation is the Suárezian whole entity as opposed to just the substantial form. By 1668 he wrote a tract on the Eucharist in which he articulated the position that the principle of individuation is the substantial form, i.e., something less than the whole entity.

Neither of the two Leibnizian principles of individuation from 1663 and 1668 are the same as Leibniz's mature view of individuation. That doctrine has its roots in an essay from 1676 entitled *Meditatio de Principio Individui*. There Leibniz considers two rectangles or two triangles coming to constitute two indistinguishable squares, as an example of different causes producing an effect that is perfectly the same. Of his two squares Leibniz asserts "neither of these can be distinguished from one another in any other way, not even by the wisest being." Based on the principle that the effect involves its cause "in such a way that whoever understands some effect perfectly will also arrive at the knowledge of its cause," Leibniz argues that "if we admit that two different things always differ in themselves in some respect as well, it follows that there is present in any matter something which retains the effect of what precedes it, namely a mind." Thus, for matter to be individuated, it has to be connected to a mind that will retain the memory or traces of its construction.

40. Leibniz (1923–), VI.1, 510; translation in Leibniz (1969), 117.

41. Leibniz (1923–),VI.1, 510; translation in Leibniz (1969), 117.

42. Ibid., VI.1, 510; translation in Leibniz (1969), 117.

Leibniz concludes: "This argument is very fine and proves that … we cannot think of anything by which matter differs, except by mind.… This principle is of great importance."[43] Of course, the mind Leibniz is referring to could be either inside or outside the thing, a universal soul or a mind, individual soul, substantial form, or individuating form, that is, a *haecceity*. Leibniz locates the principle of individuation inside the thing.

Something of his 1676 view is found as late as 1685, just before Leibniz wrote the *Discourse on Metaphysics*, in a comment on Gérauld de Cordemoy's atomist solution to the Cartesian problem of individuation. Leibniz appreciated Cordemoy's criticism of Cartesianism, but thought that Cordemoy had not gone far enough.

> These are difficulties for Cordemoy himself: let us suppose two triangular atoms come into contact and compose a perfect square, and that they rest next to each other in this way, and let there be another corporeal substance or atom, a square one equal to the other two. I ask, in what respect do these two extended things differ? Certainly no difference can be conceived in them as they are now, unless we suppose something in bodies besides extension; rather they are distinguished solely by memory of their former condition and there is nothing of this kind in bodies.[44]

There were, of course, further developments in Leibniz's view of individuation after 1685. In his mature philosophy, Leibniz rarely referred to the principle of individuation except to dissociate himself from it: "The vulgar philosophers were mistaken when they believed that there are two things different in number alone, or only because they are two, and from this error have arisen their perplexities about what they called the *principle of individuation.*"[45] He distinguished clearly his own principle from the one held in the schools, "where they torment themselves so much in seeking to understand what it is"; as he said, "the *principle of individuation* for individuals reduces to the principle of distinction of which I have just been speaking. If two individuals were perfectly similar and equal and (in a word) *indistinguishable* in themselves, there would be no principle of individuation."[46] One would have to take "principle

43. Ibid., VI.3, 491.

44. Ibid., VI.4, 1799.

45. Leibniz (1875–90), VII, 395; translation in Leibniz, (1989), 334.

46. Leibniz, *Nouveaux Essais* 2, chap. 27, in Leibniz (1875–90), V, 213–14.

of individuation" in a very general way to claim that Leibniz gave it his attention all his life, from the first of his publications to the end of his life.[47]

3. The Problem with Problems: Sorting Myth and Philosophy

Ryle's and Mates's accounts of episodes in the seventeenth century have been accepted as credible history of philosophy—or as a suitable replacement—among many in the English-speaking philosophical world. Why these accounts should be accepted as either demands a complex explanation, one that includes sociological and political and material factors. Here we will focus only on the conceptions of philosophy and its history under which ahistorical explanations are deemed acceptable. Ryle's own distinction between the "historical" mode of talking about Descartes and his largely ahistorical "official theory" encourages the thought that Ryle's account is intended as a replacement for, and not an instance of, the history of philosophy.

There are a number of assumptions implicit in the idea that "historical" explanations need not be done in the "historical mode," although one does not always, if ever, find full acknowledgment of these assumptions by their authors. Since these assumptions constitute the mythology—what everybody knows—of contemporary philosophy, they need neither to be written down nor acknowledged explicitly.[48] The most obvious assumption, as noted earlier, is that philosophy consists—or should be seen as consisting—of a set of perennial problems, and the history of philosophy, of establishing what philosophers from the past had to say about these problems and drawing implications for present day philosophy. This conception of "philosophical history" allows a particular philosopher's take on a philosophical problem to be reconstructed as a rebuttal to the position of another philosopher, regardless of whether the philosophers in questions had read each others' works, or whether one of them intended his statements to be an improvement on, or

47. The two mythic tales of "philosophical history" are not especially unusual. There are in fact numerous such stories. Every day students are taught, using Sober (2009), that Descartes's dualism is shown invalid by "Leibniz's Law," the latter being given a formulation that Leibniz would not have accepted—a double anachronism! Or one may look at A. J. Ayer (1959) where he writes that the members of the Vienna Circle chose the "epithet logical because they wished to annex the discoveries of modern logic; they believed in particular, that the logical symbolism that had been developed by Frege, Peano, and Russell would be serviceable to them" (10). "Serviceable" is hardly adequate for Schlick's view, namely, that the turning point in philosophy is an "insight into the nature of logic itself" (Schlick (1959), 54, 55); or that of Carnap, who proclaims that "Logic is the method of philosophizing" (Carnap (1959), 133). Finally, such tales about Plato abound.

48. "To know by hearsay," Thucydides tells us, "is to know by myth." *Peloponnesian War,* I, 4.1.

rebuttal of, the other. Arguments are also constructed for past philosophers that function as answers to problems that were formulated centuries after the texts undergoing "reconstruction" were written.

For such reconstructions to be possible, we must be able to translate the text from the language in which it was written to the language(s) of its present day reader(s) without losing anything of philosophical importance. For such translations to be possible there must be something about the philosophical content of the translated text that makes it markedly different from other texts in the natural language in which it was written, something that makes it possible to translate it from the language of its author into the language of its present day translator *salva veritate*, as it were. Knowing the problematic of contemporary philosophy often appears to be as important—if not more important—in judging a translation than knowing about the historical context and material culture in and by which the text was produced, preserved, and transmitted. Although authors write for, and in response to, their contemporaries, discussions of what a past philosopher has said about a philosophical problem proceed without much, if any, consideration of the forms of life or social practices represented in and by the concepts he shared with his audiences. This occurs even when the problem at issue concerns a just society, a just man, or a just act, or asks whether and how we know the natural world. These discussions often read as if we could isolate these concepts from the forms of life in the society in which the philosopher in question lived, or as if we can assume that our forms of life are the same as those in the centuries preceding us.

From philosophy's earliest days—and even before—teachings and texts that encourage and, perhaps, give rise to philosophical practices are said to be found in mathematics.[49] These expressions allegedly transcend the natural language in which they are stated, because they concern special objects or concepts that by definition are not subject to the changes in time and place that characterize natural entities, special objects not suited to the narrative syntax of natural languages in which we talk about natural entities. In the last century, some philosophers were invigorated in their hopes that the truths of philosophy and the concepts or objects that they describe could be like those found in mathematics rather than the truths, concepts, and objects found in the natural world. The advent of formal languages permitted and encouraged the representation of abstract objects and concepts without reference to time and place. Symbolic

---

49. For example, *schēma to (h)upo tinos ē tinōn (h)orōn periechomenon* can be translated as "a figure is that which is contained by any boundary or boundaries," seemingly without a change of truth value.

logic lay at the end of the long philosophical search for a neutral system of formulae, a "symbolism freed from the slag of historical languages," and for a total system of concepts.[50] Mathematical truths, and objects or concepts not suited to the narrative syntax of natural languages, were to be a part of logic. Logic combined with empiricism made possible a new "scientific philosophy."

The original celebrants of the new "scientific philosophy" did not embrace the notion of *philosophia perennis* or the history of philosophy.[51] If logical empiricism is the method of philosophy, the statements of traditional philosophy—metaphysics, ethics, aesthetics—must be rejected. Still the study of the history of philosophy was not abandoned when Logical Empiricism was transplanted to the English-speaking philosophical world, and again the reasons for this are complex, involving political, economic, and sociological factors. English language philosophers inspired by Logical Empiricism yet not willing or able to give up the study of the history of philosophy favored the approach summarized in *HPQ*'s editorial comment: treating the works of past philosophers as a means of dealing with issues of ongoing philosophical interest. The history of philosophy was exploited, as *HPQ* recommends, in dealing with present day philosophical concerns, and present day concepts, methods, distinctions, and arguments were used to illuminate historical questions. Symbolic logic's neutral system of formulae freed from "the slag of historical languages," coupled with the charge "to analyze the logic of a concept" fostered the practice of treating a concept as if it could be abstracted from the material inferential practices and forms of life that it represented. The boundary between philosophy and its history was erased. Thus were issues of ongoing philosophical interest elevated to the status of "perennial philosophical problems."

Present day philosophers may object that there is nothing new about their practice; it is as old as Plato who first promoted the idea that philosophy consists of problems that can and should be viewed *sub species aeternitatis.* They may also contend that it was Plato who, under the influence of Pythagoras, made the similarities between geometry and philosophy a cardinal point of philosophy. But these claims result from reading Plato as if he were a present day philosopher who believed in perennial philosophical problems, thereby discounting his choice to write *Sokratikoi Logoi* and what comes with it. Even the slightest amount of historical study would reveal that neither this concept of philosophy, nor the doctrinal way of reading Plato on which it depends, is as constant or as widespread a practice as many present day philosophers assume.

50. Carnap, Hahn, and Neurath (1929).

51. Schlick (1959), *passim*, and Reichenbach (1951), esp. 123 and 325.

The debate about whether Plato asserts doctrines or eschews them goes back to Antiquity. In any case, no matter how ancient, constant, or widespread this way of reading Plato may be, it is still an instance of begging the question.

The historical study needed to establish Plato's conception of philosophy—or that of Descartes or Leibniz—and how it is related to each philosopher's choice to write as he does is a complex undertaking, one that relies on material culture as well as historical texts. Historical study begins with material artifacts, including tablets and scrolls, codices and books, as well as material means for preserving and reproducing them. Generating, preserving, and studying documents, too, have a history. It cannot be the case that without documents there is no culture: human societies existed long before some enterprising members devised the "useful trick" of making marks to serve as signs for their speech and found substances on which to make them.[52] In societies that lack a writing system or have a system known only to a few members, the past is preserved through the public performance of rhythmical speech or songs and stories—what the Greeks called *muthos*—along with cultural artifacts. To the extent that we know, *muthos,* the tradition of oral performance, must still be practiced or it must have left its mark on documents made when writing and reading were first used to record speech, such as we find in Homer and Hesiod.[53] If we do not distinguish speech performed from the production of texts written and read, we may confound texts and speech acts, subsuming them both under an abstraction we call "language." In so doing, we fail to notice the differences between the two, and the priority of speech acts to texts. If we take texts rather than speech acts as the model for language, we may miss the role of the body and material culture in the forms of life and social practices that give us meaning. We may fail to see that just as a speaker conveys meaning not just by her utterance but also by her gestures and movements, her intonation and phrasing, the expression on her face and the stance of her body, the writer of a text conveys meaning by choosing to write as he does for a certain audience at a certain time in contrast to other choices. If we fail to see the importance of this choice, we may not grasp that understanding the text requires knowledge not only of the language the inscribed marks are meant to record, but also the material and historical contexts in which the text was produced and is being read, the tradition that is the source of its allusions and of which the text is a part, and the community to which it is addressed.

52. The phrase "useful trick" comes from Havelock (1981), 50.

53. That this is the case with the *Iliad* and *Odyssey* of Homer was demonstrated by Parry (1971).

This is true of philosophical texts, too, although we may pretend otherwise. As Derrida reminds us, philosophy is a genre of writing that pretends to merely inscribe speech. But it is a strange kind of speech that philosophical writing claims merely to record: speech that while grammatically tensed is logically tenseless; speech the meaning of which transcends history and context; speech about special objects described by propositions; speech that depends on confounding the properties of an inscribed text with the meaning(s) of the text inscribed. In this way arise the philosophers' claims that their discipline is the study of special kinds of objects and that philosophical concepts transcend the forms of life of the author and audience for whom they were written. That philosophical objects depend both literally and figuratively on the notion of inscription belies their special nature, as does the recognition that formal languages are parasitic on natural ones. This casts doubt on the claim that philosophical concepts can be abstracted from the material inferential practices these concepts represent, and on the practice of abstracting philosophical problems and concepts from their historical and cultural contexts, whether the text in question comes from present day philosophy or some period in its history.

The alternative is the ad hoc assumption that what we consider philosophy and its problems exist for all societies at all times. This requires that "philosophy" is but one of many names for the speculation found in nearly every known society about its origins and the origins of the world, and of its laws and customs. Such speculation occurs in poetry, folk tales, and sagas of oral, traditional cultures, usually grouped together under the term "myth." Indeed, storytelling is as universal a cultural activity as one can find, and in traditional societies those who perform it are considered "masters of truth."[54] But "myth" is understood by philosophers as Plato wished it to be understood—stories not capable of being true.[55] It is a point of pride among philosophers that what they do is not myth. Indeed, since philosophers started calling themselves "philosophers" they have insisted on philosophy's superiority to myth. Plato's Socrates insists that the distinction between *muthos* and *philosophia* is central to the very idea of *philosophia*; *muthos* is what we learn from Homer and the poets; *philosophia*, what we learn from the exercise of the intellect. Two millennia later, Carnap insists that scientific philosophy be distinguished from traditional philosophy, for its claims to be systematic are belied by its being

54. Detienne (1996).

55. Hereafter, "myth" will be used in the sense that Plato gives to it; "*muthos*," in the traditional sense in which singers are masters of truth.

descended from myth. Myth expresses our attitudes about life, the world, our society, and what befalls us, but it has no truth value.[56] Neither the content nor the syntax of myth is systematic in the way needed for knowledge. Philosophy—according to Carnap's myth—should not be expressive but descriptive as it aims to identify the logical structure of science, which, in principle, transcends history.

It is Plato's Socrates who downgrades *mimēsis* and reconceptualizes *muthos* as something false and misleading. *Mimēsis* becomes skill at painting in words or in images, and its makers have no claim to truth. At best, these imitations produce *doxa*. They cannot generate *epistēmē* because they neither recognize nor address the part of the soul having the power to conceive of abstract, intelligible objects (605b3–c4). This talk of the Forms, or special objects, is seen as support for the claim that Plato introduces the notion of *philosophia perennis*, as the Socratic question, "what is x?," is cited for his initiating the "problems of philosophy." But one can only get to a *Theory* of Forms by assuming that how one writes philosophy is not relevant to his or her philosophical beliefs. Only if one discounts Plato's desire to remain anonymous and ignores his choice to write *Sokratikoi Logoi* can we assume that Socrates is merely a mouthpiece for Plato. Only then can we pick and choose among Socrates's statements, ignoring what they mean to the audiences both in, and of, the dialogue, and ignoring as well the dramatic order of the dialogues. Only then can we overlook the criticisms of the Forms raised in the *Parmenides* and the *Statesman* and assume instead that philosophical concepts transcend the forms of life of the author and audience for whom they were written.

Plato's *Sokratikoi Logoi* are philosophical texts, but they re-present speech acts. In so doing, they bring with them the context(s) in which the texts were produced and are being read, the tradition that is the source of their allusions and of which these texts are a part, and the community to which they are addressed. They raise philosophical problems and concepts in their historical and cultural contexts and identify the material inferential practices these concepts represent. In the dialogues, Plato addresses problems and concerns he shares with his fourth-century contemporaries: we begin the search for a just life with the ways of life in which the language we speak is embedded. Thus does Plato exploit his fourth-century audience's knowledge of the characters and careers of those historical figures appearing as *dramatis personae* in the dialogues. Those who claimed the authority to speak the truth about the

56. Carnap (1959), 78–79.

meaning of justice, or love, or courage are exposed as not knowing what they claimed to know, and not brave enough to continue the search. This leaves the audience of the dialogue with the realization that this authority does not rest with a single man, no matter how famous or honored, a realization that Socrates had come to in trying to solve the riddle of the Delphic Oracle. This brings, too, the realization that none of us are what we ought to be, and that we must examine our lives in the hope of finding a way of knowing and living that enables us to be what we ought.

Plato's *Sokratikoi Logoi* reenact *philosophia* not only as a way of living but also as a way of teaching others how to live. The dialogue allows its audience to experience almost firsthand (or in a way that is second best) what other forms of writing philosophy neither encourage nor allow: the lived social practices, the normative structure of which must be made explicit in order for Plato's audiences to live in the space of reasons, and the consequences of not doing so. Socrates's interlocutors cite what "everybody knows by hearsay" simply by virtue of receiving the education that comes just from living in Athens, attending its festivals, and witnessing performances of *muthos* that have no equal. Socrates points out that "Homer says" or "everybody knows" cannot be the *reason* that something is true, that the mind is connected to it. His question "what is x?" shows the audiences in, and of, the dialogues that reasons must be conceptual structures, chains of inferences such that citing a reason for an action commits one to all that follows from the reason cited, and entitles interlocutors to attribute these commitments to her.[57]

Like the *muthos* that Plato's *Sokratikoi Logoi* are intended to replace, the dialogues are special speech. The occasion of their reenactment is nothing less than a lesson in how to live, and their reenactments do depend on the excellence of their performers. The critical difference between these performers and those who perform *muthos* is the source of their authority. It is not enough to imagine a world that provides the everyday world of human affairs with a normative structure. Authority does not rest with a single philosopher. Rather, philosophy consists of a community of enquirers who are committed to living in the space of reasons. This requires that we articulate the normative structure of our social practices, identify the chains of material inferences that count as reasons for how we know our way around the world. This is true whether the society in question exists in fourth-century Athens,

57. This echoes Brandom (1994), but he credits Plato with providing examples of this very activity.

seventeenth-century Europe, or twenty-first-century North America. That something exists besides these societies may cause them to experience similar or even the same problems, but we can only know this by examining their respective social practices, and the texts and artifacts that attest to them.

Pace those philosophers who ask us to accept *philosophia perennis* on their authority, philosophical utterances are as contingent as the problems they address. The difference between philosophy and myth lies not in the former's study of special objects that transcend the time and place and thus require a neutral system of formulae freed from the slag of historical languages. Rather, this difference lies in philosophy's challenge to the authority of myth, even when the myths being challenged are philosophy's own.

6

Philosophical Problems in the History of Philosophy: What Are They?

Leo Catana

1. Introduction

IN THE INTRODUCTION to the 1984 publication *Philosophy in History*, edited by Richard Rorty, J. B. Schneewind, and Quentin Skinner, the three editors distinguish between history of philosophy and intellectual history: the former seeks "philosophical truth" and outlines how past philosophers have reasoned about various philosophical problems; the latter seeks "historical truth" and the "meaning" of past utterances.[1] The history of philosophy is thus a problem-based discipline, whereas intellectual history is a contextual discipline.[2] The editors contend that contemporary analytic philosophers in America and Britain perpetuate this division in their analysis of the history of philosophy: they are, the editors claim, exclusively interested in philosophical questions, not in their historical contexts.[3] The editors argue that what is outside the sphere of philosophical problems, that is, historical truth and the contingency of historical contexts, should be discovered and presented by intellectual historians, not by historians of philosophy; the method of the latter, and their followers in analytic philosophy, is ill-suited to uncover such historical contexts.[4] Hence the editors endorse a division of labor in which both

1. Rorty, Schneewind, and Skinner (1984), 2, 7, 10.

2. Ibid., 3–4, 8. Grafton (2005) provides a survey of history of ideas, later to be called intellectual history. Ibid., 31: he rightly observes that the context-concept has not yet been determined accurately: "Fundamental, frequently used concepts like 'context'—a term, in the end, for information somehow distilled from the same sorts of text that it is usually invoked to explicate— require far more formal analysis than they have had."

3. Rorty, Schneewind, and Skinner (1984), 11–12.

4. Ibid., 13–14.

the history of philosophy and intellectual history are recognized as mutually beneficial. The purpose of the Introduction is clearly to establish some sort of peaceful interaction between the two disciplines.[5] In this chapter I reexamine the definitions of the history of philosophy and intellectual history assumed in the bifurcation noted earlier. I argue that the contextual task assigned to intellectual history must also be assigned to the history of philosophy, if it is going to be *history* of philosophy at all.

I see at least three problems in the bifurcation. First, it presupposes questionable assumptions about the methodological cores of the two disciplines, especially the concept of a "philosophical problem," a theme to which I return later.

Second, the desired institutional effect of the publication—to make use of the results of intellectual history for the benefit of the history of philosophy—remains to be seen. The bifurcation justifies intellectual history as contextual and history of philosophy as problem-based. Although the intended purpose was to establish some sort of mutual exchange between the two disciplines, the division of labor can also be seen as an argument in favor of a status quo. The bifurcation is thus conservative in regard to the method practiced by historians of philosophy; it is nothing but an open invitation, which historians of philosophy may easily ignore. The bifurcation is also conservative in the sense that it carries on Lovejoy's distinction from 1936 between history of philosophy, dedicated to the history of philosophical systems, and history of ideas, dedicated to the various philosophical and non-philosophical contexts in which certain unit-ideas manifest themselves in the course of history; Lovejoy's "history of ideas" was nominally and methodologically transformed into "intellectual history" in the 1960s and 1970s by Skinner and others.[6]

Third, many historians of philosophy seem to remain unaffected by intellectual historians' excavations of the historical contingencies and illocutionary meanings surrounding certain texts of the past: the former may not recognize the philosophical relevance of the uncovered contexts, nor even of the texts thus contextualized by intellectual historians, since both appear irrelevant to those problems and questions accepted as fundamental to philosophy. Or historians of philosophy may think that the locutionary meaning (not the

5. Ibid., 8–14.

6. Lovejoy (1936), 3. I have argued elsewhere that Lovejoy's distinction is rather rhetorical, and that his understanding of history of ideas is in fact relying on methodological components borrowed from nineteenth-century history of philosophy; see Catana (2010).

illocutionary) of applied terms is more relevant to their enterprise, since it has direct relevance to the philosophical problems and arguments examined.[7] Or, finally, they may feel alienated when confronted with the linguistic, historical, and contextual method practiced by intellectual historians.

The three editors' characterization of the history of philosophy as problem-based is not isolated. Nor is it obsolete, for it features in Tom Sorell's Introduction to the 2005 volume *Analytic Philosophy and History of Philosophy*.[8] Similarly, Hans-Johann Glock, an important historian of twentieth-century analytic philosophy, has recently argued that the historiography of philosophy should ideally avoid what he characterizes as excessive historicism; instead, it should aim at an account of all past philosophy as a problem-solving enterprise.[9] Glock emphasizes that this problem-oriented approach to the past is "congenial" to analytic philosophy.[10] Many other examples could be found.

7. Rorty, Schneewind, and Skinner (1984), 4, define intellectual history as a historical discipline that identifies the "meaning" of the utterances of past philosophers. However, the concept of meaning is a complex and difficult one, and some clarification would be useful here. Rorty (1984), 68, defines intellectual history as a discipline examining the intentional meaning of philosophical texts of the past: "[I]ntellectual history consists of descriptions of what the intellectuals were up to at a given time, and of their interaction with the rest of society." According to Rorty, Schneewind, and Skinner (1984), 12, analytic philosophers writing history of philosophy fail to see "what Descartes and Kant were really up to." The formulation says little about the method applied in intellectual history, though it stresses the intention of the past philosopher and his or her intervention in a social and political context. (For the emphasis on *history* in history of philosophy, see also the contributions by Mogens Lærke and Justin Smith in this volume). It does point, of course, toward Skinner's numerous articles from the 1960s onward in which John Austin's (1911–1960) and John Searle's (1932–) speech-act theory is employed on past philosophical texts. Drawing on Austin's distinction between locutionary, illocutionary, and perlocutionary speech acts, Skinner has argued that past texts should be seen as illocutionary utterances in order to be fully understood; see Skinner (2002), 79–86. In order to grasp this linguistic function, the intellectual historian should not only understand what is said in a past text, but also the social, political, and linguistic context in which it appears. Haakonssen (1996), 14, has argued that Skinner ignores the locutionary function of philosophical terms and that these play a considerable role in philosophical disciplines of the past. One could add to Haakonssen's criticism that this locutionary function is even more crucial within philosophical disciplines outside political philosophy, which does seek to intervene in social and political contexts, and which is Skinner's main interest.

8. Sorell (2005a), 1–3.

9. Glock (2008a), 869, 872–73, 875 *et passim*. Ibid., 873: Glock even makes the strong claim that "If philosophy were transformed into a cultural science or reduced to a history of ideas, it would no longer speak to the philosophical problems." That is, historical contextualization would not only be irrelevant to history of philosophy; it would dissolve history of philosophy. Ibid., 873: Glock claims that philosophers worked on non-historical problems, thereby asserting some sort of idealistic conception of a philosophical problem: "Instead, they [great philosophers, mentioned on 873] tackled non-historical problems and aspired to insights of a *non-historical* kind."

10. Glock (2008a), 884.

Although I agree with Glock's criticism of excessive historicism and appreciate his accommodation of history of philosophy within the analytic tradition, now beginning to write its own history, I do find that his problem concept calls for further discussion.[11]

Over the following pages I argue that the problem-based view of the history of philosophy found in the Introduction to *Philosophy in History* is based on an unexamined concept of a philosophical problem and a questionable distinction between internal and external elements in the history of philosophy, where the problems are seen as internal to the past philosophy, the context as external to it. Further, I argue that if one reflects upon the nature of philosophical problems in the history of philosophy, and if one realizes that the assumed internal-external distinction in history of philosophy is questionable, then historians of philosophy will be forced to accept the historically and philologically exacting task of contextualization usually assigned to intellectual historians. My entire discussion is premised on the borrowed assumption that philosophy's aim is, and has always been, to solve philosophical problems. Although I think it is sensible to approach past philosophical texts by asking "which problems did they strive to resolve?" I also maintain that philosophy's aim has varied throughout history and that reducing it entirely to a problem-solving enterprise is therefore inadequate.[12]

1. The Concept of Problem in Problem-based History of Philosophy

These three mentioned publications—Skinner, Schneewind, and Rorty's text of 1984, Sorell's of 2005, and Glock's of 2008—have two things in common. First, they do not explain the key concept in their characterization of history of philosophy as problem-based, namely, the concept of a problem, let alone the concept of a philosophical problem.[13] Glock is perhaps the one who comes closest to an explanation. He explains that these problems are

---

11. For the history of nineteenth- and twentieth-century analytic philosophy, see Hylton (1990); Soames (2003); Glock (2008b).

12. See Kranz et al. (1989); Hadot (1995); Condren, Gaukroger, and Hunter (2006).

13. Rorty, Schneewind, and Skinner (1984), 1–14, do not define what they mean by "problem." Sorell (2005a), 1–11 does not explain what is meant by a problem. Similarly Glock (2008a), 869, 872–73, 875, 877, 878, 881, 882, 884, 885, 887, 889, speaks of "problems" or "philosophical problems" without explaining what they are.

"supremely abstract and fundamental," and that analytic philosophers practicing the problem-based history of philosophy believe that "philosophy has its roots in problems of a special kind, and that its history is an evolution of these problems and of their solutions."[14] Nevertheless, this explanation is opaque and calls for further discussion.

Second, these three publications do not provide examples illustrating how such problem-based general histories of philosophy can be written successfully.[15] One is left wondering which general, problem-oriented histories of philosophy these authors have in mind, if any. The three publications do, however, point out a few publications, which either (a) examine a single past philosopher and the philosophical problems he or she struggled with (e.g., J. Bennett, *Kant's Analytic*, 1966),[16] (b), approach the entire philosophical tradition by asking one or more philosophical questions (e.g., G. E. Moore's lectures delivered 1910–11, published in 1953 as *Some Main Problems of Philosophy*)[17]; or (c), focus on distinct philosophical problems or thinkers across history in distinct publications.[18]

In these latter works we find discussions of problems but little clarification of what a problem is, or what its implications in various argumentative contexts may be. If we are to improve our understanding of the problem concept assumed in problem-based histories of philosophy, we have to explore the semantics of the concept and its employment in such histories.

---

14. Glock (2008a), 872, 884.

15. Rorty, Schneewind, and Skinner (1984), 1–14, do not provide an example of a problem-based general history of philosophy. In the same volume, one of these authors, Rorty, distinguishes between four genres in the historiography of philosophy. The first of them he calls "rational and historical reconstructions" (Rorty (1984), 49–56), claiming that it is typical of analytical philosophers (ibid., 49). This first genre is similarly problem-based (e.g., ibid., 51), but here too Rorty gives no examples of such histories of philosophy that are problem-based (ibid., 49–56).

16. Rorty, Schneewind, and Skinner (1984), 6, provide only one example of a historian of philosophy, namely, J. Bennett's monograph on Kant, but here the issue is not that of writing problem-based history of philosophy.

17. Glock (2008a), 867–97, does not give an example of a general history of philosophy that is problem-based. He may, however, be thinking of works like Moore's *Some Main Problems of Philosophy*, since he favored Moore's approach; see ibid., 884: "Moore put philosophical difficulties down to 'the attempt to answer questions without first discovering precisely what question it is which you desire to answer' (1903, p. vi [the work is not mentioned in Glock's bibliography; we find the quote in the 'Preface' to Moore, *Principia ethica*, 1903])." Glock also agrees with Michael Frede's view; see Glock (2008a), 877, 885, 889.

18. Sorell (2005a), 3, notes the series *The Arguments of the Philosophers*, ed. Ted Honderich 1970. For criticism of this series, see Garber (2001), 232 *et passim*.

The concept of a problem (Gr. *problēma*, derived from the verb *proballein*, to throw or lay before; Lat. *problema*) dates back to Classical Greek philosophy, where it was central to the methodology of philosophy. It remained integral in the ensuing philosophical tradition, reaching a high point in Kantian philosophy and Neo-Kantianism.[19] One can say tentatively that a problem consists of a disjunctive question related to a theoretical description in the domain of philosophy: does the entity S possess the property P or not-P? Or, to put it in a less narrow manner, a philosophical problem is a complex of theories and arguments that may be paraphrased by philosophers or historians of philosophy as such a disjunctive question. When one attempts to answer such a question, difficulties arise on a theoretical level, where they may concern the semantic and logical consistency between several properties attributed to the same entity. Difficulties may also arise on the level of exemplification; how do we integrate different examples into the theoretical description? In contemporary philosophy we rarely find a general definition of the problem-concept, but only instances of philosophical problems. One example is the demarcation problem, which raises the question of how to distinguish scientific from non-scientific disciplines: all these disciplines purport to present true claims about the world, but which criteria do we accept in order to separate the claims of non-scientific disciplines from those of scientific disciplines?

2. *The Concept of Problem as It Has Been Practiced in Problem-based Histories of Philosophy*

This tentative explanation of a philosophical problem—a disjunctive question related to a theoretical description—is a good match for the earliest problem-based general histories of philosophy from the late eighteenth and nineteenth centuries. Here a problem is typically dealt with in a propositional context. Georg Gustav Fülleborn (1769–1803) seems to be the first historian of philosophy to conceive the discipline history of philosophy as problem-based.[20] In his "Verzeichniss einiger philosophischen Modethematum" (1799), he signposted four problems that had been dealt with by various past

19. For the history of the problem concept, see Holzhey (1989).

20. Fülleborn (1799). For problem history, see Geldsetzer (1989), cols. 1410–11. For problem history and its origin in Bruckerian history of philosophy, see Catana (2008), 260–65. Compare with Mann (1996), 170, who claims that problem-based history "marks a radical break with all earlier attempts to treat the history of philosophy." For the alleged break, see ibid., 182–83.

philosophers: I. Can virtue be taught?[21] II. The doctrine of probability.[22] III. On the conflict between philosophical and theological truth.[23] IV. On the souls and powers of animals.[24]

Fülleborn was followed by a series of nineteenth- and twentieth-century historians of philosophy: Karl Friedrich Bachmann (1785–1855), Christian August Brandis (1790–1867), Kuno Fischer (1824–1907), Wilhelm Windelband (1848–1915), Ernst Cassirer (1874–1945), Nicolai Hartmann (1882–1950), and Harald Høffding (1843–1931), among others. The list of problems varied over time. Fischer, for instance, held that philosophy's development is determined by a stable set of philosophical problems and various philosophers' attempts to answer them.[25] He identified the following four problems as perennial: I. The problem of the world, i.e., what is nature? II. The problem of knowledge, i.e., is human sensation objectively valid? III. The problem of freedom, i.e., are human beings endowed with free will? IV. The problem of religion, i.e., which is the true religion to provide moral bliss?[26] If one compares the list of problems with that of Fülleborn, one can discern some changes, and one can also sense Fischer's interest in problems pertinent to the Kantian philosophy that he admired.

Some eminent analytic philosophers adopted this method, as in the case of G. E. Moore in his *Some Main Problems of Philosophy*, and Bertrand Russell in his *Problems of Philosophy* (1912). Moore worked on two problems: what is the nature of the external world? And what status can we assign to general ideas? Russell too posed the question of knowledge. Hans-Johann Glock makes the following statement about the philosophical problems dealt with by historians of philosophy: "These problems are supremely abstract and

---

21. Fülleborn (1799), vol. 10, 143–47.

22. Ibid., vol. 10, 147–61.

23. Ibid., vols. 11–12, 204–24.

24. Ibid., vols 11–12, pp. 224–25.

25. Fischer (1878–93), vol. 1, 15: "Die Menschheit ist ein Problem, das in der Geschichte immer vollständiger entwickelt, in der Philosophie immer deutlicher zum Vorschein gebracht, immer tiefer begriffen wird: das ist, kurz gesagt, der ganze Inhalt der Geschichte der Philosophie, ein Inhalt selbst von größter geschichtlicher Bedeutung. Erst dann sieht man die Geschichte der Philosophie im richtigen Lichte, wenn man in ihr den Entwickelungsgang erkennt, in welchem die nothwendigen Probleme der Menschheit mit aller Deutlichkeit bestimmt und so gelöst werden, daß aus jeder Lösung in fortscreitender Ordnung immer neue und tiefere Probleme entspringen."

26. Ibid., vol. 1: "I. Das Weltproblem" (17–21); "II. Das Erkenntnißproblem" (21–25); "III. Das Freiheitsproblem" (25–28); "IV. Das Religionsproblem" (28–38).

fundamental, and they include questions such as 'Can we acquire genuine knowledge?', 'How is the mind related to the body?', and 'Are there universally binding moral principles?'"[27]

It is remarkable that the kind of philosophical problems indicated by these authors—Fülleborn, Fischer, Moore, Russell, and Glock—to a large extent mirror their respective interests in contemporary philosophy. Russell's selection of past philosophers (e.g., Plato, Kant, Hume, Berkeley, Locke) reflects his interest in the questions of knowledge that arise from his epistemological position. Similarly, Moore's anti-idealism to a large extent determined the problems he chose (i.e., the problem of the external world and the problem of universals) and the past figures that he adduced. Other problems in the history of philosophy, ones that did not fit these interests, were ignored. For instance, in these writings of Russell and Moore we do not find the question of the truth-value of revealed truths in comparison to philosophical truths, a central problem to early modern thinkers like Pomponazzi and Galileo. Problem historians like Russell and Moore tend to omit an enormous range of past philosophical problems and, at the same time, to focus exclusively on those problems in the past that could be assimilated to their interests in contemporary philosophy.

Such a procedure is perfectly legitimate, as long as works of Moore and Russell are not seen as general histories of philosophy. Moore and Russell did not claim that their books were histories of philosophy covering all questions.[28] Moore contended, however, that his selection of problems was not arbitrary and not merely relative to his own interests, but *the* most important problems in philosophy.[29] Moore and Russell belonged to a generation of philosophers for whom the history of philosophy made up an important part of their education, and they clearly knew the difference between a full history of philosophy and a selective, problem-based history of philosophy.[30] Perhaps the real danger lies in the expectation that works such as those of Moore and Russell *are* in fact histories of philosophy. An expectation of this kind may lead to a denial of the possibility that there are still other problems in philosophy's

27. Glock (2008a), 872.

28. Russell (1967), vii.

29. Moore (1953), 1.

30. For history of philosophy taught at philosophy departments in the nineteenth and twentieth centuries, see Schneider's works listed in the bibliography. Our understanding of the impact that nineteenth-century histories of philosophy had on twentieth-century analytic philosophy is still very poor.

past, which may at first seem advantageous to some philosophers, at least if it epitomizes their own problems as *the* problems of philosophy. However, this selective history of philosophy may also become increasingly self-referential and cut off from problems outside philosophy thus understood. If so, is this selective procedure a service to philosophy? Or is it merely a short-lived service to those philosophers thus epitomized?

I should like to make one last observation on the practice of problem historians, namely, its historiographical dependence upon existing interpretations. We can find one example of this in Russell, who characterizes Descartes as the founder of modern philosophy. This is an interpretation that emerged with Descartes's compatriot Victor Cousin in the 1820s and 1830s. Before then, Descartes was not seen as an epistemologist. Another example is the conceptualization of Descartes, Spinoza, Locke, Berkeley, and Hume according to the scheme of "rationalism" versus "empiricism." This scheme was circulated by Immanuel Kant and subsequently integrated into many general histories of philosophy. Russell accepted it without hesitation.[31] Given that contemporary philosophers (including analytic philosophers) often premise their discussion of philosophical problems on theories and arguments with a historical narrative, as in the case of Russell framing his discussing of human knowledge within an epistemological paradigm going back to Descartes, it becomes important to those contemporary philosophers to be aware of the historiography of the historical figure in question, if they are not to fall victim of stereotypes. Of course, this also applies to scholars outside philosophy who take an interest in the history of philosophy and premise some of their arguments on developments within the history of philosophy.

To sum up, it seems safe to assume that problem-oriented historians of philosophy understand philosophical problems as disjunctive questions, although different historians arrive at different lists of perennial questions—a

31. Russell (1967), 7: "Descartes (1596–1650), the founder of modern philosophy, invented a method which may still be used with profit—the method of systematic doubt." Brucker (1742–67), vol. 5, 200–334, did not regard Descartes in this way; according to him, Giordano Bruno was the founder of modern philosophy, as Brucker understood it, namely eclecticism; see ibid., vol. 5, 38.15–20. The interpretation of Descartes as the founder of modern philosophy, insisting on epistemology and systematic doubt as the most important component in philosophy, was prepared by Kantian philosophy, and first emerged properly with Victor Cousin and his lectures in the 1820s and 1830s, subsequently published in Cousin (1841), 52–60, 81–83, 362–69, 373. In support of this view, see also Haakonssen (2004), 107. Kant (1998a), 863–65, referred key elements in the history of philosophy to the strife between "rationalism" and "empiricism." Russell (1967), 41, takes over these reductive and probably misleading interpretations of the history of philosophy.

variety suggesting the dependence of these "perennial questions" on the individual problem historian's perspective.[32]

But what ontological status do these historians assign to such problems: are philosophical problems particulars, entirely dependent upon the contingent historical circumstances of philosophy, though particulars that may variously show some local resemblances allowing the historian of philosophy to compare them? Or, alternatively, are they transsubjective entities, or even transcendent entities existing independently; entities that past philosophers "discover" and "work on" from time to time? At this point it may be useful to add that the fact that certain questions are asked repeatedly by various authors does not necessarily prove that the questions are transcendent; textual transmission and long-standing institutional frameworks may also provide much continuity in the questions posed. Also, if philosophical questions are transcendent entities, one may ask some additional questions: how many are there in all? How do we get access to them? How do we ensure that we have a complete inventory of these problems and do not mix them up with our own historically conditioned and time-bound questions?

Problem historians have not yet settled the question of the ontological status of philosophical problems. Nor is this question addressed in the three publications mentioned earlier. Glock takes a daring line, though he does not really give an answer to the question asked here. He claims that past philosophers worked on non-historical problems: "Instead, they [i.e., great philosophers] tackled non-historical problems and aspired to insights of a *non-historical* kind."[33] (Glock's italics.) The phrase "non-historical" does not mean the same as "transcendent," but the two come close in meaning, and it seems as if Glock accepts an idealistic conception of philosophical problems; they are non-historical entities.

It is surprising to see this idealistic conception of problems in the history of philosophy appear in analytical philosophy, since epistemological anti-idealism was such an important component in the classical texts of its key figures, e.g., Moore.[34] Analytical philosophers used to be fond of the empirical approach to reality, urging us to "go out in the world and look" if we want

32. For criticism of the methodology of problem-based history of philosophy, see Gadamer (1924); Krüger (1984).

33. Glock (2008a), 873.

34. Ibid., 873: Glock argues that the historicist's relativistic argument against timeless truths or problems is flawed. This leaves open the implication that philosophical problems are timeless, though it remains unproved.

information about it; when it comes to philosophy's past, however, it seems to be quite another story, since then we must rely on our apparently innate ideas about transcendent problems. It seems incomprehensible and inconsistent that analytical philosophers should not apply the same empiricist principle when it comes to philosophy's past.

Let me add one last observation about the practice of problem historians. Those philosophical problems, including the terminology used to state these problems, listed by Fülleborn, Fischer, Moore, and Glock earlier, tend to be internal to, and characteristic of, philosophy itself: here we rarely find problems pertinent to non-philosophical disciplines—problems that are then solved by philosophical tools.

The earliest of these problem historians—Fülleborn, Fischer, and Moore, for instance—articulated this idea of philosophy as a self-contained unit by means of the system concept: past philosophers strove to resolve these problems by means of their philosophical systems. Hence, in the early phase of problem-based history of philosophy we find this ancillary assumption.[35] This may explain the belief among problem historians that philosophical problems and arguments are internal in these philosophical systems and that the philosopher, or historian of philosophy, need not have to look outside these systems when analyzing and explaining these problems and arguments. If, however, the belief is false, and if huge territories of philosophy outside the early modern period—and perhaps even much early modern philosophy itself—cannot be explained by means of the system concept, then one must abandon the belief that past philosophers' textual output, including their arguments, theories, and problems, can be understood and explained solely on the basis of internal features of the assumed system. In order to deal with this question, I now turn to a related issue in sections 3 and 4: where did problem-oriented history of philosophy come from, and how did it inherit its belief that problems were internal to the system of the past philosopher?

3. Brandis Integrating the Internal-External Distinction into a Problem-based History of Philosophy

In 1815, Christian August Brandis published *Von dem Begriff der Geschichte der Philosophie*. This work is one of the most elaborate methodological texts

35. For the integration of the system concept into nineteenth-century problem-oriented histories of philosophy, see Catana (2008), 260–65. For Russell using the system concept in his problem-oriented account, see Russell (1967), 57, 71, 82–84, 90.

in the early phase of the history of philosophy, including the problem-based history of philosophy. There Brandis identified "philosophy" with "systems" of philosophy, which he called the "internal" component. Hence, the history of philosophical systems constitutes the "internal" ("innern") history of philosophy, whereas the history of "circumstances" ("Umstände") of the systems constitutes the "external" ("ausseren") history of philosophy.

The text is divided into three parts. Having made a few remarks on the relationship between philosophy and history in the preface, Brandis defines the concept of a "system of philosophy" in the first part.[36] Here he observes that philosophy has changed enormously throughout history,[37] but he nevertheless contends that all past philosophies have one thing in common, namely, that they produce systems with a unitary nature.[38] In the second part Brandis treats the "internal" history of philosophy (this part is entitled "Von der innern Geschichte der Philosophie"), and in the third part he treats the "external" history of philosophy (entitled "Von der ausseren Geschichte der Philosophie").[39]

In the second part he claims that the internal history of philosophy can be written only as an account of the philosophical systems and that this internal history makes up the core of the history of philosophy.[40] The system concept, sometimes rendered by the synonym "Lehrgebäude" (order or system of sciences), thus features prominently in Brandis's proposed methodology, especially in the preface and the first and second parts.[41] In the third part Brandis treats the external causes behind a philosopher's ideas, and here he mentions the "circumstances" ("Umstände").[42] In this third part the system concept is absent. He mentions several examples of such circumstances: the philosopher's personality, his (national) culture, the worldview typical of his epoch, and linguistic conventions of his time.[43] It is noteworthy that he does not list scientific, philosophical, or other disciplines as examples of such external features, e.g., theology, astronomy, and medicine, and their relevance

---

36. Brandis (1815), 3–26.

37. Ibid., 18.

38. Ibid., 24–26.

39. For the second part, ibid., 27–68; for the third part, ibid., 69–88.

40. Ibid., 32–35.

41. Ibid., 24–26, 32–44, 47–55, 61–62, 66–68. For "Lehrgebäude" as a synonym for "System," see ibid., 65–66.

42. Ibid., 70.

43. Ibid., 71–75.

to the propositional content of the problems and arguments advanced by a variety of past philosophers. To Brandis, philosophy is autonomous, unitary, and inward looking; it is a system that is self-dependent and its propositional content stays free of non-philosophical disciplines. One question remains, however: where did Brandis's concept of philosophy as a system come from?

Although Brandis does not refer explicitly to Johann Jacob Brucker (1696–1770), he clearly has Brucker and his system-concept in mind, transmitted directly or indirectly, when he identifies the internal history of philosophy with the history of systems.[44] Brucker's Latin work *Historia critica philosophiae* was first published 1742–44. It was the most comprehensive history of philosophy written in the eighteenth century, and it provided the key methodological concepts, the periodization, and the selection of material for subsequent historians of philosophy in the nineteenth and twentieth centuries.[45] It even made its mark on historical disciplines outside philosophy such as the history of ideas and the history of science.[46]

In the seventeenth and eighteenth centuries, the system concept had been widely used in scientific discourse, where it often denoted the order of the universe, and where it also came to denote the proper scientific method. This latter usage Brucker transferred to the methodology of history of philosophy; it became a historiographical concept.[47] In Brucker's methodology for the history of philosophy, the concept of a "system of philosophy" (Lat. *systema philosophiae*) was assigned a controlling role. It was this concept that allowed Brucker to claim that the history of philosophy was not simply history, understood as a random collection of opinions of past philosophers, but a philosophical discipline; it was "history of philosophy" (*historia philosophiae*), not only "philosophical history" (*historia philosophica*).[48] Brucker did not, to the best of my knowledge, employ the terms "internal" and "external" or their cognates. However, his employment of the system-concept did entail such a distinction, since it separates issues that are pertinent and thus internal

44. For Brandis's bibliography, see Brandis (1815), 41–42. Compare with Mann (1996), who does not recognize this as a Bruckerian concept, which we also find in another problem historian highlighted by Mann, namely, Reinhold (1791), 23, 27.

45. Catana (2008). See also Celenza (2013).

46. For its significance to history of ideas and history of science, see Catana (2010) and (2011).

47. See Ritschl (1906).

48. For Brucker's contribution to the methodological development of the history of philosophy, see Longo (2011).

to the system (namely, principles and doctrines; in Latin *principia* and *doctrinae*) from issues that are conductive to but still external to the system, namely, the circumstances (*circumstantiae*) of the system.[49]

What is meant by "system" and "circumstances"? The Bruckerian system concept denotes a limited number of general theories, so-called principles, typically of a metaphysical nature, from which a complex of philosophical doctrines is deduced, covering all branches of philosophy in an internally coherent fashion. The main task of the historian of philosophy is to reconstruct this propositional network of principles and the doctrines derived from them.[50] The system's propositional complex is thus categorized as internal (the *systema* developed by the individual philosopher). This is to be distinguished from features external to the system, namely, biographical and historical circumstances (the *circumstantiae*). Among these *circumstantiae* Brucker lists the following: the philosopher's temperament, his education, his teachers, his adversaries, his patrons, his lifestyle, the people with whom he or she lived, and similar matters.[51] This distinction between *systema* and *circumstantiae* he explains in the methodological section of the *Dissertatio praeliminaris.* He is loyal to his own methodological precepts in the accounts of individual philosophers in the remaining part of the work, where he typically begins by describing the circumstances of a past thinker and then moves on to an exposition of the thinker's system. The identification of the system's principle, or principles, marks the kernel of the exposition.[52] If we

49. Christopher Celenza has pointed me in this direction in a draft of an article of his which I read some time ago and which has now appeared in *Critical Inquiry* (Celenza (2013)).

50. Brucker (1742–67), vol. 1, p. 15.10–18: "*Ut* itaque *de sententia philosophorum sanum rectumque iudicium ferri queat, totum ex eorum scriptis systema ita eruendum est,* ut ante omnia principia generalia, quae fundamenti loco toti doctrinarum aedificio subiiciuntur, eruantur, et his demum illae superstruantur conclusiones, quae ex istis fontibus sponte sua fluunt. Quemadmodum enim hoc praecipue philosophi officium est, ut ex positis quibusdam principiis generalibus, specialia dogmata iusto nexu derivet, ita eam interpretationem merito alteri praetuleris, quae cum toto systematis habitu et connexione convenit apteque inter se cohaeret, etsi prima facie aliud dicere videatur." (Brucker's italics.) For the system concept in Brucker, see Catana (2008), 50–52.

51. Brucker (1742–67), vol. 1, 15.29–36: "Non vero ad systemata tantum ipsa, in scriptis philosophorum obvia, sed ad circumstantias quoque auctorum, temperamenti et educationis rationem, praeceptores, quos ex parte imitati sunt, adversarios, quibus sua dogmata opposuerunt, fautores, vitae genus, quod sectati sunt, gentem unde vel oriundi, vel apud quam vixerunt, et quae alia his similia attendendum est. Supra enim iam monuimus, eiusmodi circumstantias plurimum habere in ipsa systemta philosophorum influxum, quae ubi negliguntur, ineluctabilem obscuritatem pariunt." Some of these *circumstantiae* are also mentioned ibid., vol. 1, 11.21–30.

52. For instance, Plato's *circumstantiae* are discussed ibid., vol. 1, 627.1–659.21; his system of philosophy ibid., vol. 1, 659.22–728.11. Similarly, Aristotle's *circumstantiae* are described ibid., vol. 1, 776.1–800.35; his system of philosophy ibid., vol. 1, 800.36–839.33.

compare Brandis's list of "external features," we see that, by and large, it coincides with Brucker's list of "circumstances": they both include biographical and historical issues in the "external features," and they both identity the system as the core of the "internal feature." Crucially, neither counts non-philosophical disciplines as part of either the internal or the external features; both regard philosophy as an autonomous discipline whose propositional content, arguments, and theories are dependent upon internal features.

Before Brucker's *Historia critica philosophiae*, we do not find the historiographical concept of a "system of philosophy" employed in general histories of philosophy or in similar accounts of philosophy's history; the implied internal-external distinction is therefore absent from these earlier expositions. This also applies to the accounts of Brucker's immediate forerunners, e.g., Thomas Stanley's *History of Philosophy: Containing the Lives, Opinions, Actions and Discourses of the Philosophers of Every Sect* (1655–62), Georg Horn's *Historiae philosophicae libri septem* (1655), Gerhard Voss's *De philosophia et philosophorum sectis libri duo* (1658), and Johann Joensen's *De scriptoribus historiae philosophicae* (1659). The system concept and the internal-external distinction implied in it was a methodological innovation of Brucker and his contemporaries, which Brucker implemented at such a deep level of the new discipline and which Brandis took over.

I have argued elsewhere that the historiographical concept of a system of philosophy is an anachronistic invention of the eighteenth century. It is therefore inadequate in regard to Western philosophy produced before the seventeenth century, when the corresponding methodological concept was unknown.[53] Although Brucker's historiography was met with criticism in the nineteenth century, a considerable number of historians of philosophy have continued to use the concept as a historiographical tool ever since, even after nineteenth-century philosophers discarded the concept as a methodological ideal.[54] Of course, it has been revised and watered down, but in many cases it still serves as a regulative ideal. But the concept system of philosophy not only misrepresents individual thinkers in vast periods of the history of philosophy; it also creates the illusion of past philosophy as an autonomous and inward-looking enterprise, cut off from non-philosophical disciplines. The anachronism of the system concept as a historiographical

53. See Catana (2008), 35–113.

54. E.g., Copleston (1985), 2–9. See also the discussion of the historiographical concept system of philosophy in Gadamer (1998), XVIII–XXII.

concept may imply that the internal-external distinction has to be reformulated in a good deal of contemporary methodological discourse on the history of philosophy.

The fact that historians of philosophy have become accustomed to learning about past philosophers through their assumed systems invites them to believe that these philosophers really did develop systems and that the argumentative content of their philosophies is to be found within the system itself.[55] This belief is caused by the introduction of the historiographical concept system of philosophy in the eighteenth century, but it is clearly unfounded in regard to philosophies established before the seventeenth and after the nineteenth centuries; as regards the three intermediary centuries, it still remains to question whether a past philosopher's claims about system-building is mere rhetoric or actually translated into his philosophical practice. This Bruckerian background informed problem-based history of philosophy, including that of Brandis.

4. Philosophical Problems Transgressing the Internal-External Distinction

Now let me return to the theme of my introduction. Is the distinction between the history of philosophy, understood as a problem-based discipline, and intellectual history, understood as a contextual discipline, a valid one? As we have seen, Brandis introduced the assumption to problem-oriented historians of philosophy that philosophical problems were internal to the philosophy, that is, deducible solely from the system itself.

The difficulty lies in the question of what counts as "internal" and what counts as "external." Historical, biographical, sociological, cultural, and economic circumstances are typically counted as "external" factors. In contemporary debates on philosophy's historiography, it is frequently assumed, following Brucker and Brandis, that the past philosopher's social environment is to be counted as an "external" factor.[56] The internal factors, by contrast, are, first of all, the system and its propositional structure as it produces solutions to distinct philosophical problems. Hereby non-philosophical disciplines have been marginalized—disciplines that inform the meaning and reference

55. E.g., Russell (1967), 57, 71, 90.

56. E.g., Glock (2008a), 884–85.

of the terms pertinent to the problems.[57] These disciplines are counted neither among the internal nor the external factors. They fall outside the dichotomy and they are left out of sight by the historian of philosophy following this method.

If it is the task of the historian of philosophy to analyze and exhibit the philosophical problems of past philosophy, and if those problems are particulars whose semantic content transcends philosophy as a system or self-contained propositional complex, then one would have to understand not only the relevant philosophical branches, but also the relevant non-philosophical disciplines and their contribution to the problems discussed. As mentioned earlier, a philosophical problem can be seen as a disjunctive question: does the entity S posses the property P or not-P? If we want to understand the arguments for and against a given solution to the problem, we need to understand the meaning and reference of the terms S and P as they are employed in specific argumentative contexts. Depending on whether or not one accepts the universal legitimacy of the historiographical concept system of philosophy and its basic idea of philosophy as a self-contained unity, one of two options is left open.

If the system concept is accepted as legitimate, the historian of philosophy can ask "which are the principles in the system," and then figure out what was the position of the past philosopher on a specific problem. The system concept thus offers a propositional convenience, since it allows the historian to remain "inside" the system when reconstructing the past philosopher's solution. Even though such reconstructions of overarching "principles" are often arbitrary, badly documented and inconsistent, they have been persuasive,

57. The phrase "non-philosophical" disciplines can mean at least two things: (a) Those disciplines that most contemporary philosophers accept as belonging to philosophy, but formerly excluded, e.g., epistemology. Such a meaning of "non-philosophical" disciplines is clearly anachronistic and not what I mean. Cassirer thus required that the historian of philosophy should examine a past philosopher's views on all major philosophical problems, for instance, epistemology; see Cassirer (1942), 129: "For we can attribute no philosophical significance to an accomplishment that takes no definite stand on the great antitheses of metaphysics, epistemology, and ethics; which poses no definite problems and which maintains or rejects no certain solutions." However, Pico himself did not count epistemology as an independent branch in philosophy, and he certainly did not see it as a problem as philosophers came to do when we reach the Kantian age; see Pico (2004), 126.2–17, who alludes to four philosophical branches, or fields, namely, logic, moral philosophy, natural philosophy, and theology. Ibid., 128.15–22: Pico mentions these disciplines once again. (b) By "non-philosophical" disciplines one may mean those disciplines that were not normally classified among the branches of philosophy by the past philosopher himself or by his contemporaries. I mean (b) when I speak of "non-philosophical" disciplines. For the evolution of philosophy's alleged nature and its branches, see Kranz et al. (1989).

because they conform to the explanatory model endorsed by the system concept: to those trained philosophers who have been accustomed to the system concept as a didactic device, such a procedure may appear convincing, since it satisfies the need to fit a past philosopher's solutions and arguments into a system and its fundamental principles. The problem with this first option is that it is anachronistic and misleading in regard to pre-seventeenth- and post nineteenth-century philosophy; as regards seventeenth- to nineteenth-century philosophy it may be anachronistic and misleading as well.

On the other hand, if the system-concept is met with skepticism and rejected as illegitimate, then such an internal procedure has to be abandoned: it does not make sense to identify the meaning and references of S and P "within" a system if there is no system that determines what is "inside" or "outside." Then one is forced to accept a considerable amount of semantic and disciplinary uncertainty in the reconstruction of the problems, since the theoretical description of S and P may come not from philosophy alone but from non-philosophical disciplines as well. Moreover, it may not be the case that philosophy simply "imports" terminological semantics, theories, and arguments from non-philosophical disciplines and then resolves the problems "inside" philosophy; it may also happen that philosophy "intervenes" in non-philosophical disciplines and resolves problems raised within those disciplines. After all, it is not only philosophers who strive to resolve problems—theologians and other scholars and scientists do so as well. One example of this is Galileo using biblical exegesis in order to resolve the problem of the relationship between revealed truths and philosophical or scientific truths.[58]

We must therefore grasp the theoretical contributions of both philosophical and non-philosophical disciplines if we want to describe the problem at hand accurately. We cannot assume—at least not when working outside of early modern philosophy—that the information about S and its properties can be retrieved from the "principles" of a given system of philosophy, that is, "internally." Unless we endorse some sort of epistemological idealism and believe that we, as trained philosophers, have some sort of privileged and a priori access to these problems of past philosophers, we must contextualize these problems historically and philologically if we want to understand them in their own right, rather than according to our own subjective projections; there is no other way open to understand these problems or the arguments used to resolve them. For this reason, a problem-based history of philosophy

58. Galileo (1953). For Galileo's intervention, see Finocchiaro (2002).

is not incompatible with contextualization. On the contrary, a competent and historically and philologically accurate contextualization is a necessary condition of its success. For this reason, the bifurcation articulated at the beginning of this chapter, between the problem-based but non-contextual history of philosophy and problem-free but contextual intellectual history, is misconceived. It is erroneous to reserve historical contextualization for intellectual history alone, since it is indeed an integral part of the history of philosophy as well, if it intends to examine the problems of past philosophy.

This means that philology and history are integral to the method of the history of philosophy. This would indeed allow one to focus on the arguments, theories, and problems in the texts of past philosophers—though it will no longer be possible to understand these on the basis of an assumed system. Instead, it would be necessary to understand the meanings of the terms employed, the disciplines informing the terms, the argumentative force, and structure within which these terms are employed. It would also be useful if historiography were an integral part of one's training in the history of philosophy, since it is far too easy to fall victim to standard narratives about past philosophers.

According to the bifurcation stated in the 1984 Introduction and to some extent repeated by Sorell in 2005 and Glock in 2008, analytic historians of philosophy would reject such a history of philosophy because it is contextual. The way out of this impasse is to accept that even though the history of philosophy works on philosophical problems, this does not per se exclude historical and philological contextualization. On the contrary, such an integration of historical context (primarily understood as disciplinary and argumentative context) would be in agreement with the desire to focus on philosophical problems. Such a solution would not be in conflict with the anti-idealism and empiricism pervading analytic philosophy. Nor would it violate elements intrinsic to twentieth-century analytic thought, since the problem-based history of philosophy is not an invention of analytic philosophy, but one that dates back to nineteenth-century philosophy.

Acknowledgments

I should like to thank the contributors at the 2011 Montreal conference and the following persons for their comments to my paper: Line Edslev Andersen, Finn Collin, Matthew Gaetano, Mikkel Gerken, Kasper Juel Gregersen, Sofie Møller, Nikolaj Nottelmann, Joakim Kromann Rasmussen.

7

Philosophizing Historically/ Historicizing Philosophy: Some Spinozistic Reflections

Julie R. Klein

Pro captu lectoris, habent sua fata libelli
TERENTIANUS MAURUS, *DE SYLLABIS*

1. Introduction

BOOKS HAVE THEIR fortunes, notes Spinoza in the *Theologico-Political Treatise* (hereafter *TTP*),[1] drawing our attention to issues of compilation, canonization, and transmission and simultaneously alluding to the realities of censorship and destruction. So, too, do books have fates in the hand of readers; even the Bible, according to Spinoza, is not holy, but merely ink on paper, until it is read with an eye to sustaining peace.[2] Spinoza's readers are numerous and diverse, and their interpretations of his work follow suit. Looking at the current scene, a reasonably comprehensive list would include the Cartesian Spinoza, the Hobbesian Spinoza, the Judaeo-Islamic Spinoza,

1. On *fortuna libri*, see the *TTP*, VII 7, sect. 5 [101]: "*Deinde uniuscujusque libri fortunam*" as well the discussion of Euclid's *Elements* at VII, sect. 17 [111] and IX, sect. 12 [135], which speaks of the "*fortuna librorum*." Texts from the *TTP* come from Spinoza (1999). I follow Akkerman's numbering of the paragraphs in each chapter of the *TTP*, which I cite by chapter and section number. Page numbers in square brackets refer to the pagination in vol. III of Spinoza (1925). Texts from the *Ethics* (hereafter *E*) come from Spinoza (1925) and Spinoza (1985). References to the *Tractatus de Intellectus Emendatione* (hereafter *TIE*) are given according to Bruder's division into paragraphs, also used by Curley in Spinoza (1986). The *Cogitata metaphysica* (*CM*) and the *Tractatus Politicus* (*TP*) are quoted from Spinoza (1925). I have modified translations of the Letters by Curley in Spinoza (1985) and Samuel Shirley in Spinoza (1995).

2. *TTP* XII, sect. 3 [159–60].

the Protestant Spinoza, the atheist and pantheist Spinoza, the neoplatonist or idealist Spinoza, the liberal-democratic Spinoza, the Marxist (both orthodox and poststructuralist) Spinoza, the analytic Spinoza (both Anglo-American and Freudian), the ecological Spinoza, the neuropsychological Spinoza, the feminist Spinoza, and, not least of all, the Spinoza of Market Street. The list is all but guaranteed to increase as readers examine prevailing views, find new inspirations, and read Spinoza in yet new circumstances. What is the reader to do with the multiple and multiplying Spinozas? More specifically, what is the reader committed to the history of philosophy as a philosophical subject-matter to do? Unlike Dr. Fischelson, and not simply because the life of wisdom (or at least the *recta ratio vivendi* designed to lead us there) involves tenacity (*animositas*) and nobility (*generositas*) rather than scorn or anger, we cannot simply bark, "Idiots, asses, upstarts."[3] "Minds," Spinoza instructs us, "are conquered not by arms, but by Love (*Amor*) and Nobility."[4]

If Terentianus Maurus's maxim has become a cliché of the history of books, Spinoza invites us to stress the often-neglected qualification: *pro captu lectoris*, "according to the capacity of the reader." The Bible, Spinoza argues, speaks *ad captum humanum*, with various prophets and teachers adapting the central message of justice and charity to the capacities and needs of audiences in antiquity.[5] The ancient Israelites' ignorance and slave mentality account for the depiction of God as a king and legislator; in the Greco-Roman world, ethical teaching took its place alongside the rhetoric of monarchical rule. The question of the reader's capacity comes up, as well, in Spinoza's early *Treatise on the Emendation of the Intellect*, which notes the need to speak *ad captum vulgi*, "according to the capacity of ordinary people." Yielding to the capacity of the audience without abandoning what needs to be said is the way to induce a "friendly hearing of the truth (*amicas aures ad veritatem audiendam*)."[6] Listening without friendship leaves the truth unheard. Thus the speaker must seek a way to engage the audience.

---

3. Singer (1961), 11. On these affects, see Spinoza (*E*3 Definitions of the Affects XXII and XXXVI). On the *recta ratio vivendi, seu certa vitae dogmata*, see *E*5p10s and the *dictamina rationis* of *E*5p4s.

4. *E*4 App XI.

5. This principle is axiomatic in rabbinic exegesis; Christians call it accommodationism. See *TTP* II, sect. 19, [42–43], *TTP* IV, sect. 7–12, [62–68]; *TTP* XIV, *passim*, as well as Letter 19, in Spinoza (1925), III, 92.

6. *TIE*, § 17. This text echoes Descartes's *Discourse on the Method*, Parts 3 and 6; cf. Maimonides's pedagogical caution in the Introduction to the First Part of *Guide of the Perplexed* (1963), I, 15–20.

Captus refers simultaneously to the reader's intellectual ability, which is partly native talent and partly a mind-set (the Latin *ingenium* captures both), to the reader's disposition or what we might call *ethos*, and also to the reader's historical moment.[7] Reflecting on the question of capacity, that is, the ability of readers to take in, comprehend, and sustain the ideas found in books, we may ask, then, according to the capacity of the *vulgus* or according to the capacity of the philosopher, according to the capacity of the average reader or according to the brilliant interpreter? The *TTP* presents Moses, Jesus, and Solomon and their respective audiences as exemplars of different *captus*, and we have Spinoza's correspondents as well. What sort of readers are we, ourselves, and the species of readers catalogued previously? What is the extent of our *amicitia*, and what is the role of the scholarly interpreter? Faced with the list of Spinozas, most of us exclaim, "Not anything goes!" We then enumerate our scholarly methods, criteria, and standards. Interpretation without the tools of scholarship, we worry, is indistinguishable from distortion or entertaining figments of our imagination. We remind ourselves of the maxim, attributed to Terence, and quoted by Spinoza: "Nothing can be so rightly said as to be incapable of distortion or misinterpretation."[8] We will recall that Spinoza calls some readers perverse in the *TTP* Preface; he wishes that un- or anti-philosophical readers would ignore the book "rather than make a nuisance of themselves by interpreting it perversely (*perverse*)."[9] If the great theme of Spinoza's philosophy is freedom, whether as the *libertas philosophandi* found in the subtitle of the *TTP*, the affective freedom proposed in the *Ethics*, or the *libera respublica* of the *Political Treatise*, we know that freedom of interpretation, what Spinoza terms *libertas interpretandi ex suo ingenio*,[10] is inviolable, but not every interpretation makes sense. There must be some criteria according to which readings are legitimate or abusive, seriously engaged or merely glancing, philosophically compelling or not worth our time.

To address the central question of what it means to read the history of philosophy philosophically, or, in other words, to philosophize historically, I shall in this essay consider three interrelated questions prompted by the proliferation of Spinozas and reflect on them with Spinoza.

First, what is involved in philosophical reading? Given the proliferating Spinozas, competing methodologies of interpretation, and meta-hermeneutical

---

7. Curley (1986), 45–46, makes a similar point.

8. *TTP* XII, sect. 3 [159].

9. *TTP* Preface [12].

10. *TTP* Preface [11]. On *libertas philosophandi dicendique*, see also Letter 30 to Henry Oldenburg.

debates, we need to say something about the character of philosophical reading. In sections 1 and 2, I describe philosophical reading as an amalgam of technical skill, intellectual acumen, and desire; it involves both cognitive and affective dimensions. Nietzsche evokes this combination in his mini-essay on reading in the Preface to *Dawn*. He calls his own style of reading "philology": "Philology itself is never so easily over and done with anything whatsoever; it teaches to read *well*, which means to read slowly, deeply, backward and forward with care and respect, with reservations, with doors left open, with delicate fingers and eyes."[11] In Adorno's felicitous expression, philosophical thinking requires patience: "neither zealous bustling about nor stubborn obsession but rather the long and uncoercive gaze."[12] Section 1 addresses these images via Spinoza's insistence on naturalism and rejection of *praejudicia* (literally: pre-judgments) in correspondence with Willem Van Blyenbergh and ends by considering his debate with Alfred Burgh over the "true" and the "best" philosophy.

Second, how does one become a philosophical reader? In section 2, I argue that Spinoza's texts are essentially pedagogical. Rather than presuming the existence of philosophical readers, they are designed to generate philosophical readers. Spinoza writes for potential philosophers, namely, readers who can take in his critique of received views and follow his alternative path. Van Blyenbergh and Burgh exhibit the power of negative affects to obstruct thought. The case example of Spinoza's talented but troublesome student Casearius allows us to consider in more positive terms the relationship of cognition and affect in the cultivation of philosophers.

Third, what are the limits of a text? How far can we go before we pass from interpretation to original composition or arbitrary appropriation, and what is the relationship of our thinking to Spinoza's thinking? Are there, in other words, limits on interpretation? As a historian of philosophy, I strive to give an account of Spinoza's thoughts that, as much or insofar as I am able—*quatenus* is a pivotal word for Spinoza—treats him in his own terms and also engages with the relevance of his work today. Philosophical interpretation involves trying to hear what the text says, yet no one approaches the text without presuppositions. There are, in addition, the ways in which thinking inevitably exceeds what Adorno called "subordinate reflection on and adjustment to pre-given data."[13] Once we pass from enumerating factual matters

---

11. Nietzsche (2011), v. 5, 7. Nietzsche famously wrote to Franz Overbeck on July 30, 1881, to record his joy upon discovering Spinoza.

12. Adorno (2005b), 130.

13. Adorno (2005a), 9.

such as the compositional and publication history of a text and from summarizing what the text says in its own language to discussing what it means, we are engaged in interpretation; even the selection of seemingly neutral factual matters often involves judgments of relevance, and assessments of context can be tricky. After all, how far does context extend?[14] As we seek to let another philosopher's work take shape in our minds, much philosophical work on our part transpires: determining what is central and what is marginal, what is assumed and what lies outside the horizon of the work, how the arguments actually work (or don't work), the balance of borrowings, reappropriations, and innovations, and so on. We often re-read the text, discuss it with other interpreters, and revise our views. As an activity, philosophical reading, and more generally, philosophical thinking, is both receptive and productive. To use idioms from the *Ethics*, our intellectual work is affected by and affects its object, and these relations can be described in terms of fluid communication and exchange. How do we take account of this complex relation?

2. *Philosophical Readers*

Composed and transmitted in the ancient languages of Hebrew, Aramaic, and Greek, and transmitted in Latin and various languages that post-date antiquity, Scripture is unique in its variety of styles, complex history, and, strikingly, sometimes violently, divided interpreters. Most books we philosophers read are neither so obscurely sourced nor so culturally overdetermined. Nor are they so politically potent. Still, Spinoza's basic rule of interpretation, stated in *TTP* VII in the context of scientific method itself, pertains to all texts: treat them as natural phenomena.[15] Spinoza was not the first to propose methods adapted from the study of history and nature for interpreting the Bible. Luther proclaimed the freedom of the Christian to interpret the Bible rationally according to its literal sense; Calvin's hermeneutics is steeped the Renaissance humanists' emphasis on history, philology, and textual criticism; Spinoza's preferred rabbinic exegete, Abraham ibn Ezra, reasoned that Moses could not have written all of Deuteronomy.[16] Spinoza pursues the naturalistic paradigm surely, swiftly, and without any reservations, carrying it to its logical conclusion: there is nothing supra- or extra-natural about Scripture, such that there is no need for non-scientific methods. God's

---

14. This is the central question in Garber (2005).

15. See Savan (1986).

16. Spinoza calls Ibn Ezra a "*liberioris ingenii vir et non mediocris eruditionis*" (*TTP* VIII, sect. 3 [104]).

eternal word, Spinoza contends, is available in rational inquiry and true perception. Spinoza holds that Scripture teaches practical values of universal justice and charity and contains virtually no theoretical content.[17]

Examined closely, Spinozan *interpretatio* extends widely: "I say that the method for interpreting Scripture does not differ from the method for interpreting nature but agrees with it entirely."[18] Like interpreters of nature, interpreters of the Bible must develop a natural history of the text and in turn generate definitions, inferences, and conclusions. Interpretive work is both historical, in the sense of reconstructive or evidentiary, and analytical-deductive, in the sense of "regarding a number of things at once, to understand their agreements, differences and oppositions"[19] and their implications. We must construct a lexicon, grammar, and concordance; collect historical data and records; survey events; and look for patterns. Above all, just as we must seek knowledge of nature from nature itself (what other source could we have?), so too must we read the Bible on its own terms, attending to its language, circumstances of composition, canonization, and transmission history, and steadfastly resist the imposition of such extrinsic criteria as theological doctrine or philosophical scruple. *TTP* VII, sect. 22, is blunt: the "norm [of interpreting Scripture] must be nothing other than the natural light common to all, not some light above nature or any external authority."[20] Spinoza argues that extrinsic criteria distort the text, undermining any sense of evidence and whatever integrity may be discovered. Not only, then, is Scripture is amenable to scientific study. Failure to engage in properly scientific study amounts to the greatest disrespect and, worse, engenders political conflict.

To interpret Scripture naturalistically is to strive as far as we can to approach it without the distorting forces of *praejudicia*, prejudgments or prejudices. The critique of Maimonides in *TTP* VII and XV and the related critique of Judah Alfakhar in *TTP* XV are typical of Spinoza's continuous analysis of prejudice as distorting, intellectually disabling, and productive of conflict.[21] Maimonides's desire to reconcile the Bible with the principles of reason and Alfakhar's rejection of reason in favor of miracles reflect the interpreters'

17. *TTP* XIII, sect. 3 [168].

18. *TTP* VII, sect. 2 [98].

19. *E*2p29s.

20. *TTP* VII, sect. 22 [117].

21. Spinoza's criticism should not obscure his affinities for and borrowings from Maimonides. Recent studies of this relationship include Harvey (1981), 151–72; Dobbs-Weinstein (1994); and Fraenkel (2006).

respective prejudgments of Scripture's true meaning. The former embraced allegorical reading in order to accommodate Scripture to reason, undermining the obviousness and reasonableness of Scripture's essential ethical teaching and thereby creating a class of elite interpreters; the latter desired to accommodate reason to Scripture, that is, insisted on a non-rational relationship to nature and an anti-intellectual posture. Maimonides erred in one direction, and Alfakhar erred in the opposite direction. Even before Maimonides's death in 1204, his philosophical works occasioned passionate debate, and the controversies continued into the fourteenth century. Maimonides's legal works were widely respected, but critics saw the *Guide of the Perplexed* as undermining traditional beliefs about creation, miracles, prophecy, and eschatology. Maimonides's embrace of allegorical reading and his openness to Greek and Arabic philosophy, particularly Aristotle, were the issue. Maimonideans and their sympathizers were often accused of failures of character and religious observance in addition to their excesses in scriptural interpretation.

Spinoza's reference to Alfakhar evokes a tragic phase of the controversies in the 1230s. In 1232, Rabbi Solomon ben Abraham of Montpellier and his followers persuaded influential rabbis in northern France to ban the study of philosophy *tout court*. That the northern rabbis were, for various reasons, largely unfamiliar with Aristotelian philosophy was no obstacle; authorities in Castile also approved the ban. Rabbis in Provence and Aragon issued a counter-ban defending philosophy. Both sides produced sermons, letters, treatises, and legal rulings as the dispute grew. The parties' intensity now seems clearly to have arisen not only from issues of doctrinal substance and religious practice, but from the way the fact of conflicting rabbinic rulings raised questions about the nature of communal authority. Alfakhar, a physician and courtier in Toledo, was a bitter anti-Maimonidean polemicist in the 1230s but otherwise not very important in the history of Sephardic Jewry. The exchange of letters between Alfakhar and his Maimonidean opponent David Kimchi is preserved in the aptly named *Iggerot Kena'ot*, "Letters of Zealotry."[22] Most unfortunately, this phase of the controversy took place against two important actions in the ruling Christian community. First, Christians had their own controversies about Aristotelian philosophy, which had been banned in Paris in 1210. Pope Gregory IX banned it again in 1231. Second, the Albigensian or Cathar Crusade, carried out in southern France

22. See Adler's annotated translation (1996). Adler notes that Spinoza could have read the letters in Hebrew or in Johannes Buxtorf the elder's Latin translation. Christian Hebraists and Protestant Bible commentators admired Kimhi.

in this period, established a permanent Inquisition under the direction of the Dominicans. As Dobbs-Weinstein emphasizes, what Spinoza does not report in the *TTP* but must have, given his remarkable political sensitivity, considered is how the Jewish communities' internal divisions made them more vulnerable to attacks by outside authorities. The church burned Maimonides's *Guide of the Perplexed* and *Book of Knowledge*, most likely in Montpellier, in the early 1230s and burned the Talmud, probably in Paris, in 1232.[23]

In early modern Europe, reigning authorities and warring parties banned books, imprisoned and executed heretics, and produced sectarian bloodshed on a mass scale. The alliance, in other words, of church polemics with state power produced widespread suffering and destruction; religious motives and polemics were joined with long-standing political rivalries, economic competition, and other similarly non-religious reasons to devastate European populations. The European Wars of Religion, fought in the fifteenth and sixteenth centuries were, in other words, quintessentially theologico-political, multiply determined by political allegiance, nationality, and confession. Spinoza remarks bitterly in the Preface to the *TTP* that the "highest secret of monarchical government and utterly essential to it" may be "to keep men deceived, and to disguise the fear that sways them with the specious name of religion, so that they will fight for their servitude … and will not think it humiliating but supremely glorious to spill their blood and sacrifice their lives for the glory of a single man."[24] The Peace of Westphalia in 1648, roughly twenty years before the *TTP*, settled the Thirty Years' War in the heart of Europe and the Eighty Years' War in the Low Countries. Spinoza comments bluntly on the barely cooled passions of the early modern European Wars of Religion in the Preface to the *TTP*, professing amazement that the adherents of Christianity, "that is, [adherents of] love, joy, peace, moderation, and good will to all men, [oppose] each other with extraordinary animosity and [give] daily expression to the bitterest mutual hatred."[25] Spinoza calls "theological hatred" the most violent of all hatreds.[26]

While the *TTP* focuses on the political consequences of empowering prejudgments and the ease of fomenting fear and hatred amid ignorance, Spinoza's correspondence provides us with less dramatic but nevertheless interesting case studies in the power of *praejudicia*. Looking across Spinoza's texts, we can

---

23. Extant sources leave the exact dates unclear. For an overview, see Ben-Sasson (2007). Dobbs-Weinstein (2004) provides philosophical perspective.

24. *TTP* Preface, sect. 7, [7]

25. *TTP* Preface, sect. 9, [8].

26. *TTP* XVII, sect. 17 [212].

develop a clearer picture of the operations of prejudgment. As Spinoza's correspondence shows, the Dutch theologian Willem Van Blyenbergh read the sole text Spinoza published in his own name during his lifetime, *Descartes' Principles of Philosophy* (1663). This work contained a critical exposition of Descartes's would-be textbook, the *Principles of Philosophy* (1644), and, as an Appendix, Spinoza's critical lexicon of Cartesianism and Scholasticism, the *Cogitata Metaphysica*. Letter 18, from December 1664, reveals that Van Blyenbergh found much to admire and "some things which I found difficult to digest."[27] Much as he claimed to be "impelled only by desire for pure truth,"[28] Van Blyenbergh apparently wrote because he accurately perceived Spinoza's own heterodox views (which are easily found in the early works) and therefore desired not only "pure truth" but reassurance that Spinoza's views were only apparently destructive of orthodox theology. (An alternative reading would be that Van Blyenbergh wrapped his contentiousness in the rhetoric of sincere inquiry, but the difference does not much matter here.) Van Blyenbergh's queries concern classic Christian theological-metaphysical problems, including creation, evil, human freedom, and predestination. Spinoza welcomed the correspondence on a note of friendship, and, appealing to a shared devotion to truth, and replied at length to Van Blyenbergh. Spinoza's response is best described as an effort to dissolve the problems by disentangling and refuting their presuppositions; roughly put, Spinoza replies that correctly (re)conceptualizing God eliminates the very theologico-metaphysical problems Van Blyenbergh finds compelling and insoluble. The same strategy would, in principle, eliminate Van Blyneberghs's objections to Spinoza's views. The correspondence unfolds quickly, and the intellectual distance between the two men is immense. Succeeding letters show Van Blyenbergh's deep frustration with, and resistance to, Spinoza's explanations and Spinoza's sense of the futility of the whole exchange.

In Letter 20, written in January 1665, Van Blyenbergh rejected both Spinoza's specific analyses and, crucially, his unconditional reliance on the intellect. Here are Van Blyenbergh's rules of philosophizing:

> There are two general rules which always govern my endeavors to philosophize. One is the clear and distinct conception of my intellect, the other is the Word, or will, of God.... Whenever it happens that after long consideration my natural knowledge seems either to be at variance with this Word or not very easily reconcilable with it, *this Word has so much*

27. Letter 18.

28. Letter 18.

> *authority with me that I prefer to cast doubt on the conceptions I imagine to be clear rather than to set these above and in opposition to the truth which I believe I find prescribed for me in that book* [Emphasis added].[29]

Spinoza's reply is sharp and direct:

> I see that we disagree not only in the conclusions to be drawn by a chain of reasoning from first principles, but in those very first principles. So that I hardly believe that our correspondence can be for our mutual instruction. For I see that no proof, however firmly established according to the rules of logic, has any validity with you unless it agrees with the explanation which you, or other theologians of your acquaintance, assign (*tribuunt*) to Holy Scripture.[30]

Where Spinoza unreservedly affirms the "light of the natural understanding," Van Blyenbergh specifically submits intellectual apprehension to the test of dogmatic authority. Having at some length shown the contradiction generated by taking theological doctrines as premises, Spinoza says with some irony that for someone who believes that "God speaks more clearly and effectually through Holy Scripture than through the light of the natural understanding which he has also granted us," Van Blyenbergh's procedure would be correct. Spinoza instead depicts Van Blyenbergh as a servant of imagination and, consequently, of external authorities:

> As for myself, I confess, clearly and without circumlocution, that I do not understand Holy Scripture [*me S. Scipturam non intelligere*].... And I am well aware that, when I have found a solid demonstration, I cannot fall into such thoughts that I can ever doubt it. So I acquiesce in what my intellect shows me [*quod mihi intellectus monstrat*] without any suspicion that I have been deceived or that Holy Scripture can contradict it (even though I do not investigate it). For truth does not contradict truth, as I have already indicated in my Appendix.[31]

---

29. Letter 20.

30. Letter 21.

31. See *CM* II, sect. 8: "Truth does not contradict truth, nor can Scripture teach such nonsense as is commonly supposed.... Let us not think for a moment that anything could be found in Holy Scripture that would contradict the natural light." Spinoza's principle of the singularity of truth derives from Averroes, whose views Spinoza probably knew through the works of Elijah Delmedigo.

Whether out of graciousness, a sense of irony, or a desire to avoid more open conflict, Spinoza does not directly inform Van Blyenbergh that since Scripture contains virtually no discussion of matters of truth and falsity, there is no danger of a conflict with reason. Indiscreet as it seems to announce, "I do not understand Holy Scripture," surely it would be more dramatic to assert that "Holy Scripture is unintelligible." Rather than framing the discussion explicitly in terms of the nature of Scripture, Spinoza writes about his own inability to understand it.

For us, this contentious exchange raises the question of whether Spinoza's affirmation of the intellect is different in kind from Van Blyenbergh's deference to biblical prescriptions or merely an alternative prejudice. How might we explain or justify accepting one set of principles rather than another? Van Blyenbergh's answers turn on the authoritative status of religious principles. Spinoza's answer in Letter 21 turns on an account of affective life:

> If even once I found that the fruits which I have already gathered from the natural intellect were false, they would still make me happy, since I enjoy them and seek to pass my life, not in sorrow and sighing, but in peace [*tranquillitate*], joy [*laetitiâ*], and cheerfulness [*hilaritate*]. By so doing, I climb a step higher. Meanwhile I recognize something which gives me the greatest satisfaction and peace of mind [*summam satisfactionem & mentis tranquillitatem*]: that all things happen as they do by the power of a supremely perfect Being and by his immutable decree.[32]

The life of reason, which generates the idea of nature's necessity, leads to a life of contentment; intellection in particular leads to the greatest satisfaction and tranquility.[33] This appeal to the texture or quality of experience grounds Spinoza's preference for naturally derived principles: they produce joy and satisfaction. Van Blyenbergh's commitment to revealed principles and theological authority generates, by contrast, the discomforts of classically insoluble problems (e.g., predestination and freedom) and, judging from the letters, the misery of existential fear and constant moral anxiety.

These issues reappear in Spinoza's 1675 correspondence with Alfred Burgh. Burgh, who had studied with Spinoza, later converted to Roman

---

32. Letter 21.

33. E.g., *TIE* §§ 9–13; *TTP* IV, sect. 4 [59–60]; *E*5p27 (which substitutes *acquiescentia* for *satisfactio*), and *E*5p42. Spinoza instructs Van Blyenbergh that "our highest blessedness consists in love toward God," which "flows necessarily from knowledge of God" (Letter 21).

Catholicism, read the *TTP*, and implored Spinoza to follow him. In Letter 67, Burgh addresses Spinoza as a man of most subtle and acute *ingenium*, a lover of truth, and a miserable dupe of the devil. "What does all of your philosophy amount to," Burgh demanded, "except sheer illusion and chimera?"[34] Spinoza, he charged, could not even refute competing philosophies, let alone find grounds for refusing the church's instruction on matters of ultimate importance such as salvation. In reply, Spinoza goes beyond his answer to Van Blyenbergh and distinguishes claims about truth from claims about goodness. Spinoza's reply exhibits a mixture of incredulity and contempt, plus a final effort to teach Burgh. Spinoza easily undermines Burgh's stated arguments for the superiority of Roman Catholicism, and he mocks the proudly anti-philosophical Burgh's willingness to appeal to reason. If, after all, Burgh counsels the rejection or ultimate subjection of reason, why appeal to it to motivate action? Spinoza writes:

> *You appear to be willing to use reason* [*ratione tamen velle uti videris*] and ask me "how I know that my philosophy is the best of all of those that have ever been taught in this world, are now being taught, or will ever be taught in the future." But surely I have far better right to put that question to you. For I do not presume that I have found the best philosophy, but I know I understand is the true philosophy [*Nam ego non praesumo, me optimam Philosophiam; sed veram me intelligere scio*]. If you ask me how I know this, I reply that *I know it in the same way that you know that the three angles of a triangle are equal to two right angles*. That this suffices no one will deny who has a sound brain and does not dream of unclean spirits who inspire us with false ideas as if they were true. For truth is the index of itself and the false.[35]

In claiming only truth, not optimality, for his philosophy, Spinoza differentiates what Burgh had conflated. Truths, he observes, are known "in the same way" irrespective of religious views. Only sickness or fantasy—"dreaming with open eyes" is the anti-Cartesian formula Spinoza uses in *TIE* § 66—could introduce doubts about true perception, such that the theist and the atheist or heretic concur about geometry.

34. Letter 67.

35. Letter 76 (emphasis added). On truth and falsity, see Spinoza *TIE* § 46 and *E*2p43s. Spinoza's rejoinder to Burgh evokes his critique of the Cartesians.

Taking up his right to turn the question of optimality on Burgh, Spinoza contrasts intellectual assent to mathematics with judgments about religious excellence. The former is *scientia*, the latter *credulitas* or *fides*:

> But you, who presume that you have at last found the best religion [*optimam Religionem*], or rather, the best men to whom you have pledged your credulity [*credulitatem tuam addixisti*], how do you know that they are the best of all those who have taught other religions, are teaching them now, or will teach them in the future? Have you examined all those religions, both ancient and modern, which are taught here and in India, and throughout the whole world? And even if you have duly examined them, how do you know that you have chosen the best? *For you can give no reason for your faith* [*quandoquidem tuae fidei rationem nullam dare potes*]. You will say that you are satisfied [*acquiescere*] with the inward testimony of the Spirit of God, whereas others are ensnared and deceived by the Prince of wicked spirits. But all who are outside the Roman church claim with the same right for their church what you claim for yours.[36]

Spinoza all but says outright that Burgh's religious views are wide-eyed dreams. He thus avoids the question of whether there might be rational, but not demonstratively established, beliefs in addition to imaginative fantasies. He does argue, nonetheless, that adherents of all religions are equally entitled to claim their beliefs as the best, as there is, properly speaking, no knowledge that could justify anyone's exclusive claim to the truth, only *credulitas* and *acquiescentia*. Reason itself thus cannot differentiate the claims of one group of believers from another; all have an equal claim, and, given their premises, can begin to argue. In the words of *TTP* XV, sect. 7, "since we are unable to demonstrate by reason whether the basis of theology (*theologiae fundamentum*)—that men are saved by obedience alone—is true or false, can one therefore ask of us, as an objection, why do we believe it?" Answering his own question with deepest sarcasm, Spinoza writes: "I hold absolutely that the fundamental dogma of theology [*theologiae fundamentale dogma*] cannot be discovered by the natural light, or at least that no one has yet done it, and that is why revelation was most necessary."[37] We require, Spinoza argues in the *TTP*, someone to lay down the law and thereby to form the social imaginary

36. Letter 76 (emphasis added).

37. *TTP* XV, sect. 7 [185].

and social bonds. When left to prophets, the premises for such formations are imaginary. This is one reason that conflicts over religious dogma are not only inevitable but potentially intractable; competing imaginative ideas cannot be eliminated by demonstrations but only by more persuasive, or more authoritatively propagated, imaginative ideas.[38] Toward the end of Letter 76, Spinoza asks Burgh, "Suppose all the arguments [*rationes*] that you offer tell in favor only of the Roman Church. Do you think that you demonstrate mathematically [*mathematicè demonstrare*] by them the authority of that church?"[39]

If religious disputation is characterized by arguments from revealed, i.e., imaginative, premises, are there arguments for the best, or even merely the good, from rational or intellectually apprehended premises? The question is tricky, but essential, for it bears on how we read Spinoza and more generally on how we evaluate interpretations. The correspondence with Van Blyenbergh and Burgh shows that reason can dismiss some arguments and validate others, and Spinoza clearly thinks that seeing how arguments fail should cause readers to question the principles from which they are derived; his letters trace the path of unwanted implications and contradictions. If Van Blyenburgh is hopeless on this account, Spinoza does try to persuade Burgh through rational means. Throughout his works, Spinoza subjects numerous principles he regards as destructive of, and even inimical to, human flourishing to rational critique (and, when rational critique is insufficient, to withering satire). Teleology and volitional freedom are prominent examples in the *Ethics*; in the *TTP*, the doctrine of election, the idea of divine authorship of the Bible, and the reality of miracles are major examples. In each case, Spinoza argues vigorously that a fully rationalized, i.e., thorough and systematic, application of the principles leads to absurdities, individual misery, and sociopolitical suffering. Thus the negative role of reason, namely, its critical role, is quite clear.

Does reason also have a positive role? In Letter 19, to Van Blyenbergh, Spinoza explicates God's prohibitions to Adam in the Garden of Eden by reducing them to a scientific discourse. Moral and legal language, he explains, are prophetic "parables," that is, imaginative representations of nature for an unsophisticated audience. Educated readers, as Spinoza's predecessor Maimonides famously suggested, can discern an implicit rational content in the parable. If it is "bad" or "forbidden" to eat the fruit of a certain tree, the reason is simply that the fruit is toxic: "God revealed to Adam that eating of

38. *TTP* XVI, sect. 2–3 [189–90], shows that the right in question, possessed by all individuals, does not derive from reason; the fool, the lunatic, and the philosopher possess it equally.

39. Letter 76.

that tree caused death, just as he also reveals to us through the natural intellect that poison is deadly to us."[40] The rhetorical features of the story are images of causal relationships, such that what appears to be a story about withholding knowledge is a communication of knowledge by other means; the message is medical, not moral. Spinoza's analysis suggests that if our knowledge of nature were complete, the need for moral language and the related mythological images of law, prohibition, and threats would be obviated; to live well, we could simply follow the guidance of reason. *E*4p68 confirms the promise of reason: "If men were born free, they would form no concept of good and evil so long as they remained free."[41] Yet the scholium to *E*4p68 announces immediately, indeed, emphatically that the hypothesis is counterfactual: "It is evident ... that the hypothesis is false." Spinoza reminds us of *E*4p4: "It is *impossible* that a man should not be a part of Nature, and that he should be able to undergo no changes except those which can be understood through his own nature alone, and of which he is the adequate cause."[42] If we had "only adequate ideas"[43] we would be free, but adequate ideas are difficult to achieve and inevitably partial: "all things excellent [*praeclara*; literally 'preeminently clear'] are as difficult as they are rare."[44] Thus discourses of ethics and law will be with us in perpetuity; mythology, or in contemporary language, ideology, is ineradicable in the practical domain.

Letter 19 suggests that reason's dispositions concerning our natural situation can provide us with guidance about ethical models and forms of government that more fully accord with our natural situation.[45] Nature, it is clear, imposes some limits; no one can survive deadly poison, and no one can flourish in conditions of civil strife and war. Reasoning, as distinct from imagining, can clarify these limits by studying patterns and causal networks. Spinoza defines persevering in existing as a natural necessity—and thus as neither good nor evil—but achieving self-preservation involves action as well as knowledge, and action is determined by appetite or desire as well as cognitive content. Why, for example, is adapting ourselves to nature, rather than attempting to transcend nature, the desirable approach? Spinoza's argument that the paradigms

---

40. Letter 19. See also *TTP* II, sect. 14 [37] and IV, sect. 9 [63].

41. Compare *TTP* V, sect. 8 [73–74], and chap. XVI, sect. 4–5 [190–91].

42. Emphasis added. See also *E*1 Appendix, *E*4p37s2, Letter 32, and *TTP* V, sect. 8 [73–74]. Adequacy is the same in actions and ideas.

43. *E*4p68dem.

44. *E*5p42s.

45. See *E*3 Preface, *TTP* XVI, *passim*, and *TP* I, chap. 2.

of free will, creation and providence, and theologico-political governance make us miserable presumes not only a description of how nature works but also a certain model of human flourishing: one that minimizes temporal strife and fear and maximizes satisfaction and joy, one that prefers free thought to obedience, one that prefers freedom now to the promise of salvation later, and so on. His argument is that these forms of life produce more satisfaction and peace. In the *TTP* Preface, Spinoza criticizes human monarchies, themselves modeled on divine monarchy, for causing men to confuse servitude for well-being (*salus*) and shame for great honor;[46] subsequent chapters analyze the nature and production of the confusion, elaborate the implications, and propose alternative sociopolitical organizations. Spinoza appeals to his readers to explore a different path. In this sense, reason reflects on, but neither provides nor demonstrates, the first principles of the good. Spinoza's analysis of the affects and the political consequences associated with accepting certain premises must carry the weight of persuading the reader to relinquish her established views in favor of a different form of experience. The texts ask us, in effect, about which way(s) of life we desire. If, as Spinoza tells his correspondents, the philosophical life is one of joy, the philosopher is persuaded precisely by the joy that accompanies knowing.[47]

Facing the multiple (and multiplying) Spinozas in the literature, it is clear that interpreters operate according to diverse, even opposing, convictions and judgments about good readings. To be sure, as interpreters we find that reason provides procedures for interpretation; we have standards of evidence, modes of argumentation, and other articulable conventions. At the same time, we have certain desires and values in play when we read. Many of us prefer, for example, careful fidelity to the text to more drastic and dramatic interventions; inspired as such interventions may be, we demand a certain groundedness and deride departures from this norm as abusive. Our desire is to preserve the texts we inherit. Many of us have chosen contextualism rather than "presentism" or rational reconstruction. Most of us prefer systematic interpretations, though the idea of system in philosophy is actually rather recent, and we do resist readings that seem to force a text into a pre-given or alien system. The image of reason as paradigmatically deductive and systematic in the sense of complete has its own history (and a history of its demise as well).[48] When we laud systematic

46. *TTP* Preface, sect. 7, [7]

47. Only an affect can influence an affect Spinoza (*E*4p7). Cf. *CM* I, sect. 1: "Love cannot be called true or false, but only good or bad."

48. See Leo Catana's chapter in this volume.

reading, whether on a deductive model or according to a structuralist program, we express a scholarly and aesthetic preference. To the adjectives "intellectual" and "aesthetic," moreover, we must add "institutional," for the current organization of the university and our professional outlets is reflected in scholarly activities; the institutional is the sociopolitical sphere of academia. Since I follow Spinoza in thinking that the affects and politics will always be with us, I address the implications of these issues of preference and sensibility in section 3.

3. Reason and Affect, Again

The exchange with Van Blyenbergh anticipates, and the exchange with Burgh reflects, Spinoza's remarks in the *TTP* Preface about undesirable, perverse readers. Spinoza observes, "I know how stubbornly those prejudices inhere in the mind that the soul has embraced [*amplexus*] as a form of piety; and it is impossible to detach the *vulgus* from superstition as much as fear." For this reason, he continues, "I do not invite the *vulgus* and those who suffer the same passions as the *vulgus* to read these pages." Such readers do "no good to themselves" and "harm others who would philosophize more freely were they able to surmount the obstacle of believing that reason should be subordinate to theology"[49] In *TTP* VIII, Spinoza expresses concern about being too late to remove the theological prejudices that impede a proper study of Scripture:

> men will not allow themselves to be corrected on these [theological] questions but rather obstinately defend whatever they have embraced under the aspect of religion [*quod sub specie religionis amplexi sunt, pertinaciter defendant*]; hardly any place is left for reason, except perhaps among a very few (if they are compared with the rest), so extensively have these prejudices occupied their minds [*adeo late haec prejudicia hominum mentes occupaverunt*].[50]

---

49. For all these quotations, see *TTP* Preface, sect. 15 [12]. Cf. Maimonides on undesirable readers: "How then could he [the author] put down in writing [an exhaustive interpretation of a parable] without becoming a butt for every ignoramus who, thinking that he has the necessary knowledge, would let fly at him the shafts of his ignorance?" (Maimonides (1963), vol. I, 6). Descartes's Preface to the *Meditations* is equally adamant: "I would not urge anyone to read this book except those who are able and willing to meditate seriously with me, and to withdraw their minds from the senses and from all preconceived opinions. Such readers, I know are few and far between. Those who do not bother to grasp the proper order of my arguments and the connection between them, but merely try to carp at individual sentences, as is the fashion, will not get much benefit from reading this book" (Descartes (1984–1991), II, 8).

50. *TTP* VIII, sect. 1 [188]. See also *E*4p44s, which describes individuals "in whom one affect is stubbornly fixed [*affectus pertinaciter adhaereat*]."

The verb *amplector* says that individuals passionately, affectively embrace theological prejudices. When prejudices constitute an extensive portion of the mind, they crowd out rational ideas. Eschewing "complete despair," Spinoza perseveres in his efforts to educate those whose embrace of theological dogma is less fervent; perhaps not all critique is so belated as to be ineffective.

Spinoza's clearest statement of the power of prejudice is found in the early *TIE*. *TIE* § 47 assigns prejudice the same status as natural limitation: "there are men whose minds are completely blinded, either from birth or from prejudice, i.e., because of some external chance." Given Spinoza's view, articulated in *Ethics* 2, that all knowing originates in images, that is, in bodily impressions of external things and ideas of them, imaginative ideas are acquired prior to rational ideas. When imaginative ideas are endorsed by authorities, they become deeply entrenched and constitute a mind that is receptive to some ideas and closed to others. The affects associated with imaginative ideas are similarly constitutive, such that one set of ideas and its associated emotions excludes, or makes incomprehensible and repellent, another set. Not simply "pictures on a panel," Spinoza ideas are active forces,[51] which manifest themselves in cognition, affect, and action. The hostile audience is hostile not independently of or in addition to accepting the cognitive content of imaginative prejudgments; because all ideas are simultaneously cognitive and affective, the structure of prejudices is *eo ipso* the structure of resistance and hostility to alternative ideas. As *Ethics* 1 reminds us, it is often easier "to remain in the state of ignorance … than to destroy the whole construction and think up a new one"; rejecting rational alternatives to teleological interpretation as impiety or rational critique of theological claims as heresy exemplifies this pattern.[52] At *TTP* VII, sect. 1, Spinoza observes ruefully that "This is how human beings are made: that which they conceive by means of pure intellect, they defend by intellect and reason alone; and, on the contrary, the opinions that come from affects of their souls, they defend by these same affects."[53] What, then, is the power of critique? The *Ethics* is perhaps more sanguine (though hardly robustly confident) than the *TTP* in stressing that the powerful affects concurrent with reason can reshape those of imagination. Becoming more rational, if only one can engage in the process, reconfigures not merely the content of ideas but also and at the same time the mind's affective constitution.

---

51. *E*2p49s.

52. *E*1 Appendix.

53. *TTP* VII, sect. 1 [98].

In *E*2p36, Spinoza argues that imaginative ideas have their own force; one inadequate idea produces other inadequate ideas, and so on. "Inadequate and confused ideas," he writes, "follow with the same necessity as adequate, or clear and distinct ideas." The point, as the demonstration emphasizes, is that inadequate or confused ideas exist only as they are related to this or that singular mind. In contrast, since all ideas are in God (or Nature), all ideas are adequate when they are related to God. Inadequacy reflects a knower's inability to perceive them in an orderly and rationally connected way; inadequacy is, in a word, an imaginative way of thinking about nature, and, as such, subject to emendation. Considered as a pedagogy, the *Ethics* cultivates the reader's ability to attend to reasons and thus to reconsider imaginative accounts, prejudgments, and "conclusions without premises."[54] This working through is simultaneously, in affective terms, a movement from impatience, resistance, and similar states to a willingness to hear and to follow causal connections with care and attention. In the most general terms, it is a movement from passivity, sadness, and vacillation to more stable joy. In this regard, it is essential to emphasize that the *Ethics* is an ethics, not merely a treatise on metaphysics and epistemology with some attached remarks on the emotions, sociality, and politics, and a perplexing (or embarrassing) fifth part, which has something to do with immortality.[55] The *Ethics*, like the *TTP*, is concerned with knowledge, affects, and politics: the *asylum ignorantiae* protects ignorance, fear, and tyranny, endlessly replicating them in a vicious circle.

In contrast to Van Blyenbergh and Burgh, who would censure philosophical truth in the name of theological or dogmatic truth and so show themselves to be not only non- but actually anti-philosophical (or, if you wish, pseudo-philosophers or sophists), the student Casearius appears in Spinoza's correspondence as a proto-philosopher. We first learn of Casearius in a letter from Simon De Vries to Spinoza of February 24, 1663. De Vries and his friends envy Spinoza's "companion Casearius, who lives under the same roof with you, and can talk to about the most important matters at breakfast, at dinner and on your walks."[56] Spinoza dismisses the envy, noting of Casearius that "no one is more troublesome to me, and there is no with whom I have to be more on my guard." Spinoza depicts him as intellectually promising, but "boyish and unstable" and "eager for novelty rather than truth." He concludes, "I hope that in a few years these

54. *E*2p28dem.

55. On this theme, Nadler (2005) does for Spinoza what Curley (1986) did for Descartes.

56. De Vries quoted from Letter 8.

youthful faults will be emended (*emendaturum*). Indeed, as far as I can judge from his native ability (*ingenium*), I am almost certain that they will. So his nature induces me to like him."[57] Casearius's promise is clear, but the philosophical outcome is uncertain; he requires careful direction, for the development of his intellectual *captus* will be profoundly determined by his temperament and desire.

The letter thus alludes to an ethical and cognitive training regimen for becoming philosophical; Casearius, like Cartesians and other readers, requires *emendatio*. Letter 8 shows that De Vries and the circle, who are reading an early version of the first part of the *Ethics*, understand mathematics to be part of the training. Spinoza himself emphasizes the pivotal role of mathematics in the Appendix to *E*1: "the truth would have been hidden from the human race to eternity, if Mathematics, which is concerned not with ends, but only with the essences and properties of figures, had not shown men another standard of truth."[58] Ironically, however, Letters 8 and 10 ultimately suggest that, despite their recognition of mathematics as propaedeutic to philosophy, De Vries and friends actually cannot actually make use of it. Faced with Spinoza's use of the *mos geometricus*, they are full of questions about definitions and proof, and they invoke the mathematician Borelli in order to resolve their confusion. In so doing, they show an inclination to appeal to authorities and a tendency to repeat the authorities' pronouncements uncritically. In other words, De Vries and friends lack the very intellectual *captus* Spinoza identifies in Casearius. In Letter 9, Spinoza instructs De Vries that Borelli, "whose view you are too inclined to embrace, confuses all things completely," and he reworks one of Borrelli's defective examples as an illustration.[59] Letter 10 thus solidifies the suspicion that De Vries, despite his desire to know, could not understand Spinoza's views.

Lest we conclude with relief that we are not beholden to religious authorities or that Van Blyenbergh, like De Vries, was just not smart enough to appreciate Spinoza's arguments (but we are), the *E*1 Appendix reminds us that all human beings are inclined to affirm teleology, the root prejudice, and later parts of the *Ethics*, particularly the Preface to *E*4, remind us of the need for models and maxims of life to resist life's vicissitudes. If to read naturalistically and scientifically is to attempt to read, insofar as or as much as we can, without

57. Letter 9.

58. *E*1 Appendix.

59. See Letter 9. My discussion of Letter 9 has benefited from conversations with Eric Schliesser and Idit Dobbs-Weinstein.

the active forces of prejudice, and with attention to careful demonstration, Spinoza gives notice that such reading is "as difficult as it is rare."[60] The *TTP* devotes chapter upon chapter to disabusing the reader of conventional interpretations and assumptions. The *Ethics* repeatedly revisits Spinoza's critique of ideas of free will and divine monarchy precisely because these views were so pervasive and deeply held. *E*2p11s openly acknowledges the difficulty in abandoning entrenched Cartesian views of the human mind and body: "Here, no doubt, my readers will come to a halt (*haerebunt*), and think of many things which will give them pause (*quae moram injiciant*). For this reason I ask them to continue on with me slowly, step by step, and to make no judgment on these matters until they have read them through."[61] The question at these moments of the text is how a reader can open her thinking to Spinoza's ideas, both by relinquishing previous attachments and by attending to the flowing and following of unfamiliar ideas. A slightly different way of understanding *haerebunt* here would be in terms of getting stuck; the verb *injiciant* might also be understood in the sense of imposing, not merely giving, a pause. If our preconceived views leave us "stuck" and "impose a pause," the question is how to restore flexibility and movement in thinking.

While it is possible, as Spinoza suggests in *TIE* § 44 that someone could be so constituted by nature that "everything would flow to him of its own accord," it is far more often the case that we need *emendatio*, intellectual purification and healing, and affective change in order to cultivate the habits of reason and true judgment. Like citizens, nations, and governments, readers and philosophers are made or cultivated rather than born. By nature, all human beings think and feel, but different ways of thought and different affective regimes emerge in conjunction with natural history and cultivation. As Spinoza writes in his unfinished *Political Treatise*, part I, chapter 5, citizens are "not born, but made [*non nascuntur, sed fiunt.*]"[62] In other words, just as the *TIE* emends the Cartesian philosopher's ideas in order to produce someone one ready for philosophy, so too the *TTP* is designed to produce the desirable and desiring *lector philosophe* identified in its Preface. The manifest aims of the *TTP* are primarily political, but portions of the *TTP* sketch other aspects of Spinoza's thought. *TTP* III, sect. 3, for example, offers readers who can think

60. *E*5p40s.

61. Other examples of this kind of request are found in *E*1p7s2, *E*1p15s1, *E*3p2s, and the *E*5 Preface.

62. *TP* I, chap. V. Machiavelli and Hobbes hold this view. For Spinoza's distinctive use of it, see *TTP* III, sect. 6 [47] and XVII, sect. 26 [217].

"without subordinating reason to theology"[63] a mini-*Ethics* in the midst of Spinoza's methodical revision of traditional doctrines. The *Ethics*, too, is a pedagogical text, designed to produce philosophers; it starts in the prevailing discourse of its time and moves attentive readers to another place. The starting point for producing philosophers is, of necessity, with the readers' actual ideas and their concomitant forms of affective experience. Inasmuch as the Spinozan mind just is its ideas, there can be no Spinozan *epochē*, only a process of working through the philosophical language and horizon we have inherited in order to dissolve obstacles and bring our thinking to greater clarity. As we saw earlier, the *TIE* emphasizes that the philosophical pedagogue must meet the students where they are in order to prepare, step by step, for a favorable hearing of unfamiliar ideas.[64]

4. Contemporary Readers and Historical Texts

Thus far, I have focused on the issue of readers' intellectual and affective receptivity to philosophical texts. What, though, of the question of history and the historical specificity of texts and readers? As historians of philosophy, we tend to read the works of our predecessors with an eye to discovering styles of thinking, conceptual models and ways of posing questions (for to know the question is to know a lot about what will count as an answer), genealogies and lineages, and the like. At the same time, as philosophers who work historically, we remain open to the experiences of insight and reflection, to what Pierre Macherey calls, speaking of Spinoza, his actuality, that is, his philosophical liveliness for us now.[65] Where most of our predecessors thought in terms of solving problems, many of us take the interpretation of texts, at least as much as the pursuit of philosophical problems, as a principal task. We cannot, after all, engage the ideas without attending to the material history of the text: its language, its audience, its context. To the extent that we are committed historians and philologists, we, like Nietzsche, are

63. *TTP* Preface, sect. 15 [12].

64. See Alexandre Matheron's remark that reading Spinoza requires us "to rid ourselves of the bad habit of asking, 'Why is there something rather than nothing?,' as if nothingness were more intelligible than being. The question that should be asked is: 'Why are there only certain things rather than everything?'" (Matheron, (1991), 29).

65. See Macherey (1998), 125–35. Heidegger regarded Spinoza as a minor figure who wrote in a non-philosophical language; Adorno barely recognized his kinship with Spinoza; and Foucault, to my knowledge, refers to Spinoza only a few times. Jacques Derrida noted that Spinoza's philosophy destabilizes Heideggerian *Geschichte*. See Derrida (1995), 265.

Spinoza's descendants and philosophical friends. For us, most philosophical texts, to borrow Spinoza's example, are not like Euclid's *Elements*, readily comprehended by even a relatively unsophisticated reader.[66] When I say that I think that Spinoza's political ideas are potent now, or that I see his philosophy as productive for thinking about singularity, the logic of affect, or thought and extension, my way to these philosophical ideas is thoroughly material; only careful scholarship will bring me closer to Spinoza's terminology and concerns, and only diligent efforts to differentiate my own views from Spinoza's (and, a fortiori, from what I might wish Spinoza's views to be) can bring Spinoza's ideas into focus. We cannot, moreover, read Spinoza as if no interpretations or new thoughts intervened between his time and ours; no amount of historical philology or cultural reconstruction can return us to Amsterdam and the Spinoza circle, and no amount of philosophical self-scrutiny will utterly remove the post-Spinozan scales from our eyes. Can we now, for example, read without the intellectual legacy of Kant, embodied as a certain adoption of that legacy is in our training, our institutions, our very ideas of what counts as philosophical questions? Can we now think about ancient or early modern mathematics and science without our knowledge of later discoveries and interpretations of nature?

To my mind, the answer to these questions is negative. We do not—in fact we cannot—meet texts empty-handed. There is no reading without prior commitments, tacit or explicit, and the force or torsion they involve, yet what we bring to the text can be articulated and worked through. It may, moreover, change in the course of our work, for reading is a dialogical act. No one takes up philosophical texts, with the hope of remaining entirely unprovoked and unaffected by them, and no serious reader thinks that a single reading discloses the full meaning of a genuinely philosophical text. Each reader comes to the text with a singular inner library of references, habits of mind, and philosophical affinities that reflect her history and time. Spinoza captures the way experience structures the mind when he calls ideas "narratives, or mental histories of nature."[67] To the extent that each of us is historically constituted, reading is always already intertextual or, to put this point another way, inter-mental. Texts are partially constituted by readers and communities of readers. Reciprocally, minds are partially constituted in relation to texts. Until the reader takes it up, the text is merely "ink on paper"; at the same time, the ideas presented in a text shape and reshape

66. *TTP* VII, sect. 17 [111].

67. *CM* I, sect. 6.

minds. Spinoza observes in note p to *TIE* § 41, "To interact with other things is to produce, or to be produced by, other things." Viewed this way, the written text is a kind of natural limit for readers in the sense that we cannot simply ignore or override what is written, yet neither texts nor human minds are fully self-subsistent, stable, and discrete. In the language of the physics of *Ethics* 2, they are, rather, somewhat determinate and somewhat fluid, constituted by singular ratios and communicating and exchanging with others. To use the modern language of textuality, texts and minds are interwoven; the generativity of the reader's ideas encounters the generativity of the ideas available in the text.

The claim that our thinking is historically situated and shaped need not drive us to the most skeptical outcomes of historicism or to the idea that all that is left for us is anachronism. A negative answer must increase our sense of care, particularly with respect to considering changes in philosophical language, the relationship of philosophy to other sciences (especially in the case of thinkers who pre-date our own vision of the disciplines) and the wider culture in which it is set, and changes in the self-understanding of philosophers about their own activity. All of our historical-philological and reconstructive tools find their use in the hope that we are attending to what is written and what the author is thinking about. A negative answer, moreover, obligates us to give an account of our interpretive commitments, such that the same tools we use with historical texts must be used to clarify our own position as readers. To be sure, giving such an account is not without difficulties, whether we articulate them in terms of the hermeneutic circle or in terms of genealogy. Making our relation to the most canonical, "major" authors explicit is difficult precisely because their ways of thinking are constitutive of our own and, as constitutive, occlude other paths. Reading so-called minor or seemingly marginal authors is difficult because our tacit, unreflective commitments can make these authors seem incomprehensible, unphilosophical, or simply unworthy of our attention (and so unsuitable for tenure, promotion, and other professional credentials). To the extent that texts and ideas do not fit into prevailing master-narratives, canons, or the current preoccupations of our field, they are threatened with assimilation and invisibility. What is most obviously unsatisfying about the various "grand schemes" of interpretation and the "X [fill in a school or -ism] and Philosopher So-and-So" genre, is the way they impose an agenda on texts, pressing them into service and threatening to reduce thinking to acts of assimilation. No doubt thinking of this danger, Gilles Deleuze observed, "It is easy to credit Spinoza with the place of honor in the Cartesian succession;

except that he bulges out of that place in all directions, there is no living corpse who raises the lid of his coffin so powerfully, crying so loudly, 'I am not one of yours.'"[68] Committed as so many of us are to details of language and context, as interested as we may be in counter-histories or even heretical ideas, our impositions may be more subtle, but they nonetheless require the sort of careful scrutiny we extend to texts. We require, in a word, what Adorno called critique.

5. *Conclusion*

In this chapter, I have explored philosophical reading, philosophical pedagogy and resistance to philosophy, and the mutually constitutive relation of readers and texts. In so doing, I have focused on the forms of thinking and their concomitant desires and on the significance of historical and institutional structures. Philosophical readers bring themselves in an attitude of open reflection on the situation and activities of reading.

Spinoza himself wrote frequently of the joy of knowing, and so I shall end this essay on a note of pleasure. The *Ethics* famously ends by conjoining our highest joy and blessedness (*beatitudo*) or health (*salus*) with a reminder about the work required to achieve it: "All things excellent [or: most pre-eminently clear] are as difficult as they are rare" (*E*5p42s). Everyone in the academy knows that intellectual work can be difficult, even trying, and that its pleasures are profound. No discussion, I think, of philosophical reading, can do without an affirmation of pleasure. If sometimes we side with Dr. Fischelson, at least we can delight in understanding.

Acknowledgments

I am grateful to Mogens Lærke, Jeffrey Bernstein, and Helen S. Lang for their comments on earlier versions of this essay.

68. Deleuze and Parnet (1987), 15.

8

Is the History of Philosophy a Family Affair? The Examples of Malebranche and Locke in the Cousinian School

Delphine Kolesnik-Antoine

Examining the Cartesian philosophy is deeply interesting. Whether there is a close or a distant relationship, we all originate from Descartes. We are all of his blood. There is a heritage that connects him to us.[1]

1. Introduction

THE AIM OF this contribution is to study the classificatory principles that were used in the first French histories of philosophy and the enduring effects that they have today. By the first histories of philosophy in France I do not refer to those that were chronologically the very first (André-François Boureau Deslandes's *Histoire critique de la philosophie* was published in 1737).[2] I refer

1. Damiron (1846), vol. I, 3.

2. Cf. Boureau Deslandes (1737, 1756). It is important to underline the importance for the Cousinian project of Joseph-Marie Degérando's *Histoire comparée des systèmes de philosophie relativement aux principes des connaissances humaines*. The first volume appeared in 1804; the second, which mainly bears on Greek philosophy, was edited in 1823–24; the last, which contains some supplements concerning Cartesianism and modern philosophy, was published posthumously in 1847 (Degérando died in 1847). In this work, Degérendo endorses an experimental philosophy inspired by Bacon. The particularity of this philosophy is to differ both from "empiricism" (which is attributed to Locke or Condillac too often for his taste), which identifies knowledge with a simple collection of sense impressions without any recourse to speculative truths, and from pure rationalism, understood as a system that attends exclusively to abstract deductions and that avoids any reference to sensory data. This chapter does not allow me to show how Cousin adopts this framework in order to reestablish the philosophy of experience as a psychological empiricism originating in Descartes. The examples of Locke and Malebranche will, however, allow us to grasp the importance and the limits of this reestablishment.

rather to those that took the shape of systems as a result of the influence of Victor Cousin and of the lectures he gave at the Sorbonne and the École Normale Supérieure from 1815 onward, and in particular toward the end of the 1820s. This was the system of *spiritual eclecticism*, which was institutionalized in the teaching curriculum (especially in the *Concours de l'Agrégation* and the list of "good" authors that comes with it)[3] and in a teaching tradition that is still strong in France. More precisely—and the epigraph to this chapter, quoting Jean-Philippe Damiron, a key figure of the Cousinian School, testifies to this—I am interested in the primacy that a certain spiritualist image of Cartesianism enjoyed in these first histories of philosophy and how unveiling this primacy should encourage us to reconsider the heritage of Malebranche and Locke in the history of early modern philosophy.

Engaging in such a project requires two preliminary remarks. On the one hand, we must say something about the Cousinian conception of the history of philosophy in general. On the other, we must say something about the significance of the primacy of Cartesianism in that school in relation to the particular cases of Malebranche and Locke.

1. The historians of philosophy in the Cousinian school vindicate a certain form of "objectivity" of their practice. This is the case, for example,

---

3. The *Agrégation* was established in 1825 during the Restoration, by the administration of the minister of public education, Denis Frayssinous. This "competition" for gaining access to a status as civil servant within the educational system is very competitive and still exists. The aim of it is to recruit future teachers in philosophy, mainly for high schools. Cousin was the president of the *Agrégation* for a very long time. He thus contributed to the establishment of the list of authors that teachers have the right to use for their courses and give their students to read. It is also from this list that the text for one of the exams of the *concours*, the "text commentary," must be chosen. The simple fact that one author and not another figures on the list, or that one work is privileged over another, thus has great importance for the overall reception of the history of philosophy in France. This is how it appears to F. Huet, professor at the faculty of humanities at the University of Ghent, in his "Discours sur la réformation de la philosophie au dix-neuvième siècle," which serves as general introduction to J-B. Bordas-Demoulin's *Le cartésianisme ou la véritable rénovation des sciences* (1843, note 1, CXXX-CXXXI): "It is the Cartesian school that occupies most of the space on the list of modern philosophers whose works the Royal Council for Public Instruction has recently recommended to the university professors. Here is the list as it can be found in an order from 12th august 1842: Bacon, Descartes, the author of the *Logique de Port-Royal*, Bossuet, Fénelon, Malebranche, Arnauld, Buffier, Locke, Leibniz, Clarke, Euler, Ferguson, Reid. Young professors, who speak in the name of eclecticism, have taken up the task of executing this instruction, by publishing convenient editions of all the works that the council has chosen. Here are some passages from the announcements they have issued: 'We do not dissimulate our position. Quite on the contrary, we proclaim our preferences for the immortal school of spiritualist philosophers, who are strict moralist, pure and noble writers whose father is Descartes, and who never put independent thought in the service of anything except generous and salutary doctrines.... The philosophy of our time is honored to be the offspring of this great school. Descartes, Malebranche, Arnauld, Leibnitz, Bossuet, Fénelon, those are its masters' (*Bibliothèque philosophique*, chez Charpentier, éditeur)."

when they establish complete editions of the works of Plato[4] and Descartes,[5] or when they exhume new manuscripts such as the philosophical works of Père André[6] or the correspondence between Malebranche and Dortous de Mairan.[7] It is also the case when they make use of the juridical papers from Vanini's trial in order to determine the legitimacy of the accusations of "atheism" made against him.[8] However, the more the Cousinians establish themselves as a school, the more they stress the "critical" dimension of their work. Damiron even makes this the distinguishing feature of the Cousinian school in relation to German history of philosophy, and in particular in relation to Johann Jacob Brucker.[9] One must, Damiron argues, do history of philosophy not for the sake of history but for the sake of philosophy, implying that one must throw oneself heart and soul into the battle:

> There is considerable difference between historians who only tell of ordinary wars and historians who writes of the wars of mind and reason. When telling of the first kind of history, one can keep neutral, unless the violence and injustice of one side or the other is too evident. But in a war of mind and reason, one cannot, I think, stay indifferent, or tell things as if the truth did not touch us.[10]

4. See Plato (1822–1840).

5. See Descartes (1824–1826).

6. See André (1843).

7. See Malebranche (1852). Corriger: Cousin (1852).

8. See Cousin (1856).

9. On this point (albeit without stating it explicitly for reasons I will return to later), the Cousinian school adopts the method proposed by Joseph-Marie Degérando in his *Histoire comparée*. The clearest passage in Degérando on this can be found in the Introduction: "There exists, especially in foreign languages, a great number of complete or partial histories of philosophy. But almost all of those we have managed to look into place themselves on one of the following two levels: Either the historian declares himself in favor of a particular doctrine that he has been convinced by, and then presents the series of philosophical opinions as if they constituted a body of proofs destined to justify his opinion. Or, while proclaiming absolute impartiality, he limits himself to report these opinions, not only without judging them, but even without using the data given to establish any kind of result, be it theoretical or practical. The history that I present to the public has not been devised in order to justify this or that opinion.... Hence, it has been my objective to trace the facts as if I was foreign to all opinions, and I have formed an opinion only afterwards and in accordance with the sole testimony of the facts" (Degérando (1804), vol. I, xxix–xxx).

10. The passage stems from a letter from Père André to Marbeuf, dated May 3, 1719. André takes stock of the difficulties and joys he has encountered while working on his biography of Malebranche. In Cousin (1843), xli, Cousin places himself in the lineage of Père André and insists on the methodological key that the correspondence of the latter contains for writing good history.

Which classificatory principles govern such a judgmental, even passionate, history of philosophy? Cousinian eclecticism is first of all defined as rational spiritualism, i.e., as a kind of psychological empiricism that considers introspection and interior experience to be the point of departure of all knowledge. It is a spiritualism that differs from theological spiritualism, which recognizes the existence of "traditional dogma," e.g., original sin, and which refers true knowledge to revelation.[11] It also differs from sensualism which, in the various forms it has taken throughout the history of philosophy, is a variation on the idea that knowledge is rooted in the external senses.[12] It defends the primacy of the psychological method in philosophy and vindicates Descartes, insofar as Descartes applied the first rule of his method, i.e., evidence, in order to determine the existence and nature of the soul. Evidence, however, cannot be reduced to a simple logical or geometrical criterion, as Cousin himself sometimes stresses when speaking of Spinoza. It must proceed from concrete experience. It is thus in the light of a spiritualist philosophy with a particular concern for reconciling the rational and empirical dimensions of psychology that the Cousinians, in hindsight, make judgments about the value, progress, and possible incoherence of previous philosophers.

(2) With regard to the particular status that Malebranche and Locke have within the Cousinian school, given the primacy the Cousinians give to Cartesianism, it can be exemplified by the Essay Competition on the history of Cartesianism opened in 1839 by the Academy of Moral and Political Sciences. Francisque Bouillier and Jean Baptiste Bordas-Demoulin won the prize jointly, respectively, for the text that subsequently developed into the two-volume *Histoire de la philosophie cartésienne*[13] and *Le Cartésianisme, ou la véritable renovation des sciences.*[14] Charles Renouvier received the distinction "very honorable" for his *Manuel de philosophie moderne.*[15] Jean-Philibert Damiron was in charge of writing up a report on

11. This strand of spiritualism was mainly represented by De Maistre, Lamennais, and De Bonald. For an explanation of the differences between eclectic or rational eclecticism, theological spiritualism and sensualism, with regard to philosophy, ethics, politics, and aesthetics, see Damiron (1828), t. I, "Introduction," 25–29.

12. On the treatment of sensualism in the Cousinian school, see Daled (2005). Daled's book prolongs the pioneering work by Olivier Bloch (see in particular Bloch (1997), part II, chap. ii: "De Victor Cousin à Karl Marx"). On the "impurity" of the philosophy of the Enlightenment according to the Cousinians, see also Borghero (2007), 247–283.

13. See Bouillier (1854).

14. See Bordas Demoulin (1843).

15. See Renouvier (1842).

the submitted essays. He later published the text as a kind of introduction to his *Essai sur l'histoire de la philosophie en France au XVIIe siècle.*[16] When discussing the criteria of selection used in the competition, Damiron here mentions (in the third place after "The State of Philosophy after Descartes" and the determination of the Cartesian "Revolution" in the field of knowledge) the study of "the consequences and the developments of Descartes's philosophy, not only by his avowed disciples such as Regis, Rohault and De la Forge, but also by the important thinkers to whom he gave rise such as Spinoza, Malebranche, Locke, Bayle and Leibniz."[17] Malebranche and Locke are thus, at the same time, excluded from the group of "avowed disciples" of Descartes and made part of a Cartesian heritage passed over from genius to genius. What are the deeper reasons for the both privileged and illegitimate status of these two prodigal sons?

It is my hypothesis that the study of such "limit cases" allows us to overcome the opposition, often repeated by historians of philosophy, between idealist spiritualism and empiricism originating in the natural sciences. It will allow us to think a more subtle intra-empirical combat where the adversaries will eventually find each other as brothers with regard to a shared Cartesian paternity. Thus, I argue, in relation to Malebranche and Locke, the history of philosophy becomes a family affair, in the singular. The different clans are absorbed into this single family, so that the space of a complex saga opens up, where each member, in various ways, draws upon the two strands of psychology, i.e., empirical and rational, that Descartes as the first attempted to weave together.

2. *Malebranche and Locke: frères ennemis?*

The first schemas that appear when reading the reflections of Cousin himself and his followers are, with regard to Locke, a sort of deferral, and, with regard to Malebranche, an imperfect model. On this point, the Cousinians simply took over an opposition inherited from the Enlightenment (albeit in a reversed order that will prove favorable for Malebranche), namely, the opposition between the sensualist innovator promoted in Voltaire's *Lettres anglaises* and diffused among the thinkers of the French Revolution[18]

---

16. Damiron (1846).

17. Damiron (1846), vol. I, 2, note 1.

18. On this point, see in particular Cousin (1861), 10: "[Voltaire] used all his talent to promote Lockian philosophy, which he thought was that of the new era, against the exaggerated and compromised philosophies of Descartes and Malebranche."

and the overly visionary Cartesian who wrote the *Recherche de la vérité* and whose other works ended up being relatively forgotten (in particular the *Conversations chrétiennes*, the *Entretiens sur la métaphysique* and the *Méditations chrétiennes*).[19] This historiographical opposition is partly justified by the biographies of the two men, since Locke wrote some critical notes on Malebranche's conception of ideas and the vision in God that were published posthumously in 1706, only six years after Coste's French translation of the *Essay on the Human Understanding*.[20] In addition to this, the opposition was important at the time when the Cousinians were writing for two reasons. First, Locke was promoted by the adversaries of the Cousinians, the so-called Ideologues,[21] who considered Locke to be their principal father figure. We find a prominent example in Joseph-Marie Degérando's *Histoire comparée des systèmes de philosophie, relativement aux principes des connaissances humaines* from 1804. Here, Locke is presented as Bacon's prodigal son, as the founder of

19. The provision of new editions of Malebranche's works served to highlight texts that were underestimated, even ridiculed by the philosophers of the Revolution, who were more attracted by the materialist potentials in Malebranche's analyses of the fallen soul than by his psychology and moral precepts. In that regard, the explanation Bouillier provides for the fact that only the first five chapters of book two of the *Recherche de la vérité* figure on the curriculum for the *Agrégation* in 1886, is illuminating. This is "doubtless because the physiological explanations, Descartes' famous theory of animal spirits, and the play of fibres are the principal topics of the remaining [chapters]" (Bouillier (1886), v).

20. See Locke (1706). Locke was already working on his critique in 1693, at the time when he was preparing the second edition of the *Essay*. His critique is based on the second edition of the *Recherche de la vérité* from 1678.

21. On the *idéologues*, see Daled (2005), 22–23 [internal reference to Picavet, (1891), 101]: "Who were those *idéologues* to whom Bonaparte 'lent his saber' and whose oblivion in France Gusdorf has regretted? Giving in to the traditional classification of the history of philosophy under the history of writing, but with all the usual reservations, Picavet divided in 1891 the 'ideologues' or 'ideologists' into three generations. Firstly, there were those who were dead or had acquired their fame before the end of the 18th century: Condorcet, Sièyes, Roederer, Lakanal, Volney, Dupuis, Maréchal, Naigeon, Saint-Lambert, Garat, Laplace and Pinel. Secondly, there were the men who, in the schools or in public opinion, had occupied the first places under the Direction and the Consulat at whom 'one ordinarily mostly designate ideologues.' This was the most flourishing and original tradition according to Picavet: Cabanis, Destutt de Tracy et Daunou. Thirdly, there were the men who were already known in one of the two preceding periods and who continued to exercise considerable influence on their contemporaries by means of a doctrine that Picavet considered 'less distant from those that triumphed at the end of the Empire and during the Restoration.' Degérando and Laromiguière were the most important men from this generation. Thus, there were three generations where the first was an indistinct gathering according to Picavet. The second, on the contrary, divided into three branches: 'Physiological ideology,' 'rational ideology and its relations to the sciences,' 'comparative and applied psychological and rational ideology.' As for the third generation—that of Degérando—it was 'spiritualist and Christian ideology.'"

true science and of the "philosophy of experience."[22] Degérando opposes this philosophy of experience to the bad empiricism stemming from Hobbes and from the thinkers of the Cartesian school who ground knowledge in methodical doubt and innate ideas. Second, the reference to Locke contributes to the promotion of the internal senses in Scottish philosophy. In a way, Cousin is part of this movement. He did, however, have to distinguish himself from Dugald Stewart who put Locke to the task of criticizing a conception of the *cogito* deemed too deductive and rationalizing. From Cousin's perspective, Dugald Stewart's rehabilitation of the "certitude of existence" implied that Locke was separated from empirical psychology.[23] For the Cousinians, returning to the Cartesian heritage thus involved a certain number of significant displacements in the way in which the history of early modern thought was considered.

In relation to Malebranche, the Cousinians will search for other fathers than Descartes (two, even three) in order to acquit Descartes of all responsibility for the Oratorian's exaggerated idealism that the Cousinians consider to be justly denounced by their sensualist adversaries. In return, Malebranche's Cartesian heritage is reinforced via thc psychological branch:

> There is a certain number of families in the history of philosophy and all the eminent thinkers is a member of one of these. One of these families is Descartes'. Malebranche belongs to this family. He is a first-order Cartesian. His century, his country, his mindset makes him this; he belongs to the new philosophy in all aspects of his life. But if he is of

22. Degérando mainly discusses the philosophy of experience in opposition to idealism and materialism: "If, when observing human nature, one begins with this double relation, as from two primary and parallel facts, one will arrive at the doctrine developed by Locke—a doctrine which is, if you will allow the expression, the root of this new philosophical tree. However, by isolating one or the other of these two foundations and only considering a single fact, one limits oneself to observing only the internal activity of the mind, or on the contrary, noticing only its dependence on the exterior. Then two new branches will be formed, idealism and materialism, doctrines that are only the more opposed to one another that they are better suited for remaining united, in the same way as a married couple that has not been divorced enough, who even miss each other while offending each other, and who feel a secret void but still do not have the courage to get together again. I have no reservations about saying that the theory composed of this double relation is the true and legitimate philosophy of Bacon" (Dégerando (1804), vol. I, 299–300).

23. See Cousin (1833), 329–38. Cousin very directly aims at Dugald Steward and his "*Essays philosophie* [*sic*]. Edimbourg. 1810" (see ibid., 329, note 1). What he has in mind is Stewart's *Philosophical Essays*, which were indeed published in 1810 (and reedited in 1816).

> the Cartesian family, he is also of Plato's. He is this in the same way as Saint Augustine is it, that is to say, minus the paganism and plus the Christianity. He is, as it has been well said, the Plato of Christianity, and he is this with a striking originality, if not always by the breadth and fecundity of his views, then at least by their depth and loftiness. It is in psychology that he most strongly takes after Descartes and in metaphysics that he takes after Plato.[24]

On the other hand, the Cousinians also insist on the way in which Locke's heritage degenerates in offspring like Helvétius. Indeed, the heirs of Locke represent many degenerations of an original philosophy where whatever seeds of truth and wisdom originally contained in it are forgotten. Damiron writes in his *Mémoire sur Helvétius*:

> He [i.e., Helvétius] is not a man of a great philosophical family. He is not a member of Descartes' family, that goes without saying. He is not even a member of Locke's family, even though he came out of it or rather pushed to the point of excess certain points of his doctrine.[25]

When Damiron examines the pertinence of the relations established between Locke and Descartes by the competitors at the 1839 Competition, he distinguishes two argumentative approaches. The first approach, clearly exemplified by Bordas-Demoulin, consists in insisting that Locke and Descartes are related by stressing the points that remain undecided in Descartes, especially with regard to innate ideas. Then, on this basis, they show that Locke is both an unworthy and a natural heir of Descartes. The second approach,

---

24. Damiron (1846), vol. II, 593.

25. Damiron (1855), 6. Cousin himself had already developed all the aspects of this figure of thought: "The wise, honest, but too skeptical Locke was followed by the system builder Condillac. The latter in turn built the road to the hotheaded and licentious Helvétius and the elegant and cold Saint-Lambert. After them came the theoreticians of anarchy, and not long after the theoreticians of absolute power" (Cousin 2005, v). This clan strategy of exclusion is also fully at work in relation to subversive figures such as Spinoza. On this, see, for example, Cousin (1884), 392: "under no circumstances can we admit that the philosophy of Descartes is the principle of Spinoza's. They are moved by contrary mindsets. They have their origin in opposed principles and they finish with contrary conclusions. Descartes, who is completely untainted by mysticism, breathes spiritualism everywhere. Also his school, the one that descends directly from him and represents him in the seventeenth century, is highly spiritualist and theist, and has everywhere spoken up against Spinoza." On the treatment of Spinoza in the Cousinian school, and in particular in Émile Saisset, see Moreau (1978), Moreau (1979), Moreau (1983), Moreau (2013), Moreau (forthcoming).

exemplified by Bouillier, consists on the contrary in following Cousin's 1829 courses on Locke in insisting on the spiritualist dimensions of Locke's texts—dimensions that are contradictory in relation to the rest of Locke's work, but which prolong Cartesian principles on the road to truth. Damiron himself clearly inclines toward the second approach. Nobody holds that unworthy children such as Helvétius, Diderot, La Mettrie, or the Marquis d'Argens are the heirs of Descartes, the father of "true" philosophy. If, then, there is a lineage going from Descartes to Locke, it can only be established at the expense of downgrading the philosophy of the latter to a sensualist philosophy that is inconsequential to such a point that it conserves within itself, and in spite of itself, the seeds of spiritualism. But in no case can the establishment of such a paternity be established in the opposite direction, in the sense that the seeds of Locke's sensualism were present in Descartes himself. The reference to Dugald Stewart can then be retained, but only on the condition of reversing its implications. Hence, Damiron comments on the essay of Bouillier:

> The lineage from Descartes to Spinoza, as also to Malebranche, is clearly felt, but much less when it comes to the lineage from Descartes to Locke himself. It is less deep. The proof is that if Spinoza and Malebranche separate themselves from their master, it is, as Leibniz says it, by pushing further the consequences of his doctrine and not by fighting against it. Locke, on the contrary, attacks him and presents himself as his adversary. This was thus a relation that ought to be known and well defined, and the author does this with discernment and exactitude. Under the double aspect that this relation presents, the most apparent and most common aspect is that of a difference. Therefore, he [i.e., Bouillier] has mainly focused on that of resemblance, being guided in this by D. Stewart, whom he carefully cites by the way, and whom he acknowledges as having been one of the first to take into account this aspect of Locke. Consequently, according to him, if Locke comes out of Descartes, it is in relation to the method, it is the mind, it is the psychological meaning.[26]

The lineage from Descartes to Malebranche is preserved by referring the ontological considerations of Malebranche toward another paternity (that of Plato), since they compromise the primacy of empirical psychology. At the same time, the bond between Descartes and Locke ends up breaking apart

26. Damiron (1846), vol. 1, 50.

under the pressure of bad tendencies, namely, the empirical tendencies freed from their reflexive correlate, which characterize the sensualist offspring of British philosophy. But these two phenomena are clearly related. It is because Malebranche has "shocked common sense" too much that Locke has "thrown himself into the opposite extremity. He opposes empiricism to idealism as a counterweight; he contests the vision of God that has been taken up by Norris, and his polemics against innate ideas has at least the merit of bringing philosophy back to experience."[27] Through this maneuver, the Cousinian school isolates a basic core common for Locke and Malebranche, namely, the core of psychology and its two dimensions, empirical and rational. But it is exactly here, on this shared terrain, that we can envisage a new recomposed family by taking our departure in, but also opposing, the Cousinians.

3. Malebranche and Locke: Twin Brothers

The first thing to note is a curious *rapprochement* between Descartes and Locke in relation to the critique of innate ideas. In Cousin's texts, the lineage connecting Locke to Descartes is established on the basis of Locke's own testimony: "The first books that gave Locke the taste for the study of philosophy were, as he tells it himself, those of Descartes." Therefore "Descartes has the honor and merit to have contributed to the education of his most formidable adversary," since he made Locke turn away from the Aristotelian scholasticism that dominated in Oxford at the time.[28] The same line of heritage is documented in the introduction to Cousin's edition of Descartes's *Oeuvres completes*, in the context of the edition of Antoine-Léonard Thomas's 1765 *Éloge de Descartes* that the introduction includes. We must consider for a moment the eminently strategic character of this famous text.[29] In the chapter of the *Histoire comparée des systèmes de philosophie* already quoted, i.e., the chapter dedicated to the way in which Locke inherits Bacon, Degérando quotes Thomas, and in particular the long footnote 5 of the *Éloge*.[30] In this note, Thomas criticizes

27. Cousin (2005), 3–4.

28. Cousin (1861), 45.

29. On this topic, see Ferret (2008), 1–19. In this article, we also learn that, according to Grimm, the success of the *Éloge de Descartes* by Thomas was so "prodigious" that the printer of the Academy ran out of copies on the first day of its publication.

30. Degérando (1804), vol. I, 374–75, note 1. In the original edition of the *Éloge*, the note is numbered 31 (cf. Thomas (1765), 111). The numeration changes in later editions of the *Éloge*. In the 1802 edition of Thomas's *Œuvres complètes*, which was probably the one Degérando used, the note he quotes as being note 5, however, still figures as number 31 (cf. Thomas (1802, 155–56).

the way in which Descartes had put into doubt the testimony of the senses—a doubt that according to Thomas resulted only from a confusion of the senses and the faculty of judgment—and Descartes's conception of innate ideas. In his edition of Thomas's text, however, Cousin simply omits this note, justifying this by means of a curious editorial principle:

> Here I reprint the notes from the *Éloge de Descartes*, while eliminating those containing only common and bombastic philosophy and also eliminating all the elements of bad taste that one frequently encounters in almost all of them. I have scrupulously conserved the entire biographical part, which adequately relates Descartes' character, habits and long career.[31]

In conjunction with this, one should consider how Cousin endorses Thomas's contention that it is the Cartesian mind-set that, in Locke, "combats and destroys the innate ideas."[32] The idea here is that Locke picked up the central part of the argument against the Cartesian innate ideas from Descartes himself, more precisely from the Cartesian rejection of substantial forms in relation to physics. Locke simply had to repeat Descartes's argument while extending its application to the soul, the remaining substantial form in Cartesianism. Locke thus revealed himself to be more Cartesian than Descartes, indeed being against but nonetheless beginning in Descartes. The victory is handed over to the opponent and Locke is transformed into an indebted philosopher.

As for Malebranche, he is criticized for having renounced innate ideas and the *cogito*. He has proven to be a very unfaithful disciple of Descartes,[33] because he has rejected the authority of consciousness by abandoning psychology and stripping the will of all authentic causal power. In the same way and for the same reasons as he has eliminated chimerical entities from the physical universe, Malebranche has also denied to the postlapsarian soul the possibility of knowing clearly and distinctly.

The same connection is thus at work in relation to the lineages: it is the critique of substantial forms in relation to physics that serves as the model for repudiating innate ideas and for what Cousin identifies as the expulsion of the soul from the field of philosophy.[34]

---

31. Cousin (1822–1826), vol. I, 81.

32. Cousin (1822–1826), vol. I, 55.

33. Cousin (1884), 8th Lesson, 415–18.

34. Damiron (1846), vol. I, 440.

The only way now left to preserve the distinction between a "good" and a "bad" heritage in Malebranche and Locke, despite the fact that they now clearly appear as twins, is to distinguish—somewhat desperately—between two different aims of similar argumentative complexes. Bordas-Demoulin writes in *Le Cartésianisme ou la véritable rénovation des sciences*:

> Even though [Locke] and Malebranche agree on denying our knowledge of ourselves, it is not for the same reason. Subdued to the imagination, which he brings with him everywhere, Locke persuades himself that thought proceeds by images and that it cannot attain what is beneath them. When he says that he would like for someone to teach him how the act of thinking takes place, he doubtless means that he would like someone to provide an image of it. Malebranche, on the contrary, is in favor of ideas. But he believes that they only exist in God and that it is in Him that we understand everything that we understand. And since we can only apperceive in God that which is eternal, such as mathematical truths or the principles of the true or the good, and that we cannot apperceive created substances in God, Malebranche ends up holding that since we do not see the soul in God, it is unknown to us. It is the spirit of systems that leads him astray, whereas in Locke, it is the subservience of sensation. The one turns his eyes away from a light that blinding him, the other does not see it. This is the reason why Malebranche, partly illuminated in spite of himself, is more prone to contradictions.[35]

The interpretive principle here consists in criticizing Locke by reference to Malebranche's analyses of the subservience of judgment to the sense and to the imagination in books I and II of *Recherche de la vérité*. Next, and conversely, it consists in criticizing Malebranche by reference to Locke's empiricist moderation. The "spirit of systems" and the "subservience of sensations" can then explain both the argumentative complex that Locke and Malebranche share and their opposed motivations, and moreover how it all originated in Descartes.

But the Cousinians do not end their analysis here. They become even more precise. Since the aim of these analyses is to promote a rational spiritualism

35. Bordas-Demoulin (1843), vol. I, 35–41, here 40–41.

based on empirical psychology, they must imperatively distinguish themselves from the philosophy of which Locke is the most eminent representative. Hence, Cousin argues, "among all the philosophical systems, empiricism is not the one most concerned with experience,"[36] because real experience is psychological experience. But in order for this interpretation to be acceptable, they must show that Locke himself did not escape the temptations of the "spirit of systems." Moreover, they must show that a work like the *Recherche de la vérité* "is one of our best works of experimental psychology."[37] Locke must thus be blamed for not having been empiricist enough and Malebranche for having been too empiricist. The first part of this enterprise will be undertaken by Cousin himself, the second by Damiron.

1. Cousin attempts to demonstrate that, in his examination of the soul, Locke has not followed the true experimental method, i.e., the method prevalent in the natural sciences, which proceeds by induction from the observation of phenomena to the consideration of the laws that govern them, and possibly also to the consideration of their nature. In order to show this, Cousin points out that Locke has posed the question of ideas before even observing them. When doing that, Locke adopted the spirit of geometry, and not that of experimental psychology. Instead of analyzing and observing, he deduced and presupposed. He also formulated "hypotheses" concerning the possibility of reducing thought to an attribute of matter. And such prejudices have in turn brought him to falsify the experience he thought he had of his soul. Finally, Locke elevated experience into a principle of knowledge rather than considering it the condition of knowledge. By doing this, Locke became responsible for the subsequent transformation of the "philosophy of sensation" into "gross sensualism."[38]

2. The principal feature of Malebranche's character pulls him in the exact opposite direction. He rejects psychological observation on systematic grounds (the soul strictly speaking cannot be known). But in practice, he has done this better than anyone.[39] Contrary to Locke, Malebranche did in fact begin by observing the soul as a phenomenon. Afterward, however,

36. Cousin (2005), 129.

37. Damiron (1846), Vol. I, 440.

38. Cousin (2005), 146. Cousin has Helvétius in mind.

39. According to Damiron, Malebranche's religious training was an advantage in this regard: "it is maybe even particularly easy to observe for someone like him who not only has the wisdom of the philosopher, but also that of the Christian, the priest, the monk, who is accustomed by the rules of his faith to these frequent exercises of self-reflection" (Damiron (1846), vol. I, 377).

> he became caught up in a dilemma that he failed to get out of: *Describing* what the soul knows about itself through interior sentiment can never amount to a conception of knowledge placing ideas and consciousness at its centre, i.e., it can never amount to an *explanation* of the soul.[40]

The Cousinian project is thus torn between, on the one hand, the requirement to represent the great factional battles in the history of philosophy and, on the other, the concern to respond adequately to their empirico-sensualist adversaries by underlining the tensions that each philosophy contains. The result of this—when correlated with the Cousinians' conception of the history of philosophy as cyclically recurring confrontations between brotherhoods present since Antiquity—is that the project finally turns against its own original intentions. The history of philosophy becomes the history of one big, unique family, where repudiations and adoptions constantly take place. By depriving the soul and nature as a whole of causal powers and by referring all causes to God, Malebranche, for example, finds himself as the "legitimate brother" of the "miserable Spinoza."[41]

At first sight, it seems that we should, as does Thomas M. Lennon in his impressive work,[42] structure the historiography of late seventeenth-century philosophy around the great battle of the Gods and giants. According to this narrative, Locke is placed along with Gassendi and his followers in opposition to Descartes and his primary representative, Malebranche. At the end of the day, however, it is the confusion of distinctions that dominates and this should prompt the historian of philosophy to rethink the criteria of classification. In Sophie Roux's recent article on Locke's investigation of Malebranche's theory of vision in God,[43] she discusses some recent interpretations of the chapter "On Enthusiasm" in Locke's *Essay concerning Human Understanding* (IV, XIX), which was added to the fourth edition from 1700. According to

40. See in particular Damiron (1846), vol. I, 408: "This is Malebranche who by right, if not in fact, and in virtue of his maxim if not in practice, leaves psychology for ontology in a matter which nonetheless is essentially psychological, and who leaves observation for reasoning, or rather hypothesizing, and here pays for the error that he previously made when saying that we have no clear knowledge through interior sentiment, i.e. through consciousness. And what makes his embarrassment even bigger is the fact that he at the same time has said that we have no idea of the soul. But if the idea of the soul is missing and consciousness is in a state of confusion, how can we know anything about a thing which cannot be known except through consciousness and though an idea?"

41. Damiron (1846), vol. I, 520 and 596.

42. See Lennon (1993).

43. See Roux (2012).

Thomas Lennon, this chapter was written against Malebranche. According to Nicolas Jolley,[44] on the contrary, Locke was mainly trying to avoid being associated with Protestant sects. If, however, we go behind these two competing hypotheses, it becomes clear that what is at stake is the way in which our preconceptions of the relations between different philosophies determine the understanding of those philosophies themselves in their common history. Similarly, the more one insists on the antagonism between Malebranche and Locke, the less one is sensitive to the elements in Malebranche that bring him closer to Gassendi. On the contrary, the closer one investigates the use Malebranche actually makes in his philosophy of elements coming from Gassendi to describe the condition of the fallen soul, the more one becomes sensitive to the aspects of Malebranche that on the theoretical level place him closer to Locke on the genealogical tree of epistemology. This insight, moreover, has bearing on the evaluation of the arguments that Locke developed against Malebranche's theory of vision in God. On the more general level, such a change of perspective prompts us to reconsider the history of Cartesian philosophy in its entirety and to avoid caricatures of the philosophy of Descartes. Hence, as Cousin himself writes, "if the glory of Descartes is to have replaced the abstract concepts of the Schools with a living principle gathered at the source of the most intimate observation," it still remains that "he doesn't always stick to it, and the old logic often takes over again."[45] No matter from which perspective one considers them, Descartes's texts still contain different elements that are developed further by the "Cartesians" in contrasting ways.

The various criticisms that the Cousinians develop about the inadequacies of the works they study can provide us with a positive interpretive framework that is different if not outright opposed to their own, but which they nonetheless noticed and thematized very well. For example, when Cousin deplores the affinities between the theories of the soul of Malebranche and of Gassendi or Locke, it allows us to understand how it was possible for the work of the Oratorian to become a major support for the radical Enlighteners. This discovery may in turn contribute to the reinterpretation of the so-called Radical Enlightenment, until now understood through the sole figure of Spinoza.[46] It can lead us to reconsider how Malebranche recycled Gassendi's rejection of any ontological conception of knowledge and his corresponding endorsement of

44. See Jolley (2003), 179–91.

45. Cousin (2005), 3.

46. See Israel (2001).

a kind of phenomenalism, even though Malebranche appropriated Gassendi's rejection more positively as part of what he considered to be the only possible adequate description of the fallen man's condition.[47] Malebranche's rejection of the claim that we have clear and distinct knowledge of the soul can no longer be read simply negatively as the rejection of a fundamental principle of Cartesianism (i.e., the *cogito*). For this rejection is transformed into something positive through the revival of an empiricist theory that has been called for by the human condition. When Gassendi is no longer just envisaged as a simple adversary, he become a means for correcting Descartes and for grounding a form of Cartesianism that is more coherent and fits experience better. In an even broader perspective, it will lead us to reconsider the role of Cartesianism in the secularization of the soul that characterizes an entire strand of the Enlightenment, by building on the pioneering study of Diderot by Aram Vartanian,[48] or by looking into the works of someone like Maupertuis or d'Alembert.

Since Cousinianism is not construed in opposition to empiricism but in a constant critical dialogue with it, it will eventually also allow us to reevaluate Descartes himself. It allows us to recognize different tendencies in his texts that give rise to a whole spectrum of interpretations and possible objections. Moreover, it allows us to understand the way in which he chose to organize them hierarchically or even abandon some of them in response to the objections made against him. Take, for example, Dutch Cartesianism. When reporting on the essays written for the 1839 *Concours*, Damiron deplores, probably following Cousin's advice, the absence of any deeper developments of this question. He himself begins working on it in his *Essai sur l'histoire de la philosophie au dix-septième siècle*, in order to promote figures like Tobias Andreae and Johannes Clauberg and stigmatize someone like Regius whom he depicts as a metaphysical dissident and as nothing more than a copyist in relation to physics. When doing this, he displayed strong uneasiness with analyses such as those proposed by Renouvier who, in his *Manuel de philosophie moderne*,[49] underlined the existence of a Cartesian materialism among the philosophers who were also medical doctors, including Regius, La Mettrie, and Cabanis. The best proof that Renouvier's argument proved useful for the school opposed to

47. See Kolesnik-Antoine (2011); Kolesnik-Antoine (2012); Kolesnik-Antoine (2013a); Kolesnik-Antoine (2013b).

48. See Vartanian (1975).

49. This is the reworked text of the essay that Renouvier presented at the 1839 *Concours*. It was published in 1842.

the Cousinians is that it was taken up by Marx in *Die heilige Familie* (1844),[50] although Marx of course evaluated it differently from Renouvier, making it a question of reappraising and rehabilitating Cartesian materialism. From this, one sees that the isolated study of a single author (in this case, Regius) can have vast consequences, on the one hand, for our interpretation of the characteristics and the tendencies that one privileges when defining a philosophical current that we take an interest in (in this case Cartesianism), and, on the other hand, the field of vision that such an interpretive prism can open or conceal with regard to our conception of the history of philosophy in its entirety.

Let us take one last example. In one of the volumes of *La Décade*, we find a text by Destutt de Tracy where he extols the "Lockian" merits of Regius's metaphysics and deplores the exceptional oblivion of it in the history of Cartesian ideas.[51] This prompts us to follow the investigation all the way back to Descartes himself and analyze the modalities and theoretical stakes of the public construction of the Regis as a "dissident" figure, beginning with the publication of the *Fundamenta Physices* from 1646. What is a stake here is what kind of empiricism can or cannot be qualified as "Cartesian." On this point, we could turn to Johann de Castillon who, on May 31, 1770, at the Berlin Academy, proposed to "reconcile" Descartes and Locke while distancing himself from those "benign interpretations that make an author say everything one wants him to say." For, he argued, when taking a closer look at what kind of innate ideas each of these authors in fact reject, the origin of this misunderstanding becomes clear: "From where does the opposition habitually seen between them come? It comes from their disciples who, by extrapolating on the doctrine of their masters have managed to make them say the contrary of what they have said."[52] It is far from insignificant to note that this text constitutes a prime witness for Degérando and also became a reference for Bouillier when he began to elaborate his own position independent from Cousin's.

How does Bouillier proceed? We should take a look at chapter V in the first volume of the *Histoire de la philosophie cartesienne*.[53] The passage we are

---

50. See Marx (1845). See also Bloch (1997) for a precise study of the intertextual relationship between Marx and Renouvier.

51. See Destutt de Tracy (2003 [1806]), 411–412. I am grateful to Josiane Boulad-Ayoub for having brought this text to my attention. I am also grateful to François Duchesneau for having given me the possibility to explore in more detail the lineage Regius-Locke during my stay at the UQAM in October 2010. Destutt de Tracy's text can also be found in appendix to Boulad-Ayoub and Vernes (2006), 259–267.

52. De Castillon (1770), 277–282.

53. See Bouillier (1854), vol. V, 97.

interested in begins by a classic Cousinian attempt to defend Descartes, by discarding the ridiculous interpretation that most of his adversaries, and most importantly Regius, the "unfaithful disciple," proposed of the notion of innate ideas. Descartes's own response to Regius is first quoted.[54] However, as a follow-up, Bouillier underlines how the Cartesian doctrine of ideas is too "empirical." By presenting ideas "as the simple products of particular faculty of our mind and of our own nature, [this doctrine] seems to reduce them to simple modes of our thought and to ignore the divine source from which they propagate in our minds."[55] The important point is thus that, in this text, Regius's "infidelity" is not given *a priori*. His interpretation of Descartes is on the contrary given as a possible one. And it is only once Descartes has responded to the objections formulated by Regius in the *Placard* from 1647, i.e., when Descartes himself blocks this possible interpretation, that Descartes's ideas appears in their singularity in relation to Regius. By stressing this point, Bouillier highlights the important role Descartes himself played in the genesis of the spiritualist interpretation of his writings. But at the same time he opens up Descartes's texts to other possible readings that are just as legitimate when writing the history of philosophy because they are equally grounded in precise textual facts.

Bouillier's argument ends with a reference to the text by Castillon who "reconciles" Descartes and Locke. Hence, taking his point of departure as a Regius "à la Damiron," Bouillier has managed to establish a line of heritage that links a too empirical Descartes to the two canonical representatives of this strand of Cartesianism in the Netherlands and in England, namely, Regius and Locke. The lineage going from Regius to Gassendi to Locke, which was identified by the spiritualists as belonging to the clan opposed to Cartesianism, thus immediately resurfaces when one, as a historian of philosophy who is careful not to caricaturize the textual facts relied on, becomes attentive to the interpretive possibilities of Descartes's texts that only polemical and public interpretations prompted Descartes to close off (and this only sometimes, and not always). In the "wars of mind and reason" where the different "clans" of philosophy confront each other, the only weapons permitted then really are the works alone and the ways one writes their history, that is to say, how one tells their story.

54. See Garnier (1835), vol. IV, 85.

55. Ibid., 85.

4. *Conclusion*

Earlier I asked whether one could not envisage the history of philosophy as a family affair. One could answer the question by reminding the reader that, generally, a child described by the father's part of the family resembles the father, while it has the features of the mother when seen through the eyes of the mother's family. The child more or less possesses the qualities or faults of its father or those of its mother, following the clan describing it. And each new union engenders offspring that have, in certain ways and following specific proportions, family resemblances with the parents and their parents, with their cousins, their uncles and aunts or with their half-brothers and sisters. A child does, however, always end up individualizing itself, surprising those who are observing it, and thus finally does not resemble anybody but itself in the initiatives it takes or in the characteristics it has.

It is in a certain way the same with the philosophical systems studied by the historian of philosophy. If one sees the primary quality of the father, Descartes, to be a kind of subjectivism which closes itself up in abstractions and an ontological dualism of substances, and one considers his essential work to be the *Méditations métaphysiques* and the *Discours de la méthode*, excluding the *Essais*, in that case one will have difficulties seeing how all the bastard followers who endorse phenomenalist conceptions of the knowledge of both body and soul are affiliated with the Cartesian dynasty. Careful readers of *Le Monde*, *L'Homme*, of the *Principes de la philosophie*, the *Passions de l'âme* and, more generally, of polemical texts such as the *Disquisitio Metaphysica*, all the various texts that compose the dossier of the *Utrecht Controversy*, or certain parts of the correspondence—all these texts are immediately affiliated with a hidden empiricist mother whose identity one would prefer not to divulge and that one would happily reduce to the position of a maiden servant. But it is history, biographical this time, that will tell us: from a maybe hidden relation with his maiden servant, Descartes had a girl. She did not live for very long. But she still remains the only certified descendant of the philosopher.

9

The Taming of Philosophy

Michael Della Rocca

Philosophers' uncritical talk of philosophy as relying, for better or worse, on "intuitions" often manifests the misconception that our evidence in philosophy consists of psychological facts about ourselves rather than facts about the philosophical topic itself.

TIMOTHY WILLIAMSON[1]

I am not to be moved here by the charge of an insult offered to Common Sense. For not only in speculation, but in life, we must all be ready to affront that which somewhere, perhaps, in the name of Common Sense may claim our respect.... Common Sense taken ... at its worst, is in its essence a one-sidedness, which we must not be afraid to mark as stupid or even, perhaps, to denounce as immoral.

F. H. BRADLEY[2]

Don't mistake the fact that you don't like my view for an argument against it.

MICHAEL DELLA ROCCA EPIGRAPH TO THIS CHAPTER.

1. Introduction

RECENTLY—OVER THE LAST 100 years or so—something that might be called the method of intuition (hereafter the MI) has been widespread and even dominant in philosophy.[3] I will characterize this method more fully soon,

1. In Hendricks and Symons (2005), 222.

2. Bradley (1935), 640.

3. It is, perhaps, a manifestation of the length of philosophy's history and of the significance of this history to philosophy itself that the "recent" past can cover a period of more than a century.

but for a first pass, we might say that the MI is the method whereby intuitive responses (often to particular more-or-less well-described cases or examples) are central to one's philosophical theorizing: the—or an—aim of this theorizing is to arrive at an overarching theory that somehow "accommodates" these intuitive responses as well as possible. The so-called intuitions may originate in so-called common sense or be expressed in so-called ordinary language or be the result of, perhaps, a more refined, philosophical reflection or seeing, but, on any of these construals of intuitions, the—or a—goal of philosophy is often to accommodate these intuitions, to formulate a theory that somehow "respects" them and does not "ride roughshod" over them. This is the method in one way or another, and, to some extent or another, of many of my (and, I venture to say, your) favorite philosophers: e.g., Lewis, Sider, Kripke, Kamm, Nagel, Chisholm, Thomson, Fine, Moore, Putnam, van Inwagen, Schaffer, Rawls, and many, many others.

This kind of reliance on intuition has not always been as prominent in philosophy as it has been recently. Although there were, of course, prior to the twentieth century, philosophers who were more or less subservient in their philosophy to intuition and, in some cases, to common sense, and although, as I acknowledge, one can find elements of the MI in just about any historical philosopher, nonetheless, with the twentieth century and with the rise of analytical philosophy—and for reasons that we will begin to explore later—intuition came to dominate philosophy to, perhaps, a greater extent than previously. Before the twentieth century it is much easier to find philosophers—such as, in reverse chronological order, Bradley, Nietzsche, Hume, Leibniz, and (did I say?) Spinoza —who seem to be able to do philosophy without continually looking over their shoulders to check that their delicate intuitions continue to thrive in the hothouse of philosophical reflection. These philosophers and many other historical figures do not assume that their own philosophical views have to accommodate intuitions—which are, after all, facts about our psychology, our ways of thinking of the world—but instead tend to focus more directly than do more dedicated practitioners of the MI on the generally non-psychological subjects with which they are engaged. None of these philosophers, perhaps, turns his back entirely on the MI, and in recent philosophy one can find philosophers less concerned than some others with intuitions, but the general differences between recent and not-so-recent philosophy are striking.

These sweeping claims lead to the two questions that will guide me throughout this chapter: "Is it good?" and "Why now?" More subtly: in what respects is the MI to be applauded and in what respects is it to be criticized?

And why has the MI become so popular recently? I should say at the outset that I will be very critical of the MI, and perhaps as important as the challenge I make to the MI is the fact that my answers to the two guiding questions are, surprisingly, closely intertwined. The historical story I tell near the end of the chapter will help us to understand what is wrong with the MI and will clear the way for our appreciation of an alternative to the MI. Here the assiduously neglected F. H. Bradley will be pivotal to our discussion, for not only does he straddle the nineteenth and twentieth centuries and not only is he a particularly clear example of one who rejects the MI, but it is also this example that—in a negative fashion—provided much of the impetus for the ascendancy of the MI.

The story that I will tell and the assessment that I will offer are, I'm sure, skewed in important ways (I can already hear the complaints!), but this slant also provides, I believe, a provocative and needed challenge not only to certain ways of doing philosophy but also perhaps to philosophy itself.

2. *Characterizing the Method of Intuition and Its Alternatives*

Let us begin more modestly than we will end by offering a fuller characterization of the MI and of its varieties. A focal point of the MI consists of certain attitudes—intuitions—toward cases or phenomena. These intuitions concern whether such-and-such is a case of knowledge, causation, intentional action, free action, good or bad or right or wrong action, etc. Think Gettier cases, Frankfurt-style cases, trolley problems, etc. Discussions of such cases or intuitions about them have been for many years and continue to be a staple—or the staple—of the diet of many philosophers.

Often these intuitions are regarded as ordinary beliefs or as expressions of common sense (whatever that is) or as evident in the workings of ordinary language (whatever that is). This is true, e.g., of Moore, Lewis, Sider, etc., who, as we will see, make it at least part of their mission to account for ordinary beliefs. Some philosophers (e.g., Bealer) do not regard intuitions as beliefs but rather as an epistemically privileged kind of seeing or insight. The difference between the ordinary and what might be called the more refined MI is, for the most part, not relevant to my chapter. As we'll see, the criticisms I make of the MI apply in one form or another to both the ordinary and the refined MI.

For practitioners of what I am calling the MI, such intuitions often play a crucial role in constructing an overarching theory that "accommodates" such intuitions. As we'll see, the goal of such practitioners of the MI is to put intuitive responses to cases in touch with often extra-intuitive principles by means of which we can codify, generalize upon, and perhaps explain these intuitive responses.

Some philosophers, of course, eschew—on philosophical grounds—any such use of general principles. Although such philosophers reject philosophical theorizing of the generalizing sort, they nonetheless and obviously accord our intuitions a central role in whatever philosophical accounts they offer in a given domain. A prime example of such theorists are the so-called moral particularists.[4] But we can also at least conceive of similarly particularist approaches in other areas such as metaphysics or epistemology.[5] Because particularist and non-particularist purveyors of the MI each give intuitions (though in different ways) a central role in their theorizing, they will each be subject to the kinds of critiques I make against the MI.

Finally, the MI need not be focused just on intuitions about cases. One may also appeal directly to intuitions about general principles, i.e., principles that would apply to or explain a range of cases. But intuitions about cases are usually thought to be stronger than, and thus to enjoy primacy over, intuitions about general principles.[6] Whether or not this is the case, I will continue to focus on intuitions about cases. This is because such intuitions are more often discussed and because the criticisms I make concerning the version of the MI that focuses on intuitions about cases will apply to the more general version of the MI that concerns intuitions about principles as well as about cases.

The criticisms of the MI that I will offer thus all turn on the interplay between intuitions about cases, on the one hand, and principles (often, though not always, extra-intuitive principles) that are to "accommodate" such cases, on the other. Let's ask then: what kinds of interaction between principles and intuitions about cases are possible? There are three basic possibilities:

1. The first version of the MI, alluded to already, relies on intuitions about cases and dispenses entirely with principles that might govern these cases. Moral particularism would fall into this category. Intuitions about different cases are allowed to stand and are not seen as in need of buttressing by general principles that might explain how the cases about which we have intuitions are related.

---

4. See Dancy (in the *Stanford Encyclopedia*) and the essays in Hooker and Little (2000).

5. Anscombe espouses a view that might be called "causal particularism." See Anscombe (1971).

6. See McMahan (2000); Bealer (1992), 104; Bealer (1998), 205; Kagan, (2001), 46, 60.

(2) The second version of the MI is more generous than the first when it comes to principles: this version of the MI allows that there are general principles and so there can be, e.g., an overarching moral theory, but on this view, the principles are completely subservient to intuitions about cases. No principle can dictate that an intuition be revised or given up; instead the principles are completely grounded in the intuitions and any principle that conflicts with any intuition must therefore be given up. I doubt that any philosopher holds this excessively rigid view about the interplay between intuitions and principles. Indeed, it's not clear that such a view would be coherent: principles that are, as on this view, completely grounded in intuitions and have no power over intuitions might not qualify as *principles* that *govern* particular cases.

(3) The first two versions of the MI are, in different ways, inflexible when it comes to the interplay between intuitions and principles. It's in part because of its hallowed flexibility that the third version of the MI is so popular and is, perhaps, the predominant method at work in philosophy.[7] On this view, although intuitions are in *a* driver's seat and are owed *some* deference, they are not in the only driver's seat. Thus they are subject to revision and reconstrual when they conflict with well-supported principles. There is, for the method of reflective equilibrium (hereafter MRE) thus a reasonable and, one might say, fair distribution of weight between intuitions and principles: each has some, but not total, power over the other. Intuitions about cases can lead us to reject certain principles or certain proposed principles that conflict with those intuitions *and* principles can, in certain cases lead us to reject intuitions that cannot be accommodated by the principles. The intuitions are especially likely to be given up or at least modified in a case in which there is a plausible explanation of the fact that we were initially inclined to endorse the intuition.

The MRE was, perhaps, first made explicit—though not given its name—by Nelson Goodman in his discussion of the justification of deductive and inductive reasoning:

> [R]ules and particular inferences alike are justified by being brought into agreement with each other. *A rule is amended if it yields an inference we are unwilling to accept; an inference is rejected if it violates a rule we are unwilling to amend.* The process of justification is the delicate one of making mutual adjustments between rules and accepted inferences.[8]

7. DePaul (1998), 294.

8. Goodman (1983), 64; emphasis in the original.

Around the same time, John Rawls described the method in his 1951 paper, "Outline of a Decision Procedure for Ethics," and he later gave the method its name and elaborated it in *A Theory of Justice*.[9] Rawls speaks mostly not of intuitions but of our "considered judgments" "against which conjectured principles can be checked"[10] in a "process of mutual adjustment."[11]

To see the reach of the MRE, I'll point out just two examples of philosophers far removed from moral and political philosophy who nonetheless espouse this method. Thus, take David Lewis whose work has been preeminent in metaphysics and other areas. Lewis says, "a reasonable goal for a philosopher is to bring them [our intuitions] into equilibrium.... If we lose our moorings in common sense ... the trouble is that we settle for a very inadequate equilibrium."[12] Notice that Lewis, a philosopher who espouses such radical views as modal realism, counterpart theory, and perdurantism, nonetheless sees his positions as based securely in intuitions and ordinary beliefs, and he sees as his goal the establishment of a stable equilibrium. Lewis doesn't mention Rawls here, but it's clear that he means to call the Rawlsian approach to mind.

Ted Sider—another metaphysician—articulates a methodology very much in the same vein and emphasizes the accommodation of ordinary beliefs: "One ... develops a theory preserving as many of these ordinary beliefs as possible, while remaining consistent with science."[13] I'll return to these passages from Lewis and Sider.

I suspect that many versions of experimental philosophy fall within the general MRE camp. Experimental philosophy typically investigates and critiques our intuitions understood as ordinary beliefs (to see which intuitions are worth keeping) and seeks, upon that basis, to come up with principles.[14] Such accommodation of intuitions—at least of some kind—is also the goal of the MI.

George Bealer's view is not a version of MRE for Bealer, unlike Lewis, Sider, Rawls, and others, does not begin with ordinary beliefs but rather with

9. Cf. Rawls (1971). In light of the equitable distribution of weight between intuitions and principles, it is not a coincidence that this inherently fair method should be most prominently developed by the thinker who introduced the notion of justice as fairness.

10. Rawls (1951), 51.

11. Ibid., 20n.

12. Lewis (1983), x.

13. Sider (2001), xv–xvi.

14. See Alexander, Mallon, and Weinberg (2010).

a quasi-perceptual state of seeing. Nonetheless, because Bealer recognizes that even intuitions in his sense are fallible, intuitions may need to be rejected in order to accommodate principles or other intuitions.[15] In this respect, i.e., because of the mutual accommodation between intuitions and principles in his system, even Bealer's methodology resembles a version of MRE.

The versions of the MI just discussed exhaust the ways in which one may give deference (of some kind) to intuitions (of some kind) with regard to principles (of some kind). There are, of course, other ways for intuitions and principles to interact, but because these other ways put principles, as it were, in sole occupation of the driver's seat and leave no room for intuitions to determine our philosophical theories, these other ways do not count as versions of the MI. I would like to describe these other kinds of interactions briefly in part because their implausibility makes some version of the MI seem almost inevitable and in part because we may nonetheless in the end have no choice but to see whether we can avail ourselves of some version of these methods that are opposed to the MI.

> (4) The first alternative to the MI is, in effect, the flip side of (2): instead of appealing to intuitions that completely determine principles (as in (2)), according to (4) principles completely determine intuitions. That is, according to (4), if an intuition about a case conflicts with a principle we accept, the intuition must be given up. This view may not be incoherent in the way that (2) is, for there is nothing in principle wrong with principles totally governing intuitions about cases, but this view seems as inflexible as (2) and, more important, it seems highly implausible for reasons I will get to in a moment.
>
> (5) Finally, there's the view according to which principles totally dictate our philosophical theories and intuitions play no role. The intuitions play no role, not because, as in (4), the intuitions must cave in, as it were, to the principles we accept, but because even if there are intuitions, we should just ignore them in the formulation of our philosophical theories.

Does anyone endorse either (4) or (5)? I venture to say that there is not one straightforward example of a philosopher—present or past—who does so, and, as I indicated, this is especially the case among contemporary philosophers who in one way or another tend to adopt the MI. Partly for purposes of illustration and partly also because these philosophers will play a brief but important role at the end of the chapter, let me say a few words about three historical figures: Spinoza, Leibniz, and Hume. Each of these three (and there are, of

15. The fallibility of intuitions is discussed in Bealer (1992), 102, 104; Bealer (2002), 202.

course, others) seems to have little concern for accommodating common sense and seems relatively uninterested in focusing on intuitions as such. Instead, each of these philosophers is most directly concerned not with our intuitions but rather with uncovering reality itself. Intuitions as such are more or less not a focus for these philosophers. Rather, these philosophers (and others) tend to train their gaze on reality itself and their means of doing so consist of certain principles in terms of which they structure their philosophical systems.

Thus Spinoza builds his system around the Principle of Sufficient Reason (hereafter the PSR), the principle according to which each thing that exists has an explanation or is intelligible.[16] Spinoza follows this principle where it leads, regardless of whether he winds up at a place far from common sense, and with nary a glance at our intuitions as providing evidence for the theory constructed.[17]

To say that Spinoza doesn't invoke intuition as evidence for his philosophical positions is not to deny that Spinoza has rich things to say about intuitions. Indeed, for Spinoza, intuitive knowledge—i.e., knowledge of the so-called third kind—is, in some sense, the highest form of knowledge and is infallible, unlike intuitions as they are typically regarded in contemporary philosophy. My point here, though, is that Spinoza does not have as his focus the construction of a system that accommodates such intuitions; rather, what Spinoza seems more interested in accommodating is reality itself, not our intuitive thoughts about reality.

Unlike Spinoza who structures his system around one great principle (the PSR), Leibniz structures his system around two: the PSR and the Principle of Non-Contradiction (*Monadology* §§31–32). Of course, Spinoza relies on the Principle of Non-Contradiction too, but he, unlike Leibniz, does not see the PNC as independent of the PSR.[18] Employing these principles (and derivative principles such as the Principle of Continuity and the Predicate-in-Subject Principle), Leibniz arrives at shocking conclusions far from common sense. Leibniz is more concerned than Spinoza is to preserve at least some ordinary beliefs and to show how his system enables us to preserve much of what we ordinarily want to say about the world. Still, Leibniz is little concerned with making intuitions, as such, focal points in his philosophy.

---

16. See Spinoza (1994), especially Part 1, Proposition 11, Second demonstration: "For each thing there must be assigned a cause, or reason, both for its existence and for its nonexistence."

17. I have developed such a PSR-oriented conception of Spinoza's system in Della Rocca (2008).

18. See Della Rocca (2008), 276–77.

Hume is another example of a philosopher who structures his system with little attention to intuitions. Tracking down Hume's motivations and guiding principles is always a fraught matter; nonetheless, I think it is clear that, on the strength of such principles as the separability principle (according to which distinct things are separable) and the copy principle (according to which all of our ideas or thoughts derive in some fashion from experience), Hume is able to build a vast philosophical edifice that—explicitly and radically—is little concerned with common sense, except by way of pointing out that his system departs from common sense on a number of matters and by way of explaining that common sense exerts a powerful hold over our beliefs despite the force of Hume's philosophical arguments. Not even more refined intuitions are Hume's focus in his philosophical theorizing. Rather, Hume concentrates on the structure of the world and on the status of our beliefs about the world without specifically trying much to accommodate our intuitions.

Because of their distance from common sense and because they do not feel the need to consult their intuitions constantly, such philosophers may seem to reject the MI. However, even in these cases, the power of the MI is strong. Although Spinoza and company may not regularly consult their intuitions, still, such checking-in may play a crucial role in their systems, for on what basis do they start with their fundamental principles, unless they are, at some point, consulting their intuitions about these principles or about the cases governed by these principles? Further, the mere fact that each of these philosophers structures his system around principles that do not completely overlap with, and may even be incompatible with, the principles to which other philosophers give pride of place suggests that there may be some other basis besides simply reality itself on which these philosophers are relying. And here we might see an opening for the importance of intuition even in Spinoza, Leibniz, and Hume.[19]

Indeed, in this light, one may come to suspect that some version of the MI is inevitable. Without the ballast apparently provided by intuitions, what legitimate basis could one have for starting with whatever starting points one starts with? Philosophy that gives sole weight to principles as opposed to intuitions seems to be philosophy without moorings, philosophy in danger of listing dangerously from side to side, a philosophy plagued by what Lewis calls

19. Similarly, contemporary philosophers who are hostile to the MI may not coherently carry out their philosophy in an intuition-free way. I am thinking here, e.g., of Williamson who raises some important challenges to the MI. However, his positive endeavor to pursue philosophy without adverting to intuitions is unsuccessful. I hope to explore the reasons for this assessment elsewhere.

"an unstable equilibrium." For this reason, the MI, in one form or another, may come to seem inevitable, and, while Spinoza, Leibniz, and Hume may have, to some extent, freed themselves from overt appeal to intuition, nonetheless, they too must, it seems, at some level be beholden to intuitions.

This apparent inevitability of the MI only serves to make it all the more troubling that there are, as I will now explain, deep objections to the MI. By considering these objections, we will be led to a vision of how it may be possible, after all, at least to approximate a way of doing philosophy that is free of the MI.

I will thus now elicit three related difficulties with the MI, each of which is an instance of what I call the taming of philosophy, i.e., of philosophy's arbitrary limitation of its engagement with reality. These difficulties will enable me to answer the first guiding question—Is the MI good?—in the negative, and they will also lay the groundwork for the historical considerations I will invoke to answer the second guiding question—Why did the MI become so popular?

3. Is It Good? Taming and Conservatism

A standard objection to the MI in general and to the MRE in particular—though as we will see, an objection that is, in some respects, unfair—is that such a method is too conservative: it doesn't allow for the radical changes in beliefs that are sometimes required by the aspect of reality that one is investigating. The charge is that proponents of this method privilege certain starting points that are not worthy of such privileging. And the worry is that with such unjustified starting points, the whole edifice that one erects is rendered arbitrary.

This criticism is more obviously appropriate when directed against a version of the MI that privileges ordinary, commonsense beliefs. Ordinary beliefs are just ordinary, after all. Why should they get any special treatment and constrain where we wind up in our philosophical investigations? Reality may demand radical revision in our beliefs, and if we are beholden to common sense, then it may be unjustifiably difficult to make the required changes.

Such conservative—and, I think, ultimately, arbitrary—fealty to common sense is widespread in philosophy, particularly over the last 100 years, though also among certain historical figures. Thus let me just mention Berkeley and Moore as explicit proponents of commonsense philosophy who are, I believe, vulnerable to this charge of arbitrary conservatism. But let me also highlight two widely admired contemporary philosophers who, surprisingly perhaps, are subject to the same criticism. Thus consider one of Sider's methodological musings, part of which was quoted earlier:

> One approaches metaphysical inquiry with a number of beliefs. Many of these will not trace back to empirical beliefs, at least not in any direct way. These beliefs may be particular, as for example the belief that I was once a young boy, or they may be more general and theoretical, for example the belief that identity is transitive. One then develops a theory preserving as many of these ordinary beliefs as possible, while remaining consistent with science.[20]

This is an extremely conservative methodology: one may depart from ordinary beliefs, but one must not go too far; one must always return to common sense as much as possible.

Lewis gives expression to a very similar methodology. On Lewis's view (as well as Sider's apparently) one may "give up" an intuition or ordinary belief, but in order to do so one must first show how such giving up enables one to hold onto many other ordinary beliefs and to do so within a stable system of beliefs. Lewis's methodology, like Sider's, is obviously and deeply conservative. Even the most apparently exotic views, according to this methodology shared by Lewis and Sider and many others, must in the end return home and be grounded in common sense.

An explicitly and similarly conservative view (focusing on the nature of perception in particular) is embraced by James Pryor:

> [W]e start with what it seems intuitively natural to say about perception, and we retain that natural view until we find objections that require us to abandon it. This is just sensible philosophical conservatism.[21]

To point out this conservatism is not yet to criticize Lewis et al., but the criticism is not far behind, for the worry is that this privileging of ordinary beliefs is arbitrary and unjustified. Yes, it may feel good to return home to the comfort of familiar beliefs, but not all homes are worth returning to. Many of our ordinary beliefs are the products of less than reputable sources, e.g., in the case of moral opinions such as judgments that, as Peter Singer puts it,

20. Sider (2001), xv–xvi.

21. Pryor (2000), 538.

"derive from discarded religious systems, from warped views of sex and bodily functions, or from customs necessary for the survival of the group in social and economic conditions that now lie in the distant past."[22] Without a good reason for requiring a return to commonsense beliefs, a philosophy generated by this methodology seems inevitably arbitrary.

The arbitrariness is not removed by pointing out, as Lewis does, that a philosophy not anchored in common sense is unstable. This may be so, but that doesn't mean that the comforts of stability and common sense are reliably connected to the truth. It's not clear what the bearing of stability is on our grasping of reality.

The charge of unjustified conservatism has often been leveled at Rawls's MRE. Indeed, the charge by Singer recently quoted is directed against Rawls. But here the criticism is not as clearly on target, and that is because Rawls is not as beholden to common sense as philosophers such as Sider and Lewis are. Rawls can go some distance toward rebutting the charge of conservatism (and thus of arbitrariness) by pointing out, first, that the opinions about cases which he accords weight in the process of achieving reflective equilibrium are not just any judgments but our "considered judgments." Further, and especially after the original edition of *A Theory of Justice*, Rawls stresses that the kind of reflective equilibrium he has in mind is the "wide" variety according to which in one's deliberations one brings to bear not just considered judgments about cases but also background facts concerning persons and morality. Such further theoretical background may provide more room for criticism and revision of ordinary beliefs and of considered judgments.[23]

Bealer, also a proponent of the MI, like Rawls does not give pride of place to common sense or ordinary beliefs.[24] Indeed, as we saw, Bealer's focus is not on beliefs at all, but on what he sees as the kind of just seeing that is constitutive of intuitions. Because—in these different ways—they do not dwell on common sense, both Bealer and Rawls may be able to rebut (at least initially) the charge of undue conservatism or undue reliance on existing beliefs.

Nonetheless, even if they rely on intuitions of some kind which may—in different ways—be remote from common sense, both Bealer and Rawls may still face a charge of undue privileging of certain states or graspings over others. For we can ask: why should intuitions in Bealer's sense or considered

22. Singer (1974), 516.

23. See Rawls (1974–75), 7–8.

24. Bealer (1992) 103–4; (1998), 211.

judgments in Rawls's sense be our starting points or focal points?[25] It may be that reality requires a sharper, more radical departure from even our refined intuitions or considered judgments which are, as Bealer and presumably Rawls admit, fallible. There is no reason to think antecedently that we are more likely to arrive at the truth by attuning our theories to fallible intuitions—of whatever kind—than by adopting some other, extra-intuitive starting point.[26] Thus the method of refined intuition or of considered judgments in wide reflective equilibrium, just like the MI generally, may be too conservative in blocking or hampering the kind of departure from our beliefs that may be required in order to reach the truth. Thus this method may—just like the MI generally—arbitrarily treat certain starting points or focal points as good.

This closing off of certain radical options, this arbitrary limitation of one's philosophical perspective that is characteristic of the MI is what I call the taming of philosophy. The taming of philosophy in general is the ungrounded limitation of philosophy's engagement with reality, a limitation that narrows one's perspective on the world, may preclude the possibility of overturning our existing convictions, and may unjustifiably shut us off from exotic, unusual views. We will see shortly two other manifestations of this taming that the MI ushers on stage.

Of course, as I noted in the previous section, without appealing to intuitions there may be no reason for starting at whatever point one starts at in philosophical inquiry. Thus damned if you do (appeal to intuitions), damned if you don't. Or, more specifically, arbitrary if you do appeal to intuitions, arbitrary if you don't. This may be so, but even if it is, then this would merely go to support the skeptical claim that whether or not one relies on intuitions, one has no principled or justified starting point. But then as I am fond of saying in my skeptical way: so much the worse for us. The fact (if it is a fact) that any other starting point besides intuition is equally arbitrary doesn't mitigate the fact that starting with one's intuitions (of one kind or another) is itself arbitrary. Yes, it would be nice for us to have non-arbitrary starting points, but if we don't we don't, and no amount of wishing or of pinning one's hopes on intuitions or considered judgments will make it so.

So the first criticism of the MI and the first part of my answer to the question, "Is it Good?," is to point out that the MI inevitably generates a system of claims that is arbitrary and, in some respects, conservative. This is the first respect in which the MI leads to the taming of philosophy.

---

25. Cf. Hare (1973), 147.

26. Cf. Cummins (1998), 124.

4. *Is It Good? Taming and the Antiquarianism of the Present*

The first charge of taming was that this focus on our intuitions—refined or not—engenders an arbitrary conservatism in our psychological economy. The second charge of taming dwells not so much on the conservatism of the MI but on the fact that the MI centers on our intuitions, bits of our psychology. The charge is that this focus makes the MI inherently unsuited for providing an account of reality.

When one adopts the MI, one's focus is not directly on reality or the world itself; rather, one's focus is directly on our intuitions about the world, i.e., on bits of our psychology instead of on bits of extra-mental reality, and perhaps one so focuses with the ultimate goal of getting at reality through our intuitions. Thus, with the MI, philosophy becomes in the first instance more a recording of opinions or apparent insights into reality than an account of reality itself.

Timothy Williamson describes this kind of approach well:

> [Many contemporary analytic philosophers] think that, in philosophy, ultimately our evidence consists only of intuitions.... [T]hey take that to mean not that our evidence consists of the mainly non-psychological putative facts which are the contents of those intuitions, but that it consists of the psychological facts to the effect that we have intuitions with those contents, true or false.[27]

One worry about this approach is that the emphasis on our intuitions seems to be misplaced: with the MI or the MRE, we are being asked to "check" our theories against our intuitions.[28] But instead of focusing on our intuitions about the world, we should be focusing on the world itself—after all, that is what we in our philosophical theories are primarily trying to understand. This errant emphasis renders philosophical accounts that purport to be of reality unnecessarily and illegitimately subjectivist. Williamson makes a similar point in inveighing against MRE:

> [P]hilosophy is often presented as systematizing and stabilizing our beliefs, bringing them into reflective equilibrium: the picture is that in

27. Williamson (2007), 235; see also the passage from Williamson quoted as an epigraph to this chapter.

28. See Hare (1973), 145.

> doing philosophy what we have to go on is what our beliefs currently are, as though our epistemic access were only to those belief states and not to the states of the world that they are about. This picture is wrong; we frequently have better epistemic access to our immediate physical environment than to our own psychology.[29]

It's as if Rawls and other proponents of the MI are guilty of placing not so much a veil of ignorance but rather *a veil of intuitions* between us and reality. By dwelling more directly on our intuitions about the world than on the world, a philosophy guided by the MI becomes oddly detached from the philosophical subject matters with which it seeks to concern itself. Philosophy under the MI is philosophy without its moorings in reality. Earlier I said that it *may be* the case that philosophy that is not in the spirit of the MI is also philosophy without moorings, philosophy without an adequate basis for its starting points. Now we see, however, that whether or not such approaches other than the MI lack moorings, philosophy in the spirit of the MI is not well-grounded.

The problem for the MI here is another instance of the taming of philosophy. By drawing back our focus onto us and psychology, the MI detaches us from the world and so, once again, limits philosophy's engagement with reality. And, crucially as before, this limitation seems to be arbitrary and unjustified: what basis is there for thinking that certain of our intuitions should be a guide to the world? Here again, philosophy fails to be sufficiently open to the world.

And in this there is a bit of irony. In becoming in many cases more directly focused on our thoughts, than on the world, philosophy under the MI comes to resemble nothing so much as what is often derided as mere doxography, the recording of belief systems without being primarily concerned with the truth of the beliefs in those systems. Similarly, Hare likens the MRE to anthropological theories:

> [T]he only "moral" theories that can be checked against people's actual moral judgments are anthropological theories about what, in general, people *think* one ought to do, not moral theories about what one ought to do.[30]

---

29. Williamson (2007), 5

30. Hare (1973), 148.

For his part, Rawls seems (oddly) unperturbed by this kind of charge: "It [the procedure of reflective equilibrium] is, if you wish, a kind of psychology."[31] Of course, proponents of the MI will claim that they are concerned with reality, but their explicit focus on our intuitions as well as the lack of any good reason to see such intuitions as tied to the truth tends to undermine this claim.[32] I call—somewhat paradoxically—the doxography that is constitutive of the MI, its focus on what we happen to think, the MI's antiquarianism of the present.

This is where the irony comes in. Often, the MI is presented as a refreshingly direct way to do philosophy, unimpeded by such non-philosophical "distractions" as trying to understand a past philosopher on his or her own terms. Employing the MI to achieve philosophical results is seen as decidedly philosophical in a way that, often, engagement with historical figures in philosophy is not. But now—in light of this second charge of taming—it turns out that in following the MI one is less engaged with reality than one might have thought. Further, and crucially, one is less engaged with reality than one is when one grapples with and struggles to understand on its own terms the thought of a philosopher who is him or herself more directly engaged with reality instead of merely with his or her own (or anyone else's) opinions or intuitions about reality. Thus in engaging with, say, Spinoza, Leibniz, and Hume—precisely because these philosophers tend not to dwell on intuitions but on reality itself—one is more likely to be doing philosophy directly than one is when one explores the contours of one's (or Kripke's or Lewis's or Nagel's) intuitions about this or that matter. Engaging with certain historical figures in philosophy can thus be a way of doing philosophy in a less tamed fashion than is engaging with the latest journal articles that are trapped behind the veil of intuitions. In other words, in some cases, the study of the history of philosophy is a way of doing philosophy that is more philosophical than are certain current, relatively ahistorical approaches to philosophy, approaches guided more completely by the MI. In this way, relatively ahistorical approaches to philosophy are often relatively a-philosophical.

Of course, avoiding this turn inward and focusing directly on the world without relying on appeals to intuitions as evidence may not be as easy as Williamson and other opponents of the MI sometimes make it out to be. It may be, then, that—as I've skeptically said—we have no principled starting points either in our intuitions or somewhere else. But then—as I've also skeptically said—so much the worse for us.

---

31. Rawls (1974–75), 9.

32. See Williamson (2007), 211

5. Is It Good? Taming, Quine, and Revision

The third and final challenge to the MI that I will raise is another charge of taming, and it may be the most far-reaching charge yet. I will introduce this problem for the MI by focusing on the MRE in particular (or views, such as Bealer's, that resemble the MRE in important respects). Afterward, I will briefly extend this problem to the other, less common versions of the MI.

Begin with the point that the MRE is a method of bringing intuitions or considered judgments and principles into a process of, to use Goodman's phrase, "mutual adjustment." No particular intuition and no particular principle is treated as sacrosanct. Principles are not by themselves in a position to override intuitions, nor are intuitions by themselves able to overturn a principle that conflicts with those intuitions. Rather, there is an interplay at work, a "familiar give and take," as Sider puts it.[33] And we must adjust principles and intuitions so as to come up with the most coherent overall system, a system that does the best job of accommodating intuitions and also offers the most illuminating explanatory principles. But precisely because of what may seem to be its greatest virtue—its judicious balancing of intuitions and principles—the MRE faces another significant challenge. The flexible interplay between principles and intuitions means that when there is some kind of conflict between them, no one way of resolving the conflict is dictated. In the face of a conflict between an intuition and a principle, one can hold on to the intuition *come what may*, as long as one is willing to make requisite changes in the principles that one accepts and perhaps to modify, as well, certain other intuitions. Alternatively, in the face of this conflict, one can hold onto the principle *come what may* and revise or reconstrue or simply reject the offending intuition and make whatever other adjustments are required in the intuitions and principles one accepts. The general point is that because of the apparently welcome flexibility of the MRE, there is—in the case of a conflict between intuitions and principles—significant latitude: no one outcome is dictated either by the principles or by the intuitions or by the two together. This means that, for any line that one draws between intuitions and principles or between the claims that are kept and those that are rejected or modified, there are other such lines that one could equally well draw within a coherent systems of principles and intuitions.

Given this multiplicity of incompatible ways of drawing the line, whatever line we draw is going to be arbitrary and unprincipled because there

33. Sider (2001), xvi.

is no adequate basis for drawing that line as opposed to another. Drawing whichever line we draw is, in that respect, inexplicable. Or—to put the point another way—the line, the *relation*, between the principles and intuitions that we accept and those that we do not accept is ungrounded and inexplicable. And this inexplicability derives from something essential to the MRE: its flexible give-and-take between intuitions and principles.

This commitment on the part of the MRE to inexplicable distinctions of a certain kind is yet another instance of the taming of philosophy. In requiring that we arbitrarily choose one way of drawing the line between intuitions and principles as opposed to some other way, the MRE shuts us off from these other ways of gaining access to the world. The method thus necessitates an arbitrary and ungrounded limitation on philosophical perspectives on the world. Such a limitation is constitutive of the phenomenon of the taming of philosophy as I have characterized it.

One way to make the significance of this charge of taming felt is to articulate the strong analogy between this criticism of the MRE and Quine's best argument against the analytic/synthetic distinction in "Two Dogmas of Empiricism," an enormously influential paper widely regarded as one of the highlights of analytical philosophy over the last century. The argument I have in mind is Quine's argument—in sections 5 and 6 of that paper—against the analytic/synthetic distinction based on the nature of confirmation.[34]

Here is a skeletal version of this Quinean argument. Assume that there is a distinction between analytic statements that are true solely by virtue of their meaning and are not dependent for their truth on extra-conceptual facts about the world, facts that we have access to (if at all) only by virtue of experience. This is a distinction between statements we must hold onto (as long as we are to be said to understand the statement) and statements that are subject to revision or rejection in light of facts about the world that are independent of the concepts contained in the statement itself. Quine says that any such distinction is arbitrary and illegitimate for, he says, no statement is immune to revision, no statement is one that we must hold onto come what may. Any statement is such that it may be revised as long as one is willing to make the requisite changes in the system of other statements one accepts. Similarly, any statement

34. I regard his earlier arguments in that paper against the distinction as far less conclusive. There he seems merely to point out that the notion of analyticity is bound up with other equally fundamental notions such as synonymy. Quine seems to conclude that this shows that all such notions are suspect. But it's not clear why the interconnection among these notions doesn't show, instead, that they are all virtuous. See Williamson (2007), 50. The argument from confirmation, however, is not problematic in this way.

is one we may hold onto come what may as long as we are willing to make requisite changes elsewhere in our web of belief. As Quine puts the point,

> [I]t becomes folly to seek a boundary between synthetic statements, which hold contingently on experience, and analytic statements, which hold come what may. Any statement can be held true come what may, if we make drastic enough adjustments elsewhere in the system.[35]

The worry here is over the very intelligibility of the purported distinction. As Quine says, "we at present lack any tenable general suggestion, either rough and practical or remotely theoretic, as to what it is to be an analytic sentence."[36] This basic style of argumentation has influenced similar proponents of holism, such as Davidson and many others.

Quine even ties this kind of argument to—and I kid you not—the PSR. Let me set up the crucial passage I am about to quote. In critiquing Carnap's notion of logical truth, Quine argues that there is no basis for the distinction between the postulates and theorems of set theory, and, more generally, no basis for the distinction between those claims of set theory that are constitutive of the meaning of a particular term within set theory and those that are not. The point here is clearly of the same form as the claim Quine makes (later in the very same paper) that there is no basis for the distinction between analytic and synthetic statements.

When Quine describes this flexible interplay between theorems and postulates in set theory, he says first:

> In exposition we may select some of these truths [of set theory] as so-called postulates and deduce others from them, but this is subjective discrimination, variable at will, expository and not set-theoretic. We do not change our meaning of 'ε' between the page where we show that one particular truth is deducible by elementary logic from another and the page where we show the converse.

And now here comes the passage that brings tears of joy to my rationalist eyes:

> Given this democratic outlook, finally, the law of sufficient reason leads us to look upon S [the species of sentences which is so fundamental that

35. Quine (1980), 43.

36. Quine (1976a), 129; see also Quine (1976b), 105.

> one cannot dissent from them without betraying deviation in usage or meaning of 'ε'] as including *all* the sentences which contain only 'ε' and the elementary logical particles. It then follows that anyone in agreement on elementary logic and in irresoluble disagreement on set theory is in deviation with respect to the usage or meaning of 'ε'.[37]

Here Quine is saying that no principled line can be drawn between claims of set theory that constitute part of the meaning of a given term (and are, as it were, analytic) and those that do not. This is so because all statements in set theory are on the same footing, because there is no sufficient reason for differentiating their statuses. In the same way, all statements in general are on the same footing vis-à-vis analyticity because there is no sufficient reason for differentiating their statuses. For Quine, the analytic/synthetic distinction (like the postulate/theorem distinction in set theory) is to be rejected because it violates the Law (or Principle) of Sufficient Reason.

So much for Quine's reason for rejecting the analytic/synthetic distinction. Let's return to the MRE where, I believe, a similar line of argument applies. Just as any analytic/synthetic distinction is arbitrary and inexplicable and thus should, for Quine, be rejected, so too, in the interplay between intuitions and principles, any distinction between claims we keep and those we reject is arbitrary and inexplicable and, for that reason, should be rejected. Since the MRE requires drawing such an arbitrary distinction, this method should be rejected too. That is, we should stop trying to accommodate intuitions and principles in the flexible manner embraced by the MRE.[38]

So this criticism of the MRE, this third instance of taming, gets additional force from its similarity to Quine's best argument against the analytic/synthetic distinction. But, perhaps, you don't like Quine's argument against the analytic/synthetic distinction (even though it is, as I said, regarded as one of the high points of analytical philosophy). OK then, allow me to state my point about the MRE directly, without the help of Quine. The MRE requires arbitrary distinctions and inexplicable relations between claims we accept and those we reject. Such inexplicable relations are not to be tolerated because these inexplicable relations constitute a failure of the MRE to engage

37. Quine (1976a), 114.

38. This is not to say that Quine rejects the MRE. He may think that in holistically adjusting our theory in the way MRE requires we are avoiding the pitfalls of the analytic/synthetic distinction. But because such holistic adjustment is arbitrary in precisely the same way that the analytic/synthetic distinction is arbitrary and because Quine rejects the analytic/synthetic distinction on this basis, he should not endorse the MRE either.

non-arbitrarily with reality, and thus they constitute an illegitimate narrowing of philosophy's perspective on the world, another instance of the taming of philosophy. It is the very flexibility of the MRE—the very point that earns this method its august status—that leads to this objection to that method.

Of course, as before, rejecting the MRE (or something like it) and proceeding in a non-arbitrary fashion may not be realistic. And, again as before, perhaps damned if you do and damned if you don't. And again as before and again skeptically, perhaps so much the worse for us.

Briefly, we can also see that the other versions of the MI invite a similar charge of taming, even though these other versions do not depend on the kind of interplay between principles and intuitions that characterizes the MRE. On versions (1) and (2) of the MI, intuitions are, as we noted, in the driver's seat and either control principles entirely or exist without any principles at all. However, even on such a view, intuitions may come into conflict (after all, as all players in the contemporary discussion seem to agree, intuitions are fallible), and if they do come into conflict, then something has to give: the conflict needs to be resolved somehow. But given the holistic nature of psychological states and events, there is more than one way to resolve the conflict. Which resolution we adopt will ultimately be ungrounded, arbitrary, and invite charges of taming in just the way that the revisions adopted in the spirit of MRE were ungrounded, arbitrary, and invited charges of taming.

Stepping back from the three charges of taming, we can see that they all turn on the unpleasant fact that each version of the MI relies on arbitrary and inexplicable *relations*. Thus, the first charge of taming is that proponents of the MI have no non-arbitrary and principled starting points or focal points and so they can draw no principled distinction between claims that they accept as starting points or focal points and those that they do not. (This kind of taming is bound up with, as I explained, an objectionable conservatism on the part of the MI.) Thus the *relation* between claims that are accepted and claims that are not is arbitrary and inexplicable.

The second charge of taming is the more specific charge that proponents of the MI treat as evidence for whatever conclusion they reach the fact that we have such-and-such intuitions or certain special attitudes toward particular cases or principles. This focus on us and on our psychology is, I claim, arbitrary because no principled reason is given for thinking that our responses are the ones that should have primacy when it comes to reaching the truth. Because of this unprincipled focus on us, we can see the proponents of the MI as committed yet again to ungrounded and inexplicable relations: for the proponents of the MI, there is no principled reason to treat intuitive claims as particularly worthy of respect and so again there is an arbitrary line between the claims the proponent of the MI treats as epistemically valuable and those that he or she does not. The *relation* between the two classes of claims is arbitrary and inexplicable.

Similarly with the third charge of taming, we pointed out that there are unintelligible relations at play because the *relation* between the claims one revises and the claims one does not is arbitrary and inexplicable, for the proponent of the MI.

Because of the centrality of the notion of inexplicable relations in the key objections to the MI, it seems that its commitment to unintelligible relations is the basic criticism of the MI. And this commitment is the chief reason for my negative answer to the first guiding question I raised at the beginning of this chapter concerning the MI: is it good?

6. Why Now?

This insight into the crucial role that arbitrary, inexplicable relations play in the MI leads to an insight into the other guiding question, "Why now?" I noted earlier that the MI gained or regained prominence about 100 years ago with the rise of so-called analytical philosophy, and so one question I raised was this: why did the MI become so prominent with the rise of analytical philosophy and why does it continue to be prominent? A full answer to this question must contain many strands that I cannot hope to explore here. But let me isolate one particularly revealing strand that invokes some of the themes of intelligibility that I have already relied on in my (negative) answer to the question, "Is it good?"

The story I am about to tell begins on a familiar note: analytical philosophy, as we have come to know it, came into prominence with Russell's and Moore's revolt against the idealism of Bradley and others, an idealism that was, at the turn of the twentieth century, the dominant philosophical movement, at least in the English-speaking world. Now (as an irreverent supporter of Bradley might ask), why were Russell and Moore revolting? To see why, we need to look more closely at the idealism Russell and Moore sought to—and eventually did—knock off philosophy's pedestal. As Russell and Moore saw, a certain doctrine about relations lay at the heart of Bradley's idealism, and it was their rejection of this doctrine that lay at the heart of their new approach to philosophy. Thus Bradley, Russell, and Moore all shared the insight that (as Russell put it), "The question of relations is one of the most important that arise in philosophy, as most other issues turn on it: monism and pluralism, ... idealism and realism in some of their forms, perhaps the very existence of philosophy as a subject distinct form science and possessing a method of its own."[39] Fundamentally, the doctrine Bradley advanced and the others challenged was that relations are not real: relations between things—including relations of distinction—are, in some sense, merely apparent.[40] And so for Bradley, multiplicity is merely apparent and there is at most one thing in the world. Bradley's denial of the reality of relations thus quickly leads to a form of monism. For our purposes, we need not characterize the precise form this monism takes;[41] all we need to note is that Russell and Moore were opposed to monism.

In denying the reality of relations, Bradley and other idealists were denying, in particular, that there is any relation of distinction between things and thoughts about those things. This lack of a distinction between thoughts and objects of thought is characteristic of one form of idealism, and so Bradley's denial of relations also led to a kind of idealism. Russell and Moore thus were exercised both about Bradley's idealism as well as about his monism, but as Russell notes, "I think Moore was most concerned with the rejection of idealism, while I was most interested in the rejection of monism."[42]

Russell and Moore sometimes mischaracterized Bradley's thesis as the claim that all relations are internal and as merely a denial of external relations, i.e., of relations that are independent of the natures of the relata. Bradley does often focus on external relations in his critique of relations, but that critique is as much a challenge to the notion of relationality as such: both internal and external relations come under attack. I will continue to speak of Bradley's attack in these more general terms.[43]

Why does Bradley reject the reality of relations? Bradley's famous (notorious) regress argument is responsible. The most straightforward way to present the argument is as an expression of the demand that relations be grounded, i.e., they must be explained by some thing or things. Bradley's argument, then, turns on the claim that there is no legitimate way for relations to be

---

39. Russell (1956a), 333.

40. See especially Bradley (1968), chapters 2 and 3, Bradley (1935), and Candlish (2007), chapter 6.

41. For some relevant distinctions, see Schaffer (2010).

42. Russell (1956b), 54.

43. Candlish (2007) is very good at distinguishing the more general and less general forms of Bradley's critique and at showing that Bradley intends the more sweeping attack, despite some potentially misleading things Bradley says.

grounded or explained. Why not? Consider a relation, R between relata *a* and *b*. Given the demand for grounding that Bradley accepts, this relation must be grounded in some thing or things. But in what things? R cannot be grounded in *a* alone (to the exclusion of *b*) because that would be arbitrary: *b* is equally eligible to be a ground for R. Similarly, R cannot be grounded in *b* alone. So what, then, is R grounded in? It's natural to say that R is grounded in *a* and *b* not separately, but in *a* and *b together*, i.e., in the fact that *a* and *b co-exist*, i.e., in the fact that *a* and *b* are related somehow. But this is to ground R in another relation, which simply raises the question of the ground of a relation again, and we are off on Bradley's regress.

Here's another way to see Bradley's point: R, the relation between *a* and *b*, must be grounded and it seems that it must be grounded in part in *a*. But grounding is itself a relation, so in order for *a* to be related to *b*, there must be a grounding relation between *a* and R. Call this further relation, R'. But R'—a relation between *a* and R—must itself be grounded. So there must be another relation R" that grounds the relation between *a* and R', but R" must be grounded, etc. And so again we have a regress.[44]

Bradley's notorious (famous) argument has been challenged and, less frequently, defended, but I cannot enter into a full-blown defense here. The point I want to stress is that Bradley's argument proceeds from the demand that relations be explicable and that they be grounded—and Bradley explicitly sees his argument this way. Here is Bradley focusing on external relations in particular:

> [I]f the terms from their inner nature do not enter into the relation, then, so far as they are concerned, they seem related for no reason at all, and, so far as they are concerned, the relation seems arbitrarily made.[45]

Also, throughout chapters 2 and 3 of Book I of *Appearance and Reality*, Bradley is concerned with, as he puts it, the intelligibility of relations and with giving a "rational account" of them.[46] And he expresses this concern both about external relations *and* about internal relations.[47] In insisting that relations be

44. I have presented the Bradleyan regress in these ways and defended this argument from some objections in Della Rocca (2012).

45. Bradley (1968), 514; see also 517.

46. Ibid., 19.

47. Ibid., 24, 26–27.

explicable and should be rejected because they are not explicable, Bradley articulates a claim that is a general version of Quine's more specific rejection of relations of distinction between analytic and synthetic statements. Indeed, it's worth noting that Bradley—more than fifty years before Quine's paper—argues against the analytic/synthetic distinction for reasons that are continuous with his reasons for the rejection of relations.[48]

Others also regard Bradley's argument as proceeding via something like the PSR.[49] But, most important for our purposes, *Russell* and *Moore* also see Bradley's argument this way. Russell is more explicit on this point. Citing some of the same passages that I just quoted, Russell points out[50] that Bradley's regress argument depends on the rejection of brute or inexplicable relations and on the PSR (or, as Russell calls it just as Quine does, "the Law of Sufficient Reason"). Seeing Bradley's use of the principle as the source of Bradley's monism and idealism, Russell attacks this source. He flatly rejects the PSR and embraces inexplicable relations. Russell says (correctly, I believe) that Bradley's view on relations

> seems to rest upon some law of sufficient reason, some desire to show that every truth is "necessary." I am inclined to think that a large part of my disagreement with Mr. Bradley turns on a disagreement as to the notion of "necessity." I do not myself admit necessity and possibility as fundamental notions: it appears to me that fundamentally truths are merely true in fact, and that the search for a "sufficient reason" is mistaken.[51]

Given the fundamentality of Russell's rejection of the non-reality of relations to his critique of Bradleyan monism and idealism, and thus given its fundamentality to his role in the formation of analytical philosophy, it is no exaggeration to say that Russell's rejection of the PSR made possible his role as one of the founders of analytical philosophy.

The same is true of Moore's role as a generator of analytical philosophy. Moore too sees Bradley's denial of the reality of relations as fundamental to Bradley's system, and he goes after Bradley at precisely that point. Moore obviously has no problem with ungrounded or inexplicable relations. In his early,

48. See Bradley (1922), 185.

49. See, e.g., Campbell (1931), 25; Hylton (1990), 56; Candlish (2007), 46–48; van Inwagen (2009), 44–45.

50. In Russell (1956b), 58, and Russell (1910a), 164–65

51. Russell (1910b), 374.

landmark essay, "The Nature of Judgement" (1899), an essay that, as Russell acknowledges was a major influence on Russell, Moore makes his acceptance of ungrounded relations clear in the context of his treatment of the relations between a thinker and concepts or possible objects of thought. Moore points out, in effect, that this relation is an external relation: "It is indifferent to their [concepts'] nature whether anybody thinks them or not."[52]

The general claim that there may be external relations, relations not grounded in the natures of the relata (or in anything else) emerges more clearly in Moore's 1919 paper "External and Internal Relations." That relations hold is, Moore says, often a mere matter of fact:

> It seems quite obvious that in the case of many relational properties which things have, the fact that they have them is *a mere matter of fact*.[53]

In these passages, Moore's commitment to the rejection of the PSR is apparent and so is his commitment to ungrounded or inexplicable relations. And these commitments form the basis of Moore's attack on Bradleyanism and form the basis of Moore's contribution to the rise of analytical philosophy.

Fair enough, you might say, but so what? What does all this stuff about Russell's and Moore's fundamental commitment to the inexplicability of at least some relations and to the falsity of the PSR have to do with the prominence of the MI in philosophy as we know it today?

First, note that Moore is, in a way, the patron saint of the MI. The intuitions that Moore shows deference to are, above all, intuitions in the form of the dictates of so-called common sense. Thus Moore says in another landmark essay, "A Defence of Common Sense" (1925): "the 'Common Sense view of the world' is, in certain fundamental features, *wholly* true."[54] For Moore, intuitions of common sense must be accommodated: "to speak with contempt of those 'Common Sense beliefs' which I have mentioned is quite certainly the height of absurdity."[55] Moore thus espouses a version of the MI in which intuitions (about cases in particular) are accorded primacy, and principles that go against commonsense beliefs have no legitimate role to play.[56]

---

52. Moore (1993c), 4.

53. Moore (1993b), 88, emphasis in original; see also 99.

54. Moore (1993a), 118.

55. Ibid., 119.

56. See also Moore's equally influential essay, "Proof of an External World."

Russell also is a fan of the commonsense version of the MI, though his endorsement is a more nuanced one that gives deference to science as well. Although Russell supports his rejection of monism "on empirical grounds" informed by science,[57] we also find Russell explicitly rejecting the PSR and monism in part on the basis of something like common sense. Thus, he rejects the PSR by appealing to ways of defining necessity that "account for its common uses,"[58] and in a classic statement of the MI, he says, "Pluralism is the view of science and common sense and is *therefore* to be accepted if the arguments against it are not conclusive."[59]

So Moore and Russell adhere to the MI and, in different ways, defer to common sense.

By contrast, Bradley is no fan of common sense and is much more willing than either Moore or Russell to go against our intuitions. Thus, we find Bradley acknowledging that the acceptance of external relations is a deliverance of common sense:

> At first sight obviously such external relations seem possible and even existing. They seem given to us … in change of spatial position and gain also in comparison. That you do not alter what you compare or rearrange in space seems to Common Sense quite obvious, and that on the other side there are as obvious difficulties does not occur to Common Sense at all.[60]

In rejecting external relations, as he does, Bradley is thus explicitly going against common sense. In a striking expression of non-deference to common sense, one that I have quoted more fully as an epigraph to this chapter, Bradley says, "I am not to be moved here by the charge of an insult offered to Common Sense."[61] Although inveighing against common sense in these ways doesn't by itself mean that Bradley rejects the MI in general, he certainly comes closer to doing so than do either Russell or Moore.

OK then, Russell and Moore embrace a version of the MI, and Bradley seems more or less hostile to the MI. But, again, so what? What bearing does

57. Russell (1910a), 338–39.

58. Russell (1910b), 374.

59. Russell (1927), 264, my emphasis; see also Russell (1956c), 178.

60. Bradley (1968), 514.

61. Bradley (1935), 640.

this interesting difference have on the other interesting difference, lately noted, between Bradley, on the one hand, and Russell and Moore, on the other, viz., the difference whereby Russell and Moore accept inexplicable relations and Bradley does not? To answer this question, recall that, as I have argued, inexplicable relations are fundamental to the MI (in any version). Further, as I have also argued, the key objections to the MI stem from this very commitment to inexplicable relations. In this light, we can see that once Russell and Moore—in their youthful, headlong effort to avoid Bradleyan idealism and monism—rushed to embrace inexplicable relations, the way was paved for them to adopt some version of the MI. Not only was the commitment to inexplicable relations necessary for adopting the MI, but it was also practically sufficient in this context for adopting the MI. Given that Bradley's metaphysical views were, as we have just seen, bound up with his methodology which was in tension with the MI, it follows that in attending to Bradley's metaphysics it was only natural for Russell and Moore to address themselves to methodological matters. In particular, once Russell and Moore focused on the interaction between principles and intuitions, once inexplicable relations were allowed on the table, and once the major objections to the MI were thus off the table, there was, if I may put it this way, no reason for Russell and Moore *not* to adopt the MI, and so they did. In this context, in which, among other things, they succumbed to the allure of inexplicable relations, the MI was indeed almost inevitable.

And not only was it almost inevitable, it became so thoroughly ingrained among philosophers who followed in the footsteps of Russell and Moore that the problems with the MI did not even show up on the radar screen of most philosophers in the soon-to-be-dominant analytic tradition. Thus, as we saw, certain contemporary philosophers such as Pryor channel Moore and praise philosophical conservatism without any apparent pangs of conscience. Indeed, we find more and more philosophers—right up until the present—pursuing philosophy behind what I have called the veil of intuition. For these philosophers who feel the now almost instinctive aversion to Bradleyan monism—an aversion that is more or less part of the collective unconscious (or collective conscious) of analytical philosophers—some version of the MI is completely natural and any apparent alternative is well-nigh unthinkable.

In this light, it is not surprising that many contemporary philosophers who reject something like Bradleyan monism are explicitly fans of the MI.[62]

---

62. For example, Lewis—a proponent of the MI—is an atomist who rejects any form of monism. Schaffer—also a proponent of the MI—endorses a form of monism but rejects the much more radical form to be found in Bradley. See Schaffer (2010).

In this light also, we can begin to see that philosophers such as Quine who promote (perhaps unknowingly) Bradley-esque arguments concerning relations are, like Bradley himself, to be seen as less in line with the MI than are most contemporary philosophers. Because of this Bradleyan connection, such philosophers may stand outside the analytic tradition in an important respect. Thus Quine's Bradley-esque argument in "Two Dogmas"—in addition to being seen as a high point of analytical philosophy—may also be, in fact, the beginning of the end of analytical philosophy, for it has influentially embodied a kind of argumentation that runs counter to the presuppositions on which analytical philosophy was founded and which have, for better or worse, largely dominated philosophy ever since.

To be clear: my claim is not that Quine in "Two Dogmas" and philosophers such as Davidson who argue in this vein were directly influenced by Bradley. At the time of "Two Dogmas," practically no one—except perhaps Richard Wollheim—was reading Bradley. Nor am I saying that Quine and others explicitly rejected the MI. Rather, my claim is that the similarity between Quine's argument and Bradley's reveals Quine (and others) to be out of step both with the MI and with the originating force of analytical philosophy.

So we have at least a partial answer to the second guiding question: why now? Why has the MI been so popular over the last 100 years or so? The answer—or an answer—is that the rejection of Bradleyan monism required the acceptance of inexplicable relations that paved the way for the adoption of the MI. And, as we saw, we also have an answer to the first guiding question: is it good? Is the MI a good method for philosophical inquiry? The answer I offered is that this method is highly problematic because, in several ways, the pursuit of the MI embroils its practitioners in inexplicable relations, relations of a kind that Quinean arguments have taught us to be wary of and, more generally, inexplicable relations that seem to make the pursuit of philosophy more arbitrary than we might have expected or would have desired.

One might also think that seeing the problems with the MI and seeing the far-from-inevitable philosophical presuppositions that, once adopted, give rise to the MI may make embracing an alternative to the MI all the more feasible. But, unfortunately, that doesn't seem to be the case, for, as we saw, the alternatives to the MI seem unworkable because these alternatives do not rely on intuitions and it may seem that doing philosophy without the guidance of intuitions is every bit as arbitrary as starting with intuitions. As I've said, perhaps it's damned if you do (start with intuitions), damned if you don't. More specifically: arbitrary if you do, arbitrary if you don't. And, as I've also said, perhaps so much the worse for us.

If there is no principled way to proceed, then we face the real possibility and prospect that philosophical inquiry itself cannot be coherently pursued. I think that this, perhaps grim, skeptical possibility is one that we philosophers must, if we are to be honest, take seriously. The very possibility of philosophical inquiry is thus, I believe, something that should always be in question for philosophers.

7. Two Lifelines

But, against this stark backdrop, there are some flickers of hope, two lifelines, that emerge from the criticisms and historical account of the MI that I have presented.

The story I have told about the origins of analytical philosophy indicates that the acceptance of inexplicable relations by Russell and Moore created a context in which the MI could thrive. We also saw that it is the MI's commitment to inexplicable relations that is the culprit behind the taming of philosophy that the MI brings on. So a possible way to try to avoid the MI and these difficulties is to strike at their root, i.e., to reject the embrace of inexplicable relations and to challenge the rejection of the PSR.[63] A philosophy guided more completely by a concern with intelligibility and the PSR is thus a philosophy more removed from the inexplicability that leads to the MI and to the taming of philosophy. Again, we may never reach a point at which each move in our philosophy—including its starting points—is dictated solely by a concern to maximize explicability and to avoid arbitrariness, but we can, perhaps, approximate this ideal to greater and greater degrees. The motto here is, to the extent that a philosophy is guided by the PSR and by the goals of maximizing intelligibility and explicability and avoiding arbitrariness, it is a philosophy untamed. So being guided by intelligibility is the first lifeline.

But how can such a philosophy be carried out? This brings me to the second lifeline. To help us figure out what such an intelligibility-focused philosophy might look like, to figure out how far we can go in untaming philosophy, one suggestion is to look to certain philosophers at work before the veil of intuitions descended on philosophy, philosophers who, in some cases—though in imperfect fashion—placed a concern with explicability and intelligibility at the heart of their philosophical systems. In philosophy's past—more so, perhaps, than today—we may find thinkers who are willing to be guided by a concern with intelligibility and who may be our guides in untaming philosophy.

---

63. I have defended the PSR in Della Rocca (2010).

In this light, it is no surprise that some of the philosophers who are furthest from the MI have also been philosophers most concerned with intelligibility and the PSR. Thus, as we saw, Spinoza and Leibniz who (in different degrees) are far removed from the MI also—and not coincidentally, I would say—structure their systems around the PSR and explicability. Hume, too, as we saw, is far from the MI and, while he explicitly rejects and argues against the PSR,[64] his system is also shot through with a concern with intelligibility, and he grapples throughout with the strength of the PSR whose implications he understands better than most other philosophers.[65] It is to philosophers such as these—philosophers most engaged with the power of intelligibility, explicability, and the PSR—to whom we should turn for guidance in seeking to undo the taming of philosophy. Thus a return to certain areas of the history of philosophy is my second lifeline.[66] By engaging with these figures from philosophy's past, we may be, as I argued, pursuing philosophy more directly than we do when we practice the method of intuition and are caught up in what I called the antiquarianism of the present. There are other weighty reasons to engage with the history of philosophy, but this one—correcting the distortion of philosophy brought on by the rise of analytical philosophy—is perhaps one of the most timely.

So my suggestions are two: let intelligibility be your guide and engage with historical figures who—writing before the veil of intuitions tamed so much of philosophy—also let intelligibility be their guide. Can these suggestions lead to successful philosophical inquiry? I don't know. But they are, perhaps, our best hope for attaining a philosophy that is, as far as possible, untamed.

Acknowledgments

This chapter was presented at a workshop on methodology in the study of the history of philosophy at Concordia University in Montréal in October 2011. For generous and helpful comments, I would like to thank Eric Schliesser, Mogens Lærke, Justin Smith, Sungil Han, Leslie Wolf, Rebecca Newberger Goldstein, Barbara Sattler, George Bealer, Allison Glasscock, Laurie Paul, Paul Franks, Omri Boehm, Joshua Knobe, Carol Rovane, Julia Borcherding, my colleagues at a Yale faculty lunch presentation, and the loyal critics in my memorable seminar at Yale in the spring of 2012.

---

64. See, especially, Hume (2000), I.3.3.

65. For this reading of Hume, see Della Rocca (forthcoming).

66. I call this lifeline: "phone-a-friend."

10

Philosophic Prophecy

Eric Schliesser

The myth of physical objects is epistemologically superior to most in that it has proved more efficacious than other myths as a device for working a manageable structure into the flux of experience.

W. V. O. QUINE

[Philosophy] is an investigation of utopian concepts that transcend the empirical.

JOSÉ BENARDETE

1. Introduction and Summary

THE MAIN TASK for philosophers is introducing, clarifying, articulating, or simply redirecting concepts as—to echo Quine's poetic formulation—"devices for working a manageable structure into the flux of experience."[1] In what follows I sometimes use "coining concepts" as shorthand for this task. When the concepts are quantitative they are part of a possible science (or pseudo-science); when the concepts are qualitative they can be part of a possible philosophy (and other important projects). Of course, in practice, concepts are often stillborn, while others have multiple functions in fields of inquiry that may straddle philosophy and science.

In this chapter I argue that historians of philosophy must, among other things, coin concepts that disclose the near or distant past and create a shared horizon for our philosophical future. In virtue of our expertise we can often do so by drawing on previously orphaned concepts.

The more narrow aim of this paper is to introduce two concepts, "Newton's challenge to philosophy" and, especially, "philosophic prophecy," that are

1. Quine (1961 [1951]).

suitable to philosophers who engage with texts in a scholarly fashion. I do so by re-telling the story of early analytical philosophy and its connection to the reception of Spinoza.

By "Newton's challenge to philosophy," I mean the following: from about 1700 onward, "natural science" is increasingly taken to be authoritative in settling debates within philosophy; it is a concept that focuses attention on the (contested) authority of science and its various manifestations within philosophy.[2] By "philosophic prophecy," I mean the structured ways in which concept formation by philosophers can shape possible futures, including that of philosophy.

In what follows, I first develop and characterize philosophic prophecy more precisely. In order to illuminate the concept, I contrast it with several related, more familiar concepts. Second, I offer brief critical comments on two alternative approaches to the history of philosophy promoted by Quentin Skinner and Michael Kremer in order to make more precise the approach favored here. Third, I offer a fresh narrative about the prehistory and origin of analytical philosophy.[3] My story focuses on Ernest Nagel, who, I claim, is the philosophic prophet of analytical philosophy. Along the way, I explore the shared origins of analytical philosophy and analytical history of philosophy in the anti-Spinozistic writings of George Boole and Bertrand Russell. I oppose Nagel's and Russell's narratives in light of Moritz Schlick, the founder of the Vienna Circle. I adopt Schlick's bold and unappreciated vision of the task of philosophy in scientific age(s).[4] I focus on his identification of philosophical legislation with qualitative concepts.

2. A. Philosophic Prophecy[5]

What a man thinks of himself, that it is which determines, or rather indicates, his fate.

HENRY DAVID THOREAU

The magnificent cause of being, // The imagination, the one reality //
In this imagined world

WALLACE STEVENS

2. Schliesser (2011a).

3. Della Rocca (this volume) also offers a new account of the origins of analytical philosophy. My approach can explain his as an instance of philosophic prophecy.

4. See Schlick, (1936), especially 343.

5. This section draws on material I published before in Schliesser (2011b).

In this section, I characterize philosophic prophecy. I introduce the concept, first, by explaining how it relates to two other better known concepts—the so-called self-fulfilling prophecy and the self-refuting prediction—to which it bears a close family resemblance. Then I give a list of ten characteristics of philosophic prophecy (with references to texts that instantiate these). I conclude this section by contrasting philosophic prophecy with two other concepts—so-called noble lies and Straussian esoteric readings—with which it can be easily mixed up.

According to Robert K. Merton, a self-fulfilling prophecy is,

> in the beginning, a false definition of the situation evoking a new behavior which makes the original false conception come true. This specious validity of the self-fulfilling prophecy perpetuates a reign of error. For the prophet will cite the actual course of events as proof that he was right from the very beginning.[6]

Merton points to bank runs based on false rumors as examples. By contrast, self-refuting predictions start out as a true description of the situation that evokes behavior making the originally true conception eventually come out false. An example is the promotion of investment products based on the lack of correlation between two real estate markets that help bring about some such correlation.[7] Self-fulfilling prophecies and self-refuting predictions take it for granted that publicly expressed ideas can have an effect on the world.[8] In particular, their impact can change the truth-functional status of descriptions of the world. Of course, not all utterances are like this. Planetary orbits are generally not meaningfully impacted by the claims we make about them. Even in the social sciences there is a class of theorems that shows that there are successful, non-trivial predictions that need not change the underlying system.[9] Let us leave aside writings that do not impact the subject matter of which they speak.

Here I focus on a further class of writings that can impact the world. Philosophic prophecies are structurally akin to self-fulfilling prophecies.

6. Merton (1996),185.

7. Soros (2009), 25–80, has renewed interest in this issue.

8. See, for a paradigmatic statement, Keynes (1936), 383–84.

9. Grunberg and Modigliani (1954) and Muth's (1961) characterize precise (and infrequent) circumstances in which this can take place. As Wade Hands points out, Simon (1954) does something similar. See Hands (1990). For recent work on these matters, see U. Mäki (2011).

Philosophic prophecies conceptualize a merely possible, even improbable, situation and evoke behavior that makes the original conception come out true, or approximately true. To be sure, the outcome (that is, the approximate truth described in the prophecy) of it is a contingent fact, i.e., the existence of a philosophic prophecy is necessary, but not sufficient for an intended outcome.[10]

In order to characterize philosophic prophecy more fully, I distinguish ten features of it:

1. It is "secular" prophecy. By this I mean to distinguish it from biblical and other religious prophecy. It is prophecy by philosophers.[11] The content of philosophic prophecy may well be religious (on a suitably broad understanding of it) even theological in character. For example, Bacon's *New Atlantis* offers a narrative of an island society that is indirectly controlled by a secret scientific community that presents itself as a priestly society; the whole narrative is infused with religious themes and motifs.[12] Salomon's House must have seemed very implausible to Bacon's initial readers. But within forty years, in Thomas Sprat's official *The History of the Royal Society of London*, the opening poem already treats Bacon as a prophetic visionary "like Moses," who had shepherded his flock past "the barren wilderness" to the "very border" of the "promised land" of the Royal Society.[13]

2. Philosophic prophecy is not primarily about offering predictions; it is about creating a possible future. Of course, predictions can enter into the content of a philosophic prophecy. Rhetorically, even negative predictions can be intended to produce an alternative outcome. Consider, for example, Adam Smith's claim in *Wealth of Nations*: "To expect, indeed, that the freedom of trade should ever be entirely restored in Great Britain is as absurd as to expect that an Oceana or Utopia should ever be established in it. Not only the prejudices of the public, but what is much more unconquerable,

10. This does not rely on some invisible hand mechanism because of the role of contingency that I assign to the consequences of philosophic prophecy. Of course, the possible includes the actual so some philosophic prophecies are trivially true, but those may not be much remarked upon.

11. Of course, some figures in the Old (Jeremiah, Job) or New Testament (Paul) engage in philosophy, and I allow that the whole Bible contains quite a lot of philosophy. See Hazony (2012).

12. Harrison (2007), 179.

13. See stanza V of Cowley's poem. See Sprat (1667), 35, and especially 151–52.

the private interests of many individuals, irresistibly oppose it."[14] Although Smith's words can be taken as a mere statement of fact, they are more likely intended to rouse (part of) "the public" so that they overcome their own prejudices and the private interests of others. He is inviting readers to see themselves as members of a community with public interests. One reason to doubt that Smith, who taught rhetoric, is making purely factual claims (that there was once freedom of trade in Britain, but it is beyond belief that there should again be freedom of trade) is that except in this passage, there is no evidence that he thought that there ever was a genuine "freedom of trade" in Great Britain. In context, Smith is talking primarily about guild and settlement laws that hinder poor people from moving into areas and about industries that offer opportunities for employment. Moreover, he is explicitly comparing his advocacy of free trade with projects (James Harrington's *The Commonwealth of Oceana* and Thomas More's *Utopia*) that are themselves also instances of philosophic prophecy. In doing so, he highlights the crucial difference between his project and theirs: his proposal requires no constitutional changes to existing institutions and practices nor does it presuppose dramatic improvements in human nature. All that is required is a change of public perception about what seems possible and reasonable as well as incremental ("slow gradations," and "with a good deal of reserve and circumspection")[15] policy changes.

3. In accordance with the teleological conception of philosophic prophecy, philosophic prophecy is a necessary, albeit almost never sufficient, condition for the prophesied future. So, without the prophecy, the prophesied future would not have come about. Befitting a teleological concept, philosophic prophecies can fail, too. "Philosophic prophecy" is not a success term.

4. Philosophic prophecy appeals to the imagination often by way of narrative (e.g., Thoreau's *Walden;* cf. Descartes's autobiography in the *Discourse on Method* and the account of his three dreams in Baillet's *La vie de monsieur Des-Cartes*),[16] dialogues, poetry, history,[17] travel reports (e.g. Bacon's *New Atlantis*), mythic history (e.g., *Phaedrus* 224–30, or David

---

14. Smith (1976), 4.2.43. I am quoting by paragraph, not page number, here. http://oll.libertyfund.org/title/220/217458/2313890.

15. Smith (1976), op cit. http://oll.libertyfund.org/title/220/217458/2313887.

16. Browne (1977) and Keevak (1992).

17. See Kant (1963).

Lewis's embrace of "Sellars' myth"),[18] the introduction of novel or transmutation of existing vocabulary, etc. (Think of all that is conveyed by the Platonic category *muthos*.) Here I intend a contrast with rational persuasion by way of (formal/deductive/structured) argument (viz., Platonic *logos*). The point is not that philosophers sometimes illustrate their claims by way of poetic imagery. Rather, philosophic prophecy makes something—however improbable—conceivable that was in some sense previously inconceivable. A nice discussion of what I have in mind can be found in the writings of Benardete, in a comment on Shakespeare's *Macbeth*:

> Newton's first law of motion describes how every body would act if it were free of all impressed forces. Owing to universal gravitation there is, and can be, no such body. Revealing the nature of every body 'as it would be found in trials to which it cannot be exposed,' Newton's first law is to be seen as a true contrary-to-fact conditional in the subjunctive mood. No mere 'mirror of life,' it is in his subjunctive not indicative mood that the poet can emulate the physicist. Although oracular witches are contrary to nature, the poet may invoke them in the antecedent of a contrary-to-fact conditional and thereby reveal, in the consequent, what no mirror of life could reveal.[19]
>
> What is true here in Shakespeare's tragedy is also true of philosophic prophecy: new concepts can reveal an otherwise invisible reality. By "invisible reality," I do not primarily mean very small or very distant objects. Rather, in science and in philosophy, we sometimes use concepts to denote/delineate/define hard-to-imagine counterfactual situations. In particular, concepts in philosophic prophecy make visible *intentional* objects. In virtue of the productions of the imagination and people's subsequent attitudes, philosophic prophets (help) create, in part, new possible social realities by which we navigate the "flux of experience."[20]

I do not mean to suggest that the content of the philosophic prophecy is irrational or in opposition to reason. On the contrary, in general, philosophic

18. Lewis (1999) 258–59. Mea culpa: I have lost track of who first called my attention to this passage.

19. Benardete (1970). Benardete, in turn, is quoting the critic Johnson (hence the quote marks around, "as it would be found in trials to which it cannot be exposed").

20. I do not endorse the Quinean idea that regimentation of scientific discourse is the main task of philosophy.

prophecy is meant to reinforce the claims of reason. In particular, philosophic prophecy often simultaneously intends to promote the cause of reason as well as justice, humanity, etc. The motive, if discernible, behind philosophic prophecy is a kind of philosophic philanthropy, that is, to "refresh life."[21]

5. One reason I refer to the "imagination" is that philosophic prophecy often consists of claims the truth of which cannot be established at the time of articulation, but that avoid (obvious) falsehoods. A prominent deployment of this strategy is offered by Spinoza's "tenets of universal faith" in chapter 14 of his *Theological-Political Treatise*. According to Spinoza, many of these tenets "have not even a shadow of the truth, so long the person who accepts them does not know them to be false."[22] Daniel Garber glosses this as follows: "This is quite crucial: a belief can be efficacious in producing obedience *only* if it is genuinely believed to be true. As soon as it is known to be false, it is no longer capable of supporting the practice of obedience."[23] Garber fails to notice that there is a gap between not knowing that something is false and genuinely believing that it is true. The tenets can be beyond what is rationally knowable. What is crucial is that the contents of philosophic prophecy ought to avoid knowable falsehood. So, existing knowledge and extrapolations from it are important constraints on philosophic prophecy.[24]

6. Another reason I refer to the "imagination" is that philosophic prophecy is, thus (ultimately), accepted on trust, or even faith.[25] Philosophic prophecy is in part accepted by virtue of the authority of the prophet. It is often designed to contest the magisterial authority of other schools, narratives, etc. This is why we often find it interwoven with origin myths or programmatic texts, etc.

7. The previous, sixth characteristic is related to a very useful criterion that allows discerning whether one is dealing with an author who engages in, or is taken to engage in, philosophic prophecy: she or he nearly always articulates a dialectic between true versus false philosophy or true versus

---

21. Benardete, (1996), 194.

22. Spinoza (1925), III, 176.

23. Garber (2008), 173.

24. With our extreme and increasing intellectual division of labor and the often highly esoteric content consequent of it, much specialized knowledge is becoming practically unknowable to nearly all outsiders.

25. I thank Ben Nelson for discussion of this point.

false philosophers (teachers/experts, etc.). A prominent early modern example of this rhetoric can be found in David Hume, who diagnoses a dialectic between false and true philosophy. Admittedly, for us, the locution "true philosopher" sounds awkward, but Hume also uses it.[26] In particular, it is especially characteristic of philosophic prophecy to invent or restructure intellectual traditions around such a dialectic. For example, in a polemic with the analytical heirs of Russell, Jonathan Schaffer attempts to restore the respectability of monism; he does so by creating an "intellectual pedigree tracing from Parmenides, Plato, and Plotinus, to Spinoza, Hegel, and Bradley" to himself.[27] This pedigree is to be contrasted with Russell's contemporary analytical heirs:

> It will prove useful to begin with Russell's claim that pluralism is favored by *common sense*. This claim is the source of the contemporary dismissal of monism as being obviously false. Russell declares: "I share the common-sense belief that there are many separate things; I do not regard the apparent multiplicity of the world as consisting merely in phases and unreal divisions of a single indivisible Reality."[28] Russell then frames the debate as a debate between the commonsensical empiricist pluralist who can see that "there are many things" and the wild-eyed rationalistic monist who would argue a priori that there is only one thing.[29] Here is the birth story of analytical philosophy and what has sounded like the death knell for monism. But analytical philosophy—for all of its many virtues—was born in sin.[30]

Schaffer's moralized pedigree is enlisted, in part, to reframe and, thereby undo Russell's moralized conceptual framing of an opposition between common sense (empiricist) pluralism and the dreams of wild-eyed rationalistic monism. Russell is indeed a master of philosophic prophecy. Here is also an implicit example of the dialectic between true and false philosophy in Russell's writings: sometimes the opposed view is systematically unnamed. Russell (1914) does not name "Hegel's modern disciples" (note the implied magisterial relationship) in the main body of the text, and when Russell does quote one of them for saying that "Reality is not

26. For scholarly treatment, see Livingston (1998), chapter 2, especially.

27. Schaffer (2010), 32.

28. Russell (1985), 36.

29. Russell (1985), 48.

30. Schaffer (2010), 46. For similar rhetoric, see Della Rocca (in this volume).

merely one and self-consistent, but is a system of reciprocally determinate parts," the author's name (Bernard Bosanquet) only appears in a footnote. One of the main targets, Francis Bradley, never gets mentioned.[31]

8. The core presupposition of philosophic prophecy is that our unforeseen actions can be the intended outcome of past design. Although the content of philosophic prophecy can be rich in detail, it need not anticipate the exact variety of ways in which history unfolds. Rather, what philosophic prophecy relies on is a kind of shared conceptual horizon between the prophecy and the prophesied future.[32] To put this in less poetic terms: the way some problems or issues within (and outside) philosophy are conceived today may be indebted to how issues were framed in some philosophic prophecy. So, this fully allows all manner of contingency because the author(s) of such a prophecy need not anticipate in what contexts issues are debated, or who is included in the debate, etc.

9. Philosophic prophecy works often by introducing a set of conceptual oppositions that help *delimit* how philosophic problems/controversies/questions are treated subsequently. I have in mind something akin to a Kuhnian paradigm. For example, Hobbes's fiction of a "state of nature" has shaped the subsequent tradition even in works that aim to refute or get around it.

10. The present list of characteristics portrays an ideal type. It does not purport to offer necessary and sufficient conditions. The concept is, in the first instance, developed to facilitate descriptive analysis and classification within philosophical history of a wide range of otherwise very different philosophers operating within very different milieus. By organizing our source material in light of a concept such as philosophic prophecy we may also alter the meanings of philosophy

One might think that philosophical prophecy has little to do with the substance of philosophy given that I have aligned it with the imagination, trust, faith, *muthos*, etc. Moreover, one may worry that if philosophic prophecy succeeds, it may well be a partial consequence of social authority of the prophet (and her interpreters, etc.). But even if we grant the assumptions behind such objections, I do not see why in writing the history of philosophy we

31. For context, see Candlish (2007).

32. Even if one were to accept that authorial intentions are fixed in light of context (and define this non-arbitrarily), meanings need not be so fixed. In particular, philosophic prophecy, once successful, "shapes" meaning into the future.

should only focus on what is commonly thought philosophical. The contextualists have taught *us* this would impoverish our craft; we may also miss important features of an author's philosophy if we ignore such supposedly extra-philosophical features.[33] So, even within philosophy, we need concepts that help us gain clarity on the ways in which philosophical thought can function both inside and outside philosophy. In particular, when we are dealing with (potentially) canonical or once canonical authors, their "prophetic" role plays a significant part in their status.

Within the Western philosophical tradition, Plato's dialogues are probably the origin of the genre of philosophic prophecy: Socrates is contrasted with false authorities (the best of whom are Sophists), and Plato's characters use narratives that are full of claims that are not knowably false and which enhance philosophical doctrine. Nevertheless, philosophic prophecy is by definition not the activity of offering noble lies, which consists in affirming claims known to be false. I also distinguish the application of philosophic prophecy from the practice promoted by some of Leo Strauss's followers of locating unstated esoteric doctrines in a text. It is not impossible that some esoteric doctrines are sometimes conveyed by means of philosophic prophecy.[34] Yet, in philosophic prophecy the *exoteric* text is doing the work of shaping the thought of future generations.

This last point helps explain why the approach proposed here is entirely compatible with other, more prevalent scholarly methods in writing the history of philosophy. So, while here I focus on the way a particular concept functions in texts and their effects, this is not meant to rule out the significance of arguments or the many contextual and material conditions that structure the reception of these. On the contrary, my focus here on authority is meant to open the door to investigations of all kinds of practices that are significant in philosophical history. Philosophic prophecy is a tool that can be promoted by historians of philosophy. This is naked self-interest, too; we should keep imagining practices of the history of philosophy that keep history of philosophy within philosophy.

Moreover, not all philosophic prophecies need to have been successful up until now to be worthy of our consideration. On the contrary, sometimes our present focus on a previously ignored or hidden prophecy may be just the condition to generate a new, shared intellectual horizon.

Before I re-tell the history of the origins of analytical philosophy, I briefly contrast my approach to the history of philosophy with two influential

33. See Goldenbaum, this volume, for a nice treatment of Kant and theology.

34. I do not share the prevalent hostility to Leo Strauss (see Goldenbaum and Smith in this volume).

alternative approaches. I do so in order to make precise the manner and philosophical motives for the approach defended here.

3. Methodological Contrasts

In this section,[35] I polemically reject two opposing methodologies.[36] First, I engage with Skinner's self-consciously "philosophical" methodological (1969) article.[37] This influential essay promotes the idea that in doing history of philosophy we encounter "alien problems."[38] We find an echo of Skinner's view in Bernard Williams' advocacy that history of "philosophy … can help us in reviving a sense of strangeness or questionability about our own philosophical assumptions."[39] Now, to understand my approach, one must grasp that concept formation is a way to create *shared* meanings between us and the past where there might not have been any before.[40] Second, I engage in critical reflection on Michael Kremer's criticism of approaches to the history of analytical philosophy, which presuppose that recent philosophy is necessarily a progressive enterprise.

Skinner's approach is focused on authorial intent.[41] While intentions may matter quite a bit in moral evaluation, philosophy and its history are not primarily morality plays. In this volume, Mogens Lærke offers many criticisms of Skinner's focus on intentions and urges us to focus on meanings instead.[42] On the whole I endorse Lærke's arguments. But even so I focus on a peculiar

35. This section has benefited from discussion with Michael Kremer, Dennis Des Chene, and audiences in Brighton, Groningen, Madrid, and Montreal. I am especially grateful for critical comments by Susan James, Quentin Skinner, James Harris, Knud Haakonssen, Steve Nadler, and David Teirra.

36. Skinner (1969), 3–5. In a recent interview, Skinner describes his (1969) as "a kind of polemical squib." www.artoftheory.com/quentin-skinner-on-meaning-and-method/

37. Skinner (1969), 4.

38. Ibid., 52.

39. Williams (2006 [1994]), 260.

40. See also Vermeir, this volume.

41. Skinner (1969), 49.

42. Moreover, Lærke and Vermeir (also this volume) take effective aim at Skinner's claim that the historian must attempt to fix an author's intentions in the form of an *unrecoverable* counterfactual ("no agent [that is the subject of historical inquiry—ES] can eventually be said to have meant or done something which he could never be brought to accept as a correct description of what he had meant or done"). Vermeir, Lærke, and Justin Smith all repair (and transform) Skinner's methodology (and variants on it) such that the history of philosophy can become a properly autonomous and professional activity. They accept the intellectual division of labor within philosophy, while I see this as a threat to philosophy.

authorial intent—one that is tacitly ruled out without argument by Skinner[43] and implicitly presupposed by Lærke's method:[44] philosophic prophecy is a species of philosophical utterances that Skinner overlooks.

Contra Skinner, who asserts a sharp distinction between the history of philosophy and "our own immediate problems,"[45] the approach I advocate here focuses on the way our problems may well be deliberately caused, in part, by past philosophers, even if the way we articulate our problems would be unfamiliar to them. As an aside, my approach can be rearticulated entirely without mention of intentions—philosophic prophecy can be analyzed in terms of highly structured possible consequences of texts; what matters is that these texts played a constitutive role in transforming a merely possible, even inconceivable, conceptualization of a situation into a situation in which the original conception comes out true, or nearly enough true.

Let's grant, for the sake of argument, Skinner's claim that it is a "general truth" that there are no "timeless concepts." From this rejection of timeless concepts, Skinner insists that all concepts are relative to a particular society. (See his awkward locution about concepts "which have gone with different societies.") With this move, Skinner also explicitly embraces a doctrine of contingency such that there are no perennial questions in philosophy and only individual answers to individual questions (within a culture).[46] I offer three related criticisms:

First, in arguing against timeless concepts, Skinner proceeds entirely by ridicule.[47] But he offers no argument for ruling out potentially *durable* concepts. For the purposes of my project, all that is required is that concepts can sometimes transcend the culturally enclosed audience of their first publication. Second, Skinner's meaning-relativism need not entail the kind of contingency he identifies. Even without timeless concepts the existence of certain conceptual connections between concepts across different societies

43. Skinner (1969) assumes that one's intended audience is one's near contemporaries.

44. Lærke (this volume) takes controversies as a primitive in his methodology. My approach focuses on how some concepts become the shared, but *potentially tacit*, background assumptions that make controversies possible.

45. Skinner (1969), 53.

46. See ibid., 53.

47. Ibid., 51–52. Here is Skinner's self-evaluation: (upon his re-reading of Skinner 1969) he "was struck, if I may say this, that it was very funny. I thought it had a lot of quite good jokes in it. And yes, maybe that had a certain shock value, because it was a satire amongst other things." www.artoftheory.com/quentin-skinner-on-meaning-and-method/. Now, one might argue (as Mogens Lærke did in private correspondence) that this is itself a sign of (successful) philosophic prophecy.

may not be *entirely* contingent at all—they may be the product of human agency.[48]

Skinner's approach fits comfortably with a method of case study that is extremely popular among contemporary historians. Among its practitioners, each and every case is viewed as unique so that no general claims can be extracted from these. In historical context one can understand this strategy as a wedge against Marxist views of historical determinism. It is a savvy way to deflect interference from outsiders, who have no reason to be concerned about "history," which provides *only* a "lesson in self-knowledge."[49] But why should we restrict the scope of the "lessons" that philosophical history can teach?

Third, Skinner's approach comes at a very dangerous cost: it cannot fully comprehend claims of meaning in history by, say, nationalists and religious thinkers and peoples. His approach has to reinterpret such claims in terms of intended meanings that are in some sense unintelligible or irrational—this is one reason I recoil from Skinner's and his followers' emphasis on the alien-ness of the past. To put this uncivilly: the strangeness—even when intended in non-judgmental fashion—one finds elsewhere may also be a sign of one's own parochialism or, worse, pusillanimity. By treating the past as *essentially* strange, Skinner promotes political and philosophical quietism about the past and future (in accord with the Wittgensteinian roots to his thought).

Skinner proceeds as if the professional historian stands outside history speaking to fellow historians; he promotes a "positivist" understanding of history to be sorted by the expert historian.[50] And in doing so, he is in no position to decide what facts matter to the history of philosophy, except those taken from a preexisting and *paradigmatic* tradition or expert judgment. While such an attitude is scientifically respectable, it is fundamentally at odds with philosophy, which must also be capable of questioning the tradition from within which its puzzles and problems are articulated; otherwise there are unexamined assumptions in the philosophical enterprise. It is, thus, a

---

48. For example, in treating Hume and Adam Smith on the nature of property, I argue that they develop a style of argument that captures the conceptual presuppositions that generate, in part, the social conditions of possibility of the existence of an institution, even long after the initial conditions that first gave rise to the possibility have passed. See Schliesser (2006).

49. Skinner (1969), 53. In a recent interview Skinner calls attention to his anti-Marxism: "the most novel thing I was trying to say, which was that it was meant to be a critique of the then very prevalent Marxist theories of ideology." www.artoftheory.com/quentin-skinner-on-meaning-and-method/.

50. Cf. the defense of positivism by Smith (this volume).

category error for a philosopher to follow Skinner's path (cf. his use of "moral error").[51]

In his (1969) paper, Skinner briefly discusses and dismisses an alternative view (which he associates with Hegel) that the best way to write history of philosophy is from the "present," which is, after all, the most highly evolved. Soames's massive *Philosophical Analysis in the Twentieth Century* heartily embraces that Hegelian perspective. In a forthcoming paper, drawing on some distinctions from the historian of mathematics, Ivor Grattan-Guinness (1990), Kremer has adopted the phrase "a royal road to me" for that kind of presentist history "which aims to provide an 'account of how a particular modern theory arose out of older theories instead of an account of those older theories in their own right,' thus confounding the questions 'How did we get here?' and 'What happened in the past?'"[52] Kremer goes on to suggest that "philosophical history is always in some sense a 'road to me,' but only becomes objectionable if it is treated as a 'royal road to me.' Properly carried out, philosophical history will shape its practitioner philosophically."[53] That is to say, in effect Kremer criticizes Soames for writing a history of his [and Kripke's] prejudice(s), or to put this more politely (and closer to Kremer's own words), Soames does not merely mischaracterize the past; in Soames's approach we cannot be surprised by the past.[54]

According to Kremer, Soames's self-congratulatory history of progress (the royal road to me) is not properly a philosophical activity—Soames's enterprise is too uncritical of present (local) orthodoxy. As opposed to Soames-style "royal road to me," Kremer embraces "untimely" history of philosophy (quoting Bernard Williams, who is echoing Nietzsche), that is, a kind of "road to me."[55] In particular, untimely history of philosophy either up-ends present philosophy (this is why surprise matters so much to Williams) or makes the past useful to one's present (by making one revise/improve one's philosophical orientation/doctrine, etc.).

51. Skinner (1969), 53.

52. Kremer (forthcoming), 32. Kremer is quoting Grattan-Guinness (1990),157.

53. Kremer (forthcoming), 32.

54. The "royal road to me" can produce very illuminating (or deviously misleading) history of philosophy in, say, Quine's little history at the start of "Epistemology Naturalized" (Quine 1969). It draws an interesting distinction, and then tells a surprising, yet self-serving story about it. But it is not easy to distinguish philosophical royalty from royal imposters.

55. Kremer (forthcoming), 23.

I find Michael Kremer's defense of philosophical history as a species of philosophy very congenial. For Kremer, philosophical history just is philosophy. In particular, Kremer's philosophical scholar gets transformed by the practice of history. Later I discuss Ernest Nagel, who has something like this in mind when he speaks of "intellectual catharsis" that history can provide. Even so, I draw four contrasts with Kremer in order to help make more precise my position.

First, I do not deny that the past can be strange initially. But we should *also* be *willing* to try to locate or originate similarities. In particular, second, we can introduce or reorient concepts that make shared horizons between the past and our future possible. These concepts may be rooted in the past. But, third, these concepts also make a shared future possible for us and our past—it is a historical-philosophical fact that many of the most interesting philosophers of the past have coined concepts that our present activities articulate and, in doing so, help generate our futures (and not just the present). Or, to put it a bit more paradoxically: even if this way of proceeding need not be the only avenue for philosophical historians, some concepts can—if we are wise—give us a "new" past that is worth articulating and clarifying for the sake of our future.[56] Fourth, in doing so, we may also risk re-writing what it is to be philosophical. This last remark is no doubt very cryptic, but one way to put this point is that Kremer writes entirely from *within* our tradition, while the historian of philosophic prophecy has to question tradition.

In what follows, I engage in some philosophic prophecy—both by reconstructing past philosophic prophecy and by proposing my own narrative that is designed to extend and alter the contours of the tradition I am describing—by re-telling the history of analytical philosophy and analytic history of philosophy, where I also use the concept for descriptive purposes. I do so by critically examining an earlier, extremely influential, attempt at philosophic prophecy, namely, Ernest Nagel's attempt to establish the nature and boundaries of analytical philosophy. Along the way, I show how he is indebted to Boole's treatment of Spinoza. I then turn to Schlick to promote an alternative vision of analytical philosophy. Nagel and Schlick are both very *good* philosophic prophets; one offers a mostly false and one a mostly true prophecy.

56. A philosophical historian is in a symmetric relation with the material she studies—sometimes her activity is a preselected means of the subject matter. To get a sense of what I have in mind, reflection on the final paragraph of Stone (2006) may be useful.

4. *Ernest Nagel: The (False) Prophet of Analytical Philosophy*

A stranger frequently hears important truths at the fireside

TOCQUEVILLE

If we are going to reform the way we do history of philosophy in a manner that is exciting philosophically, that is, in a way that will actively shape the future of philosophy, then we need to understand the ways in which we are prevented from thinking of history of philosophy as a species of philosophy. In particular, we need to disarm practices that insulate philosophers from the activity of history of philosophy that have deep roots in analytical philosophy.[57]

I do so by calling attention to three texts that help explain the origins and ways of analytical philosophy, including the role of rational reconstruction within it. The linchpin of my analysis is Russell's (1914) treatment of Spinoza, but also George Boole and, especially, Ernest Nagel, figure largely in the account.[58]

The way we think about the origins of analytical philosophy can be traced to a remarkable two-part narrative published in 1936 by Nagel.[59] Ostensibly it is an informal report from his tour of the continent.[60] But he is probably the first to characterize "analytical philosophy" as a movement in the sense that became influential the next decades.[61] He is the first to pick out the schools of

57. This section is very indebted to ongoing criticism from Jeff Bell.

58. My narrative fails to do justice to the important role of Susan Stebbing. See Beaney (forthcoming).

59. Nagel (1936a) and (1936b) are not unknown in the burgeoning, historical literature of the origin of analytic of philosophy (e.g., Richardson (2002), but I know of no work that treats these as a source of study in its own right. I thank Greg Arnold-Frost for repeatedly calling my attention to these pieces.

60. Nagel insists that he is "reporting less what certain European schools of philosophy *profess*, and more what I got out of a year's study abroad" (1936a, 5). In so doing, Nagel insulates himself against empirical refutation.

61. "Analytical philosophy" had a different meaning/use familiar to Nagel's readers. Nagel's essay is almost certainly responding to Sidney Hook (1930). By "analytical" (152) or "analysis" (142, 149) Hook does not mean what Nagel (and thus, *we*) mean by it. Hook identifies Edmund Husserl's program with analysis (on 152ff.). Martin Heidegger is also treated as somebody who engages in "analysis" (154), as do the students of Wilhelm Dilthey (153). To be an "analyst" in Hook's lingo means, besides adopting a taxonomic method, that one keeps one's eyes on "the object" (152). I thank Jeff Bell for calling my attention to Hook's piece. See his blog posts, www.newappsblog.com/2011/10/cc12-hooks-impression-of-german-philosophy-circa-1930.html and www.newappsblog.com/2011/10/schools-and-traditions-or-husserl-and-realism-pt-i.html.

thought that came to be associated with it (the Cambridge of Bertrand Russell, Ludwig Wittgenstein and G. E. Moore; the Vienna Circle with special focus on Rudolf Carnap, who was then in Prague; and the Polish logicians in Lvov and Warsaw). In particular, Nagel deliberately "excluded mention of the men whose thought does not bear directly on questions of logic and method."[62] He also emphasizes what the different schools "have in common, methodologically and doctrinally."[63] He writes:

> In the first place, the men with whom I have talked are impatient with philosophic systems built in the traditionally grand manner. Their preoccupation is with philosophy as *analysis*; they take for granted a body of authentic knowledge acquired by the special sciences, and are concerned not with *adding* to it in the way research in these sciences adds to it, but with *clarifying* its meaning and implications. Philosophy for these men holds out no promise of settling questions which only the empirical sciences are competent to settle; nor does it assume the function of legislating what sort of things it is permissible or possible for the empirical sciences to investigate. Those who seek in philosophy a substitute for religion or a key to social salvation will not find it here. The intellectual temper cultivated by these men is that of ethical and political neutrality within the domain of philosophic analysis proper, however much they may be moved by the moral and social chaos which threatens to swallow the few extant intellectual oases upon which they stand.[64]

Nagel then goes on to emphasize the common concern with "method" which "dominates all these places" as well as the fact that "students whose primary interest is the history of ideas will find that, with some important exceptions, they will profit little from talking with these men."[65] Finally, he ascribes to them a minimal, albeit non-trivial "common doctrine," that is "the men to whom I refer subscribe to a common-sense naturalism. They do not believe that the everyday world is an illusion, or that science or philosophy reveal a contrasting reality."[66] I trust this characterization is familiar to most

---

62. Nagel (1936a), 5.

63. Ibid., 6.

64. Ibid., 6

65. Ibid., 6.

66. Ibid., 7.

contemporary readers in English-language philosophy. This is how *we* have been taught to think about where analytical philosophy comes from.[67]

Yet, there is plenty of further evidence in Nagel's narrative to suggest that we are in the realm of philosophic prophecy. Let me offer two pieces of evidence.

First, Nagel is not a dispassionate bystander. Quite to the contrary, he contrasts "the shining sword" of "analytical philosophy" favorably with unnamed opposing schools described as "a romantic irrationalism that has completely engulfed Europe";[68] and its "community of seers";[69] and also, "traditional speculative philosophy frequently cultivates mystification and conscious irrationalism."[70] Nagel relies here on a version of the dialectic between true and false philosophy, but with two twists: (i) within his account of analytical philosophy there is a further contrast between the "gentle force of a luminous mind" of Carnap[71] and the secretive, homoerotic cult surrounding Wittgenstein.[72] (This is not the only such implied contrast; within the discussion of the Vienna Circle, "Schlick and Waismann" are treated as a foil for Carnap; their views do not receive sustained discussion.) (ii) Though he admires analytical philosophy greatly and wants to further its progress as part of a scientific philosophy against the American followers of traditional philosophy,[73] Nagel is also a critic:

> [I]t seems to me that a better knowledge of the history which they condemn would have saved many of the analytical philosophers from serious error; for, it will be seen, the latter frequently discuss the traditional problems however disguised they may be by a different terminology. Moreover, the historical approach, when wisely cultivated, can

67. There are also accompanying shared origin myths that persist within analytical philosophy. See Candlish (2007), 4–18, for a fascinating treatment. For a different approach, see Dummett (1994).

68. Nagel (1936a), 5.

69. Nagel (1936b), 6.

70. Nagel (1936a), 9.

71. Nagel (1936b), 44.

72. Cf. Nagel (1936a), 10: "It is easy for anyone at Cambridge to perceive excellent reasons for the fascination that both men [Moore and Wittgenstein] exercise upon their students. It is not easy, without lapsing into the personal and impertinent, to convey those reasons to strangers to Cambridge." (See also ibid., 16–17.)

73. Richardson (2003).

> frequently produce the same kind of intellectual catharsis and dissolution of pseudo-problems as does the analytic method.[74]

Second, Nagel hints clearly enough that he is drawing the domain of analytical philosophy rather narrowly. So, despite the fact that he treats analytical philosophy as hostile to the history of philosophy, Nagel is fully aware that one of the main heroes of his narrative, Jan Lukasiewicz, is deeply immersed in the "history of logic" and—non-trivially given my present focus on the constructive role of history of philosophy—has made important contributions to modern logic because of it.[75] Because Nagel excludes anything other than "logic and method," even Moore's work in ethics is passed over in silence. Nevertheless, Carnap's views on ethical statements are treated extensively and found wanting ("perhaps the least satisfactory part of Carnap's views is his analysis of the propositions of ethics and esthetics").[76]

In Nagel's 1936 pieces the rejection of ethics is unmotivated. But we can glean the conceptual oppositions that make this rejection possible by turning to one of Nagel's heroes, Russell's treatment of Spinoza:

> The ethical work of Spinoza, for example, appears to me of the very highest significance, but what is valuable in such work is not any metaphysical theory as to the nature of the world to which it may give rise, nor indeed anything which can be proved or disproved by argument. What is valuable is the indication of some new way of feeling towards life and the world, some way of feeling by which our own existence can acquire more of the characteristics which we must deeply desire. The value of such work, however immeasurable it is, belongs with practice and not with theory. Such theoretic importance as it may possess is only in relation to human nature, not in relation to the world at large. The scientific philosophy, therefore, which aims only at understanding the world and not directly at any other improvement of human life, cannot take account of ethical notions without being turned aside from that submission to fact which is the essence of the scientific temper.[77]

---

74. Nagel (1936a), 7.

75. Ibid., 50.

76. Ibid., 48ff.

77. Russell (1914).

Russell sharply distinguishes between Spinoza's ethics and metaphysics. Throughout his writing, Russell systematically defends the beauty and nobility of Spinoza's ethics but denies it is philosophical for four significant reasons: (i) Spinoza's metaphysics of substance has been disproved by science and can, thus, be discarded. This is an instance of Newton's Challenge to Philosophy. Russell echoes eighteenth-century Newtonian criticism of Spinoza, especially Samuel Clarke.[78] (ii) Because Spinoza's metaphysics is discredited, his ethics is not really founded on or supported by argument, but by feeling and "maxims."[79] (iii) The feeling that Spinoza's ethics promotes is according to Russell oriented toward practice, and (iv) Russell denies that philosophy is fundamentally concerned with practice but rather with understanding.

Now, crucially, Russell's philosophy is fundamentally a denial of philosophical freedom—it is about "submission to fact." There is, in Russell, no sense in which a philosophical legislator has any freedom to develop or determine conceptual structures from indeterminate reality. It is, in fact, a determined submission because Russell self-consciously prevents himself from entering into certain feelings—he is a "cool critic" and deliberately "unsympathetic." This is a decision by Russell. It is his self-command. But oddly enough, in order to reject Spinoza (and Henri Bergson), Russell invokes scientific facts even though he also insists that, when it comes to philosophy, one should not rely on the fallible and potentially outdated content of science. Thus, Russell's targets outstrip the resources he has left available to himself and his intellectual heirs.

But why would Russell have thought that Spinoza's ethics is not really founded on or supported by argument? Had he done an analysis of Spinoza's arguments in the *Ethics* and found them wanting? I suspect Russell remembered chapter 13 (and 14) of Boole's (1854) masterpiece.[80] Boole writes, "The analysis of [the *Ethics*'] main argument is extremely difficult, owing not to the complexity of the separate propositions which it involves, but to the use of vague definitions, and of axioms which, through a like defect of clearness, it is perplexing to determine whether we ought to accept or to reject. While the reasoning of Dr. Samuel Clarke is in part verbal, that of Spinoza is so in a

78. Schliesser (2012b).

79. Russell (1912) uses similar arguments to dismiss Bergson.

80. Elsewhere, Russell credits Boole with having discovered "pure mathematics," or formal logic (Russell, 1918, 74). Boole is not mentioned by Ray Monk in his biography of Russell; this is emblematic for a more general problem in the way "early analytic" is treated from within by even its most able historians.

much greater degree; and perhaps this is the reason why, to some minds, it has appeared to possess a formal cogency, to which in reality it possesses no just claim."[81] What are these remarks doing in this brilliant book that, regardless of its technical limitations, invents "pure mathematics"?

If we remember George Boole (1815–1864), it is because we sometimes talk of logical connectives as Boolean operators. Specialists in the history of logic are, of course, aware that he is something like the Copernicus of modern logic, but we have forgotten that he set in motion a way of thinking that has become deeply entrenched within analytical philosophy, including analytic history of philosophy. Let me illustrate this with a few remarks on chapters 13–14, where Boole (also) invents what we now call the "rational reconstruction" of argument in symbolic form in the history of philosophy.[82] Boole begins chapter 13 as follows:

> 1. The general order which, in the investigations of the following chapter, I design to pursue, is the following. I shall examine what are the actual premises involved in the demonstrations of some of the general propositions of the above treatises [Clarke's *Demonstration* and Spinoza's *Ethics*—ES], whether those premises be expressed or implied. By the actual premises I mean whatever propositions are assumed in the course of the argument, without being proved, and are employed as parts of the foundation upon which the final conclusion is built. The premises thus determined, I shall express in the language of symbols, and I shall then deduce from them by the methods developed in the previous chapters of this work, the most important inferences which they involve, in addition to the particular inferences actually drawn by the authors. I shall in some instances modify the premises by the omission of some fact or principle which is contained in them, or by the addition or substitution of some new proposition, and shall determine how by such change the ultimate conclusions are affected. In the pursuit of these objects it will not devolve upon me to inquire, except incidentally, how far the metaphysical principles laid down in these celebrated productions are worthy of confidence, but only to ascertain what conclusions may justly be drawn from given premises; and in doing this, to exemplify the perfect liberty which we possess as concerns both the choice and the order of the elements of the

81. Boole, (1854), 145.

82. The phrase "rational reconstruction" is traced back to Carnap's *Aufbau*. See Beaney (forthcoming).

> final or concluding propositions, viz., as to determining what elementary propositions are true or false, and what are true or false under given restrictions, or in given combinations. 2. The chief practical difficulty of this inquiry will consist, not in the application of the method to the premises once determined, but in ascertaining what the premises are.[83]

Boole offers a careful analysis of the arguments on both sides of the Clarke-Spinoza dispute. I offer three general comments on the significance of Boole's treatment of it.

First, the main stated point of Boole's exercise is to illustrate the philosophical power of his technical tool. Even with the limitations of Boole's symbolic logic, the arguments by Clarke and Spinoza become transparent and clear in a way that may have never before been seen and were probably not so seen again until Jonathan Bennett's *A Study of Spinoza's Ethics* (1984)—our exemplar of history of philosophy as rational reconstruction. While early modern philosophers talked about "clear and distinct" knowledge, inspecting ideas always remained a suspect method as the Newtonian critics of Descartes and Spinoza insisted. In fact, it's from Boole that philosophers learned how analysis could provide clarity.

Second, Boole concludes chapter 13 with the following remark:

> It is not possible, I think, to rise from the perusal of the arguments of Clarke and Spinoza without a deep conviction of the futility of all endeavors to establish, entirely a priori, the existence of an Infinite Being, His attributes, and His relation to the universe. The fundamental principle of all such speculations, viz., that whatever we can clearly conceive, must exist, fails to accomplish its end, even when its truth is admitted.[84]

The principle, whatever we can clearly conceive, must exist, is closely connected to and in certain respects an implication of the principle of sufficient reason (the PSR). This is not true in all thinkers, of course, but "Spinoza related the idea of a sufficient reason in turn to the divine intellect so that there was a sufficient reason for the existence of something if and only if it were conceivable by God."[85] Without mentioning the principle of sufficient

83. Boole (1854), 184.

84. Ibid., 216–17.

85. Kane (1976), 27. I thank Daniel Schneider for the reference. I am grateful to Schneider, Alan Nelson, Michael Morris, and Omri Boehm for discussion.

reason as such, Boole's criticisms sets the stage for Russell's rejection of the PSR in his dispute with Bradley.[86]

Third, Boole conceives of his enterprise of developing symbolic logic in moral terms (this is undeniable in the last pages of the book). In the preceding quote, it shows up as a hint by way of "the perfect liberty which we possess as concerns both the choice and the order of the elements of the final or concluding propositions." In part, our philosophical *freedom* consists in logical-conceptual ordering.[87] Coining concepts is meant to subsume Boole's vision of philosophical liberty as opposed to Russellian submission to fact.

Let us return to Nagel.[88] His narrative self-consciously excludes more than history of philosophy and ethics. Nagel addresses the issue in his first footnote:

> I am excluding Broad from this account, partly because being the only philosopher at Cambridge who publishes at any length. Broad is adequately known through his writings, partly because discussions at Cambridge do not for the moment center around him, and partly because I myself am only mildly interested in the themes with which he is at present occupied.[89]

We may have *forgotten*, but between 1925 and 1935 Broad published major books in the philosophy of mind, free will, ethics, history of philosophy, and even an extensive engagement with John McTaggart's metaphysics. Nagel concludes the note with, "For lack of space I must also forego comment on the Peircean-pragmatic turn which the discussions of induction and probability have taken in the cases of Braithwaite and the late Frank Ramsey." This omission is significant for two additional reasons:

(i) If he had included Richard Braithwaite and Ramsey, he would have had to pay attention to what we can call analytical philosophy of social science, not just in Cambridge, but also at Vienna (e.g., Otto Neurath). A focus on Ramsey would have forced him to consider the ways in which analytical philosophy and Cambridge political economy in the wake of Henry Sidgwick

---

86. See Della Rocca, this volume.

87. This anticipates Carnap's voluntarism. See Jeffrey (1995).

88. Nagel (2011), 40–41, certainly recognized the significance of Boole to Alfred North Whitehead and Russell.

89. Nagel (1936a), 10, n. 1.

overlapped. (Moore and Russell were students of Sidgwick.) Nagel's grouping and the way it is given cohesion internally and externally was an act of philosophical legislation.[90] But once set in motion, and with the aid of forced exile and deaths of many leading lights of Nagel's analytical philosophy, the narrative became self-reinforcing (especially since Nagel became a leading organizational and philosophical figure in the Unity of Science movement and North American philosophy more generally).[91]

(ii) The omission is also surprising in light of one of the primary themes of Nagel's two-part essay: the continuity between Charles Sanders Peirce and analytical philosophy (e.g., "Much of this reads like a page from Peirce").[92] In particular, "Without being aware of it, they have taken seriously Peirce's advice that expert knowledge of some empirical subject-matter ought to be part of a philosopher's equipment."[93] Nagel is in favor of scientific philosophy[94] and before long his branch pragmatism will be assimilated to the analytic movement he has delineated.

5. *Schlick and Coining Concepts: A Counter-History of Analytical philosophy*

Einstein dramatically changed the shape of physics at the start of the twentieth century. In doing so he also caused a crisis in Kantian "scientific philosophy," which was perceived to have committed itself fatally to the a priori necessity of Euclidian geometry and the Newtonian science of motion. The

90. This being so, it helps explain why subsequent generations have had such a hard time giving necessary and sufficient definitions of "analytical philosophy" (even if it can be identified by shared myths). It also helps explain why multiple narratives on the origin of analytical philosophy will always be possible.

91. Nagel's efforts were contested. See, for example, Taube (1937), 205–10. Dennis Des Chene objects that the paucity of citations to Nagel's piece undercut my claims about its significance. I agree it is important to identify possible transmission mechanisms, including oral traditions in graduate education. (For a nice example of this, see Carus (2007), 265 n. 13, where Howard Stein is reported on Carnap's teachings.) Nagel occupied a position in a leading department that spanned decades; he also had students who wrote influential treatments: for example, Pap (1949), which was widely discussed and cited, could well be one of the crucial transmission mechanisms for Nagel's views.

92. Nagel (1936a), 18.

93. Ibid., 30; see also 37.

94. Besides the pragmatists, the then dominant Neorealists were also promoting scientific philosophy in America. For their manifesto (which anticipates the Vienna Circle manifesto in uncanny ways), see Edwin B. Holt, Walter T. Marvin, W. P. Montague, Ralph Barton Perry, Walter B. Pitkin, and Edward Gleason Spaulding (1910).

series of philosophical episodes associated with this scientific revolution instantiates the significance of what I call "Newton's Challenge to philosophy." Recall I mean by this that "science" is authoritative in settling debates within philosophy.

One of the great martyrs of philosophy, Moritz Schlick (who was assassinated in 1936), took these developments so seriously that at one point he even admitted that "I am not writing for those who think that Einstein's philosophical opponents were right."[95] This is an exemplary instance of Newton's Challenge to Philosophy in practice. In context, Schlick is using the example of Einstein to introduce and defend his brand of verificationism (which he calls "true positivism") in response to criticism by C. I. Lewis, who according to Schlick mistakenly attributes a *false* "solipsistic" positivism to the members of the Vienna Circle (a solipsism that Schlick, in turn, associates with Hans Vaihinger).[96]

The fact that Schlick categorizes his opponents rather than just focusing on the arguments, suggests that we are dealing with a demarcation project of the kind philosophic prophets engage in. Schlick's scientific philosophy *also* embraces a vantage point for philosophy that can reflect on science from *without*, without accepting science's claims merely on authority. The mature Schlick does so as an "unrelenting" or "true" "empiricist."[97] In particular, he explicitly contrasts his "true" empiricism with the presumably false empiricists, who are "theoretically minded men who take their stand *within* science."[98] These false empiricists embrace a "rationalist attitude" that mistakes science for reality.[99] In context, the explicit target is Carl Hempel.[100]

---

95. Schlick (1936), 343.

96. Ibid., 358ff.

97. Schlick (1935), 65–70.

98. Ibid., 69; the emphasis is Schlick's.

99. Ibid., 69: "Science is a system of propositions; and-without being aware of it-these thinkers substitute science for reality; for them facts are not acknowledged before they are formulated in propositions and taken down in their notebooks. But Science is not the World. The universe of discourse is not the whole universe. It is a typical rationalistic attitude which shows itself here under the guise of the most subtle distinctions. It is as old as metaphysics itself, as we may learn from a saying of old Parmenides." See also Benardete (1964), 224.

100. Given the subsequent ways the Carnap-Quine debates evolved, it is important that *here* Schlick does not mainly defend the distinction between, within, and without science in terms of the analytic-synthetic distinction. Rather, he relies on a distinction between the authority of first-person experience and the authority of textbook experience. The distinction is also consistently deployed in Schlick's better known work of 1932.

My main interest in focusing on Schlick can be found in his response to the impact of Einstein on philosophy. Appealing to Socrates's practice, the mature Schlick sharply distinguishes between two intellectual enterprises: science should be defined as the "pursuit of truth" and philosophy as the "pursuit of meaning."[101] Schlick introduces this distinction in order to be able to insist that great scientists are properly philosophical when they *discover* new and proper meanings of concepts (his favorite example is Einstein's analysis of simultaneity). These concepts are about possible circumstances. Hence, the articulation, clarification, and reorientation of concepts that do not merely describe what is, but rather what could be, is on this account an essentially philosophical activity. Schlick's position is a salutary corrective to a focus on professional practices that are *subsequent* to the intellectual division of labor.[102]

In addition, in one of his earliest writings (1910), Schlick sharply distinguishes between the development of quantitative and qualitative concepts. According to the young Schlick, the former are concepts of science, the latter of philosophy.[103] Once practitioners of a field of inquiry are capable of deploying quantitative concepts in a stable, theory-mediated measurement practice, it is well on its way to being a science.[104]

So, according to my reading of Schlick, coining, articulating, and clarifying concepts is a distinct philosophical activity that can take place within and outside the sciences. When the concepts are quantitative, they are part of a possible science; when the concepts are qualitative, they are part of a possible philosophy.[105] A focus on designing concepts is very close to Carnap's conceptual engineering.[106] I understand many of the canonical works in early analytical philosophy as well as the near canonical works by Ramsey and Neurath as exemplifying the coining of concepts with a great deal of philosophical precision, sophistication, and lasting influence.

---

101. Schlick (1931), 15; emphasis in original. See also Lærke, this volume.

102. We can be maximally tolerant about the way in which concepts are introduced and articulated (e.g., poetry, mathematics, historical enquiry, etc.).

103. The Vienna Circle was founded in 1922. Some might object to treating pre-1915 Schlick as part of analytical philosophy.

104. So, philosophers can generate formal tools for the sciences, but it is a category mistake when these tools substitute for reflection within philosophy.

105. That is to say, the fruits of attempts at so-called formal philosophy must be judged by their utility for or function in science, not philosophy.

106. See Carus (2007), especially chapter 10.

I have set Schlick's verificationism aside. Even so, he may be thought to be an unlikely hero of my story. For it might seem that Schlick sharply distinguished between philosophy (concerned with truth of past systems of thought) and history (concerned with beauty, brilliance, and historical significance).[107] Schlick's particular conception of the *historian*'s task will be rejected by nearly all contemporary historians. I have no desire to revive either Schlick's particular understanding of history or the merely instrumental role that "knowledge of the past" has in his particular vision for the progress of philosophy. I prefer to endorse Nagel's pro-attitude toward history. I admire his focus on the "wise cultivation" of history that makes self-awareness as well as "intellectual catharsis and dissolution of pseudo-problems" possible."[108] We can reflexively practice the history of philosophy by way of developing and studying qualitative concepts that help shape not merely our understanding of philosophy's past, but also our future.

Acknowledgments

I thank Yoram Hazony, Dario Perinetti, Donald Rutherford, Ursula Goldenbaum, and, especially, Dennis des Chene, Justin Smith, and Mogens Lærke for very helpful discussion of an earlier draft of this chapter. I also thank Lynn Joy for encouraging this project at a crucial stage. In Brighton, Madrid, Nijmegen, and Montreal several audience members called my attention to important similarities between my approach and projects they were familiar with within continental philosophy. I hope more qualified readers will explore these similarities.

107. See Schlick (1931).

108. After Nagel's critical review of Hans Reichenbach's *The Rise of Scientific Philosophy*, Carnap wrote Reichenbach as follows: "Usually the deep reverence of philosophers for traditional philosophies is due to their low standard with respect to clarity and exactness of thinking, caused by a lack of training in scientific thinking. It seems a pity that Nagel seems somewhat infected by this, also he has done a good deal of study in science" (Carnap to Reichenbach, September 19, 1951; Pittsburgh University Archives Document number: HR 037-17-03).The original is in English. I thank Alan Richardson for calling my attention to this passage.

11

Philosophical Systems and Their History

Alan Nelson

1. Introduction

IN THIS CHAPTER,[1] I advocate an old-fashioned, somewhat conservative methodology for certain subjects in the history of philosophy. I am not going to argue for its superiority to other methodologies. I hope only to contribute to securing its place on the current menu in light of certain pressures to which it is subject. The method I have in mind strives to interpret important historical figures in philosophy as presenting philosophical *systems* of thought. This kind of systematic interpretation, as I shall call it, begins with the supposition that the philosophy being interpreted is itself systematic. Sometimes a philosopher's intentions are obvious; Spinoza's *Ethics*, for example, is manifestly systematic. In these cases the task of systematic interpretation is to understand how to minimize the shortcomings of the philosophy from the perspective of its author. There are other cases in which a philosopher gives some indications that a system is being presented, but the texts themselves do not seem to bear it out. In these cases, the method I am advocating sets the task of recovering the obscured systematicity. Section 2 gives a positive characterization of systematic interpretations. Section 3 notes some of the special obstacles that these interpretations must overcome if they are to be successful. Section 4 gives a brief sketch of how one might systematically approach Locke's *Essay Concerning Human Understanding*. That text is a good test case because Locke professes systematicity, but historians have produced daunting arguments for the conclusion that the text fails to present a coherent system.

1. Citations to Descartes's works are from Descartes (1984–91) and are abbreviated by CSM(K) followed by the volume and page numbers. CSM(K) contains marginal page references to the canonical edition of Adam and Tannery.

2. *What Is Systematic Interpretation?*

Once it is supposed that we are dealing with a systematic philosophy, we can characterize some methodological prescriptions for taking the supposition seriously. There is, of course, no algorithm for producing systematic interpretations—I'll be offering no more than rough guidelines. There are some philosophers who are generally regarded as being, in some sense, very systematic thinkers: Plato, Aquinas, Descartes, Spinoza, Leibniz, Kant, etc. The focus here is on early modern thinkers, but I think there are much more recent systematic thinkers as well: Donald Davidson, David Lewis, and Gilles Deleuze are good examples, but there are many others.[2] So far many readers will find what I've said platitudinous, at least while making allowances for the traditional aspects of the methodology. What might be more controversial is my claim that most interpreters, even those striving to produce internal accounts of authors' intended meaning, do not adhere to the guidelines I take to govern systematic interpretation.

To begin, systematic interpretation can be contrasted with both interpretations that emphasize contextual analysis of texts and those emphasizing instead rational reconstructions of arguments. Certainly, these both have important roles to play in improving our understanding of the history of philosophy. Systematic studies, in tension with contextualist approaches, purport to recover the doctrines intended by the great philosophers of the past. What is more, they maintain a sharp contrast between the great and not-so-great by making clear the explanatory power of the systems devised by great thinkers. "Greatness" is found primarily in the texts themselves and not in their reception. The systematic method also differs from rational reconstruction because it focuses on how the various doctrines of a thinker cohere instead of on how those doctrines are argued for. *Arguments* are understood as themselves internal to a philosophical system; what counts as a plausible premise or as a convincing argument is not to be objectively adjudicated from a historian's perspective

---

2. The terms "systematic interpretation" and "systematic philosophy" are, perhaps, not ideal in light of Leo Catana's (2008) tracing of the history of the historiographical concept of a system. He argues that the application of a particular, specialized concept of a system has often been anachronistically imposed on historical figures. Catana acknowledges, however, that some philosophers beginning in the seventeenth century with Descartes might appropriately be characterized as systematic in another sense. It is relevant, for example that Descartes intended his "system" to span all the sciences. A similar point applies to Catana's convincing argument that the distinction between questions internal to a text and those external to it is fraught with methodological difficulties (see Catana, this volume). But these difficulties are mitigated in those special cases in which a text explicates its own conception of internality. Again, the canonical figures of the Descartes-Kant period maintain that all human knowledge (save, perhaps, the deliverances of faith) are internal to their systems.

outside the system. And what does count as a good argument within a system of philosophy need not line up very closely with modern post-Fregean logic. Keeping this in mind, the systematic historian aims to clarify without reconstruction why the "arguments" (hereafter I'll omit scare quotes for this and related words) found in texts were supposed by their authors to be fully convincing. In some thinkers, logic itself is intertwined with other substantive, proprietary doctrines about cognition and ontology.[3]

Of course this sounds strikingly anti-Analytic, and that does not trouble the systematic interpreter. But we can and should distinguish (a) systems of philosophy that are not "Analytic," from (b) "Analytic" styles of exposition for the presentation of non-"Analytic" systems. In my opinion, systematic interpretations are best presented in an analytic vein. By that I mean the use of stylistic techniques such as interspersing textual quotations with interpretive analysis and footnoting interpretive claims (which might be presented in numbered lists) with citations of the target text and secondary literature. This style of presentation is, however, not essential to systematic interpretation.

With that as background, some characteristics of philosophical systems and interpretations that respect that systematicity can be enumerated. Or, to put it another way, I can enumerate some of the constraints on a historical interpretation of a systematic philosopher if that interpretation is to count as systematic in the sense being developed.

(1) *Systematic interpretations minimize significant doctrinal inconsistencies.* This might seem too obvious, but when dealing with great thinkers, *apparent* inconsistencies of a serious order are easy to find and hard to remove. For example, Descartes's thinking about corporeal substance seems riddled with obvious problems. The essences of material things are said to be clearly and distinctly perceived,[4] but the precise volume changes from instant to instant and its determinate value is not knowable. And various simple paradoxes have been suggested regarding motion in a Cartesian plenum-universe.[5] Or consider that Leibniz's monads are simple substances, but they seem to be temporally atomized into successive states.[6] And one of the most notorious problems in recent Leibniz scholarship concerns the

3. For a discussion of how logic itself is sensitive to other features of Descartes's system of philosophy, see Rogers and Nelson (forthcoming).

4. CSM II, 3.

5. E.g., Kenny (1968), 214.

6. This problem is trenchantly posed in Whipple (2010) and then given a systematic resolution.

difficulty in reconciling Leibniz's systematic claims about foundational simple substances with texts that suggest a central role for divisible corporeal substances.[7] Yet another example is provided by Locke's statement in the *Essay* that all ideas are either simple or complexes obtained by operations of the mind on simple ideas.[8] This seems to conflict with the apparent introduction of abstract ideas as a third distinct category.[9] These examples can be multiplied ad libitum, so I will mention just one more. Spinoza's centrally important theory of attributes is fraught with problems so severe that it has seemed to many commentators that it must be set aside and ignored if other aspects of Spinoza's philosophy are to be better understood.[10]

A systematic interpreter takes these apparent inconsistencies as prominent problems, assumes there is a solution, and then works to solve them. Why assume that most apparent inconsistencies in the texts are resolvable? I find it very unlikely that these geniuses left major inconsistencies in their thinking and did not notice them. This naturally raises the suspicion that systematic interpreters are engaged in hagiographic apologies for their historical heroes. But if we find an interpretation resolving the contradiction, that should count as a very powerful consideration in its favor. This kind of systematic evidence should outweigh the evidence of surface readings that display apparent textual inconsistencies. The systematic interpreter's counter-charge to hagiography is that those spurning systematic interpretations are uncharitable. They are not uncharitable in the Davidsonian sense that they fail to interpret the targeted texts as agreeing with *us*, where the first person plural is constructed from the interpreters' point of view. On the contrary, apparent surface inconsistencies are sometimes interpreted as real inconsistencies precisely because the interpreter constrains the text to agree with us on important points. (Descartes must hold that ordinary material objects are substances, Leibniz must hold that monads unfold through a series of discrete, successive states, etc.) Systematic interpretations charitably maximize consistency even if this means minimizing a philosopher's agreement with "us."

---

7. For a recent, detailed treatment, see Garber (2009).

8. Locke (1975), 2.2.2, 119. Locke's *Essay* is cited by book, chapter, and section separated by periods and followed by the page number in Locke (1975). I have selectively modernized Locke's typography.

9. Ibid., 2.12.1, 163.

10. On this topic there are no fewer than three competing interpretations that are systematically inspired: Gueroult (1968), Gueroult (1974), Melamed (2013), and Shein (2009).

2. *Key concepts tend to be tightly linked conceptually and not subject to independent analysis.* Systematic philosophers rarely use a "divide and conquer" strategy on philosophical problems. As an example, consider Descartes's treatment of the currently popular question of whether it is consciousness or representation that is the deepest mark of the mental. He frustrates those trying to reconstruct his position one way or the other. He characterizes thought as essentially encompassing both and does not prioritize either. Descartes tightly links the form of thought of which we are immediately aware (ideas) with the immediate awareness itself.[11] Of course, Descartes does not permit unconscious representation. But neither does he allow consciousness without objects. It is not possible to think nothing. We might regard this running together of these features of thought as an unfortunate oversight, or we can instead systematically interpret him as quite deliberately holding that thought is simple and unanalyzable yet (characteristically for a "rationalist") representing diversity.[12] Furthermore, these conceptual linkages often do more than prevent independent analyses. This is the next point.

3. *Systematic philosophers often link key concepts without any priority relations among them.* Even when rational reconstructionists are prepared to admit that a philosopher tightly connects important concepts, they sometimes often aim to establish which concepts are foundational and which derivative. When a convincing reconstruction of this sort is not to be found, it is implied that this is due to error, oversight, or confusion in the texts. Good examples of this come up in the interpretation of Spinoza's mature philosophy. One of these is Spinoza's linking of causation with dependence and involvement in the fourth axiom of the first part of the *Ethics*. Or consider Locke's apparently "circular" characterization of power and cause.[13] Again, we could lament the lack of analyses that successfully isolate the concepts. But we can assume instead that the philosopher has deliberately linked the concepts. It is also interesting to note in this regard Descartes's claim concerning the axioms introduced in his geometrical exposition of the *Meditations:* "Nevertheless, many of these axioms could have been better explained, and indeed they should have been introduced as theorems rather than as axioms, had I wished to be more precise."[14]

11. CSM II, 113–14.

12. CSM I, 195–96.

13. Locke (1975), 2.7.8, 131; 2.21.1–2, 233–34; 2.26.1–2, 324–5.

14. CSM II, 116.

4. *Systematic philosophers in the early modern period take a dim view of the power of language to express truth and systematic interpreters respect this.*

This tenet is given classic expression in Berkeley's *Principles of Human Knowledge*:

> Unless we take care to clear the first principles of knowledge, from the embarrass and delusion of words, we make infinite reasonings upon them to no purpose.... Whosoever therefore designs to read the following sheets, I entreat him to make my words the occasion of his own thinking, and endeavor to attain the same train of thoughts in reading, that I had in writing them. By this means it will be easy for him to discover the truth or falsity of what I say. He will be out of danger of being deceived by my words, and I do not see how he can be led into an error by considering his own naked, undisguised ideas.[15]

Berkeley's position is that the acts of will and perceptions of ideas that constitute thought have a structure that is very difficult to communicate to others with language. This position is shared by many early modern thinkers. They are not interested in something like Kant's Table of Judgments in his first *Critique* which tabulates logical structures of thought that correspond rather nicely to the grammatical structure of language. Now that we have an understanding of formal logic far beyond Kant's it is even more compelling to theorize that language can be made to express thought with great exactitude. We have no temptation to do philosophy solely by recourse to our own wordless "naked, undisguised ideas." Berkeley had the extreme position that such words as "cause," "substance," "object," "property" (or "mode"), etc. as used by other philosophers purport to correspond to abstract ideas, but necessarily fail to do so. But consider philosophers with positions less extreme in this respect—Leibniz and Hume for example. A systematic interpreter of these two will find it very implausible that the word "cause," for instance, picks out some one thing that the two are disagreeing about. She will instead work to recover how the word is used within the very different systems of Leibniz and Hume.

Here is a concrete example of what I have in mind drawn, again, from Descartes. An interpretive issue that has drawn much attention is whether Descartes might have regarded the human being as a (finite) substance.

---

15. Berkeley (1948–57), Vol. 2, 40, (Introduction, Section 25).

Is he a dualist or a "trialist"? This seems like a deep issue: is the human being *really* a *substance*? But here is another way of looking at matters. *Modulo* questions about interaction, Descartes is quite clear on the basic ontology of the human being. It is a composite of thought and extension whose intimacy is experienced in the sensations that arise from neither the mind nor the body alone, but from their being joined by God's infinite power. So the right question to ask is whether the *word* "substance" is apt for the human being. To answer we note that the word is rightly applied to a thinking thing or to an extended thing. That can be fleshed out by enumerating some of their features: independence from other beings except God, being the subject of characteristic modes, etc. So the question becomes, "Does the human being sufficiently resemble the paradigms of thought and extension to deserve application of the term, 'substance'?" It is not independent in the right way (since it depends on each of its components as well as on God), but it does have characteristic modes, namely, sensations. The score is tied at one. A systematic interpretation sees little interest in linguistic legislation here. The metaphysical facts are before us; the particular linguistic description is optional.

5. *Systematic interpreters tend to see thoughts of great thinkers as growing in detail from early works to later works instead of seeing them as changing through well-defined stages.* This characteristic of systematic interpretations depends on distinguishing (i) the doctrine held by the philosopher being interpreted, from (ii) the biographical facts about how the philosopher arrived at that doctrine, from (iii) how the philosopher contrives to write in order to persuade others of the doctrine. The goal is to retrieve as fully as possible the first of these—the doctrine. Of course, the doctrine is accessed primarily from the texts, and biographical considerations are often relevant to recovering the doctrine. But sometimes the three can come apart in important ways and the systematic interpreter is sensitive to this.

An illustration is provided by the dispute over whether Spinoza held the doctrine that the mind's ideas should be arranged according to the order of exposition in his *Ethics*. I think the prevailing view is that Spinoza maintained that a well-ordered intellect must have the same structure as the text of the *Ethics*. This reading leads, however, to some striking inconsistencies. In the early propositions of Part I we find assertions about more that one substance before Spinoza goes on to demonstrate that there is only one. And at the sixteenth proposition of the first Part and its demonstration we find a significant reference to the infinite intellect, but it is not until the second Part that we get a demonstration (from the axiom that Man thinks!) that God is a thinking thing. If these difficulties are to be removed, Spinoza's underlying doctrine must be given priority over the structure of the text. This method enables us to understand why Spinoza would cut himself considerable slack in the formal exposition of the text. Some departures from full rigor are probably intended to help along the reader; others might have been impossible to avoid without making the text unacceptably long or complex.

Once the systematic interpreter has this picture of a stable doctrine underlying the text, there is less pressure to see changes over time in the philosopher's mode of expression as reflecting deep shifts in the doctrine. Malebranche's introduction of efficacious ideas is a good test case here. Most Malebranche scholars take this to be a deep shift in Malebranche's thinking regarding the soul's union with God and its cognition of bodies. Malebranche explicitly characterizes the causal role of divine ideas in sensory cognition about twenty years after writing the *Recherche*. But from a systematic perspective, the doctrine of efficacious ideas is a straightforward corollary of Malebranche's signature occasionalism.[16] If God is the true cause of all change, then he is the cause of our having sensations appropriate to bodies in our vicinity. Since God's ideas are not distinct from God in any robust sense, attributing the cause of sensations to God's ideas does not do much to specify the original doctrine that sensations (and everything else) are caused by God. The result is a more sympathetic picture of Malebranche. In response to objections to his original presentation, he restated his view in slightly different terms. He did not scramble to adjust what he regarded as faults in the original doctrine. Needless to say there will be some clear cases of sharp doctrinal change (e.g., Wittgenstein's abandonment of most or all of the system of the *Tractatus*) and some cases that are very hard to judge (e.g., Leibniz on the centrality of corporeal substance).

6. *Systematic interpreters give much weight to authors' claims about their own systems*. And as a corollary, it is assumed that systematic philosophers regarded themselves as very successfully traversing their philosophical agendas. So we find some philosophers making grandiose claims about the scope and power of their systems. At the end of the *Principles* Descartes writes of his scientific hypotheses,

> And perhaps even these results of mind will be allowed into the class of absolute certainties, if people consider have they have been deduced in an unbroken chain from the first and simplest principles of human knowledge.[17]

16. See Nolan (2008).

17. CSM I, 290–91.

Keeping in mind that he is here describing, for example, how magnetic phenomena are to be understood as the effects of imperceptible grooved particles screwing through iron, this might seem to be faintly ridiculous—or outright bluster. And here is perhaps my favorite, even though it is not an early modern text, taken from Wittgenstein's Preface to the *Tractatus*: "On the other hand, the *truth* of the thoughts that are here communicated seems to me unassailable and definitive. I therefore believe myself to have found, on all essential points, the final solution of the problems."[18] And here from the first sentence of the preface to Berkeley's *Principles*, "What I here make public has, after a long and scrupulous inquiry, seem'd to me evidently true, and not unuseful to be known,"[19] and we are told in the preface of the *Dialogues* that the reader should find "Many intricate points made plain, great difficulties solved, several useless parts of science retrenched, speculation referred to practice, and men reduced from paradoxes to common sense."[20]

On the other hand, writers in the empiricist tradition tend to go in the opposite direction and prominently announce how little they mean to accomplish. Probably the most famous example of this is Locke's claiming in the "Epistle to the Reader" in his *Essay* to be an underlaborer clearing away rubbish in the path of the great thinkers. This is followed up in the main text by copious references to the low candlepower of the light of our intellect and so on. These pronouncements are cheerfully ignored by those who write tomes on Locke's metaphysics, but they are taken at face value by systematic interpreters and serve as powerful constraints on how the system is to be understood.[21] Statements like these from systematic philosophers are plentiful and easy to find, but they are also easy to discount. Perhaps the discounting now comes naturally because we have learned to school our own philosophical ambition even within its currently restricted purview. I shall give just one more example from Kant's *Critique of Pure Reason*. Although in one way Kant's program shares Locke's famous modesty about the limits of knowledge, neither philosopher is modest about his execution of the program. Here is Kant:

> I have not avoided reason's questions by pleading the incapacity of human reason as an excuse; rather I have completely specified these

18. Wittgenstein (1974), 5.

19. Berkeley (1948–57), Vol. 2, 23 (*Principles*).

20. Berkeley (1948–57), Vol. 2 p. 168 (*Dialogues*).

21. The case of Locke's *Essay* is taken up in section 4 of this chapter.

> questions according to principles, and after discovering the point where reason has misunderstood itself, I have resolved them to reason's full satisfaction.... [I] make bold to say that there cannot be a single metaphysical problem that has not been solved here, or at least to the solution of which the key has not been provided.[22]

The last section of this chapter discusses a plan for interpreting Locke as having this combination of modesty about the scope of philosophy and great confidence in the excellence of the results within that scope.

7. *Systematic philosophers are often, as a matter of principle, satisfied with explanations that are thin and unsatisfying from a non-systematic perspective.* Let us return to Descartes and his grooved magnetic particles. If we suppose that he really meant it when he said that this mechanism for explaining the results of experiments had been deduced with geometrical rigor from first principles, how could that work? One suggestion would be to take him actually to be committed to the theory of deduction that he expounds. If a deduction is rigorous when one clearly and distinctly perceived that the conclusion has the same nature as the premise,[23] that clears the path to an understanding of Descartes's point of view. If we can imagine iron filings on a table in the vicinity of a lodestone as moving as the result of grooved particles, we are basically home free. For grooved particles are taken to have no relevant properties aside from their size, shape, and motion. So their nature—to be extended in certain ways—is (or at least can be) clearly and distinctly perceived. And extension itself is one of the primary principles that can be intuited straightaway after appropriate training. Thus, grooved particles, and for that matter the motions of the iron filings, are in Descartes's special sense deduced from a first principle. That oversimplifies matters a bit because Descartes also thinks that further principles about God and about human sensory perception are required for an absolutely complete deduction. Descartes saw this additional systematicity as a strength. It would be seen as philosophical weakness by a non-systematic interpreter. She could claim that Descartes failed properly to separate physics, perception, and metaphysics.

This story Descartes sketches is obviously not a "deduction of phenomena" in Newton's sense. And because that is the sense in which we are accustomed to evaluate claims that something has been explained, Descartes's

22. Kant (1998b), 101.

23. CSM I, 56–7.

explanation inevitably strikes us as woefully inadequate. Nevertheless, the texts quite clearly indicate that Descartes is fully satisfied with his scientific deduction. He has succeeded on his own terms, as disappointing as that might seem to post-Newtonians.[24] I am not suggesting that we always turn a blind eye to ways in which a philosopher's system turns out to be inadequate. But we are also missing something if we do not understand why the philosopher did regard it as adequate. There is, therefore, something inadequate in an *interpretation* that tries to make sense of something important in a philosophical system by making it internally inconsistent with other important features of the system. This is likely to happen, I am suggesting, when we try anachronistically to impose our own standards of explanatory adequacy. We should instead work with the author's own standards, especially when these are explicitly stated.

3. Obstacles to Systematic Interpretation

With this sketch of some of the features of systematic interpretations in place, a complementary list can be made. The following list characterizes some entrenched procedures which, when adhered to, tend to block systematic interpretations.

1. *The anachronistic tendency to understand supposed examples of common sense as philosophical data points instead of illustrations of philosophical theories.* Many of our contemporaries tend to see examples in the style of "Charlotte and Sebastian are walking down the street" as exhibiting truths revealed by "intuitions."[25] These intuitions then serve as data points for reconstructing arguments, and perhaps in the distant future these arguments might lead to a full theory of the collected data. But systematic philosophers very often use such examples in a diametrically opposed fashion. In these cases, they serve as loose illustrations of theoretical points that are "already" settled by a philosophical system. So the theory is conceptually and epistemically prior to any homely examples that are adduced to illustrate it. Taking loose illustrations to be data points establishing fixed doctrine can lead to misinterpretations. This is how I see the following passage in Descartes's Third Meditation.

> With regard to the clear and distinct elements in my ideas of corporeal things, it appears that I could have borrowed some of these from my idea

---

24. For discussion of this feature of Descartes's system, see Nelson (forthcoming, 2013).

25. For some discussion of this tendency, see Della Rocca, this volume.

of myself, namely substance, duration, number and anything else of this kind. For example I think that a stone is a substance, or is a thing capable of existing independently, and I also think that I am a substance.[26]

This passage might be regarded as smoking gun evidence proving that Descartes held that stones are substances in just the same sense that thinking things are. But a systematic interpreter can easily find other reasons for Descartes's introducing the example at this point in the *Meditations.* At this point in the work, Descartes's meditator is still sifting through his suspect ideas. Moreover, the quoted passage does not exactly say that the meditator clearly and distinctly perceives that a stone is a substance. It says that the clear and distinct idea of substance is included as an element in the meditator's idea of corporeal things. And that idea might still be quite confused. And in the second quoted sentence, the meditator *thinks* [*cogito*] that the stone is a substance; it does not say that he clearly and distinctly perceives it to be so. The important question of whether Descartes takes individual bodies to be substances or not should be answered systematically.[27]

This example from the Third Meditation brings out the importance of attending to a systematic philosopher's expository strategy. A substantial philosophical text cannot be absorbed in a glance; one must read it through, usually from beginning to end. So it is very difficult to find an uncontroversial starting point and serially build up a theory point-by-point. The significance of examples that are adduced early in a text can be fully evaluated only in light of the entire text (and often related texts are also required). It is noteworthy that works that do, in fact, try to lay out a philosophical system in a format resembling a mathematical demonstration often turn out to be more, rather than less, difficult to understand. The examples of Spinoza's *Ethics* and Wittgenstein's *Tractatus* have already been mentioned.

2. *The anachronistic lure in pedagogy to present great philosophers as taking varied perspectives on "problems" or issues that are somehow simply given.* This anti-systematic tendency gives us the problem of causation, the problem of free will, the problem of personal identity, etc. As suggested earlier, a systematic philosopher's doctrine concerning (for example) causation cannot be isolated from the doctrines concerning substance, infinity, determination, law, etc. This means that causation, for example, what causation is, depends on

26. CSM II, 30–31.

27. For discussion, see Sowaal (2004) and Smith and Nelson (2011).

how it is embedded in surrounding notions and this will vary from author to author. So the systematic philosopher will not immediately reject an interpretation of Spinoza that identifies the "logic" by which one idea follows from others with the causation by which one thing is determined by others. This interpretation, whether it is ultimately a good one or not, cannot be immediately convicted of attributing to Spinoza some kind of category mistake. The systematic interpreter will not say, "That is not genuine causation." Similarly, Leibniz's holding that everything that happens to an individual is included in that individual's complete concept does not force an interpretation according to which Leibniz does not allow for genuine freedom. Nor was Leibniz somehow trying to analyze "genuine" freedom into an impoverished basis. The systematic interpreter must allow for what Robert Sleigh has called "replacement."[28] Leibniz can be interpreted as replacing what he regarded as a faulty concept of freedom (for instance) with what he took to be the correct one—real, genuine freedom. Leibnizian freedom might look deterministic to those working in other philosophical frameworks, but why shouldn't Leibniz himself have regarded his opponent's conception as a mirage?

I am criticizing a kind of essentialist *assumption*. If we are to accept that Aristotle and David Lewis are both investigating some univocal notion, causation, for example, then we are owed an argument to that effect. And it will not do to appeal to common sense. Common sense itself has a great deal of plasticity as we can see from Berkeley's taking himself to be its defender.[29] A systematic interpreter supposes in this case that even if we could isolate some commonsensical notion of causation, it is being *replaced* by Aristotle and Lewis. It might be alleged that systematic interpreters are themselves victims of realist, essentialist assumptions at another level. Are they not assuming that there is a fixed system of doctrines expressed in the writings of a great philosopher waiting to be fully articulated? This worry could have some bite if two mutually inconsistent systematic interpretations were supported by a single group of texts. We would then have something analogous to the much discussed problem of the underdetermination of theory by evidence. These interesting questions are beyond the scope of this chapter, which is simply to characterize systematic interpretations and some of their virtues.[30]

---

28. Sleigh (1990), 9.

29. See Bordner (2011) for a treatment of some of the subtleties in Berkeley's doctrines regarding common sense.

30. See Lennon (1993), 378–92, for some very helpful perspective on various forms of essentialism, realism, and relativism in histories of philosophy.

It is clear how all this connects with pedagogy. If a teacher is to convey something interesting about an assortment of historical figures within the compass of a single university course, it will be scarcely possible to give each a systematic treatment of the sort I am describing. That would require the luxury of courses devoted to just one or two figures or perhaps even to one or two texts. And even with that luxury it is hard to resist setting up philosophical debates *across* systems. An example of this attractive plan is the presentation of Leibniz and Locke as (virtually) arguing about the status of innate ideas. And how convenient it is to present Descartes and Malebranche as contesting the nature of ideas, and Locke, Hume, and Kant as contesting causation, and so on. This rubric greatly facilitates the setting of exam questions, topics for essays, and even for dissertations. What begins as a practical constraint on course and curriculum design calcifies into a de facto orthodox style of developing interpretations of historical figures.[31]

3. *Pedagogical pressure to teach generalized critical skills and cutting edge advances.* An essentialist conception of perennial philosophical problems coheres well with the unrelenting critical stance toward texts with which many philosophers wish to imbue their students. It is common for departments of philosophy to take responsibility for teaching subjects such as "critical reasoning," "scientific reasoning," "informal logic," and decision theory. Part of what presumably qualifies philosophers for these subject matters is the special role that "analytic technique" plays in their treatment of any topic within the purview of philosophy departments.

With this attitude in place, students approaching historical texts are encourage to engage critically with them as they read. If the students carry this to an extreme they will ask themselves after every paragraph, or even every sentence: "Do I agree?" "Has the author conclusively established her point?" Of course, asking these questions is much facilitated if they are based on intuitions about *cause, essence, freedom*, etc. that do not depend on any specific theoretical background. For students not yet practiced in consulting their intuitions, they can get help by seeing how the historical figures themselves debated the perennial issues. Students reading Leibniz's *New Essays on the Understanding* need not worry that Locke will pull an intellectual swindle because Leibniz will keep him honest and vice versa. If

31. Of course, it is compatible with the point under discussion that *comparing* philosophical *systems* can be of great value. Understanding Descartes on the innate idea of extension helps one to see what Berkeley is denying; understanding Hume on causation clarifies the point of Kant's Second Analogy in his first *Critique*, and so on.

one still fears being sold a bill of goods by one of these philosophers, then Kant can be brought in to adjudicate, and so on. And naturally, the last word on *cause, essence, freedom,* etc. is not likely to be found in any old text. The very best way to assess Plato critically is to see how he fares against what philosophers have come up with in the last five years or so.

Systematic interpreters are wary of such debates, useful though they might be in class. Even when the form of a point-by-point debate does not need to be reconstructed (e.g., as in the third and fifth sets of objections and replies to Descartes's *Meditations* or Leibniz's *New Essay*) the degree of philosophical engagement between systems is easy to exaggerate. That "debate" between Descartes and his opponents Hobbes and Gassendi can be held up as a paradigm of philosophers arguing past one another.[32] Those three are, to varying degrees, systematic philosophers and each is arguing from within his own system. There are few extra-systematic topics that they can productively debate.

4. *Professional pressure to publish quickly and regularly.* The project of developing a systematic interpretation requires familiarity with a very substantial body of texts and secondary literature. It will also usually involve pursuing many interpretive ideas that turn out to be dead-ends. Long-range projects can be very risky in many academic environments, especially for younger scholars. Someone doing history of philosophy and seeking tenure is probably well advised to publish some articles even if he or she is also writing a book. And these articles and books should probably be on well-defined, familiar kinds of topics. Examples of topics that are most likely to please publishers' readers and journal referees include responses to existing secondary literature, examinations of one or two arguments found in just a few pages of text, and first looks at works by minor figures or understudied passages and texts. Work of this kind is easier to peer-review than is work that engages the history of philosophy systematically. And when work of this kind is written and then published it reinforces the norms that encourage it in the first place. I do not mean to suggest that young scholars are getting bad advice. I am only trying to explain why we do not see more systematic interpretations if they have the virtues that I am claiming for them.

4. *A Program for Systematic Interpretation: Locke's* Essay

In this section, I consider some of the special impediments blocking a systematic reading of Locke's *Essay*. Let us first attend to Locke's own characterization

32. Grene (1985), ch. 6, makes this case for the Descartes-Gassendi exchange.

of his project. His purpose is epistemological: "This, therefore, being my purpose to enquire into the original, certainty, and extent of humane knowledge; together, with the grounds and degrees of belief, opinion, and assent ... [33] It is therefore worthwhile to search out the bounds between opinion and knowledge; and examine by what measures, in things, whereof we have no certain knowledge, we ought to regulate our assent, and moderate our perswasions."[34] This inquiry proceeds within the theory of ideas Locke develops. "It ['idea': AN] being that term, which, I think, serves best to stand for whatsoever is the object of the understanding when a man thinks...."[35] According to his theory of ideas, the understanding is furnished with some of its ideas via the senses and some via the mind's reflection on its operations on its ideas (and some via both routes).

The linchpin of the theory of ideas is the distinction between simple and complex ideas. "The better to understand the Nature, manner, and Extent of our Knowledge, one thing is carefully to be observed, concerning the Ideas we have; and that is, that *some* of them are *simple*, and *some complex*."[36] Locke introduces simple and complex ideas as mutually exclusive and as exhaustive of the objects of thought. Simple ideas are absolutely simple; "each in itself uncompounded, contains in it nothing but *one uniform appearance,* or conception in the mind, and is not distinguishable into different ideas."[37] "When the understanding is once stored with these simple ideas, it has a power to repeat, compare, and unite them even to an almost infinite variety, and so can make at pleasure new complex ideas."[38] This means that the epistemological project will proceed by examining the complexes that constitute our knowledge and tracing the operations of the mind by which they are produced from simples. "But as the mind is wholly passive in the reception of all its simple ideas, so it exerts several acts of its own, whereby out of its simple ideas, as the materials and foundations of the rest, the others are framed."[39] Locke names this the "historical, plain method" (hereafter HPM):

> It shall suffice to my present purpose, to consider the discerning faculties of a man, as they are employ'd about the objects, which they

33. Locke (1975), 1.1.2, 43.

34. Ibid., 1.1.3, 44.

35. Ibid., 1.1.8, 47.

36. Ibid., 2.2.1, 119.

37. Ibid., 2.1.1, 119.

38. Ibid., 2.1.2, 119.

39. Ibid., 2.12.1, 163.

> have to do with: and I shall have on this occasion, if, in this historical, plain method, I can give any account of the ways, whereby our understandings come to attain those notions of things we have....[40]

The completeness of the HPM depends on taking items of knowledge and opinion to be complex ideas,

> Since the mind, in all its thoughts and reasonings, hath no other immediate object but its own ideas, which it alone does or can contemplate, it is evident that our Knowledge is only conversant about them.[41]

Knowledge, then seems to me to be nothing but *the perception of the connexion and agreement, or disagreement and repugnancy of any of our ideas.* In this alone it consists.[42]

Part of the appeal of the HPM is undoubtedly the way in which it parallels the method of corpuscular natural philosophy.

> The dominion of man in this little world of his own understanding being much the same as it is in the great world of visible things; wherein his power, however managed by art and skill reaches no farther than to compound and divide the materials that are made to his had; but can do nothing towards making the least particle of new matter, or destroying one atom of what is already in being.[43]

Of course, it has not escaped the notice of commentators that Locke emphatically states these methodological commitments. Until recently, however, no one has attempted to interpret the project as successfully pursuing Locke's announced method. R. Aaron, for instance, posed some very influential challenges to those who would develop a systematic interpretation.[44] These challenges have since been strengthened and multiplied instead of being addressed on Locke's behalf. Aaron's thesis is that Locke relaxed, and sometimes just for-

40. Ibid., 1.1.2, 43–4.

41. Ibid., 4.1.1, 525.

42. Ibid., 4.1.2, 525. Locke takes opinion, also called judgment, to be the "taking" or "presuming" of ideas to agree or disagree instead of the perceiving of them to agree or disagree (4.14.3, 4.14.4) 653. The question of whether Locke is able to adhere to these claims will be taken up shortly.

43. Ibid., 2.2.2; 120.

44. Aaron (1971) is the third edition; the first edition was published in 1937.

got, the compositional theory of ideas required for the HPM. Here is a partial list of Aaron's complaints.

1. The characterization of simple ideas is inadequate. Example: Simple ideas are like perceptual atoms, but the simple idea of a particular shade of red, call it *red**, is an abstract idea because it can have numerous instances. But abstract ideas result from operations of the mind, so they should be complex.[45]
2. Locke's project exceeds his stated modest bounds. Example: Locke is concerned to presenting an introspective psychology.[46]
3. Not all the objects of thought can be characterized as compounds of simple ideas. Example: Introspection takes thought itself as an object; the role of simple ideas of reflection is left completely unclear.[47]

Aaron is entirely justified in raising these questions. Despite the book's great length, Locke is often far from explicit. The *Essay* could not get through the process of modern peer review without being thoroughly rewritten. There are texts that prompt Aaron's criticisms and there are no overlooked texts in which Locke explicitly answers them. Any interpretation, however, is going to involve some small glosses of the text and some extrapolations from it. If we can find the ones under which Locke's progress is as successful as he thinks it is, then those glosses and extrapolations are to be preferred.

To address Aaron's first complaint, let us try to defend the strict simplicity of Locke's simple ideas. A point that has been familiar at least since Plato is that true simples cannot be *described* or *defined*—a description or definition would articulate some complex structure.[48] Simples can only be named, but even the name *Red** (for a definite simple idea of a determinate red), for example, is somewhat awkward because it is capable of being applied to more than one simple. But this does not yet make it an abstract, or general name, nor does it mean that the idea *Red** is an abstract idea. Similarly, the name "top quark" applies to any number of top quarks which are strictly simple and accordingly qualitatively indistinguishable one from another (at least according to our best current physics). *Red** would name an abstract idea only if instances of *Red** differed qualitatively while sharing *Red**-ness. But why

45. Ibid., 110–12.

46. Ibid., chap. 4.

47. Ibid., 129–33.

48. Locke (1975), 3.4.7; 422.

should Locke be committed to that? Perhaps because he characterizes simple ideas as "containing one uniform appearance"?[49] This might strongly suggest that *Red**, for example, will "appear" as a uniform patch of a certain shape and texture. As Berkeley noted, an idea with color, shape, and texture is not happily characterized as simple.[50] To resolve this difficulty, we need to examine the sense in which simple ideas are "appearances."

Let us begin by remembering that Locke wants his theory of ideas to be in the service of an epistemological theory. It is not primarily a phenomenological or psychological theory. Locke does hold that when we think the mind is aware of its ideas. But this does not mean that the theory of ideas is to be developed on the basis of introspective data. Instead, the theory must posit a stock of simple ideas of sensation and reflection that are sufficient for tracing the experiential origins of any given complex idea. The task is *not* to begin with the simples and show how from them to construct the complexes. Instead, we begin with the complexes and then use the HPM to work backward from them until we reach simples. This procedure was familiar from natural philosophy. The natural philosopher does not show step-by-step how to construct a steel rod from an unimaginably large number of individual iron corpuscles and charcoal corpuscles. Instead, he gives an analysis of how a steel rod could be composed of an arrangement of those *kinds* of corpuscles. This analogy also shows how we might never be aware of individual simple ideas qua simple ideas even though in another sense we are aware of nothing but (compounded) simple ideas. When we look at a steel rod, there is one sense in which we are seeing nothing but iron and carbon corpuscles even though we cannot see individual corpuscles.

This elucidates the sense in which simple ideas are "appearances" as follows. *Red** is not experienced as a shaped, textured, patch of color. *Red** is not experienced as such, in isolation, qua simple.[51] Again, this is analogous to our not seeing individual physical atoms when we look at an object entirely composed of atoms. When one does experience a colored patch of that shade of red, then at least one instance (probably many instances) of *Red** is a component of that complex. One might still wish to pursue Aaron's complaint by asking why Locke uses the word "appearance" if the simple idea does not appear in experience as such.

49. Ibid., 2.1.1, 525.

50. For a comparison of Locke, Berkeley, and Hume on simple ideas, see Nelson and Landy (2011).

51. Nelson and Landy (2011).

Locke could respond first by reiterating that according to his theory of ideas, *Red** is a component of what is experienced even though it is not experienced *as* simple. Second, there is a quite different sense in which simple ideas are appearances. They are ways in which substances appear to the mind. Substances have powers to furnish the mind with simple ideas. While simple ideas are not resembling images of substances, they nevertheless are "real,"[52] "adequate,"[53] and "true"[54] representations of them. So a simple idea of *Red** is a way in which a substance appears to an observer—it is part of what constitutes the observer's complex idea of that substance. Third, he could remind us that his project is ultimately to explore the limits of knowledge that is based in experience—experience that is analyzed by the theory of ideas. His overall project begins by laying out the technical apparatus of his theory of ideas. Then, after defining knowledge and opinion in the terms of that theory, Locke proceeds to demonstrate the power of the HPM to account for test cases of knowledge and reasoned opinion, while ruling out purported cases that are not properly grounded in ideas. The theory of ideas is confirmed by its explanatory adequacy for these phenomena. It is not designed to yield a phenomenological theory of experience. This perspective on Locke's project thus addresses Aaron's second complaint as well.

The example of Aaron's third complaint is well put by M. Bolton in this way:

> Book II, Chapter I names sensation and reflection as the sources of simple ideas. This suggests that we have experience of our own mental operations on a par with our sensory experience of things in the world. But, in fact, Locke does not treat them just alike. Whereas the perception of external things and their qualities is mediated by ideas, for Locke, ideas do not mediate perception of one's ongoing mental acts, or so I suggest.[55]

The main textual problem is that Locke writes,

> By *reflection* then, in the following part of this discourse, I would be understood to mean, that notice which the mind takes of its own

52. Locke (1975), 2.30.2, 372.

53. Ibid., 2.31.2, 375.

54. Ibid., 2.32.9, 387.

55. Bolton (2007), 85. Bolton's article is an excellent up-to-date source for obstacles to a systematic reading of the *Essay*.

> operations, and the manner of them, by reason whereof, there come to be ideas of these operations in the understanding.[56]

This suggests, as we have seen before, that Locke is characterizing an aspect of phenomenology that is revealed by introspection. Bolton concludes that simple ideas of reflection have no representative function in experience comparable to that which sensory ideas have.[57] If that is indeed what Locke means to be doing, then the prospects for interpreting Locke as making essential use of his theory of ideas are not good. There is, however, a surprising resource at Locke's disposal. Locke holds that we are aware of our thought so that when the mind operates on its ideas to form complexes, the mind is aware of these operations. Now suppose that this awareness *is* mediated by a simple idea of reflection, as seems to be required for systematicity. Suppose further that this simple idea of reflection becomes a component of the complex idea generated by the operation of the mind. So, for example, the mind constructs a complex idea of relation by combining the ideas of the relata with the simple idea of *comparison*.[58] The result is that when the mind is aware of the result of the operation (the complex idea), it is thereby aware of its components including the simple reflective idea *comparison*. As we have seen, this does *not* mean that the mind is aware of this simple idea as such—it is not aware of it qua simple.[59] It appears awkward for this reading that Locke refers in the passage quoted earlier to the "notice that the mind takes of its own operations" because this suggests that the reflective simple is generated by an act of introspection and not by the operation that produces some complex idea. But the quoted passage goes on to mark "the manner of them [the operations], *by reason whereof, there come to be ideas of these operations in the understanding*" (emphasis added). This phrase should be read as saying that it is the mind's operating, rather than its "noticing" that generates the simple idea of reflection. The "notice taken" of the operation of the mind can be quite analogous to the way in which the simple idea *Red** is noticed as a component of the experience of an apple. Namely, it is a component of the complex idea resulting from the operation in question. We might further strengthen the parallel between the reflective *comparison* and the sensory simple *Red** by marking how each can figure into abstract ideas. Just as one might compare the complex ideas

56. Locke (1975), 2.1.4, 105. See also 2.1.19, 115; 2.6.1, 127, and 2.27.9, 335.

57. Bolton (2008), 86.

58. Locke (1975), 2.25.7, 322.

59. This method of handling simple ideas of reflection is explored in detail in Brown (2006).

of various red objects to generate the abstract idea associated with the name "red," one might compare various acts of comparing to generate the abstract idea associated with the name "comparison." The simple idea *comparison* can be a component of an abstract idea named "comparison" just as the simple idea *Red** can be a component of an abstract idea named "red." That, in turn would explain why young children and animals do not have abstract ideas.[60]

In light of these considerations, I submit that Locke may well succeed in preserving both the simplicity of his simple ideas and a tight parallel between sensation and reflection as required by his system. These proposed sketches of solutions to the difficulties raised for a systematic reading of the *Essay* require much more work (as do the characterizations of the problems they are meant to solve) in order to be convincing. There are, moreover, many additional challenges to such an interpretation that I have not even mentioned.[61] I hope only to have shown that the methodology of systematic interpretation is not a dead-end and is worth pursuing with appropriate texts such as Locke's *Essay*. There is no need to take the particularly well-known and difficult obscurities in that text to rule out the possibility that we might make good on Locke's own pretensions to systematicity. It is worthwhile to recover that Lockean perspective even if the system that emerges strikes us as philosophically inadequate.

Acknowledgments

I thank the participants in the Workshop at Concordia University and, especially, the editors of this volume for helpful suggestions. Some of this material was presented at a workshop organized by Marc Bobro on early modern philosophy and pedagogy at the 2011 meeting of the Pacific APA. I have also benefited from discussing with Ken Brown, Matt Priselac, and Patrick Connolly the systematic interpretations of Locke they are developing. Krasi Filcheva, David Landy, and Larry Nolan also gave me helpful advice.

60. Locke (1975), 2.11.8–2.11.12, 158–60.

61. Some of these are taken up and addressed systematically in Priselac (2012).

12

Charitable Interpretations and the Political Domestication of Spinoza, or, Benedict in the Land of the Secular Imagination

Yitzhak Y. Melamed

A fool hath no delight in understanding, but that his heart may discover itself.

PROVERBS, XVIII 2

1. Introduction

IN A BEAUTIFUL recent essay, the philosopher Walter Sinnott-Armstrong explains the reasons for his departure from evangelical Christianity, the religious culture in which he was brought up. Sinnot-Armstrong contrasts the interpretive methods used by good philosophers and fundamentalist believers:

> Good philosophers face objections and uncertainties. They follow where arguments lead, even when their conclusions are surprising and disturbing. Intellectual honesty is also required of scholars who interpret philosophical texts. *If I had distorted Kant's view to make him reach a conclusion that I preferred, then my philosophy professor would have failed me.* The contrast with religious reasoning is stark. My Christian friends seemed happy to hide serious problems in the Bible and in their arguments. They preferred comfort to intellectual honesty. I couldn't.[1]

1. Walter Sinnott-Armstrong (2007), 73; italics added.

To what extent can we, historians of philosophy, claim the virtue of intellectual honesty? Speaking frankly, I do not find the practice criticized by Sinnot-Armstrong's philosophy professor rare or unusual at all. We very frequently distort the views of past philosophers in order to reach the conclusions we prefer. We just call it "Charitable Interpretation."

In this essay, I discuss and criticize the logic behind so-called charitable interpretations in the history of philosophy. This phenomenon is ubiquitous and is not at all restricted to a particular philosophical strand or ideology. Analytic philosophers and postmodernists, Marxists, liberals, secularists, and fundamentalists, we all engage in the very same domestication project. Even more disturbing than the sheer ideological pervasiveness of this phenomenon is the fact that, on many occasions, *superb* philosophers and historians take part in this fairly childish endeavor.

In the first part of this chapter, I discuss the general logic of charitable interpretations in the history of philosophy, mostly by addressing discussions in metaphysics and epistemology. In the second part, I focus on the somewhat less noticed use of charitable interpretations in the study of political philosophy and point out the quintessential role ideology plays in these discussions. In both parts, I concentrate mostly on the interpretation of Spinoza's thought.[2] I do so not because I have special fondness for Spinoza ("guilty as charged," I admit), but because Spinoza is such a beast (and may I add, an enchanting beast) and attracts a disproportionate share of the domestication efforts from historians and philosophers of all creeds and persuasions. In the third and final part of the paper, I will begin to outline an alternative *methodology*, which suggests that past philosophers can be most relevant to our current philosophical discussion, to the extent that they provide us with *well-motivated challenges to our commonsense beliefs*. Such challenges have the invaluable virtue of being able to undermine our most fundamental and

2. Unless otherwise marked, all references to the *Ethics,* the early works of Spinoza, and Letters 1–29 are to Spinoza (1985) (abbreviated C). In references to the other letters of Spinoza I have used Spinoza (2002) abbreviated S). I have relied on the Spinoza (1925) critical edition for the Latin text of Spinoza (abbreviated G). I use the following standard abbreviations for Spinoza's works: *DPP* = *Descartes' Principles of Philosophy* [*Renati des Cartes Principiorum Philosophiae Pars I & II*]; *CM* = *Metaphysical Thoughts* [*Cogitata Metaphysica*], *KV* = *Short Treatise on God, Man, and His Well-Being* [*Korte Verhandeling van God de Mensch en deszelfs Welstand*], *TTP* = *Theological-Political Treatise* [*Tractatus Theologico-Politicus*], *TP*= *Political Treatise* [*Tractatus Politicus*], Ep. = *Letters*. Passages in the *Ethics* will be referred to by means of the following abbreviations: a(-xiom), c(-orollary), p(-roposition), s(-cholium) and app(-endix); "d" stands for either "definition" (when it appears immediately to the right of the part of the book), or "demonstration" (in all other cases.) Hence, *E*1d3 is the third definition of part 1 and *E*1p16d is the demonstration of proposition 16 of part 1.

secure beliefs and force us to engage with the most fundamental questions. What more can we expect from good philosophy?

Before I begin my crusade against the Marxists, secularists, analytic philosophers, and all the other gangs mentioned earlier, let me point out one view or method that I will *not* criticize. I have *nothing* against anachronism, at least not against intentional, well-crafted anachronism. Intentional anachronism is used in a very creative way in music (see the works of Arvo Pärt and Michael Nyman). It has been put to some very impressive uses in literature (as in Christoph Ransmayr's 1988 novel, *Die letzte Welt* [*The Last World*], or in Shakespeare's Roman tragedies), and in principle, I see no reason that it cannot be used in a similarly fruitful manner in philosophy. I am not a historicist, though I have respect for the consistent upholder of this view, and my crusade attempts to save *philosophy*, not history, from the intellectual laziness of domestication efforts. However, it will turn out that in order to have the best *philosophical* profit from past philosophical texts, it is crucial to read them in a historically precise manner.

2. Part One: "Be Aware of the Charitable Interpreter": Charitable Interpretations, the History of Philosophy, and Gettier's Fallacy

The logic of charitable interpretations is rather simple. Suppose a Past Philosopher (PP) makes a statement S. We believe that S, read literally, is clearly unacceptable. Since we appreciate PP as a great mind, we cannot believe that he or she could have uttered such foolishness. Thus, instead of ascribing S to PP, we ascribe S', which is different from, and sometimes even utterly opposed to S. Let us look at a few examples.

In his 1984 book on Spinoza's *Ethics,* Jonathan Bennett suggested that Spinozistic modes should not be interpreted as tropes, since tropes "are nonsense."[3] In his 2001 *Learning from Six Philosophers*, Bennett confesses that he changed his mind and that he now thinks that "tropes are just fine."[4] So far, so good—I have nothing but admiration for a philosopher's willingness to persistently reexamine his views. But strikingly in 2001, Bennett also argued that we should interpret Spinoza's modes as tropes. Why? Did Bennett's change of mind regarding the value of tropes change the views presented by Spinoza in

3. Bennett (1984), 94.

4. Bennett (2001), I 145.

his 1677 text? Why did the change in Bennett's evaluation of trope theory have to be accompanied by the ascription of this view to Spinoza as well?

Let us have a look at a second example. In an impressive recent article, Jonathan Schaffer provides some intriguing arguments in support of Priority Monism, the view according to which there is exactly one *basic* (i.e., independent) concrete thing, *the universe*.[5] Schaffer contrasts Priority Monism with the much more radical Existence Monism, which asserts that everything that is, is exactly one concrete thing. Priority Monism allows for the universe to have a plurality of (proper) parts since, according to Schaffer, the whole is prior to its parts, and the existence of a plurality of dependent things (the universe's parts) is consistent with Priority Monism. Existence Monism does not allow for the universe to have parts insofar as it rules out the existence of *any* plurality of concrete things, even if these are *not* independent things. At this point, Schaffer asks whether the monism of historical figures such as Spinoza, Hegel, Plotinus, Proclus, Lotze, Royce, Bosanquet, Bradley, and Blanshard is Priority or Existence Monism. He answers:

> It seems to me that the priority reading should be preferred to the existence reading if the texts in question can sustain it, on the grounds of interpretive charity. After all, Existence Monism is a radical view, conflicting with such seeming truisms as Moore's "Here's one hand … and here is another."[6]

The logic of this argument should be familiar: Existence Monism is crazy. Spinoza and Hegel and Parmenides, etc., were "Great Minds." We should do our best to avoid ascribing "crazy views" to "Great Minds."

I am not going to address, here, the question of whether Spinoza is, or is not, a Priority Monist.[7] (Let me just note, in passing, that Spinoza does not seem to share Schaffer's conviction that the whole is prior to its parts. On the contrary, Spinoza argues on many occasions that parts are prior to their wholes.[8] Thus, the priority of Spinoza's one substance to its modes cannot

5. Schaffer (2010), 66. Cf. Schaffer (2008).

6. Schaffer (2010), 66.

7. I tend to believe that Schaffer's important distinction between Priority and Existence Monism is not sharp enough and that as a result, certain views such as Spinoza's could be placed in either camp depending on one's precise interpretation of the priority relation at stake. I discuss this issue briefly in Melamed (2012b), 216.

8. See *DPP* 1p17d; *CM* II, v, G I 258: C 324; *KV* I, ii, G I 25 and G I 30; Ep. 35, S 856; and *E*1p12d. For discussion of these passages, see Melamed, "Spinoza's Mereology."

be the priority of the whole to its parts.) I brought the example of Schaffer's distinction in order to demonstrate the logic of charitable interpretations and the manner it is used to domesticate past philosophers.

Let us quickly consider a third and final example. In an important recent article on Spinoza's necessitarianism, Edwin Curley and Gregory Walski write:

> We defend the view that Spinoza is committed to allowing for the existence of a plurality of possible worlds .... We think this ought to be the default interpretation of Spinoza. It is, as Bennett says "tremendously implausible" that this is the only possible world.[9] We operate on the methodological principle that views which are tremendously implausible should not be attributed to the great, dead philosophers without pretty strong textual evidence.[10]

Let me note briefly that, for all I can tell, *no* view should be attributed to *anyone* "without pretty strong textual evidence." Still, the gist of Curley and Walski's view is quite clear. They state the methodology of charitable interpretation in a very transparent and helpful manner: our default attitude should be such that we try to avoid ascribing radical and implausible views to great, dead philosophers.

What is wrong with this methodology? Later, I will suggest that in a sense this methodology involves a cult that resists the ascription of errors to great minds in a manner not very different from the fundamentalist's refusal to allow for any errors in the literal reading of the Bible. But before we address these lofty issues, let me discuss a few mundane points.

First, the implausibility of a belief is usually measured by its agreement with our so-called commonsense intuitions. Such intuitions might be, more or less, common, but they are rarely held by everyone (by the way, how common should they be in order to be counted as commonsense intuitions? 60 percent? 70 percent? 98 percent? Is there a meta-commonsense intuition about how common an intuition should be in order to count as bona fide common sense?). I, for one, have no commonsense intuitions as to whether this is

9. In fact, Bennett makes a more hesitant claim: "the view that this is the only possible world *seems on the face of it to be* tremendously implausible" (Bennett (1996), 75; italics added). Bennett's formulation itself is a bit odd (if a claim is "tremendously implausible," why qualify it as only *seeming* to be so, and if it only *seems* implausible, then probably it is not *tremendously* implausible).

10. Curley and Walski (1999), 242.

the only possible world, or whether there is a plurality of possible worlds, or whether parts are prior to their wholes, or wholes are prior to their parts. In fact, on both issues, I understand both sides of the debate. Now, you might claim that I am too corrupted by philosophical studies and speculation, and that we should follow our so-called pre-philosophical intuitions. Yet, it seems to me very odd that we should give preference to the intuitions of the butcher and shopkeeper rather than the philosophically informed person, especially when the issues at stake are *philosophical* (and not butchery or shopkeeping).

Second, the methodology of charitable interpretation is a major stumbling block to the understanding of philosophers belonging to cultures distant in either time or space. The intuitions of thinkers belonging to such cultures are often different—sometimes radically different—from our own, and by adhering to the imperatives of charitable interpretation, we risk becoming deaf to their unique voices. The charitable interpreter will do his best to reinterpret these bizarre voices in a manner that is most familiar to him. By doing so, he compromises the recognition of the other person's subjectivity and deprives himself of knowledge and appreciation of human diversity. The charitable interpreter will do his best to multiply himself in space and time by enforcing his own views "as much as the text can sustain it" on the writings of other thinkers. How uncharitable!

Third, charitable interpretation deprives us of the most profitable use of past philosophers, i.e., the rather rare opportunity to encounter well-argued and well-thought challenges to our most fundamental beliefs. It is precisely because the writings of past philosophers come from cultures that are significantly different from our own (and hence share many fewer of our commonsense intuitions than writings of our contemporaries) that they can provide us with these challenges. A philosophical narcissist will try to find his image everywhere, but a thinker who is not lazy and whose thought is still flexible and alive should welcome a challenge that may lead to questioning his or her most obvious beliefs.

Charitable interpretation of past philosophers is used much more frequently than in the few cases in which it is stated honestly and transparently (as in the examples I provided). It often appears in the form of the claim that a past philosopher is *relevant* to the extent that his claims are vindicated by contemporary philosophy or science. Thus, for example, one could find Leibniz praised for advocating the relativity of time and space. Of course, such praises commit an obvious Gettier fallacy.[11] Assuming that

---

11. See Gettier (1966).

the theory of relativity is true, Leibniz indeed held a justified, true belief, but it is certainly not true *by virtue* of the reasons Leibniz had in mind, since he did not believe in an upper limit to possible velocity. Thus, even though the theory of relativity agrees with Leibniz's belief in the relativity of space, this does not at all vindicate Leibniz's views, since the agreement is merely coincidental.

My point about "vindication" leads us to another crucial feature of the use of charitable interpretation among late twentieth-century analytic historians of philosophy—namely, its apologetic nature. Analytic philosophy began with a ban that seemed to commit the old history of philosophy and metaphysics to the flames.[12] Of course, the dons of Cambridge and Oxford could not dispense with Plato and Aristotle, and even Kant was relatively immune from this wholesale condemnation, but for the great metaphysician of the modern period, it was a lengthy and painful process (which is still incomplete) to reclaim philosophical respectability.

Historically speaking, it is clear why figures such as Spinoza and Hegel were reintroduced into the mainstream of analytic philosophy through a domestication project that reinterpreted the two as harmless, mostly commonsense, philosophers. I am not convinced that this apologetic process was strictly inevitable.

When analytic philosophers of the sixties and seventies asked, "why should we care about the philosophies of Spinoza and Hegel?" they posed a *legitimate* question, which undermined traditional values and conventions that many contemporary Europeans took for granted (to my mind, the naive question "why should we care about it?" is fair in almost *any* context). Unfortunately, the answer supplied by many contemporary historians of philosophy was little more than an attempt to acquire a kosher stamp. These answers frequently took the form of "Spinoza's philosophy is important because he advocates an attractive view" that was in vogue at that time (such as holism, the deductive-nomological model, anomalous monism, and these days, metaphysical monism). I find such answers disappointing. I do not need Spinoza in order to examine these views. Quine, Hempel, Davidson, and Jonathan Schaffer are good enough. I need Spinoza in order to examine precisely the positions that were *not* presented by other philosophers. I need Spinoza in order to examine *Spinoza's* views.

12. On the emergence of analytic philosophy and its rejection of the substantially metaphysical theories of the British Idealists, see Michael Della Rocca's chapter in this volume and Soames (2003), vol. 1, 94–95.

3. Part Two: "Spinoza Got It Right": Charitable Interpretations and the History of Political and Religious Thought

Over the past few decades, Spinoza has been claimed by a variety of ideologies, each being attracted to one element of his thought, and subsequently attempting to enlist him among its ranks. The poor seventeenth-century philosopher has had to undergo a series of posthumous conversions that could be proudly compared with the modest achievements of the great old inquisitors of the past. The late Emilia Giancotti-Boscherini, a superb Marxist Spinoza scholar, labored with great diligence and talent to show that Spinoza's thought truly belongs to the school of modern materialism.[13] Graeme Hunter, a Protestant scholar, has recently argued that Spinoza's thought was "internal to Protestant Christianity" and that Spinoza did not entertain any "heretical doubts about the divinity of Christ."[14] In terms of pure public relations, it seems that the most successful posthumous conversion is the common custom today to refer to Spinoza by his given Hebrew name, "Baruch," in spite of the simple fact that we have *no trace* of evidence showing that Spinoza *ever* used this name in his adult life. Whether and to what extent Spinoza's Jewish upbringing played a significant role in his thought is an important question that needs to be addressed through careful study of his work and the works of his teachers. Renaming Spinoza "Baruch" is nothing but an instant and cheap gesture of political correctness. Still, the most *important* and *elaborate* Spinozist conversion is the recent attempt to bring Spinoza under the holy wings of Enlightenment Secularism.

In a series of recent books, Jonathan Israel, an outstanding economic historian,[15] has argued that the values of modernity owe their origin to Spinoza's philosophical school, which he terms "the Radical Enlightenment." Thus, for example, in his 2006 *Enlightenment Contested*, Israel writes:

> "Modernity" conceived as an abstract package of basic values—*toleration, personal freedom, democracy, equality racial and sexual, freedom of expression, sexual emancipation, and the universal right*

13. Giancotti-Boscherini (1978).

14. Hunter (2005), 83. For discussion of Hunter's claims, see Melamed (2012a).

15. See Israel's 1986 masterpiece study, *The Dutch Republic* and *European Jewry in the Age of Mercantilism*.

> *to knowledge and "enlightenment"*—derives ... from the Radical Enlightenment.[16]

The association of Spinoza with modern liberalism is commonplace among today's writers (especially among Jewish writers). Thus, Steven Nadler argues: "Spinoza was an eloquent proponent of a secular, democratic society, and was the strongest advocate for freedom and tolerance in the early modern period."[17] According to Leo Strauss, Spinoza is responsible for "the decisive impulse toward ... modern republicanism which takes its bearings by the dignity of every man,"[18] and if we believe Rebecca Goldstein, "Spinoza fundamentally insisted on the separation of church and state," thus anticipating and indirectly influencing the founding fathers of America.[19]

Obviously, I cannot provide here a comprehensive account of Spinoza's political thought. Still, before joining this "Spinoza Got It Right!" celebration of Benedict the secularist, feminist, liberal, humanist, democrat, and egalitarian, let me suggest a preliminary and cursory fact-checking. In the following few pages, I will concentrate on the "package of basic values" suggested by Israel, since it seems to present in a condensed and transparent manner a very common recent image of Spinoza. Was Spinoza indeed a champion of "toleration, personal freedom, democracy, equality racial and sexual, freedom of expression, sexual emancipation, and the universal right to knowledge and 'enlightenment'"? Let's see.[20]

A. "*Separation of Church and State.*" In the *TTP*, Spinoza argues that the state's "supreme powers [should be] the interpreters of religion and religious

---

16. Israel (2006), 11; italics added. Cf. Israel (2010), vii–viii, for a restatement of the very same basic values of the so-called Radical Enlightenment. Anticipating the response that perhaps Israel intended to ascribe these values only to Spinoza's *followers* in the Radical Enlightenment and their interpretation of Spinoza (and not to Spinoza himself), let me note, first, that if indeed (as I will shortly show) Spinoza was very far from advocating Israel's "basic values of the Radical Enlightenment" it is not at all clear in what sense Spinoza can be associated with the "Radical Enlightenment" (whatever this term means). Second, let me point out that Israel actually attributes this package of values *directly* to Spinoza. For the ascription to Spinoza of support for democracy and egalitarianism, and objection to oligarchy, see Israel (2010), 2, 92–94, and Israel (2006), 231, 252, 561. For descriptions of Spinoza as a champion of "comprehensive toleration," "freedom of worship," and "liberty of expression," see Israel (2006), 155, 157, 231, 252, and Israel (2010), 92. This is merely a small selection among many similar passages.

17. Nadler (2012).

18. Strauss (1965), 16.

19. Goldstein (2006), 11.

20. For a complementary overview of Spinoza's critique of metaphysical humanism, see Melamed (2010a).

duty."[21] Indeed Spinoza repeatedly argues in this work that no one should be allowed to preach publicly on issues of religion, unless he is first granted permission to do so by the sovereign. In this context, Spinoza writes:

> But if anyone should ask now "By what right could Christ's disciples, who were private men, preach religion?" I say that they did this by right of the control they had received from Christ over unclean Spirits (see Matthew 10:1). For above, at the end of Ch. 16, I explicitly warned that everyone was bound to keep faith even with a Tyrant, except that person to whom God, by a certain revelation, had promised special aid against the Tyrant. So it is not permissible for anyone to take this as an example, unless he also has the power to perform miracles.[22]

In order to avoid any misunderstanding of Spinoza's sardonic claims, let me make clear that he did not believe in ghosts or unclean spirits, and since he deemed the belief in unclean spirits to be simple nonsense,[23] it seems that "the right against unclean spirits" was no better. Christ's disciples could preach in public without permission from the Romans, since they *believed* that they had a right (or power) against unclean spirits (a right or power which may or may not have saved them when they were *justly* persecuted by the Romans). However, Spinoza adds, those who are not granted such a special "right" are not allowed to preach in public without securing the permission of the sovereign.[24] This seems to be a rather bizarre notion of the separation of church and state, but perhaps in other texts, Spinoza is more conventional in endorsing the "basic values of modernity."

The *Political Treatise* is one of Spinoza's two incomplete works written at the very end of his life. In this work, Spinoza envisages a "National Religion."

> Although everyone ought to be given the freedom to say what he thinks, nevertheless large assemblies ought to be prohibited. And so those who are devoted to another religion ought to be allowed, indeed, to build as many houses of worship as they wish, provided they are small, modest, and somewhat dispersed. But it is very important that

21. *TTP*, chap. 19, G III 232.

22. *TTP*, chap. 19, G III 233.

23. See Spinoza's amusing correspondence with Hugo Boxel, Eps. 51–56. For Spinoza's claim that "true Christians" should not believe in ghosts, see *TTP*, chap. 2, G III 43.

24. For further discussion of this passage, see Melamed (2012a), 142–44.

> the temples which are dedicated to the national Religion [*patriae Religioni*] be large and magnificent, and that only Patricians or Senators be permitted to officiate in its chief rituals. So only Patricians should be permitted to baptize, to consecrate a marriage, lay on hands, and without exception, to be recognized as Priests, and as defenders and interpreters of the national Religion.[25]

Some commentators cite this passage as evidence of Spinoza's support for religious tolerance.[26] We will shortly deal with this notion of "religious tolerance," but for the time being, let me just point out that in this text as well, Spinoza's alleged support for the separation of church and state seems to be highly idiosyncratic, given his endorsement of national religion and the allocation of priestly functions to the … Senators.

B. *"Toleration."* In the passage just quoted, Spinoza suggests that the state should allow the existence of other houses of worship (apart from those of the national religion), provided that these other religions are *systematically* discriminated against. Indeed, Spinoza is willing to tolerate disgraced and lowered religions that will attest to the glory and success of the national religion. You may call this tolerance if you wish;[27] but, according to this notion of tolerance, any government that falls short of exterminating or expelling the believers of a minority religion should be praised as genuinely tolerant. Hence, according to this notion of tolerance, we should praise (for example) St. Augustine's "tolerance" toward the Jews, and today's people of Switzerland for their generous willingness not to exterminate Muslims as long as their mosques and minarets "are small and modest" (as Spinoza says) in comparison with the temples of the state's majority religion.[28]

Moreover, apropos of tolerance, only rarely does Spinoza address the issue of excommunication. Yet, in one of these rare references, Spinoza stipulates that excommunication should be *supervised* by the state.

---

25. *TP*, chap. 8, G III 345.

26. Israel (2006), 155.

27. This is essentially the medieval notion of tolerance, by which Muslims and Christians (when the latter were not engaged in strict extermination) treated each other and Jews; it is also how Jews imagined they would treat Muslims and Christians when they gained power (see Maimonides, *Mishne Torah*, Hilkhot Melachim, VI, 1). Under this model, the other is conceived as a parasite whose unfortunate presence is not to be eradicated by force. One may expect human beings to treat each other in a more decent way, for example, by celebrating the presence of the other and valuing a multiplicity of competing, unsubordinated, cultures. Such a celebration of multiculturalism has no trace in Spinoza.

28. See Cumming-Bruce and Erlanger (2009).

> No one has the right and power without the authority or consent of the sovereign to administer sacred matters or choose ministers, or decide to establish the foundation and doctrines of a church, nor may they without that consent give judgments about morality, and observance of piety, *or excommunicate* or receive anyone into the church, or care for the poor.[29]

Notice that in this passage Spinoza lists excommunicating among the *legitimate* and common functions of the church, alongside almsgiving and establishing doctrines of faith. Spinoza stipulates that all functions of religion should be supervised by the state, but he does *not* have any in-principle objection to the use of excommunication. On the contrary, he seems to treat it just like any other legitimate function of the church. Thus, it seems that Spinoza's notion of tolerance is just as idiosyncratic as his view of the separation of church and state.

C. "*Equality Racial and Sexual, and Sexual Emancipation.*" In the Third Chapter of the *TTP*, Spinoza scolds those who believe that "nature produced different kinds of men,"[30] but it would be too quick for us to conclude from this that Spinoza is in favor of racial equality. Spinoza's writings are not free of contemporary European prejudices, and his depiction of Islam[31] (and to a lesser extent, Judaism) seems to be a perfect reflection of the bigotry common among his contemporaries.

It is difficult for me to see in what sense Spinoza can be described as supportive of sexual emancipation. His attitude toward sexuality is, for the most part, highly negative. Consider, for example, the following passage:

> He who imagines that a woman he loves prostitutes [*prostituere*] herself to another not only will be saddened, because his own appetite is restrained, but also will be repelled by her, because he is forced to join the image of the things he loves to the shameful parts [*pudendis*] and excretions [*excrementis*] of the other. (E3p35s)

Describing a woman who refuses one's love as "prostituting," and her lover's sex organs and semen as "shameful parts and excretions," does not seem to me

29. *TTP*, chap. 19, G III 235; italics added.

30. *TTP*, chap. 3, G III 47.

31. For Spinoza's rather ridiculous depiction of Islam as allowing no doubts or religious controversies, see *TTP*, Preface, G III 7. Unlike Spinoza's intimate knowledge of at least some core divisions of Jewish literature, his brief discussion of Islam discloses nothing but ignorance and prejudice.

to be in the spirit of the sixties, but who knows? Perhaps we should charitably interpret "prostituting" as nothing over and above lovemaking (for how could a great mind like Spinoza think that genitals are "shameful"?).

Much more telling and important is Spinoza's attitude toward "sexual equality." At the very end of the extant part of his *Political Treatise*, Spinoza claims, "Women and servants... are under the authority of their husbands and masters."[32] He goes further, and argues:

> Women do not, by nature, have equal right with men, but they necessarily submit to men, and so it cannot happen that each sex rule equally, much less that men are ruled by women. [33]

Along the same lines, Spinoza argues that in a monarchy—one of the three legitimate forms of government according to Spinoza—"under no circumstances should daughters be permitted to inherit the state."[34]

The exclusion of women from the polity is just one feature of a broader attitude toward women in Spinoza's work. In general, for Spinoza, the adjective "womanish" is strongly pejorative, as, for example, in his description of vegetarianism as an "empty superstition and womanly compassion [*muliebri misericordia*]" (*E*4p37s1).[35]

D. "*Universal Right to Knowledge and Enlightenment.*" Discussing Maimonides's attempt to reinterpret Scripture so that it agrees with philosophical truth, Spinoza scolds Maimonides's "excessively audacious" method and criticizes him for depriving the masses of the opium of anthropomorphic religion.[36] Spinoza does not believe in educating the masses in a transparent

32. *TP*, chap. 11, G III 359.

33. *TP*, chap. 11, G III 360.

34. *TP*, chap. 6, G III 306. Compare with this sober note by Margaret Wilson (1999, 193n26): "It seems to be widely agreed that Spinoza is quite derogatory in what he states and implies about the mentality of non-male humans. Ruth Barcan Marcus and Anne Jaap Jacobson have both suggested to me that it is worthwhile to consider the relations between major philosophers' views about non-male humans and their views about non-human animals. I think they are probably right." Let me just add that, as we have just seen in Spinoza's discussion in *E*3p35s, he does not hold in high regard the physicality, or carnality, of non-male humans.

35. For other pejorative references to women see *TTP*, Preface, G III 5, and chap. 3, G III 57.

36. See *TTP*, chap. 7, G III 115–16: "It completely takes away all the certainty the multitude can have about the meaning of Scripture from a straightforward reading of it."

manner so that the common people can advance beyond the anthropomorphic imagery of scripture and learn the true nature of things:

> Men must be led in such a way that they do not seem to themselves to be led, but to live according to their own temperament and from their free decree.[37]

The main function of religion in Spinoza's ideal state is to manipulate and control the masses, and it is essential for this purpose that the simple-minded citizens *not* be aware of the manner in which the sovereign manipulates them. *Sapere aude* [Dare to Know], the (somewhat pompous) slogan of Kantian Enlightenment, is not the advice Spinoza would offer to the masses. Achieving true knowledge is frequently detrimental to the masses. For Spinoza, the masses should be taught primarily to be *obedient*, and insofar as knowledge may impede obedience, it should *not* be taught to the masses.

> We should say that a person believes something piously or impiously only insofar as either his opinions move him to obedience or he takes a license from them to sin or rebel. As a result, if anyone becomes stiff-necked by believing truths, his faith is really impious; on the other hand, if he becomes obedient by believing falsehoods, it is pious.[38]

E. "*Democracy.*" Democracy is one of the three legitimate forms of government that Spinoza examines in his *Political Treatise* (the other two being aristocracy and monarchy). As far as I can see, Spinoza prefers both democracy and aristocracy to monarchy, though it is not at all clear what his preference is between democracy and aristocracy. Spinoza's very qualified support for democracy does not stem from any principled egalitarianism. For the most part, he despises and fears the masses. "The mob is terrifying if unafraid," Spinoza warns in the *Ethics* (*E*4p54s), and the whole structure of his political philosophy rests on the foundational observation that "it is impossible that most people will be eager to live wisely" (*TP* Ch. 10 | III/356). Spinoza's main motivation for supporting democracy relies on the rather naive form of realpolitik which assumes

---

37. *TP*, chap. 10, G III 356.

38. *TTP*, chap. 13, G III 172. See also *TTP*, chap. 14, G III 176: "Faith does not require tenets which are true as much as it does tenets which are pious, i.e., tenets which move the heart to obedience, even if there are many among them which have not even a shadow of the truth, so long as the person who accepts them does not know them to be false."

that a large group of people with a vast variety of conflicting desires is unlikely to agree on extremely irrational policies. "The will of a very large council," says Spinoza, "cannot be determined so much by inordinate desire as by reason."[39] Spinoza's fear of Caligula- or Nero-like rulers is the main reason for his rejection of monarchy. Democracy and aristocracy, he thinks, do not allow insanity to take hold of the state, simply because it is impossible for the insane to agree on a common madness. Naïveté is not typical of Spinoza, but on this issue, the events of the twentieth century clearly refuted him.

Our cursory review of Spinoza's compliance with Jonathan Israel's package of basic values of modernity shows that Spinoza's performance was hardly satisfactory. Spinoza expresses reserved support for democracy though the underlining reasoning behind this view is not particularly impressive. We also saw that Spinoza advocated a complete assimilation (rather than separation) of religion and state, that he viewed women as essentially inferior to men, that he viewed human sexuality in derogatory terms, and that his notion of tolerance was essentially the medieval notion that stipulated systematic discrimination against religious minorities. At this point one may wonder how serious and highly intelligent historians could ascribe to Spinoza the package of liberal values mentioned. As I just noted, there is *some* basis for Israel's sweeping generalizations, but the actual picture is far more complex. What makes serious historians engage in such an apparently reckless hermeneutics? For all I can tell the main motivation behind this practice is to show that Spinoza's political thought is *relevant* to today's discourse, or that Spinoza was the source of what we deem to be fair and right. We interpret Spinoza charitably (i.e., bending the text so that it can be read as expressing a desirable and respectable political view) since we highly appreciate his genius. A great political philosopher should advocate "decent" views (i.e., views that are similar to ours).

We can present this point in the form of a question: if indeed Spinoza was no feminist, no egalitarianist, and supported systematic discrimination against religious minorities—*why should we care or study him at all?* I find this question both legitimate and important, and the following section will be dedicated to outlining a surprising answer to this question; but let me state from the very beginning that I completely agree with the claim that we engage with past philosophers to the extent that we consider them relevant to our thought. The question is: *what makes a past philosopher relevant?*

39. *TP*, chap. 8, G III 336. See also *TTP*, chap. 16, G III 194.

4. Part Three: Philosophical Relevancy

The claim that we should care about past philosophers to the extent that their thought is relevant allows for a variety of ways by which past philosophers can be relevant. Yet, it rules out one position that is somewhat mischaracterized in the existing literature on the methodology of the history of philosophy. The so-called antiquarian approach is supposed to justify our engagement with past philosophers as a practice that is done for its own sake, or simply in order to record the views of past philosophers as historical facts, regardless of whether their thoughts are relevant to our discussions. This is an enchanting view, but for all I can tell, this "method" was never pursued outside of some short stories by Borges and his likes. A historian (any historian, not only historians of philosophy) who is interested in recording facts regardless of whether these facts are relevant to us should be engaged in the history of the rhinos in twelfth-century Sumatra just as much as he or she is engaged in twentieth-century political history. Qua facts, the number of teeth of any twelfth-century rhino is just as good as the rhetorical capacities of a certain Adolf Hitler, or the sex drives of Rasputin. Oddly enough, however, there are very few dissertations on our poor twelfth-century Sumatran rhino, and quite a few on Hitler and Rasputin. To put things simply: there is no history that is not motivated by what the historian finds relevant to his or her life. Otherwise, we would be picking our subject matter by random choice of a space-time unit (e.g., the space of this room in January 12, 1012). The choice of subject matter by a historian of *philosophy* is not different. We pick a topic that, in one way or another, we deem to be relevant to us.

There are many manners in which past philosophers can be relevant to us. We can study past philosophers in order to uncover the genealogy of our current values and beliefs. In this manner we learn the causal trajectory of our common beliefs, and what seems to us natural and obvious is exposed as a historical construct, attached to certain concrete circumstances. Alternatively, we can turn to the history of philosophy in order to import and revive unjustly abandoned notions or views held by past philosophers. Thus, analytic philosophers of the second half of the twentieth century imported the medieval distinction between *de re* and *de dicto* modality. A third view may suggest that past philosophies could be used in order to compare and contrast similar views across the centuries. Thus, one can profitably observe the similarities and differences between Spinoza's and Davidson's versions of the holism of the mental. This can be—if conducted properly—a legitimate and fully conscious anachronistic exercise.

While I have much sympathy for each of the aforementioned motivations for the study of past philosophers, I would like to suggest another, somewhat surprising, reason that I find compelling. We should engage in the study of good past philosophers, *not in spite, but because* of the fact that frequently past philosophers argue for views that are significantly different from ours. We should consciously challenge ourselves in a dialogue with philosophers whose views are both (a) *well argued*, and (b) *different from ours*. Such a dialogue is likely to make us probe our most basic beliefs, expose our own blind spots, and reevaluate what we take to be obvious and natural. Past philosophies give us the rare opportunity to challenge ourselves in dialogue with "justified, *wrong*, beliefs," or more precisely, beliefs that appear to be well justified and that we still deem to be wrong. Instead of searching for anticipators of our own views, we should look for well-justified alternatives that can challenge our views. I stress that we should engage with *well-argued* views of past philosophers, because we should not adore any whimsical non-sense of the great past philosophers. We should treat past philosophers with the same critical attitude with which we treat our peers, yet we should do our very best to let them speak *in their own voice*, and avoid bending the text so that it can express the views we find attractive. For that reason, it is crucial that before we generate our critical dialogue with past philosophers we should carefully reconstruct their views with maximal historical precision. We should be maximally attentive to the text and strive to reject the temptation of charitable interpretation, not because anachronism is wrong in itself, but rather because it deprives us of the rare opportunity to challenge ourselves in a critical dialogue with intelligent views that are different from ours. Thus, precise *historical* reconstruction is a major prerequisite for using past philosophers in the most profitable manner *philosophically*.

If the text of Spinoza's *Theological Political Treatise* suggests that the state should use religion as a political tool for the manipulation of the masses, we should not bend the text so that it can be read as separating state and religion. We should be open to the idea that Spinoza might be an acute political philosopher, having strong arguments in favor of his position, while not agreeing with us. Once we realize that, we should go deeper and seek for our and Spinoza's reasons. Posing such a contrast—especially in moral and political issues—is likely to make us question premises that usually we barely consider, or even realize.

5. Conclusion

Before concluding this chapter let me address the question of whether there are *any* cases of legitimate charitable interpretations of past philosophers. I believe there are; a wholesale ban on charitable interpretations would seem to stem from an attitude that sanctifies the text and idolizes its author. Unfortunately, I am not aware of any philosophical author who is immune from error, and for that reason I think we must be open to the possibility that the text may contain an error (whether it is mere a slip of pen or a more substantial error) which has to be emended. Yet, I contend that charitable interpretations of past philosophers should be severely restricted and very cautiously pursued. The most (and possibly the only) legitimate application of charitable interpretation would be in the case of internal consistency within the same text, i.e., when an author makes explicitly contradictory claims within the same text. But even in such a case, we should be very careful before turning to the aid of charity. First, we should keep in mind the possibility that the author is *intentionally* toying with the law of non-contradiction. If we have any evidence that the author does not accept the standard formulation of the law of non-contradiction, we should abstain from employing charity. Second, we should consider the possibility that the author changed her mind while writing the text. This possibility should be given more consideration when we are dealing with textual units that are rather long, and in cases where we have evidence that the author revised her earlier statements in a later period. Third, we should consider the possibility that the internal inconsistency in the text may result from unresolved deliberation by the author. In such a case, we should note the tension and consider various resolutions. Pointing out tensions and internal contradictions in the thought of a philosopher may advance us quite a bit not only in obtaining the precise historical facts, but also (and more important) in uncovering the logical space of the issues at stake.

In this chapter I have criticized the attitude common among contemporary historians of philosophy (and some philosophers) who strive to reconstruct the texts of past philosophers so that they appear respectable and agree with the common views and intuitions of our contemporaries. I have argued that this practice deprives us of the most philosophically profitable use of past philosophers, i.e., their ability to challenge our own well-fortified intuitions. There is a significant relation between one's methodology in studying the history of philosophy and one's preferred methodology of philosophical inquiry. Philosophical conservatism and slavish adherence to so-called commonsense intuitions, while they do not strictly necessitate the use of charitable interpretation of past philosophers, seem to play a significant role in motivating the appeal to charity. This is not the place for a detailed discussion of the value of philosophical intuitions. Still, let me suggest briefly that even if the appeal to intuitions were unavoidable (and I am not yet convinced that this is indeed the case), it would by no means imply that intuitions should be instantly accepted; rather than uncritically consumed they should be used as a crucial ingredients of philosophical *slow cooking*. They should be challenged, tested, and modified time and again.

One finds a very similar philosophical sensibility in Spinoza's famous discussion of miracles in the *TTP*.

> But since miracles were produced according to the capacity of the common people who were completely ignorant of the principles of natural things, plainly the ancients took for a miracle whatever they were unable to explain in the manner the common people normally explained natural things, namely by seeking to recall something similar which can be imagined without amazement. *For the common people suppose they have satisfactorily explained something as soon as it no longer astounds them.*[40]

What precisely went wrong in the *vulgus*' attempt and failure to explain miracles? Obviously they erred, according to Spinoza, by "being ignorant of the principles of natural things"; but why did they *stay* ignorant in spite of their genuine attempt to trace the causes of miracles? Why did they not look for the natural explanations of miracles? The *vulgus* were definitely not wrong in trying to find a causal explanation for miracles; Spinoza openly argues that we ought to try to explain things through their proximate causes.[41]

What went wrong in the method of the "common people" was that they did not go far enough in their attempt to explain the nature of things. Instead of stubbornly seeking the explanation for each fact, they felt content once an extraordinary fact was shown to be the result of a *familiar* phenomenon, while paying no attention to the need to explain the familiar. In a way, they were rudimentary commonsense philosophers who asked for an explanation for what appeared to be against common sense and were completely reassured

40. *TTP*, chap. 6, G III 84; italics added.

41. *TTP*, chap. 4, G III 58. The last three paragraphs of this chapter are a modified version of Melamed (2010b, 130–31).

once the unfamiliar turned out to be a result of the common. For Spinoza, our familiarity with a phenomenon does not render it intelligible; the familiar or common, just like the extraordinary and uncommon, demands a clear explanation.

Acknowledgments

I would like to thank the participants at the workshop in Montréal, where this chapter was first presented, for their helpful comments. I am also indebted to Eckart Förster, Zach Gartenberg, Michah Gottlieb, Zeev Harvey, Nick Kaufmann, Mogens Lærke, John Morrison, and Oded Schechter for their very helpful comments on earlier versions of this chapter.

13

Mediating between Past and Present: Descartes, Newton, and Contemporary Structural Realism

Mary Domski

1. Introduction

MY GOAL IN this chapter is to address a practical worry that the editors raise in the Introduction to this volume. The worry is one that belongs to many contextualist historians, and it is directed at appropriationist attempts to bring early modern philosophy into conversation with contemporary philosophy.[1] In brief, the general worry is that creating a dialogue between past and present involves *revising* the philosophy of the past so that it fits the model and speaks the language of the present. Or put differently, the central worry is that we are apt to *distort* the historical record precisely by assuming a unity between the past and present practice of philosophy when, in fact, contextualist evidence strongly suggests that no such unity exists. Take Descartes as an example. Contextualist studies have shown us that Descartes's philosophical program is premised on essential connections between metaphysics, epistemology, physics, and ethics—on a unity between disciplines that, currently, we take to be isolated from one another.[2] Thus, according to the contextualist critic, to bring any single part of Descartes's program into conversation with

1. Throughout the chapter, I adopt the editors' general characterization of the aims that distinguish "appropriationist" and "contextualist" views of history. For the appropriationist "the history of philosophy is held to be a source of ideas and arguments that may be of use in current philosophy, and it is to be studied as a way of advancing in the resolution of problems of current interest." In contrast, the contextualist maintains that "the history of philosophy is to be studied and understood for its own sake and on its own terms, even when the problems of interest to the figures in this history have since fallen off of the philosophical agenda." (p. 1 of this volume.) Other contributors to this volume discuss whether and how the contextualist historian can successfully capture the meaning of historical texts. This is not an issue I broach here.

2. Cf. Garber (1992).

twenty-first-century philosophy (e.g., to try to draw lessons for contemporary metaphysics from Cartesian metaphysics) requires that we revise and thereby distort what Descartes's philosophy actually is.

The problem of revisionism and distortion is especially pronounced for those who adopt the "conceptual resources" view of history, a view according to which the past is a storehouse of answers and strategies that can be introduced into current philosophical debates. Roughly put, this version of appropriationism takes our current philosophical questions and debates as fixing the terms of discussion such that the framework that defines our current philosophical inquiries defines *the* language of philosophy. Taking this approach, learning from the history of philosophy requires translating the language of the past into the language of the present, and it is this process of translation that is the primary target of the contextualist critic. In brief, her fundamental concern is that the language of past philosophy cannot faithfully be captured by our current language. There will be a loss in translation, and a significant one at that.

My goal is to offer a way around this contextualist worry by abandoning the "conceptual resources" model of history and offering an alternative characterization of how appropriationism might succeed. Specifically, I urge a marriage of contextualism and appropriationism that embraces the contextualist claim that philosophical practice is itself contextually defined, i.e., that the standards for doing philosophy are supplied by, and can only properly be understood in reference to, the historical situation in which philosophy is and has been practiced. Moreover, the main project of the form of appropriationism I propose is not to translate the language of the past into the language of the present but to identify in just what sense past philosophy is *different* from contemporary philosophy. The task, in other words, is to take a reflective stance on the past and present practice of philosophy and *mediate* between the different languages they speak in order to gain an enhanced perspective on the questions and concerns that define contemporary philosophy. This approach to creating a meaningful dialogue between the history of philosophy and contemporary philosophy is inspired by proposals made in Margaret Wilson's celebrated 1992 "History of Philosophy in Philosophy Today; and the Case of the Sensible Qualities." Briefly considering one of Wilson's examples of how contemporary philosophy might benefit from attention to early modern philosophy will help me clarify the position I aim to defend.[3]

3. In section 3 of her paper, Wilson offers five lessons that we can draw from her contextualist treatment of early modern approaches to sensible qualities. I focus on her fifth lesson, which is presented under the subheading "Metaphilosophical issues."

The example is presented after Wilson offers her rich and insightful overview of the seventeenth-century treatment of sensible qualities, as she reflects on how different their projects are from our current ones. She draws attention to the peculiar aims of the early moderns and remarks that seventeenth-century writers "were, above all, explaining and advocating a view of the relation between sense experience and physical reality which they saw as rivaling and replacing recently dominant Aristotelian-Scholastic assumptions, a view consistent with a dramatically more successful and fundamentally different science of nature. Now clearly [she's quick to point out], late-twentieth-century philosophers are not doing *that*."[4] However, recognizing that there is such a difference between the past and present does not end the story. Instead, recognizing that we are working in a different philosophical-scientific context—one in which philosophy and science are no longer "seamlessly combined" but are regarded "as two distinct modes of intellectual activity"[5]—allows us to bring into relief a question that plays centrally, though often implicitly, in contemporary debates concerning sensible qualities: What *is* the relationship between philosophy and science? As Wilson rightly urges, until this question is addressed we will have no good answers to the related questions of whether philosophy should model its investigations on science, of whether incorporating scientific claims into philosophical discussion will render philosophy a science, and most important, of whether it is at all possible to sustain a unique place for distinctively philosophical inquiries into the nature of sensible qualities.

Following Wilson's lead, then, history can serve as a resource for the present, but not in the standard way whereby we assume that the answers to our current questions are waiting for us in the historical record. What Wilson illustrates is that history can open up a way of understanding what is *missing* from current discussions, because the practice of past philosophy—the unique language that the historical figures speak—points us to some fundamental relationship that informs our present philosophical inquiries. To see, in particular, that philosophy and science are no longer "seamlessly combined," as they were for early modern thinkers, motivates reflection on the nature of philosophy's connection to science and also brings us to recognize that our answer to this question could change the character of our current enterprises and, at best, place them on more solid philosophical ground. Thus,

4. Wilson (1992), 242.

5. Ibid., 242.

in opposition to the contextualist critic described earlier, who claims that the differences between past and present prevent meaningful dialogue between the historian of philosophy and the contemporary philosopher, Wilson shows us that further reflection on the very differences that separate the past from the present can open a space for contemporary philosophers to identify and address questions, the answers to which can illuminate the very philosophical foundations on which our current debates rest.[6]

In what follows I want to extend this lesson from Wilson and examine a relationship we now take for granted in our philosophical discourse about science: the connection between mathematics and the physical sciences. Given the history of science we have inherited (here, think of physics from Newton onward), we accept that mathematics is the language of physical science, that to do physics is to trade in mathematical formalism. Borrowing Wilson's terminology, mathematics and physics are for us, and for good historical reasons, "seamlessly combined," and their essential connection, if you will, is often taken as a given in current discussions concerning the representative power of physical theories (as I will elaborate later). Of course, such was not the case in the seventeenth century. The marriage of mathematics and physics was, in that period, an open question that required argument, and I aim to show that attention to these early modern arguments can open up a way for better understanding our practices in contemporary philosophy of science and, specifically, for enhancing current discussions of whether and in what sense our mathematically formulated physical theories are true (or approximately true) representations of the natural order.

To make my case, I narrow my focus on the contemporary debate between epistemic and ontic structural realists. This is a debate in which the history of philosophy and the history of science continue to play a central role, where those on both sides have taken a "conceptual resources" stance toward history and looked to the past for directives on how they might clarify their philosophical positions on scientific theories. As beneficial as this approach has been for proponents of epistemic and ontic structural realism (as well as their critics), my goal is to show that a different approach to history—and to the relationship between the past and present—might positively change the character of the current debate. Specifically, by examining Descartes's and

6. It is neither Wilson's contention nor my own that history provides the *only* way to reach a reflective stance on our current philosophical practice. The point of her remarks, which I endorse, is that recognizing that contextualist approaches to history *can* offer insight into our current practices gives us good reason to reject the claim that contextualist history cannot (and thus should not) be brought into conversation with contemporary philosophy.

Newton's arguments for merging mathematics with physical science, I aim to show that contemporary structural realists could benefit from attending to an issue that informed the seventeenth-century debates concerning the mathematization of nature, namely, the role that epistemic and ontological commitments play in the development of our scientific theories.

2. *History in Current Debates about Structural Realism*

The natural starting point for discussion of contemporary structural realism is John Worrall's 1989 "Structural Realism: The Best of Both Worlds." Worrall's ambitious goal in this essay is to develop a version of scientific realism that can explain the "approximate truth" of our best scientific theories and address the challenge of Larry Laudan's (1981) so-called pessimistic meta-induction. The basic problem that Laudan highlights is a problem that emerges from the history of scientific theory change. This history reveals that empirical success is retained at moments of theory change, i.e., that the same set of empirical phenomena is often explained by two succeeding theories (e.g., both Newtonian mechanics and Einsteinian relativity can explain planetary motion). However, at these same moments there is no evident cumulative progress at the *theoretical* level (e.g., Newtonian mechanics and Einsteinian relativity are grounded on incompatible theories of space and time). As such, the historical record seems "to supply good inductive grounds for holding that those theories presently accepted in science will, within a reasonably brief period, themselves be replaced by theories which retain (and extend) the empirical success of present theories, but do so on the basis of underlying theoretical assumptions at odds with those presently accepted."[7] The challenge, then, to any realist account of scientific theories is to explain in what sense theoretically incompatible theories can be said to be true, or even approximately true, of nature. How, for instance, can a realist maintain that both Newtonian mechanics and Einsteinian relativity capture something true about nature when, clearly, they make opposing theoretical claims about the natural order?

In response to this historical problem, Worrall adopts an approach to what theories represent that moves us beyond the common realist claim that our theories represent natural objects. His position is one explicitly inspired by remarks from Henri Poincaré's *Science and Hypothesis* (1902; English translation 1952), and it is a position according to which (1) scientific theories represent nature through their mathematical equations (or structure), and

---

7. Worrall (1989), 149.

(2) what these equations represent are the *relations* between natural objects. As Poincaré puts it, the equations of our scientific theories "express relations, and if the equations remain true, it is because the relations preserve their reality." Thus, when we talk of objects such as *motion* or *electric current*, say, we are using mere "names of the images [that] we substitute for the real objects which Nature will hide for ever from our eyes. The true relations between these objects are the only reality we can attain."[8] Following Poincaré's suggestions here, Worrall responds to Laudan's challenge by focusing on the mathematical structures that get carried over from one theory to the next, and claims that the continuity in mathematical formalism gives warrant to the realist claim that truth is preserved at moments of scientific theory change.

While Worrall makes a compelling case on behalf of realism, James Ladyman (1998) points out that there is an ambiguity in Worrall's presentation of structural realism such that it can be read as either an epistemic or a metaphysical position. The epistemic reading is supported by the claims that Worrall appropriates from Poincaré, and it is a reading according to which our scientific theories capture the relations between natural objects *because* our epistemic makeup limits us to knowledge of such relations. In other words, even if the natural ontology includes objects, our theories do not and cannot capture the essences of these objects precisely because we are not epistemically fitted to know them. Proponents of the epistemic version of structural realism thus maintain that our best scientific theories are *approximately* true insofar as they are (potentially) incomplete representations of a more robust natural ontology.[9]

In his 1998 paper, Ladyman forwards an alternative form of structural realism that is also suggested by Worrall's treatment, one Ladyman there calls *metaphysical* structural realism but which has since been dubbed *ontic* structural realism. The basic claim of this position is that our scientific theories capture the structure and relations of nature because, in brief, relations are all that actually exist. To clarify this position, Ladyman turns to the history of science and draws on Hermann Weyl's group-theoretic approach to relativity theory. Ladyman emphasizes that what is objectively and metaphysically true of nature—what is true about the structure of nature itself—is captured

8. Poincaré (1952), 162; emphasis in the original. I have argued elsewhere (Domski, preprint) that Poincaré's remarks point to a neo-Kantian position about scientific theories, not a realist one, as Worrall claims.

9. I say "(potentially) incomplete representations," because some defenders of epistemic structural realism are agnostic about the existence of individual objects.

by the mathematical formalism of Weyl's theory. Specifically, what we see in Weyl's version of relativity is that the metaphysics of nature is "*given by* the invariance structure of theories."[10] Here we can clarify a fundamental difference between ontic structural realism and epistemic structural realism: on Ladyman's score, our best scientific theories capture the structures of nature as epistemic structural realists contend, but our theories succeed in capturing this structure because *what is objective* and *all* that is objective is precisely what the theory *represents* as objective. In other words, it is not our epistemic limits that determine what our theories represent; our theories capture the real relations and structure of nature, because this objective metaphysical structure is all there is to know.[11]

To be sure, there's much more that could be said about structural realism, but the examples I use highlight the role that history continues to play in the current debate.[12] We notice in particular that history is treated as a "conceptual resource": it continues to serve as a source of scientific theories and philosophies of science that help clarify current positions as well as the problems surrounding currently held positions. As noted earlier, my goal is to reveal that history can play a different role and to show, in particular, that, starting from a contextualist stance on the seventeenth century, we can expand the terms of the current structural realist debate and move the discussion beyond the question of *why* our best theories capture structural, or relational, aspects of the natural ontology—whether because of our epistemic makeup or because of the natural ontology itself. By looking at Descartes's and Newton's competing arguments for why it is appropriate to mathematize nature in order to understand nature, I hope to show that structural realists could benefit from addressing the extent to which the epistemic and the ontological determine the development of our physical theories. To make my case, I focus on Descartes's *Principles of Philosophy* (1644) and Newton's *De Gravitatione* (written prior to 1687), texts in which Descartes and Newton address why mathematics is appropriate for our inquiries into nature.

---

10. Ladyman (1998), 421.

11. As Ladyman puts it, "A crude statement of ESR [epistemic structural realism] is the claim that all we know is the structure of the relations between things and not the things themselves, and a corresponding crude state of OSR [ontic structural realism] is the claim that there are no 'things' and that structure is all there is" (Ladyman 2009).

12. For other, more recent examples, see French and Ladyman (2003) for their appeal to the history of quantum theory to support their version of ontic structural realism and also Brading and Skiles (2012) for their use of Descartes and Newton to challenge French and Ladyman's argument. See Ladyman (2009) for a comprehensive overview of the different forms of ESR and OSR.

3. Descartes and Newton on the Appropriateness of Mathematics for Physics

a. Descartes's *Principles*

The now standard reading of the physics included in Descartes's *Principles* is a reading that rightly emphasizes the metaphysical foundations on which the program rests.[13] What we find, in particular, is that in the Cartesian "metaphysical physics" Descartes establishes an essential connection between God's activity and our human knowledge of the natural world according to which our metaphysically certain knowledge of God, as established by natural reason (and as presented in Part 1 of the *Principles*), grounds and explains what is *true* of the external world.

To appreciate how metaphysics and physics are merged in the Cartesian program, consider Descartes's presentation of his second law of nature, according to which "all motion is in itself rectilinear; and hence any body moving in a circle always tends to move away from the centre of the circle which it describes."[14] Initially, Descartes explains the truth of this law in terms of God's activity and tells us that

> The reason for this second rule is the same as the reason for the first rule, namely the immutability and simplicity of the operation by which God preserves motion in matter. For he always preserves the motion in the precise form in which it is occurring at the very moment when he preserves it, without taking any account of the motion which was occurring a little while earlier.[15]

Descartes then clarifies how this metaphysical justification for the second law is connected with our *perception* of natural motions as he discusses the motion of a stone in a sling:

> For example, as the stone A turns in the sling rotating along the circle ABF [Figure 13.1], in the instant that is at point A, [the stone] is indeed

---

13. This reading has recently gained increasing popularity in large part because of Garber's (1992) treatment of the Cartesian program.

14. Part 2, Article 39; AT VIII, 63; CSM I, 241–42. Following now standard citation format, I use "AT" to refer to Descartes (1964–1975) and "CSM" to refer to Descartes (1984–1991).

15. Part 2, Article 39; AT VIII 63–64; CSM I, 242.

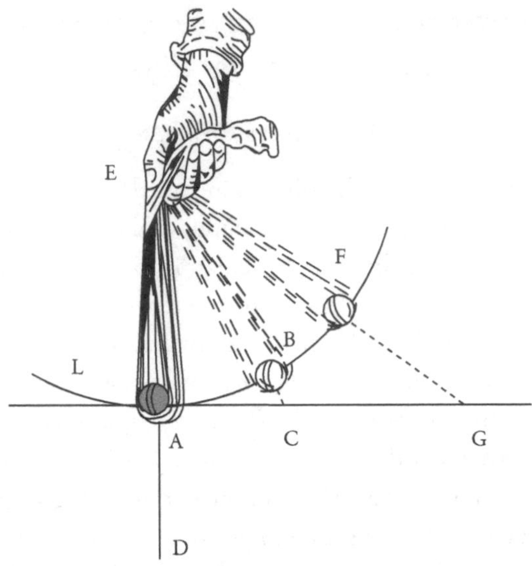

FIGURE 13.1. The Sling of *Principles* Part 2; AT VIII, 64.

> determined to move itself in some direction, namely along a straight line toward C, assuming that AC is tangent to the curve. On the other hand, we cannot imagine that [the stone] has the power to determine itself in any circular movement: even if the stone comes from L towards A following a curved line, we cannot at all understand [*intelligi*] how there could be the slightest part of this power to move in a curve in the stone when it is at point A. Of this we have confirmation from experience, because when the stone leaves the sling, it does not in any way tend toward B but advances directly toward C. From this it follows that any body that is moving circularly perpetually tends to recede from the center of the circle it describes, as it is indeed sensed in our hand from the experience of twirling the stone in the sling.[16]

As Descartes presents it, the stone's tendency to move in a straight line at each moment of its motion in the sling illustrates how God's simple and immutable activity is presented to our intellects and to our senses. Namely, it is because God's activity is simple and immutable (and thus directed in a straight line) that there are limits to what we can imagine and understand of the stone as

16. Part 2, Article 39; AT VIII 64–65. This part of Article 39 is not presented in CSM I. I completed the translation above with assistance from Christian Wood.

it completes its motion. Put differently, God's simple and immutable activity is that which explains the *true* and *proper* tendency to motion found in the stone, and because there is such a true and proper tendency, we have a *metaphysical* explanation for why our empirical perceptions of the motion of natural bodies have the character they do.

This law and Descartes's other two metaphysically grounded laws of nature are the centerpiece of Part 2 of the *Principles* and provide the first step of physical inquiry. The second step comes in Part 3, where the goal is to explain *all* the natural phenomena that appear to our senses. To achieve these explanations, we do not begin from the metaphysical truths established in Parts 1 and 2. Instead, as emphasized in Article 45 of Part 3, our investigation commences with the natural effects we sense, and from these effects we reason to causes.[17] That is, we begin with the complicated (or unclear and indistinct) phenomena presented to our senses, and our task is to parse through this complexity and identify possible and intelligible physical causes of what we witness.

Importantly, in the section that transitions us between Parts 2 and 3, Descartes asserts that the physical, effect-to-cause inquiry of Part 3 is mathematical and claims that "The only principles which [he will] accept, or require, in physics are those of geometry and pure mathematics." He explains further:

> I freely acknowledge that I recognize no matter in corporeal things apart from that which the geometers call quantity, and take as the object of their demonstrations, i.e. that to which every kind of division, shape and motion is applicable. Moreover, my consideration of such matter involves absolutely nothing apart from these divisions, shapes and motions.... And since all natural phenomena can be explained in this way, as will become clear in what follows, I do not think that any other principles are either admissible or desirable in physics.[18]

To understand the *mathematical* character of the physics presented in Part 3 requires attention to how the mathematical principles that Descartes mentions play an explanatory role. What do such mathematical principles

---

17. Part 3, Article 45; AT VIII, 100; CSM I, 256. Of course, Descartes requires that our explanations be consistent with and proceed in accordance with the truths established in the earlier parts of the *Principles*. The point here is that these explanations do not necessarily or deductively follow from those metaphysical truths.

18. Part 2, Article 63; AT VIII, 78–79; CSM I, 247.

explain? And why should we rely on these principles when we already have a metaphysically firm foundation for our physics? On my reading of Part 3, the epistemically exact principles of mathematics offer us an intelligible though still possible account of natural phenomena, which cannot be known exactly. In other words, mathematics offers us a guide for picking out what is intelligible in a complex natural system, and in this sense, the mathematical theory of Part 3 (if we even want to call it a theory) does not offer an absolutely true account of nature as metaphysical considerations of God's activity do. In line with the methodological directives presented in Article 45 of Part 3, mathematical principles offer a possible and intelligible story of the causes at play in nature.

To see what I have in mind, consider again the motion of the stone in the sling but now as it is presented in the physics of Part 3:

> *57. How the same body can be said to strive to move in different directions at the same time.* Often many different causes act simultaneously on the same body, and one may hinder the effect of another. So, *depending on the causes we are considering*, we may say that the body is tending or striving to move in different directions at the same time. For example [see Figure 13.1], *the stone A* in the sling EA which is swung about the centre E *tends to go from A to B, if we consider all the causes which go to determine its motion*, since it does in fact go in this direction. But *if we concentrate simply on the power of moving which is in the stone itself, we shall say that when it is at point A it tends towards C*, in accordance with the law stated above [namely, the second law of nature] (supposing, of course, that the line AC is a straight line which touches the circle at point A). For if the stone were to leave the sling at the exact moment when it arrived from L at point A, it would in fact go from A towards C, not towards B; and although the sling may prevent this outcome, it does not prevent the "striving." Finally, *if we concentrate not on the stone's total power of moving but only on the part which is checked by the sling, and we distinguish this from the remaining part which produces the actual result*, we shall say that when the stone is at point A, it tends to move simply towards D, or that it "strives" to move away from the centre E along the straight line EAD.[19]

19. Part 3, Article 57; AT VIII, 108–109; CSM I, 259; emphasis added.

Notice here the emphasis that Descartes places on the choice we have when we consider the stone's motion and its tendency to motion: we can "consider all the causes which go to determine its motion" *or* we can "concentrate simply on the power of moving which is in the stone itself," *or* we can concentrate only on the part of that power of motion checked by the sling and "distinguish this from the remaining part which produces the actual result." In Part 2, where Descartes was using this same example to explain the second law of nature, there was no choice in our treatment of the stone's tendency to motion; on that metaphysical account, we were considering the *true* and *proper* tendency to motion at each instant of the stone's path, and this tendency is produced by God's simple and immutable act of conserving the stone's motion. However, here, in the context of the physics, we start from the variety of causes acting on the stone and make a choice such that what we understand of the stone's motion depends on which cause of motion we choose to consider.

Descartes's different uses of the sling in Parts 2 and 3 help clarify how he connects metaphysical certainty and mathematical certainty with our understanding of nature. On the one hand, Descartes's *metaphysics* has established that every essentially extended body is attributed a true and proper tendency to motion, and on the other hand, Descartes's *physics* is aimed at explaining the variety of causes of the motions we witness in nature by appeal to the clear and intelligible principles of motion offered by mathematics. Insofar as the principles of mathematics indicate which motions are intelligible, easy, and simple to our human intellects, these principles are regulative: they guide us to physically possible explanations of natural motion, explanations that must of course be consistent with the rational, metaphysical certainty of God's simple and immutable activity but that extend our understanding beyond this metaphysical certainty so that we can comprehend the multitude of physical causes acting on a moving body. As a result, even though mathematics plays a central role in Descartes's physics—even though what is mathematically intelligible directs our investigation into natural motions—mathematics by no means lends any certainty to our physical investigations. To the contrary, mathematics enters our natural investigations—and should enter our investigations—to offer an intelligible guide for selecting among possible explanations for the variety of motions we perceive. In Newton's *De Gravitatione*, we find something different: the mathematically intelligible *is* what is naturally certain and, moreover, the mathematically intelligible directs us to metaphysical truths of nature.

b. Newton's *De Gravitatione*

De Gravitatione is a short but complicated text. According to the opening lines, the main topic of the work is the science of weight and equilibrium. However, there is much more besides, including several arguments against the physics of Descartes's *Principles* and important claims regarding God's presence in nature. I focus on Newton's claims regarding space to establish a fundamental contrast between the interplay of mathematics and metaphysics in the Cartesian and Newtonian programs: whereas, for Descartes, gaining genuine knowledge of what is true of the essentially extended spatial bodies in nature requires *metaphysically* certain knowledge of God's preservation of nature, for Newton, it is our *mathematically* certain knowledge of the real form of space that grounds our knowledge of natural bodies and also our knowledge that these bodies are essentially and fundamentally related to the divine.

In *De Gravitatione*, Newton's account of space comes in two distinct parts: he first describes what space is *not*, and then proceeds to detail what space *is*. When he tells us what space is not, he claims that space is not a substance, "because it is not absolute in itself, but is as it were an emanative effect of God and an affection of every kind of being."[20] Space is also not an accident, because "we can clearly conceive extension existing without any subject," and finally, space is not nothing at all, because "it is something more than an accident, and approaches more nearly to the nature of substance."[21] Newton then elaborates,

> There is no idea of nothing, nor has nothing any properties, but we have an exceptionally clear idea of extension *by abstracting the dispositions and properties of a body* so that there remains only the uniform and unlimited stretching out of space in length, breadth, and depth. And furthermore, many of its properties are associated with this idea; these I shall now enumerate not only to show that it is something, but also to show what it is.[22]

Over the next several pages, Newton proceeds to explain what space is and enumerates six properties associated with this idea of extension, some of which I will treat in the following.

---

20. Newton (2004), 21.

21. Ibid., 22.

22. Ibid., 22; emphasis added.

According to the passage that transitions us from what space is *not* to what space *is*, Newton claims that he has identified the properties that belong to space (as it exists in the natural ontology) by examining the "exceptionally clear idea" of space (i.e., our mental representation of space). And as just noted, this idea of space is generated "by *abstracting* the dispositions and properties of a body." With this remark Newton suggests that having the idea of space depends on first having an idea of body, and moreover, he suggests that these ideas of bodies somehow communicate the existence and nature of an extra-mental entity that we term space, or extension. To get a better handle on the "abstraction" that is at play here, and to see how it enables Newton to draw a connection between our knowledge of space and our knowledge of bodies, we can turn to the introduction of *De Gravitatione*, where Newton employs the notion of "abstraction" to explain how he will present the science of weight and equilibrium. He claims that he will "largely abstract [this science] from physical considerations" and "demonstrate its individual propositions from abstract principles, sufficiently well known to the student, strictly and geometrically."[23] He then clarifies that in the mathematical science of weight and equilibrium, body is "that which fills place," and he specifies further that "body is here proposed for investigation not in so far as it is a physical substance endowed with sensible qualities, but only in so far as it is extended, mobile, and impenetrable." He continues,

> I have not defined [body] in a philosophical manner, but abstracting the sensible qualities ... I have postulated only the properties required for local motion. So that instead of physical bodies you may understand abstract figures in the same way that they are considered by geometers when they assign motion to them, as is done in Euclid's *Elements*, Book 1, 4 and 8.[24]

Roughly speaking, abstraction is presented here as a process of selection and reduction: Newton ignores the sensible qualities that are associated with bodies and focuses only on those features that are "required for local motion." Reducing bodies to these features leaves us entities to which only a select group of properties are attached: they are reduced to "abstract figures" which are merely "extended, mobile, and impenetrable." As a result, Newton can

23. Ibid., 12.

24. Ibid., 13.

treat bodies "strictly and geometrically" because he has invoked a process of abstraction that allows him to focus on those properties that can themselves be "strictly and geometrically" known.[25] In other words, in Newton's mathematization of the real, he focuses on the mathematical features that *actually* and *really* belong to natural bodies, and moreover, he learns through empirically gathered evidence that bodies have these mathematical features: by rationally considering the empirically derived idea of body, Newton discovers that among the properties that belong to all bodies are the very ones studied in the mathematical sciences, and in geometry in particular.[26]

So, when Newton claims that our "exceptionally clear idea" of space (i.e., our mental representation of space) is gathered "by *abstracting* the dispositions and properties of a body," his suggestion is that to arrive at our idea of space, we begin with a sensuous conception of body as that to which sensible properties are attached, and then we abstract these sensible properties and focus only on those required for local motion. By doing so, we generate a representation of body as that which is extended, mobile, and impenetrable, and, consequently, we can generate an "exceptionally clear idea" that represents "the uniform and unlimited stretching out of space in length, breadth, and depth," an idea which corresponds to the form of space that is actually related to the bodies of sense-experience. As a result, we have at our disposal a representation of space that can be strictly and geometrically known, and moreover, our *knowledge* of this representation underwrites our knowledge of the mathematical features of the *real* bodies in nature.

Turning to Newton's so-called affection thesis, he also forwards an essential connection between *existence* and *spatiality* such that to exist is to bear some relationship to space: "Space [as he says] is an affection of a being just as a being. No being exists or can exist which is not related to space in some way."[27] Moreover, because existing things are related to space (and duration), they are rendered quantities, or better, they are rendered quantifiable; one can

---

25. In light of Newton's claim that he is focusing on those "properties required for local motion," there remains some ambiguity about whether these properties are the only essential properties of bodies. It could very well be that there are more "real" properties that belong to bodies, and Newton has simply chosen to focus on the sub-set that explains a body's motion. Contrast Janiak's remarks in Newton (2004), 13, Note 2. For my present purposes, we need only accept that extension, mobility, and impenetrability actually and really do belong to bodies.

26. I argue in Domski (2012) that Newton's use of "abstraction" is best understood when put into conversation with the neo-Platonic commitments that inform the treatment of space in *De Gravitatione*.

27. Ibid., 25.

assign a quantifiable value to an object based on the size of the space in which it is present. As Newton puts it,

> certainly both [space and duration] are affections or attributes of a being according to which *the quantity of a thing's existence is individuated to the degree that the size of its presence and persistence is specified.*[28]

Newton then tells us that, since God is present at all positions of space, He has an infinite degree of being, and since created bodies are located in some bounded region of space, their degree of being has a finite value. As such, it is in virtue of the fact that *all* existing things have a relation to space that they have a specifiable degree of being. Put differently, the uncreated creator, created minds, and created bodies all bear a relation to the naturally real form of space, and therefore, they are rendered quantifiable and subject to possible mathematical investigation.

At first blush, this account of body and spatiality sounds rather Cartesian. Descartes defines bodies as essentially extended—material substance and extension are in fact identical—and then claims that these bodies have a size associated with them based on their extension. Newton's characterization is importantly different: what is essential to bodies is their existence, and this existence can be measured in relation to the space they occupy. In other words, the degree of a body's being is not a result of its presence in space; rather, it is in virtue of their presence in space that the degree of each existing being is *measurable*. To put the difference in simpler terms: for Descartes, it is because bodies are spatially extended that they exist (as material substances), whereas for Newton, it is because bodies exist that they are spatial and are thereby rendered quantifiable.

To further clarify the non-Cartesian character of Newton's natural philosophy, note that, for Newton, it is in virtue of their presence in space that we know, with the same certainty that we know space is infinite, that all existing, created things are related to God. This suggestion emerges when Newton lays forth the final of the six properties associated with our "exceptionally clear" idea of space:

> 6. Lastly, space is eternal in duration and immutable in nature because it is the emanative effect of an eternal and immutable being. If ever space had not existed, God at that time would have been nowhere;

28. Ibid., 25–26; emphasis added.

> and hence he either created space later (where he was not present himself), or else, which is no less repugnant to reason, he created his own ubiquity.[29]

The main point here is that knowing the eternality of space derives from understanding the nature of God as creator: to create, a creative being must be somewhere, i.e., the creator must be present in space. However, in the next part of the passage, Newton appeals to our intuitively certain knowledge that space itself must exist:

> Next, although we can possibly imagine that there is nothing in space, yet we cannot think that space does not exist, just as we cannot think that there is no duration, even though it would be possible to suppose that nothing whatever endures.[30]

The existence of space is taken to be manifest to our reasoning: when we think and reason about space, we are *forced* to think its existence. Why must this be so? Recall the origin of our "exceptionally clear" idea of space: the idea of space originates from consideration of the ideas we have of actually existing things. Since the ideas of these existing things reveal their presence in space, these ideas also reveal that space exists. However, recall also that our *knowledge* that space necessarily exists does not depend on sensory evidence per se; this necessity derives from our rational consideration of the idea of space. And because we know space necessarily exists, we know that it is necessarily and always related to God—to a divine being that exists necessarily and eternally. In this way, the intuitive, mathematically certain knowledge gathered from rational consideration of our idea of space is knowledge that space is always and in every region of its infinite expanse related to the divine.[31] In turn, our knowledge of the mathematical form of space that is constitutive of nature underwrites our knowledge that all existing things are related to God, an eternal and immutable being who is everywhere in space.

Though my overview of Descartes's and Newton's mathematical approaches to nature has been extremely brief, this treatment helps clarify the sense in which their natural philosophical programs are competing ones.

---

29. Ibid, 26.

30. Ibid., 26.

31. Cf. Domski (2012) for further discussion.

Both Descartes and Newton, like the majority of early modern thinkers, embraced an ontology according to which God is foundational: for both, all existing things, including bodies and the space that bodies occupy, depend on God for their existence and are connected to God for as long as they exist. However, from an epistemic point of view, where the question at hand is why we should use mathematics in our investigations of the natural order created and sustained by the divine, Descartes and Newton offer opposing answers. For Descartes, knowledge of God precedes knowledge of bodies; to even know how to properly engage with the natural order, we must first know how God conserves nature. Mathematics is introduced only after knowledge of this metaphysical foundation is in place, and mathematics is introduced as a regulative guide, as a tool that makes intelligible the causes of phenomena that cannot be known with metaphysical certainty. For Newton, in contrast, epistemic priority is granted to the natural and, specifically, to the mathematical aspects of the natural. We interact with nature first, and from this interaction, we abstract a form of space that is mathematically intelligible and that grounds what can be known "strictly and geometrically" about nature. In this way, the mathematically intelligible is what is *naturally* certain, and moreover, the mathematically intelligible grounds our knowledge of God's relationship to space and to nature at large. In briefer terms, for Descartes, the "order of knowing" proceeds according to the "order of nature"; the path to understanding what is physically real follows the ontological hierarchy that begins with the creator and ends with the created. For Newton, in contrast, the "order of knowing" proceeds according to what is mathematically certain; we begin with our knowledge of the mathematical features of nature, and of space in particular, and from this starting point, we extend our knowledge to other aspects of the natural order. Newton, of course, accepts the same ontological scheme as Descartes; ontologically, God is metaphysically prior to the motions studied in physics. What Newton rejects is the suggestion that this ontological scheme supplies an epistemic map, as it were, for our inquiries into nature.

4. Descartes, Newton, and Structural Realism

Returning now to the structural realism debate, notice that if we adopt a "conceptual resources" approach to history, the reading I just offered makes it is very tempting to align Descartes with epistemic structural realism and Newton with ontic structural realism. For Descartes, mathematical physics supplies us knowledge of real causal relations (as we saw in his presentation of the sling in Part 3 of the *Principles*), but the objects between which these relations hold are not *mathematically* accessible. The ontologically prior objects (i.e., the relata of the causal relations) are only knowable through our metaphysical inquiries, and thus, as epistemic structural realists urge, our mathematically formulated physical theories capture real relations because these are the only physical reality we are mathematically and epistemically fitted to know. For Newton, on the other hand, the spatial relations captured by his mathematical physics correspond to the metaphysically true spatial structure of nature. Of course Newton does not go so far as to say that structure is all there is; for him there are objects. But in the spirit of ontic structural realism, Newton claims that such objects are knowable in structural terms; they are knowable as objects with the essentially spatial and geometrically knowable features of extension, mobility, and impenetrability that are expressed by the mathematical formalism of our physical theory. So just as Descartes and Newton disagree about whether mathematical knowledge exhausts our knowledge of nature, about whether mathematics grants us access to *all* that really exists, so too do proponents of epistemic and ontic structural realism disagree about whether the mathematical structure of a scientific theory offers us exhaustive insight into the natural ontology. Descartes and the epistemic structural realists tend toward the negative, and Newton and ontic structural realists tend toward the positive.

It is here, of course, that we hit upon the worries of revisionism and distortion voiced by the contextualist critic. As indicated at the outset of the paper, this critic would protest that the questions surrounding the fit between theory and nature are not as similar as I just presented them, and that drawing such connections between Descartes, Newton, and structural realists rests on a revised and distorted view of the issues with which these early modern thinkers were engaged. For although we might say that Descartes, Newton, and the structural realists are all wrestling with the question "What is the extent of our mathematical knowledge of nature?," or "What do our mathematically formulated physical theories capture about the natural order?," the precise meaning of the question is contextually defined, and reading Descartes and Newton in their proper historical context reveals a deep dissimilarity between the concerns of these early moderns and the structural realists. We can return to my treatment of Descartes and Newton to see what fuels this worry. As we saw, answering the question of how far our mathematical knowledge of nature extends hinges on Descartes's and Newton's competing accounts of how we are to relate our mathematical knowledge of nature to our knowledge of God—the one being that is for both of them metaphysically invariant and ontologically essential. Descartes distinguishes *metaphysical* certainty from mathematical certainty and thereby distinguishes our foundational knowledge of God's existence and conservation of nature from our mathematical knowledge of the causes that govern the phenomena we sense. Newton, in contrast, takes our *mathematical* knowledge of the spatial framework of nature to be foundational, and what results is a physical theory that rests on our mathematically exact knowledge of real spatial relations. For him, mathematical certainty is the *only* brand of certainty introduced in the order of knowing nature, such that even our certainty of God's relationship to the natural, spatially situated order of things is a form of mathematical certainty. Of course, these are not issues for contemporary structural realists. Given the context of the current debate, where the marriage of mathematics and physics is taken for granted, there is no, and need not be, discussion of the differences between metaphysical and mathematical certainty, let alone any discussion of God's place in the metaphysical and epistemic order of things. Thus, as the contextualist critic would urge, the apparent similarity between the questions of the early moderns and the contemporary structural realists is *merely* apparent and can only be maintained by taking God out of the early modern picture. To do this is to commit a cardinal sin of history, for as the critic would protest, early modern philosophy without God is simply *not* early modern philosophy.

However, this need not be the end of the story. Following Wilson, recognizing that the terms of past and present debates are contextually defined, and thereby different in fundamental respects, can set the stage for further dialogue between past and present. In Wilson's example, noticing that the disciplinary context of the early moderns was essentially different from our own—noticing, in particular, that in their historical context they could regard the connection between philosophy and science as their disciplinary given while we no longer can—reveals the importance of giving philosophical consideration to why we should maintain the ties between philosophy and science now that the nature of these disciplines has changed. A similar lesson can be gathered for contemporary philosophy from a contextualist treatment of Descartes and Newton, though in this case, the tables have been turned. It is part and parcel of *our* historical situation to take for granted the relationship between mathematics and physics, a relationship that the early moderns found to be philosophically problematic and requiring justification. My claim is that attention to the early modern arguments for the connection between mathematics and physics motivates reflection on what precisely it means for us to embrace this connection as our given. To be clear, I am not urging that we consider *whether* this connection should be our given. I am urging that we make the effort to *clarify* what our commitment to this relationship entails. What precisely are we committing to when we accept mathematics as the language for our physical theories?

In this regard, Descartes and Newton can be especially instructive, because the importance of such a question can be seen in their attempts to justify their mathematical programs for physics. Though their claims are couched in terms of God and our human-knowing place in a divinely created natural order, their arguments show that to argue for mathematical physics was to address general questions about the nature of the relationship between mathematics and physics. A primary question: what are we assuming about the epistemic power of mathematics when we merge mathematics with physics? For instance, are we assuming that mathematics can be appropriately applied to *any* sort of natural ontology? Or does our commitment to mathematics as the language of physics itself entail that we limit the scope of the ontology that might populate the natural order? Descartes's and Newton's answers to these questions fueled their confidence in mathematical physics and also, as we saw, informed their positions on the extent of our mathematical knowledge of nature. They recognized that developing their respective physical theories could not be isolated from questions concerning the nature of mathematical knowledge or from questions concerning the relationship between mathematical knowledge and natural knowledge.

The lesson I want to urge for the structural realist is that although these questions no longer have the urgency that they did for Descartes and Newton, they are questions that can help clarify their respective positions on what our physical theories represent. Take, for instance, the basic claim of the epistemic structural realist: the mathematical structure of our theories captures metaphysically real relations, because these relations are all we are epistemically fitted to know. A question we can now consider is whether these epistemic limitations are imported through the mathematics we are using. Are we only capable of knowing real relations in physics, because the mathematical language of the physics is itself limited to expressing relations? Building off of Poincaré, is the basic claim of the epistemic structural realist that the true relations between objects "are the only reality we can attain" because these true relations are the only reality that our *mathematical formalism* can attain? Turning to the ontic structural realist, different questions present themselves. Their basic position is that our theories capture the real relations and structure of nature, because this objective metaphysical structure is all there is to know. At first glance, it would seem that this structuralist ontology could itself justify our use of mathematical formalism in physics: we do and should use mathematics in physics, because mathematics offers a structural, relational language, as it were, that is fit to capture the metaphysically basic structures of nature. In other words, it is an ontological commitment that explains our continued use of mathematics in physics. But if this is the sort of argument the ontic structural realist would present, further issues arise, namely, is there evidence we can marshal for this structural metaphysics that is independent of our mathematical physics? Those such as Ladyman and Steven French have examined the representative power of mathematically formulated theories (such as from Weyl and from quantum mechanics) to support their claim that what is objectively real is represented as objective in the mathematics of these theories. Yet if the very use of mathematics in physics is justified by a structuralist metaphysics, then the fact that these theories represent the real structures of nature should be no surprise and would not itself give *reasons* for adopting the basic ontic structural realist position. As such, ontic structural realists must either abandon the history of the physical sciences as a source of support for their position or provide a different account of why it is appropriate to adopt mathematics as the language of the physical sciences.

Cashed out in more general terms, the lesson from Descartes and Newton is that what a mature, developed scientific theory represents, and what such a theory indicates about our epistemic access to nature and about the metaphysical structure of nature, is the product of a philosophically informed *process* of theory construction. To cast our physics in mathematical form is to adopt some epistemic and ontological attitude toward nature, mathematics, and the relationship between them. Seen in this light, the structural realist claim that our best scientific theories are approximately true representations of the structure of nature motivates consideration of the metaphysics, epistemology, and philosophy of mathematics on which this philosophical outlook is grounded. It motivates consideration, that is, of the very philosophical foundations on which the debate rests.

Let me conclude by reiterating the primary aim of my discussion. I am not claiming that Descartes and Newton provide us the right (or only) answers to questions about what our mathematically formulated physical theories represent about nature. Nor is my point that attention to these historical actors can somehow correct our current practice. My point is that a contextualist reading of Descartes and Newton can reorient our current discussions and enhance the terms of the current debate between epistemic and ontic structural realists. *Must* we turn to history to gain this deeper perspective on our current practices? Here I grant that the answer is no. But the main question at hand is whether we *can* turn to history for such a perspective, and in this regard, I hope I have said enough to address the worries of revisionism and distortion and to show that, with the proper mediation, contextualist history can illuminate our current philosophical circumstances and possibly even motivate us to reorient our philosophical priorities.

Acknowledgments

I am grateful for the feedback I received on this paper at the "Philosophy and Its History" workshop (Concordia University, October 2011) and also from colleagues at the University of Pittsburgh's Center for Philosophy of Science, where I was a visiting fellow during the spring 2012 semester. Special thanks to Dan Garber, Mogens Lærke, Justin E.H. Smith, and especially Eric Schliesser for their critical comments. I am also indebted to Steven French for his feedback on an earlier draft of this paper and would like to acknowledge the Pitt Center for Philosophy of Science for their generous support.

14

What Has History of Science to Do with History of Philosophy?

Tad M. Schmaltz

1. Introduction

MY TITLE IS of course modeled on Tertullian's famous question, "What has Athens to do with Jerusalem, or the Academy with the Church?" As it happens, the answer to this question—Tertullian's protest notwithstanding[1]—is: a lot, insofar as pagan philosophy and Christian thought were significantly interrelated in late antiquity. One need consider here only the Christian conception of the Second Person of the Trinity as *Logos*. Yet it must be granted Tertullian that Athens and Jerusalem are nonetheless distinguishable insofar as Christian thought involves core commitments that pagan philosophy does not share. For instance, whereas the doctrine of the resurrection of the body was central for Christian thinkers (as Tertullian himself insisted), such a doctrine was only a curiosity for pagan philosophers. Though the analogy is not perfect, I argue that we can say in a similar way that history of philosophy is naturally linked to, but at the same time has commitments that distinguish it from, history of science.[2]

Discussions of the relation of history of science to philosophy have tended to focus not on history of philosophy, but rather on philosophy of science. There is an extensive literature on whether the history and philosophy of science is an integrated field or merely a "marriage of convenience" between fundamentally

1. The quote from Tertullian continues: "Away with all attempts to produce a mottled Christianity of Stoic, Platonic, and dialectic composition!"

2. One complication for the analogy is that whereas pagan philosophy and Christianity were intellectual competitors in late antiquity, I hope to show that the same need not be said of history of science and history of philosophy with respect to the early modern period.

different disciplines.[3] Because the question of the relation to philosophy of science has been so important to the development of history of science, I begin with a brief consideration of it. What the history of this relation reveals is an evolution of history of science away from philosophy of science and toward social history. I attempt to explain this evolution in terms of the increasing importance to history of science of the disciplinary demands of history.

I then turn to the question of the relation of history of philosophy to current philosophical work, particularly in the "analytic" tradition that is dominant in Anglophone philosophy. The opposite sides of the debate over this question are represented by those who contend that philosophy can advance only through a consideration of its history, on the one end, and those who counter that the history of philosophy is separate from, and largely irrelevant to, current philosophical research, on the other. We will discover—what for our purposes is a particularly significant feature of the debate—that both sides invoke a comparison to the relation of history of science to current scientific practice. In fact, there is reason to think that history of philosophy is neither essential to nor separate from philosophy. This suggests that the relation of history of philosophy to philosophy is best conceived in terms of the relation of history of science not to science, but rather to history.

Finally, I consider a particular case study of the relation of history of science to history of philosophy that focuses on the early modern period. Recent scholarship on the history of philosophy has emphasized the anachronistic nature of the separation of science from philosophy especially during the seventeenth but even well into the eighteenth century. Such an emphasis may seem to suggest a need to fully integrate history of early modern science into the study of early modern philosophy. But I argue that in considering the disciplinary context of the relation between history of science and history of philosophy, we can see that what is called for is collaboration rather than assimilation.

2. *The History of History of Science*

About fifty years ago, history of science was emerging as a distinct discipline in the Anglophone world.[4] The situation was complex, with no

3. I borrow the term "marriage of convenience" from Giere (1973), a review of Stuever (1970). For recent explorations of the prospects for an integrated study of the history and philosophy of science, see the essays collected in Mauskopf and Schmaltz (2012).

4. My remarks in this section draw on the introduction I have co-written with Seymour Mauskopf to Mauskopf and Schmaltz (2012).

unified development of the history of science across the various disciplines.[5] Nonetheless, it is fair to say that the field as a whole was dominated at this point by scientists and philosophers, and not historians. Even Alexandre Koyré, the author of the *Études galiléennes*,[6] which became the foundational work in modern historiography of science, was professionally a philosopher.[7] While not sundering ties to the historical profession, historians of science early on felt the need to associate with philosophy in order to establish a distinct professional and institutional identity. The predominant association was with philosophy of science, understandably enough given the shared focus on science.

But there are considerations beyond the obvious one of commonality of subject matter that can explain the early connections between history of science and philosophy of science. One was that historians of science tended to adopt an "internalist" approach to science that focuses on the logical development of a theoretical system. This was undoubtedly due to the impact of Koyré's studies of the Scientific Revolution. Perhaps reflecting his philosophical training, Koyré viewed this watershed episode in strongly intellectualist terms, delineating it as "intellectual mutation," in which even experimentation played little or no role, much less social and cultural contexts.[8] This intellectualist approach was coupled with a strong guiding belief in scientific progress, perhaps expressed with the most sophistication in Charles Gillespie's *The Edge of Objectivity*.[9] Intellectualist and progressivist perspectives on science were certainly something that historians and philosophers of science had

5. Thus, in some cases, work in the history of a scientific discipline took place from within that discipline (particularly in social sciences such as economics and psychology, but also in astronomy) whereas in other cases that work was largely external to that discipline (particularly in natural sciences such as physics and chemistry). Thanks to Eric Schiesser for reminding me of this complexity. See also note 24.

6. Koyré (1939).

7. Indeed, from its beginnings in nineteenth-century France, history of science developed in close relation to the various histories of philosophy influenced by Johann Jakob Brucker's foundational *Historia critica philosophiae* (1742–44). For more on this early relation of history of science to history of philosophy, see Catana (2011). In this article, Catana is drawing on his discussion in Catana (2008) of the emergence of the discipline of the history of philosophy from the work of Brucker.

8. There also was an "externalist" strain in early history of science, reflected in the focus on the social and economic roots of science in the work of historians such as Edgar Zilsel and J. D. Bernal. However, one scholar has concluded with respect to such figures that their "effect on historical writing... was not very great" (Young (1990), 83). I do think there is a more pronounced emphasis on external factors in more recent history of science, for reasons that I hope to make clear in what follows.

9. Gillespie (1960).

in common, and the fact that there was this shared perspective on a common object serves to explain the perception of the propriety of a "marriage" between the two fields.

Then came Thomas Kuhn's *Structure of Scientific Revolutions*. Kuhn argued in this work—first published in 1962—that a philosophical account of science must attend to the historical facts concerning scientific practice. *Structure* did not emerge ex nihilo, of course; this text was anticipated by earlier expressions of dissatisfaction with the dominant emphasis in philosophy of science on the "context of justification" and on the relative lack of interest in the discipline in the "context of discovery."[10] One thinks here of the work of figures such as Stephen Toulmin and Norwood Russell Hanson that predates *Structure*.[11] Nonetheless, Kuhn's text served as the primary trigger for a movement in the philosophy of science to take the history of science seriously.

At the same time, though, the publication of *Structure* provided the occasion for history of science to disengage itself from philosophy of science. There are two features of *Structure* that are crucial for the disengagement. The first is the turn in this text against a progressivist view of scientific development. This turn is reflected by Kuhn's introductory comment that

> Aristotelian dynamics, phlogistic chemistry, or caloric thermo-dynamics... were, as a whole, neither less scientific nor more the product of idiosyncrasy than those current today.[12]

As Kuhn made clear in the body of the text, scientific change had to be seen as consisting not in smooth advance, but rather in epochs of paradigm-guided "normal science" punctuated by episodes of revolutionary paradigm change. Theory and practice in a science in its postrevolutionary state were "incommensurable" with the prerevolutionary aspects of the same science. Given this new account of science, it was impossible to delineate a steady, cumulative "advance" over time for a science that went through a revolution. At the end of *Structure*, Kuhn pushed the argument further, urging that it is impossible to define scientific "progress" in terms of closer and closer approximation to natural "truth."

10. This distinction, famously introduced by Hans Reichenbach, is between the objective relations of theory to evidence ("context of justification") and the subjective ways in which these relations are discovered ("context of discovery"); see Reichenbach (1938), 36–37.

11. See Hanson (1958) and Toulmin (1961).

12. Kuhn (1970), 2.

The second feature important for the reception of *Structure*—which is more implicit in the text itself—is reflected in Kuhn's comment in the preface that a consideration of scientific change must be "set in the sociology of the scientific community."[13] Kuhn himself admits in a postscript to the 1970 edition of his text that

> if this book were being rewritten, it would ... open with a discussion of the community structure of science, a topic that has recently become a significant subject of sociological research and that historians of science are also beginning to take seriously.[14]

Whereas the first feature of *Structure* encourages a kind of anti-progressivist historicism that denies the possibility of any neutral comparison of different scientific paradigms, the second feature encourages a kind of "externalist" emphasis on the social context of science. Both of these features of Kuhn's text—more than its emphasis on the philosophical value of history of science—attracted the attention of historians of science. The increasing historicism and externalism of work in history of science led to tensions in the former marriage of this discipline to philosophy of science, resulting in at best a marriage of convenience, and at worst an outright divorce.[15]

The influence of both features of *Structure* on history of science was mediated by the work of a group of sociologists, mainly British, who in the early 1970s introduced a program they called "sociology of scientific knowledge" (SSK). SSK had eclectic roots—the philosophy of Wittgenstein and sociology, anthropology, and perhaps Marxist historiography, among others. But it was the impact of Kuhn's *Structure* that proved crucial. The Edinburgh formulation of SSK, termed the "Strong Programme" by David Bloor and Barry Barnes, was grounded upon a number of methodological principles. Most fundamental was the prescription that science be subjected to empirical study not different in kind from such study of other aspects of human culture. Associated with this was a second prescription, the "symmetry postulate." Particularly important methodologically in the analysis of scientific

13. Ibid., vii.

14. One can well ask, as Keith Jones has in the title of his article, "Is Kuhn a sociologist"; see Jones (1986). After all, *Structure* itself is predominantly intellectualist in orientation. Koyré's name is the first to be mentioned in this text, and the focus of the discussion there is on intellectual rather than social issues (thus the admission in the "Postscript" of a need to make sociological considerations more prominent).

15. Cf. the literature cited in note 3.

controversy, this postulate prescribed that neither side of the controversy be assumed to have intrinsically superior scientific merit or epistemic privilege.[16]

These prescriptions could be seen—and were seen by their formulators—as conclusions developed from Kuhn's perspective on scientific change. What was particularly influential in Kuhn was the view of science as involving the imprinting of "paradigms" on the student through scientific training. In SSK this view was transmuted into scientific "practices," carried on by scientific "sub-cultures," with no one having methodological or epistemic superiority. Moreover, the old talk of scientific "discovery" was to be replaced by talk of natural knowledge "construction."[17] Historians of science increasingly saw their concerns as naturally linked to the project in SSK of offering normatively neutral contextual explanations of past and present scientific constructs. This shift serves to explain the increasing association of history of science with interdisciplinary "science studies" programs influenced by the SSK approach.

There was the view in SSK that explanations in terms of social causes are to supplant, and not merely supplement, explanations in philosophy of science in terms of rational considerations. The argument here typically involves an appeal to a strong version of the so-called Duhem-Quine thesis of the underdetermination of theory by evidence.[18] According to this version, rational considerations cannot constrain theory choice, and the conclusion often drawn from this is that only social factors can in fact account for adherence to scientific theory.[19]

No doubt certain historians of science were, and are, sympathetic to this line of argument. However, the ambition in SSK to replace philosophy of

---

16. These features of SSK reflect the emphasis of many of its proponents on the anti-progressivist elements of Kuhn's account of science (e.g., his rejection of a smooth advance to "better" theories), and such elements have also caught the attention of historians of science. Since I think that the emphasis on external factors serves more clearly than anti-progressivism to distinguish history of science from history of philosophy, I focus more on the former here. The issue of anti-progressivism is perhaps more relevant in the case of the relation of history of science to philosophy of science.

17. See Barnes (1990).

18. I say "so-called" to reflect the view that there is no single version of this thesis common to Duhem and Quine; see Pietsch (2012).

19. For instance, Barnes offers sociological explanations of science as a replacement for the "individualistic *rationalist* account of evaluation in science" that one finds in the work of "rationalist philosophers." In arguing against rationalist account, Barnes appeal specifically to the fact that "theory ... is underdetermined by experience, in science as much as in any other context" (Barnes (1990), 62–63).

science seems to rest on a questionable theoretical basis,[20] and in any case there is a less contentious motivation for the disengagement of history of science from philosophy of science. Kuhn has indicated this motivation in an insightful essay, "The Relations between History and History of Science," which perhaps deserves more attention than it has received. In this essay, Kuhn argues that in contrast to the case of history of philosophy, which belongs in philosophy, the natural home of history of science is history rather than the scientific disciplines it studies. He recognizes that at the time he was writing (1971), history of science was something of "a discipline apart," only tenuously incorporated into history. But he suggests that this separation is increasingly being overcome by the emphasis in history of science on the sort of sociocultural considerations that are more familiar to historians. Thus he notes that

> perhaps partly because of their increasing contact with historians, [historians of science] are turning more and more to the study of what is often described as external history. Increasingly they emphasize the effects on science not of the intellectual but of the socioeconomic milieu, effects manifest in changing patterns of education, institutionalization, communication, and values.... Because historians will find themselves at home with the studies that result than they have with older histories of science, they are particularly likely to welcome the change.[21]

It may well not be the case that the relations between history and history of science have improved as much as Kuhn predicted in this passage. Yet though I am something of an outsider here, my sense is that his hope for a more complete integration of history of science into history has been shared by many of his fellow historians of science.[22]

For some, the sort of move in history of science away from philosophy and toward history that Kuhn indicates is ill advised. Thus, Larry Laudan has

---

20. For philosophical critiques of the ambition to replace philosophical accounts of science, see Friedman (1998), Kitcher (1998), and Zammito (2004), ch. 5. Kuhn himself was critical of the more radical claims of SSK, singling out in particular the rejection within this movement of the causal significance of "scientific values"; see Kuhn (1977), xxi, and Kuhn (2000), 106.

21. Kuhn (1977), 159–60.

22. It should be noted, however, that there is a recent debate among historians of science over the relation of history of science to history, on the one hand, and to science studies, on the other; cf. Daston (2009) and Dear and Jasanoff (2010). My own Kuhnian view of the relation of history of science to history is somewhat closer to Daston's position than to the position of Dear and Jasanoff.

claimed that history of science has gone astray in abandoning its former stance "that science needed to be understood in cognitive terms" and in emphasizing "social and institutional studies" that involve concerns that are "subordinate and secondary."[23] To be sure, in his essay on the relation of history to history of science, Kuhn himself chastises historians for failing to give due weight to accounts in history of science of the internal development of scientific disciplines. To this extent, Laudan's point that history needs to attend more to the cognitive aspects of science is well taken. However, Kuhn's complaint seems consistent with his praise for increased attention in history of science to the institutional and socioeconomic contexts of this development. A concern with such factors will indeed be subordinate and secondary if the goal is integration with philosophy in general, and with philosophy of science in particular. But as Kuhn indicates, it is not subordinate and secondary if the goal is integration with mainline work in history. And I can see no compelling reason to think that history of science must ally itself with philosophy, as it once did, rather than with history, as it has increasingly attempted to do.

Admittedly, the situation for history of science remains complex. There are still associations with programs in history and philosophy of science, and at the same time with science studies programs.[24] The divided state of history of science helps to explain its current precarious institutional position; it is not always clear, in terms of practitioners of the established disciplines, precisely *who* history of science is *for*. However, Kuhn indicates that one solution to this problem is for history of science to associate itself more closely with history by emphasizing the sort of social factors that are of more secondary and subsidiary interest with respect to other perspectives on science. As we will see, this sort of solution has implications for how we answer the question of what history of science has to do with history of philosophy.

2. *The Relation of History of Philosophy to Philosophy*

In *Philosophy in History*,[25] an important collection of essays on the relation of philosophy to its history to which the current volume is naturally seen as a kind of successor, certain contributors argue for the essential importance of

---

23. Laudan (1990), 47, 51.

24. In some cases (e.g., psychology, economics, astronomy) the history of the discipline remains in the discipline itself. However, my sense is that this is the exception rather than the rule, and that as the history of the science becomes increasingly professionalized it increasingly distinguishes itself from the relevant science.

25. Rorty (1984).

history of philosophy for current analytical philosophy. Thus, Charles Taylor defends the view in Hegel that "philosophy and the history of philosophy are one," and thus that philosophy itself is "inherently historical."[26] One reason Taylor provides for the need for historical study in philosophy is that current philosophical dogmas are to some extent conditioned by past views that have been forgotten. History allows for a reassessment of these dogmas by recovering their forgotten sources. As Taylor puts it,

> in order to undo the forgetting, we have to articulate for ourselves how it happened, to become aware of the way a picture slid from the status of discovery to that of inarticulate assumption, a fact too obvious to mention.... That is why philosophy is inescapably historical.[27]

In his contribution to the volume, Alasdair MacIntyre also cites Hegel when insisting on the centrality of history of philosophy to philosophy. In support of a Hegelian point of view, he invokes a comparison of philosophy to the natural sciences. According to MacIntyre, the Kuhnian view of the "incommensurability" of different scientific paradigms reveals that natural science can establish the rational superiority of its solutions only by explaining the limitations of past theories. For this reason, "the history of natural science is in a certain way sovereign over the natural sciences."[28] However, current philosophy depends in the same way on history for the justification of its practices. MacIntyre therefore concludes that "the history of philosophy is on this view that part of philosophy which is sovereign over the rest of the discipline."[29]

But is philosophical advancement as dependent on history as Taylor and MacIntyre contend? There are reasons to doubt that this is the case. Taylor has pointed to a possible use for history in philosophy in uncovering hidden assumptions, and we will consider an interesting example of this use presently. However, one may well question whether history is indispensable for this task. Insofar as the assumptions are embedded in current practices, it seems that, at least in principle, non-historical reflection of those practices could reveal them.[30] Moreover, there seem to be plenty of examples from current

---

26. Taylor (1984), 17.

27. Ibid., 21.

28. MacIntyre (1984), 44.

29. Ibid., 47.

30. See the similar point in Secada's review of *Philosophy in History* (Secada (1986), 410).

philosophy of cases where success does not depend on the sort of appeal to history that Taylor recommends. Often discussions of topics in analytic philosophy depend crucially on the tools of logical analysis, recent moves in an ongoing debate, and perhaps suggestive results from current empirical science; consider, for instance, recent treatments in epistemology of the "Sleeping Beauty Problem," or in philosophy of science, interventionist accounts of causation.[31] In at least some, and perhaps many, cases of such discussions, historical studies of past views seem to be beside the point.

A focus on the example of the practice of contemporary analytic philosophy also can serve to undermine MacIntyre's view of history of philosophy as sovereign over philosophy. In Kuhnian terms that MacIntyre's discussion encourages, current analytic philosophy is largely a "normal scientific" kind of practice devoted to problem solving. In at least some cases, the rules of the practice seem to be sufficiently well defined and stable to allow for an assessment of success in terms of internal standards. And indeed, in this respect this sort of philosophy seems to be like the natural sciences, in which, pace MacIntyre, the results are at least sometimes acceptable even without an appeal to the court of history.

A radical version of this line of argument leads to the conclusion that history of philosophy is in fact largely incidental to philosophy. Such a conclusion is reflected in the quip—which MacIntyre attributes to Quine—that "there are two sorts of people interested in philosophy, those interested in philosophy and those interested in the history of philosophy."[32] One way to defend this conclusion is by defining philosophy in terms of the task of providing solutions to current problems. Insofar as historians of philosophy are not focused on such a task, according to this view, they are indeed interested in something other than philosophy.

In support of this sort of view, Gilbert Harman explicitly invokes a comparison of philosophy to science. Tom Sorell reports that in an email exchange on the issue of the status of history of philosophy, Harman defends the claim that "history of philosophy tends not to be useful to students of philosophy" by appealing to the fact that

> it is not particularly helpful to students of physics, chemistry, or biology to study the history of physics, chemistry, or biology. Of course, it

31. On the Sleeping Beauty Problem, see Sorensen (2006); on interventionist views of causation, see Woodward (2008).

32. MacIntyre (1984), 39–40. MacIntyre's counter to this quip is memorable: "the people interested in philosophy now are doomed to become those whom only those who are interested in the history of philosophy are going to be interested in in a hundred years' time" (ibid., 40).

> may be helpful for students of physics to start with classical mechanics before taking up relativity theory and quantum mechanics. But it tends not to be helpful for them to read Newton.[33]

Harman himself emphasizes that he says that history of philosophy only *tends* not to be useful to philosophers, and he notes that he in fact has interests in the history of moral philosophy.[34] Yet one suspects that he has such interests primarily because he thinks that the history of moral philosophy contributes directly to current debates concerning issues in moral philosophy. In any event, his conception of philosophy in terms of the normal scientific practice of problem solving can encourage the view that history of philosophy can count as philosophy only to the extent that it contributes directly to this task.

However, this view of the contribution of history of philosophy to philosophy seems to be overly restrictive. Even if Taylor does not show that the use of history to uncover hidden assumptions is somehow essential for philosophical advancement, I think it still must be granted to him that history can be useful to current philosophy when it is used in this way. I find confirmation of this point in a recent discussion of the relation of history of philosophy to philosophy by the late Margaret Wilson.[35] Defenses of the philosophical value of the history of philosophy tend to emphasize what past views have in common with, and therefore can contribute to, currently received philosophical positions. Yet Wilson has emphasized—in a rather iconoclastic manner—that history can also reveal that defenses of such positions retain assumptions from the past that are no longer clearly justified. Her example is recent treatments of the distinction between primary and secondary qualities, which tend to appeal to standard early modern accounts of this distinction. According to Wilson, greater attention to the context of these accounts reveals assumptions that are at least questionable in light of subsequent scientific developments. For instance, the early modern notion of primary qualities assumes that such qualities can be both universal features of macroscopic objects and basic explanatory posits of physics. However, this assumption must now be questioned given the fact that the basic posits of recent physics do not seem to be intelligible directly in terms of features given to us in ordinary perceptual experience.[36] Moreover, recent developments in the color sciences provide

33. Sorell (2005b), 44.

34. Idem.

35. See the related emphasis on the importance of Wilson's article in Mary Domski's contribution to this volume.

36. Wilson (1999), 477–78.

reason to question the early modern assumption that secondary qualities are given in basic sense experience, prior to any intellectual processing.[37] Though Wilson does not herself cite Taylor with respect to these points, they seem to illustrate his claim that history can advance philosophical discussion by revealing the origins of hidden assumptions of current views that require further critical evaluation.[38]

The conception of philosophy entirely in terms of the normal scientific practice of problem solving also seems to be overly restrictive. For though one can find this sort of practice particularly in discussions in analytic philosophy, still even analytic philosophy includes as an important part of itself a sort of meta-reflection on its practices that is not common in the sciences. Even when history of philosophy considers views only tenuously connected to current debates, it can contribute to this sort of reflection. Indeed, at the same time that Wilson stresses the differences between the contemporary issues concerning sensible qualities and early modern discussions of this topic, she also notes that attention to the latter raises metaphilosophical questions concerning the relation of philosophy to science. As we will see, there was no sharp distinction between philosophy and science in the early modern period. But in light of their current disciplinary separation, there is a question of how these two are to be related. In recent discussions there has been an attempt to "naturalize" philosophy by drawing on the results of the empirical sciences. As Wilson asks, however, even if it is the case that "philosophical work, at least in some areas, is no longer supposed to be independent of scientific results and theory, then what is its specific and peculiar role in telling us in what, say, the nature of color consists?"[39] Here reflections on the differences between early modern philosophy and the current state of the discipline can lead us to address in a more self-conscious way questions about the relation between philosophy and science today.[40] Thus, even if philosophy is not "inherently historical" in

37. Ibid., 479.

38. I therefore dispute Catherine Wilson's suggestion that this discussion supplies a reason for philosophers of sensible qualities "to avert their eyes from the whole messy business of the history of theories of color" (Wilson (2005), 63). What Margaret Wilson's discussion seems to me to supply is a reason to think that history can be useful in the sort of way that Taylor emphasizes.

39. Wilson (1999), 481.

40. See Daniel Garber's related point that it is precisely the historian who emphasizes how much current philosophical practice differs from past practices who is in a position to show "how philosophical problems, as well as the very concept of philosophy, have changed over the years," and therefore to "make us look more carefully at our own current situation, at what our relations to the larger world really are, and … make us aware of what the possibilities for the future might be" (Garber (2005), 145).

the way that Taylor and MacIntyre contend, history of philosophy does have something to contribute to philosophy beyond providing formulations of or solutions to problems currently of interest to analytic philosophers.

But what marks out history of philosophy as philosophical is not merely that it can contribute to current philosophy in various ways; after all, it seems that other kinds of history could contribute as well, at least in principle. What is distinctive about history of philosophy is rather that it has a fundamentally philosophical orientation. Admittedly, it can be difficult to explicate the nature of this orientation. Indeed, it is notoriously difficult to formulate a general characterization of philosophy that clearly distinguishes it from other kinds of theoretical practice (as illustrated by the difficulty of determining the relation of philosophy to science). Nonetheless, we can perhaps understand the philosophical nature of history of philosophy by contrasting it with other kinds of approaches to the history of thought. For instance, historians of ideas tend to view past thought primarily in terms of intellectual influences and effects. Though such influences and effects are also important for the historians of philosophy, their main concern is to enter into that thought in order to discern whether there is anything there that is profound or richly problematic. I believe that Yves Charles Zarka is indicating this sort of difference when he notes that history of ideas "unrolls the complex course of human thought as if it took place in front of neutral observers," whereas "philosophical historiography goes beyond that in order to bring to light, by means of what a text says, the object at which is aimed, that which it invites us to think about."[41] History of philosophy therefore goes beyond history of ideas insofar as it not only places past thought within its intellectual context, but also grapples with that thought itself as an object of philosophical scrutiny.[42]

History of philosophy is perhaps even more clearly contrasted with an approach to the history of thought that focuses on its social dimensions. Such an approach is reflected in the following emphatic claim of the German historian Reinhart Koselleck:

> There is no such thing as a history which is not, in some way or other, connected to human relationships, to various forms of association, or

41. Zarka (2005), 157.

42. Cf. Kristeller: "The historian of philosophy will stress the relation of a given idea to the entire context of the thought of the philosopher who expresses it and to that of his contemporaries, predecessors, and successors in the history of professional philosophy," whereas "a historian of ideas who does not have a primary concern with philosophy will treat the same ideas rather within the context of the surrounding non-philosophical thought with which they may be more or less connected" (Kristeller (1964), 13).

> to social stratification; so much so that to characterize history as "social history" expresses a permanent, irreducible, somehow anthropological claim, which is hidden behind every form of historiography. And there is no such thing as a history that does not have to be conceived as such before it can materialize as history.[43]

For Koselleck, this sort of view of history is opposed to "the concepts of the history of ideas and intellectual history that were studied independently of their socio-political context, for their own value."[44]

In commenting on this conclusion, Zarka highlights its implication that history of philosophy "would be swallowed up in the context of history in general."[45] The focus on the social dimensions of past thought would leave out philosophical analyses of the thought itself. In opposition to Koselleck's reduction of history to social history, Zarka insists on the possibility of a "philosophical history of philosophy" that "seeks in the end to bring to light what a thinker was giving us to think about when he wrote what he wrote."[46] It is this focus on philosophical engagement with the content of past thought that distinguishes philosophical history of philosophy from Koselleck's social history.

We have seen that both of the opposing sides in the debate over the relation of history of philosophy to philosophy invoke a comparison of the relation of history of science to current science, with MacIntyre taking the latter relation to show that history of philosophy is sovereign over philosophy, and Harman taking it to show that history of philosophy is for the most part irrelevant to philosophy. But the points from Kuhn that I discussed toward the end of the previous section serve to render this comparison dubious. For as Kuhn indicates, history of science is not related to science in the way in which history of philosophy is related to philosophy. In the latter case, the history finds its home in the discipline that is its subject. But this is not the case with the history of science. Rather, Kuhn takes the maturation of this field to involve an increasingly closer association with history. Insofar as the focus of history of science is on the historical and social setting of scientific practice, it does not seem to contribute directly to the practice itself. This point supports Harman's claim that the

43. Koselleck (1997), 101.

44. Ibid., 103. Passages cited in Zarka (2005), 154. I consider Zarka's response presently.

45. Zarka (2005), 155.

46. Ibid., 158.

history of science is "not particularly helpful to" students of the particular scientific disciplines.[47] But history of science is not particularly helpful in this way because it is not primarily *for* scientists. This distinguishes history of science from history of philosophy, for the latter is primarily in the service of the discipline it concerns.

In light of Kuhn's remarks on the increasing association of history of science with history, it seems that the more appropriate analogue of the relation of the history of philosophy to philosophy is the relation of the history of science to history. In order to be responsible to history, history of science must emphasize the ways in which scientific practice connects to social and institutional history. Narratives concerning these larger contexts provide history of science with its direction and its point. But though history of philosophy certainly can overlap with and learn from this sort of history, its primary concern is to engage the philosophical arguments and projects themselves rather than to relate these to larger social forces. In short, whereas it is a distinctive feature of history of science that it is *history* of science, it is a distinctive feature of history of philosophy that it is history of *philosophy*.[48]

3. Science and Philosophy in Early Modern Thought

The question of the relation of history of science to history of philosophy is especially pressing given a recent change in Anglophone scholarship on metaphysical and epistemological topics in the early modern period (roughly, the seventeenth and eighteenth centuries). This change is reflected in two influential studies—published the same year—that cover different ends of this period, namely, Daniel Garber's *Descartes' Metaphysical Physics* and Michael Friedman's *Kant and the Exact Sciences*.[49] Garber presents a Descartes who is concerned with offering metaphysical principles for a new mechanistic science, whereas Friedman makes clear Kant's concern that metaphysics take into account results in the sciences. In a way, both draw attention to Newton as a pivotal figure: Garber, implicitly, by emphasizing those features of Descartes's physics that anticipate the appeal in Newton's *Principia*

47. I think there is a contrast here with recent philosophy of science, which has tended to focus on the conceptual foundations of contemporary developments in particular scientific fields, and thus is in a better position to contribute to ongoing debates within scientific disciplines.

48. A further parallel is that both history of science and history of philosophy have a somewhat troubled relation to their parent disciplines, though the inclusion of history of philosophy in philosophy seems to be more secure than the inclusion of history of science in history.

49. Garber (1992) and Friedman (1992).

to "mathematical principles" and natural laws, and Friedman, explicitly, by emphasizing Kant's interest in providing metaphysical foundations for his reconstructed version of Newtonian mechanics. Both works have prepared for the recent reconsideration of Newton's role in the transformation of the relation between philosophy and science during the early modern period. Thus Newton, who has always been a central figure for the history of early modern science, is increasingly a central figure for the history of early modern philosophy as well.[50]

As Gary Hatfield claims in his review of the work of Garber and Friedman, there is a new sense among scholars of early modern philosophy that "deep engagement with intellectual history and history of science is a necessary condition for reading the texts of theoretical philosophy."[51] We have considered the suggestion that history of philosophy must be absorbed into social history. However, the question that Hatfield's claim raises is whether the history of early modern science can be absorbed into a properly contextualized study of philosophy during this period. In addressing this question, I will set aside Kant and the post-Newtonian period and focus on pre-Newtonian early modern philosophy.

An initial relevant fact here is that there was no clear distinction between early modern science and philosophy. In some ways our science corresponds to the Aristotelian discipline of "natural philosophy," often itself identified during the early modern period with "physics." But the Aristotelian physics dominant among early modern scholastics differs markedly from current physics in at least two crucial ways. First, the former has much broader scope insofar as it concerns not only local motion, but also the orbits of the planets, the nature of the earth, the organization of plants and animals (including the human body), and even the nature of the human soul. Moreover, it includes a consideration of the conceptual foundations of the study of nature that we would now be inclined to assign to philosophy of science rather than to science itself.

This sort of physics also differs from physics in our current sense insofar as more traditional scholastics distinguished it from "mixed mathematical" disciplines such as astronomy, optics, and mechanics. The basis for this distinction was that these disciplines focus either on mere mathematical description

50. Hatfield (1996a), 131. On the emergence of Newton as a figure for history of philosophy, see, for instance, Janiak (2008).

51. Which is not to say that Garber and Friedman were the first in the Anglophone world to emphasize this sort of view; one can find anticipations, for instance, in works such as Smith (1952) and Buchdahl (1969).

or on the operations of artifacts, and thus do not provide the sort of causal explanations of natural processes that are distinctive of physics.[52] There was a shift in the relation of these disciplines to natural philosophy during this period, which certainly is an important part of the "Scientific Revolution." However, these shifts cannot be neatly divided into their "scientific" and "philosophical" elements.

A consideration of the case of Descartes serves to illustrate the difficulty of finding such a division during this period. Even a cursory examination of Descartes's *Principles of Philosophy* reveals that he retained the broad conception of natural philosophy. Garber's discussion of Descartes's metaphysical physics focuses on the second part of this text, "Of the Principles of Material Things," which includes the identification of body with extension, the analysis of bodily alteration in terms of local motion, and the introduction of the laws of nature and rules governing collision. But the third part, "Of the Visible Universe," includes particular hypotheses concerning the motion of the sun, moon, planets, and comets, and the fourth part, "Of the Earth," includes hypotheses concerning the formation of the earth, the nature of the elements and minerals, and the cause of magnetic attraction.[53] Moreover, Descartes had intended to include, but never completed, further parts concerning the nature of plants, animals, and the human body. For Descartes, as for the more traditional scholastic followers of Aristotle, all of these topics were to be covered by natural philosophy, as opposed to being relegated to specialized scientific disciplines.

Descartes was in some sense a scientific "revolutionary," but his revolt was not clearly "scientific" as opposed to "philosophical." For his primary concern was to reform Aristotelian natural philosophy by introducing new foundational principles for it. There was in Descartes a radical simplification of scholastic ontology, a replacement of prime matter and substantial and accidental forms with parts of quantity and their states of motion and rest. But there was no separation of physics and the other sciences from a general "philosophy of nature." For such separation, we need to wait for the full impact of Newton's

52. For a discussion of the complexity of the relation between physics/natural philosophy and mixed mathematics during this period, see Hatfield (1996b).

53. The first part, "Of the Principles of Human Knowledge," indicates the basic metaphysical and epistemological constraints on natural philosophy.

Principia Mathematica, itself a work in "natural philosophy" (thus its full title, *Philosophiae Naturalis Principia Mathematica*).[54]

But if, as the case of Descartes and even Newton illustrate, it is anachronistic to separate investigations that we recognize as scientific from those that we take to be philosophical, one might well wonder whether there remains any point to separating the history of science during this period from the history of philosophy. To be sure, it is not a decisive consideration that the distinction between history of science and history of philosophy would not have made sense in the early modern period. After all, there was no notion during this period of history of philosophy as we understand it; history of philosophy as a sub-discipline of philosophy came into being only toward the end of the eighteenth century.[55] But the crucial question is whether it now makes sense for us to fully integrate history of early modern science into history of early modern philosophy.

The case for integration is perhaps strengthened by recent work in the history of early modern science. One example I have in mind is the work of William Newman and Laurence Principe on the importance of the practice of alchemy to the emergence of the "corpuscular philosophy" during the seventeenth century.[56] The approach in this work, which is similar to an older "internalist" history of science, might seem to be indistinguishable from the work of a contextualist historian of early modern philosophy. However, there is some question whether this sort of work is perfectly in line with what Zarka calls "philosophical history of philosophy." In contrast to the case of philosophy of science, the issue here is not really the anti-progressive tendencies of such work in history of science; progressivism just does not seem to be a particularly prominent issue in recent work in the history of early modern philosophy. What is more relevant is the fact that internalist history of science tends to reflect a historicist line in restricting itself to an understanding of past views in their own terms, with no regard for any ultimate philosophical

54. Grant has concluded from the fact that Newton at one point proposed to publish only the first two books of his *Principia* under the title, *De Motu Corporum libro duo*, that "the argument that Newton did not believe that he was doing natural philosophy in the Principia gains credibility from Newton himself" (Grant (2007), 315). However, Newton's decision to retain the reference to natural philosophy in his title can be explained by the fact that he included a third book, "the system of the world," and thus did not restrict his discussion to a mathematical treatment of motion that abstracts from its application to bodies within our solar system.

55. As indicated in Frede (1988). Cf. the work of Catena cited in note 7.

56. Newman and Principe (2002) and Newman (2006). See also the discussions in Dear (1995) and Meli (2006) of early modern developments in mathematics and mechanics, respectively.

assessment of them. Though it perhaps need not preclude such an assessment, this sort of history of science is not particularly concerned—as philosophical history of philosophy typically is—to provide it.[57]

A further consideration is that though internalist work in history of science can perhaps be allied with contextualist history of philosophy, it is more closely affiliated—by means of both internal references and external institutional arrangements—with a more externalist social history of science. And this latter kind of history appeals to a sort of "context" that is different from the sort of context of primary interest to philosophical historians of philosophy. Peter Galison indicates the relevant difference here when he notes:

> When philosophers talk about the context of an argument (say, by Descartes), they often mean bringing into the argument not only the text in question but also the texts of surrounding philosophers (issuing from the late sixteenth century, for example) addressing related issues. When historians speak about context, they often have in view the non-textual environment, which might be political, institutional, industrial, or ideological—as in "The context of Oppenheimer's remarks on atomic research was the detonation of the Soviet atomic bomb."[58]

Galison's comment concerns the relation of history of science to philosophy of science, but I think it has clearer application to the case of the relation of the former to history of philosophy. For historical context is obviously important to history of philosophy in a way in which it is not to philosophy of science.[59] And the sort of context that is important for history of philosophy does indeed tend to differ in just the way Galison suggests from the sort of context that tends to be important for social history of science. History of philosophy, as a branch of philosophy, focuses primarily on the philosophical context of a particular text, as provided in other texts. In contrast, social history of science, as a branch of history, is concerned primarily with the non-textual environment of most interest to historians. Of course, this is to say neither that philosophical historians of philosophy are uninterested in the social context, nor that social historians of science are uninterested in the

57. Thanks to Sy Mauskopf for pressing me to consider this difference between history of science and history of philosophy.

58. Galison (2008), 113.

59. After all, much of current philosophy of science has a "presentist" orientation that current history of philosophy, particularly in its contextualist version, does not.

philosophical context. It is a matter rather of where the priorities lie: is the philosophical upshot of the text the main point, or is the concern rather with social connections and implications?

To appreciate this distinction, let us consider the case of Galileo, the subject of Koyré's seminal work in the history of science. This is a particularly important case for historians of early modern philosophy who focus on developments in natural philosophy. It is well known that Galileo insisted on the title of Chief *Philosopher* and Mathematician when he joined the court of the grand duke of Tuscany. Yet Galileo, more than Descartes, suggested the need for a re-conception of the Aristotelian category of natural philosophy. Whereas we have seen that Descartes relied on a traditional Aristotelian framework for his presentation of natural philosophy in his *Principles*, Galileo's indication at the start of his *Discorsi* (*Discourses ... on Two New Sciences*) is that he looked to the work of the artisans in the Venice Arsenal in constructing new sciences concerning the strength of materials and various kinds of motions. Thus in marked contrast to Descartes, Galileo's emphasis was not on providing a systematic metaphysical alternative to the Aristotelian conception of nature. Rather, his concern was to use the techniques of the mixed mathematical discipline of mechanics to provide anti-Aristotelian solutions to a delimited range of problems concerning bodies.[60]

This contrast was not lost on Descartes. In commenting on his recently purchased copy of the *Discorsi*, he notes in a letter to his friend Mersenne that though he approves of the fact that Galileo "abandons the errors of the Schools and tries to use mathematical methods in the investigation of physical questions," nonetheless Galileo "has not investigated matters in an orderly way, and has merely sought explanations for more particular effects, without going into the primary causes in nature; hence his building lacks a foundation."[61] Which is to say, Galileo's work is not informed by a systematic kind of natural philosophy of the sort that Descartes claimed to provide.[62]

Thus, the case of Galileo is obviously relevant to the task of assessing the conceptual bases for and the implications of early modern views of natural philosophy. However, it should not be assumed that this task is always of central concern to historians of science. Indeed, an indication that it is not

---

60. Cf. Hatfield: "In the strict (seventeenth-century) sense of the term, Galileo did not propound a physics, even if he did apply mathematics to natural philosophical questions" (Hatfield (1996b), 503).

61. Descartes (1964–75), 2:380.

62. For a consideration of Descartes's critique of Galileo, see Shea (1978).

is provided by one of the most prominent studies of Galileo in recent history of science, Mario Biagioli's *Galileo, Courtier*. The chief aim of this work, according to Biagioli, is "to provide a detailed, sometimes microscopic, study of the structures of [Galileo's] daily activities and concerns and to show how these framed his scientific activities."[63] Though Biagioli is concerned with the "social and cognitive legitimation" of Galileo's natural philosophy,[64] he is not particularly concerned with providing an analysis of this philosophy or relating it to its intellectual competitors.[65] His focus is rather on how specific features of aristocratic court culture conditioned Galileo's presentation of himself as a philosopher. *Galileo, Courtier* seems to be a fairly clear example of history of science that is for history rather than for philosophy.

It should be evident by now that this comment is not meant as a criticism of Biagioli's work. Which is not to say that the discussion in *Galileo, Courtier* is unproblematic; indeed, in his review of this text and in his subsequent exchange with Biagioli, the historian of science Michael Shank seems to me to have noted several significant problems.[66] But what is relevant for my purposes is less the content of Biagioli's work than its form. And surely there can be no question (as there is none for Shank) of the value of placing Galileo's work in its sociopolitical context. In fact, it seems that this approach could have value even for the historian of philosophy who is focused primarily on the philosophical significance

63. Biagioli (1993), 3.

64. Ibid., 353.

65. It is noteworthy, for instance, that Biagioli tends to set aside Galileo's work on mechanics since "his interest in mechanics did not fit the court environment particularly well" (Biagioli (1993), 4). But see Biagioli's very interesting discussion in ch. 3 of Galileo's disputes with his Aristotelian adversaries over the buoyancy of objects in water.

66. Shank (1994), with the exchange consisting in Biagioli (1996) and Shank (1996). As Shank indicates, his reservations concern mainly Biagioli's "practices as a historian" (Shank (1996), 109), and his initial review and the subsequent exchange focus on details of interest primarily to historians, such as the plausibility of Bialgioli's claim that the link between Cosimo I and Jupiter was important for Galileo's dedication in *Sidereus nuncius*, and the defensibility of Biagioli's argument that the "fable of sound" in the *Assayer* reveals that this text is a courtly work. Biagioli's reply notwithstanding, I find much of Shank's original objections concerning the historical details to be persuasive. However, I also think that what is of more of interest to historians of philosophy is Shank's side remarks in his initial review that Galileo's commitment to Copernicanism was not as dependent on his courtly identity as Biagioli contends, and that Galileo's work on mechanics was more central to his conception of philosophy than Biagioli allows (Shank (1994), 236–37). As Shank notes, moreover, Biagioli's account of incommensurability in ch. 4 is philosophically contentious. See, for instance, Biagioli's radically historicist claim there that "all that matters is that an impossibility of communication was claimed by the members of a group. Whether or not they were right in their claims is not something that can be legitimately judged from any point of view external to that culture or group" (Biagioli (1993), 212).

of Galileo's views. For one lesson that history of science—in both its internalist and externalist versions—has to teach history of philosophy is that past views do not exist in some ahistorical heaven of ideas, but rather are offered at particular historical moments by particular individuals who have been conditioned by and are reacting to particular intellectual traditions and are struggling to succeed in particular social situations. In light of this lesson, historians of early modern philosophy ought not only recognize that there is room for social historical studies such as Biagioli's work on Galileo, but also attempt to engage with and learn from such studies where they can.

The answer to our target question, then, is that history of science certainly has something to do with history of philosophy, and increasingly so given recent developments in scholarship on early modern philosophy. But just as there is reason to insist on the contextualization of the thought of historical figures, so too we must view in context the ways in which we approach that thought. When we view both history of science and history of philosophy in this way, we can recognize that practitioners of those fields do not always have the same aims and interests. Whereas there is a special connection of history of science to social history, the primary commitment of history of philosophy is to philosophy. These differences reveal why history of science, even of early modern science, cannot simply be a branch of history of philosophy, just as history of philosophy cannot simply be a branch of social history.

Of course, disciplines and institutions change, and it does not seem impossible that both history of science and history of philosophy will evolve in such a way that some sort of unification of the two areas will make sense. But in current circumstances, perhaps the ideal model for the relation of history of science to history of philosophy is one involving the interaction of parties that to some extent operate independently of each other. In commenting on the relation between history of science and philosophy of science, Kuhn has proposed that the two fields "continue as separate disciplines," adding that "what is needed is less likely to be produced by marriage than by active discourse."[67] I would suggest that we say something similar with respect to the relation of history of science to history of philosophy.

67. Kuhn (1977), 20.

Acknowledgments

Thanks to the participants in the workshop for this volume for helpful comments on an earlier version of this chapter, and to Matt Evans and the editors of the volume for additional suggestions that led to several improvements. Special thanks to my friend and former Duke University colleague Sy Mauskopf for comments on and extensive discussion of various drafts of the chapter.

Bibliography

Aaron, Richard. 1971. *John Locke*, 3rd ed., Oxford: Oxford University Press.

Adler, Jacob. 1996. "Letters of Judah Alfakhar and David Kimhi," *Studia Spinozana* 12, 141–67.

Adorno, Theodor W. 2005a. "Why Still Philosophy," in idem, *Critical Models and Catchwords*, translated by H. W. Pickford, New York: Columbia University Press, 5–18.

——. 2005b. "Notes on Philosophical Thinking," in idem, *Critical Models and Catchwords*, translated by H. W. Pickford, New York: Columbia University Press, 127–34.

Alexander, Joshua, Ronald Mallon, and Jonathan M. Weinberg. 2010. "Accentuate the Negative," *Review of Philosophy and Psychology* 1:2, 297–*314*.

Ankersmit, F. R. 1994. *History and Tropology*, Berkeley: University of California Press.

Anscombe, G. E. M. 1971. *Causality and Determination*, Cambridge: Cambridge University Press.

Anstey, Peter R. and Stephen A. Harris. 2005. "Locke and Botany," *Studies in History and Philososophy of Biological and Biomedical Sciences* 37, 151–71.

Auerbach, Erich. 1967. *Gesammelte Aufsätze zur romantischen Philologie*, edited by F. Schalk, Bern: A. Francke.

Augustine. 1993. *On Free Choice of the Will*, translated by T. Williams, Indianapolis: Hackett.

Ayer, A. J. 1959. "Introduction," in *Logical Positivism*, edited by A. J. Ayer, New York: Free Press, 3–30.

—— 1999. "Die andere Frau. Synchrone und diachrone Betrachtungen zu Gal 4.21–5.1," in *Antijudaismus im Galaterbrief? Exegetische Studien zu einem polemischen Schreiben und zur Theologie des Apostels Paulus*, Novum Testamentum et Orbis Antiquus 40, Freiburg: Universitätsverlag/Göttingen: Vandenhoek & Ruprecht.

——1990. "Sociological Theories of Scientific Knowledge," in *Companion to the History of Modern Science*, edited by R. C. Olby, G. N. Cantor, J. R. R. Christie, and M. J. S. Hodge, London: Routledge, 60–73.

Basso, Sebastien. 1621. *Philosophiae naturalis adversus Aristotelem. In quibus abstrusa veterum physiologia restauratur, et Aristotelis errores solidis rationibus refelluntur*, Geneva.

Bealer, George. 1992. "The Incoherence of Empiricism," *Aristotelian Society Supplementary Volume*, 66, 99–138.

——. 1998. "Intuition and the Autonomy of Philosophy," in *Rethinking Intuition: The Psychology of Intuition and Its Role in Philosophical Inquiry*, edited by M. DePaul and W. Ramsey, Lanham, MD: Rowman and Littlefield, 201–39.

——. 2002. "Modal Intuition and the Rationalist Renaissance," in *Conceivability and Possibility*, edited by T. Gendler and J. Hawthorne, New York: Oxford University Press.

Beaney, Michael. Forthcoming-a. "The Historiography of Analytical philosophy" in *The Historical Turn in Analytical Philosophy*, edited by Erich Rech, Basingstoke: Palgrave Macmillan.

——. Forthcoming-b. "Analytical Philosophy and History of Philosophy: The Development of the Idea of Rational Reconstruction," in *The Historical Turn in Analytical Philosophy*, edited by Erich Rech, Basingstoke: Palgrave Macmillan.

Beck, Lewis White. 1995. *Foundations of the Metaphysics of Morals and What Is Enlightenment*, Upper Saddle River, NJ: Prentice Hall.

Bell, Jeff. 2011a. "CC#12: Hook's 'Impression' of German Philosophy circa 1930." www.newappsblog.com/2011/10/cc12-hooks-impression-of-german-philosophy-circa-1930.html.

——. 2011b. "Schools and Traditions; or Husserl and Realism, pt. I." www.newappsblog.com/2011/10/schools-and-traditions-or-husserl-and-realism-pt-i.html.

Benardete, José. 1964. *Infinity: An Essay in Metaphysics*, Oxford: Oxford University Press.

——. 1970. "Macbeth's Last Words," *Interpretation* 1, 63–75.

——. 1996. "One Word of the Sea: Metaphysics in Wallace Stevens," in *Wallace Stevens Journal* 20:2, 181–98.

Benjamin, Walter. 1999. *The Arcades Project*, translated by H. Eiland and K. McLoughlin, London: Belknap Press.

Bennett, Jonathan. 1984. *A Study of Spinoza's Ethics*, Cambridge: Cambridge University Press.

——. 1996. "Spinoza's Metaphysics," in *The Cambridge Companion to Spinoza*, edited by D. Garrett, Cambridge: Cambridge University Press, 61–88.

——. 2001. *Learning from Six Philosophers: Descartes, Spinoza, Leibniz, Locke, Berkeley, Hume*, 2 vols., Oxford: Oxford University Press.

Ben-Sasson, H., Jospe, R., and Schwartz, D. 2007. "Maimonidean Controversy," in *Encyclopedia Judaica*, 2nd ed., vol. 13, 371–81.

Berkeley, George. 1948–57. *The Works of George Berkeley, Bishop of Cloyne*, edited by A. Luce and T. Jessop, London: Nelson.

Biagioli, Mario. 1993. *Galileo, Courtier: The Practice of Science in the Culture of Absolutism*, Chicago: University of Chicago Press.

——. 1996. "Playing with the Evidence," *Early Science and Medicine* 1, 70–105.

Bloch, Marc. 1941. *Apologie pour l'histoire ou métier d'historien*, Paris: Librairie Armand Colin.

Bloch, Olivier. 1997. "Marx, Renouvier, et l'histoire du matérialisme," in *Matières à histories*, Paris: Vrin, 384–441.

Boas, Franz. 1943. "Recent Anthropology," in *Science* 98, 311–313, 334–337.

Boileau, Nicolas. 1682. *Traité du Sublime a Monsieur Despreaux. Où l'on fait voir ce que c'est que le Sublime & ses differentes especes*. Paris: Chez Pierre Prault.

Boivin, Nicole. 2008. *Material Cultures, Material Minds: The Impact of Things on Human Thought, Society and Evolution*, Cambridge: Cambridge University Press.

Bolton, Martha. 2007. "The Taxonomy of Ideas in Locke's *Essay*," in *The Cambridge Companion to Locke's* Essay Concerning Human Understanding, edited by L. Newmann, Cambridge: Cambridge University Press.

Boole, George. 1854. *An Investigation of the Laws of Thought, on Which Are Founded the Mathematical Theories of Logic and Probabilities*, Cambridge: Macmillan.

Bordas-Demoulin, Jean-Baptiste. 1843. *Le Cartésianisme, ou la véritable rénovation des sciences*, Paris: J. Hetzel.

Bordner, Seth. 2011. "Berkeley's 'Defense' of Common Sense," *Journal of the History of Philosophy* 49: 31, 5–38.

Borghero, Carlo. 2007. "Clio et Atena. Le origini 'impure' della storiografia filosofica del primo ottocento," *Giornale critico della Filosofia Italiana* 3:2, 247–83.

Boucher, David. 1985. *Revisionist Methods for Studying the History of Ideas*, Dordrecht: Springer.

Bouillier, Francisque. 1854. *Histoire de la philosophie cartésienne*, Paris: Durand/Lyon: Brun et Cie.

——. 1886. "Introduction," in Nicolas Malebranche, *Traité de l'imagination: deuxième livre de la Recherche de la vérité*, Paris: Garnier, I–XXI.

Boulad-Ayoub, Josiane and Monique Vernes. 2006. *La Révolution cartésienne*, Quebec: Mercure du Nord/Les Presses de l'Université de Laval.

Boureau Deslandes, André-François. 1737, 1756[2]. *Histoire critique de la philosophie*, Amsterdam: François Changuion.

Brading, Katherine and Alexander Skiles. 2012. "Underdetermination as a Path to Structural Realism," in *Structural Realism: Structure, Object, Causality*, edited by Elaine Landry and Dean Rickles, New York: Springer, 99–115.

Bradley, F.H. 1968. *Appearance and Reality*. Oxford: Clarendon Press.

—— 1922. *The Principles of Logic*, vol. 1, 2nd edition. London: Oxford University Press.

——. 1935. "Relations," in Bradley, *Collected Essays*, vol. 2, Oxford: Clarendon Press, 628–76.

Brandis, Christian August. 1815. *Von dem Begriff der Geschichte der Philosophie*, Copenhagen: G. Bonnier.

Brandom, Robert. 1994. *Making It Explicit*, Cambridge, MA: Harvard University Press.

Braudel, Fernand. 1969. *Écrits sur l'histoire*, Paris: Flammarion.

Brett, George S. 1908. *The Philosophy of Gassendi*, London: Macmillan.

Brown, Kenneth. 2006. *The Strict Interpretation of Locke's Theory of Ideas*. Ph.D. dissertation, University of California, Irvine.

Browne, Alice. 1977. "Descartes's Dreams," *Journal of the Warburg and Courtauld Institutes*, 40, 256–73.

Brucker, Johann Jacob. 1742–67. *Historia critica philosophiae a mundi incunabulis ad nostram usque aetatem deducta*, 5 vols., Leipzig: B. C. Breitkopf, 1742–44. Appendix, 1 vol. Leipzig: Heir of Weidemann and Reich, 1767.

Buchdahl, Gerd. 1969. *Metaphysics and the Philosophy of Science, the Classical Origins: Descartes to Kant*, Cambridge, MA: MIT Press.

Burkert, Walter. 1972. *Lore and Science in Ancient Pythagoreanism*, translated by Edwin L. Minar Jr., Cambridge, MA: Harvard University Press.

——. 1977. *Griechische Religion der archaischen und klassischen Epoche*, Stuttgart: Kohlhammer.

——. 2004. *Babylon, Memphis, Persepolis: Eastern Contexts of Greek Culture*, Cambridge, MA: Harvard University Press.

Campbell, Charles A. 1931. *Scepticism and Construction: Bradley's Sceptical Principle as the Basis of Constructive Philosophy*, New York: Macmillan.

Candlish, Stewart. 2007. *The Russell/Bradley Dispute: And Its Significance for Twentieth-Century Philosophy*, Basingstoke: Palgrave Macmillan.

Carnap, Rudolph. 1959. "The Elimination of Metaphysics through the Logical Analysis of Language," translated by A. Pap, in *Logical Positivism*, edited by A. J. Ayer, New York: Free Press, 60–81.

Carnap, Rudolf, Hans Hahn, and Otto Neurath. 1929. *Wissenschaftliche Weltauffassung*, Vienna: Artur Wolf Verlag.

Carus, André. 2007. *Carnap and Twentieth-Century Thought: Explication as Enlightenment*, Cambridge: Cambridge University Press.

Cassirer, Ernst. 1932. *Die Philosophie der Aufklärung*, Tübingen: J. C. B. Mohr.

——. 1942. "Giovanni Pico della Mirandola. A Study in the History of Renaissance Ideas," *Journal of the History of Ideas* 3, 123–44, 319–46.

Castillon, Johann de. 1770. "Descartes et Locke conciliés," in *Histoire de l'Académie royale des sciences et des lettres de Berlin (avec Mémoires)*, Berlin: Haude et Spener, Libraires de la Cour et de l'Académie Royale, 277–82.

Catana, Leo. 2005. "The Concept 'System of Philosophy': The Case of Jacob Brucker's Historiography of Philosophy," *History and Theory* 44, 72–90.

——. 2008. *The Historiographical Concept 'System of Philosophy': Its Origin, Nature, Influence and Legitimacy*, Leiden: Brill.

——. 2010. "Lovejoy's Readings of Bruno: Or How Nineteenth-Century History of Philosophy Was 'Transformed' into the History of Ideas," *Journal of the History of Ideas* 70:1, 89–110.

——. 2011. "Tannery and Duhem on the Concept of a System in the History of Philosophy and History of Science," *Intellectual History Review* 21:4, 493–509.

Celenza, Christopher S. 2013 "What counted as philosophy in the Italian Renaissance? The history of philosophy, the history of science, and styles of life," *Critical Inquiry* 39(2): 367–401.

Chartier, Roger. 2009. *Au bord de la falaise. L'histoire entre certitudes et inquiétude*, Paris: Albin Michel.

Clark, Andy. 2008. *Supersizing the Mind: Embodiment, Action, and Cognitive Extension*, Oxford: Oxford University Press.

Clark, Stuart. 1997. *Thinking with Demons. The Idea of Witchcraft in Early Modern Europe*, Oxford: Oxford University Press.

Condren, Conal, Stephen Gaukroger, and Ian Hunter. 2006. *The Philosopher in Early Modern Europe: The Nature of a Contested Identity*, Cambridge: Cambridge University Press

Copleston, Frederick. 1985. "Introduction," in *A History of Philosophy*, New York: Image Book, vol. 1, 2–9.

Cousin, Victor. 1822–26. *Œuvres de Descartes*, edited by V. Cousin, Paris: Chez F.G. Levrault, Libraire.

——. 1822–40. *Œuvres de Platon*, edited and translated by V. Cousin, Paris: Bessange Frères.

——. 1833. "Sur le vrai sens du *Cogito, ergo sum*," in *Fragments philosophiques*, 2nd ed., Paris: Ladrange, 329–38.

——. 1841. *Cours de l'histoire de la philosophie*, Paris: Didier.

——.1843. "Introduction," *Œuvres philosophiques du Père André*, Paris: Adolphe Delahays, 1843, I–CCXXXVI.

——. 1852. "Correspondance entre Malebranche et Dortous de Mairan," in *Fragments de philosophie cartésienne, pour faire suite aux Fragments philosophiques*, Paris: Didier, 262–348.

——. 1856. "Vanini ou la philosophie avant Descartes," in *Fragments de philosophie cartésienne*, Paris: Didier.

——. 1861. *Philosophie de Locke*, Paris: Didier.

——. 1884. *Histoire générale de la philosophie depuis les temps les plus anciens jusqu'au XIXe siècle;* 11th ed., Paris: Librairie Académique Didier/Emile Perrin, Libraire-Editeur.

——. 2005. *Philosophie sensualiste au XVIIIe siècle*, Elibron Classics, 2005, V (re-edition of the 5th ed., Paris: Didier et Cie 1866).

Craig, Edward. 1999. *Knowledge and the State of Nature*, Oxford: Oxford University Press.

Cumming-Bruce, Nick and Steven Erlanger. 2009. "Swiss Ban Building of Minarets on Mosques," *New York Times*, November 29, 2009.

Cummins, Robert. 1998. "Reflection on Reflective Equilibrium," in *Rethinking Intuition: The Psychology of Intuition and Its Role in Philosophical Inquiry*, edited by M. DePaul and W. Ramsey. Lanham, MD: Rowman and Littlefield, 113–27.

Cunning, David. 2010. *Argument and Persuasion in Descartes'* Meditations, New York: Oxford University Press.

Curley, Edwin. 1986. "Dialogues with the Dead," *Synthese* 67, 33–49.

Curley, Edwin and Gregory Walski. 1999. "Spinoza's Necessitarianism Reconsidered," in *New Essays on the Rationalists*, edited by R. J. Gennaro and C. Huenemann, Oxford: Oxford University Press, 241–62.

Dagron, Tristan. 2009. *Toland and Leibniz*, Paris: Vrin.

Daled, Pierre F. 2005. *Le Matérialisme occulté et la genèse du "sensualisme." Ecrire l'histoire de la philosophie en France*, Paris: Vrin.

Damiron, Jean-Philibert. 1828. *Essai sur l'histoire de la philosophie en France au XIXe siècle*, Paris: F. Didot.

——.1846. *Essai sur l'histoire de la philosophie en France, au XVIIe siècle*, Paris: Hachette.

——. 1855. *Mémoire sur Helvétius*, Paris: A. Durand.

Dancy, Jonathan. "Moral Particularism." *Stanford Encyclopedia of Philosophy*, http://plato.stanford.edu/entries/moral-particularism.

Dascal, Marcelo, ed. 2006. *The Art of Controversy. Gottfried Wilhelm Leibniz*, Dordrecht: Springer.

Daston, Lorraine. 2009. "Science Studies and the History of Science," *Critical Inquiry* 35, 798–813.

Daston, Lorraine, and Peter Galison. 2007. *Objectivity*, New York: Zone Books.

Daston, Lorraine, and Katharine Park. 1998. *Wonders and the Order of Nature, 1150–1750*, New York: Zone Books.

Davidson, Donald. 1984. *Inquiries into Truth and Interpretation*, Oxford: Oxford University Press.

Dear, Peter. 1995. *Discipline and Experience: The Mathematical Way in the Scientific Revolution*, Chicago: University of Chicago Press.

Dear, Peter and Sheila Jasanoff. 2010. "Dismantling Boundaries in Science and Technology Studies," *Isis* 101, 759–74.

Dégerando, Joseph-Marie. 1804. *Histoire comparée des systèmes de philosophie relativement aux principes des connaissances humaines*, 3 vols., Paris: Chez Henrichs.

Deleuze, Gilles and Claire Parnet. 1987. *Dialogues*, translated by J. Tomlinson, New York: Columbia University Press.

Della Rocca, Michael. 2008. *Spinoza*. London: Routledge.

——. 2010. "PSR," *Philosophers' Imprint* 10:7, 1–13.

——. 2012. "Violations of the Principle of Sufficient Reason (in Leibniz and Spinoza)" in *Metaphysical Grounding: Understanding the Structure of Reality*, edited by Fabrice Correia and Benjamin Schnieder, Cambridge: Cambridge University Press, 139–64.

——. Forthcoming. "Playing with Fire: Hume, Rationalism, and a Little Bit of Spinoza," in *The Oxford Handbook of Spinoza*, edited by Michael Della Rocca, New York: Oxford University Press.

DePaul, Michael. 1998. "Why Bother with Reflective Equilibrium?" in *Rethinking Intuition: The Psychology of Intuition and Its Role in Philosophical Inquiry*, edited by M. DePaul and W. Ramsey, Lanham, MD: Rowman and Littlefield, 293–309.

Derrida, Jacques. 1974. *On Grammatology*, translated by G. C. Spivak, Baltimore: Johns Hopkins University Press.

——. 1981. *Dissemination*, translated by B. Johnson, Chicago: University of Chicago Press.

——. 1995. "'Eating Well,' or the Calculation of the Subject," in *Points … Interviews, 1974–1994*, edited by E. Weber, Stanford, CA: Stanford University Press.

Descartes, René. 1964–1975. *Œuvres de Descartes*, edited by C. Adam and P. Tannery, 11 vols., Paris: Vrin.

Descartes, René. 1984–1991. *The Philosophical Writings of Descartes*, 3 vols., edited and translated by J. Cottingham, R. Stoothof, M. Murdoch, and A. Kenny, Cambridge: Cambridge University Press.

Destutt de Tracy, Antoine. 2003 [1806]. "Sur les lettres de Descartes," in *La Décade philosophique, littéraire et politique*, 1 June 1806 (re-edited in *La Décade Philosophique comme système, 1794–1807)*, edited by J. Boulad-Ayoub, Rennes: Presses Universitaires de Rennes 2003, vol. I, 411–17.

Detienne, Marcel. 1996. *The Masters of Truth in Archaic Greece*, translated by J. Lloyd, New York: Zone Books.

Diggins, John Patrick. 1984. "The Oyster and the Pearl: The Problem of Contextualism in Intellectual History," *History and Theory* 23:2, 151–69.

Dobbs-Weinstein, Idit. 2004. "The Maimonidean Controversy," in *History of Jewish Philosophy*, in *Routledge History of World Philosophies*, vol. 2, edited by D. Frank and O. Leaman, London: Routledge, 331–49.

——. 1994. "Maimonidean Aspects in Spinoza's Thought," *Graduate Faculty Philosophy Journal* 17: 1–2, 153–74.

Dohm, Christian Wilhelm. 1781. *Über die bürgerliche Verbesserung der Juden*, Berlin-Stettin: Nicolai.

Domski, Mary. 2012. "Newton and Proclus: Geometry, Imagination, and Knowing Space," *Southern Journal of Philosophy* 50:3, 389–413.

——. Preprint. "The Epistemological Foundations of Structural Realism: Poincaré and the Structure of Relations," delivered at the Research Workshop of the Division of History and Philosophy of Science, University of Leeds.

Doyle, Arthur Conan. 1976. "Silver Blaze," in *The Complete Short Stories*, London: John Murray-Jonathan Cape.

Dummett, Michael. 1994. *Origins of Analytical Philosophy*. Cambridge: Harvard University Press.

——. 2004. *Truth and the Past*, New York: Columbia University Press.

Durkheim, Émile. 1915. *Elementary Forms of Religious Life*, London: Allen and Unwin.

Editors. 1984. "Editorial Statement," *History of Philosophy Quarterly* 1, 1.

——. 2011. "Editorial Statement," *History of Philosophy Quarterly* 28, 3.

Einstein, Albert and Leopold Infeld. 1971. *The Evolution of Physics*, Cambridge: Cambridge University Press.

Eskildsen, Kasper Risbjerg. 2008. "Leopold Ranke's Archival Turn: Location and Evidence in Modern Historiography," *Modern Intellectual History* 5:3, 425–53.

Evans, Richard J. 2000. *In Defence of History*, London: Granta Books.

Evans-Pritchard, Edward Evan. 1962. *Social Anthropology and Other Essays*, New York: Free Press.

Femia, Joseph V. 1981. "An Historicist Critique of 'Revisionist' Methods for Studying the History of Ideas," *History* 20:2, 113–34.

Ferret, Olivier. 2008. "Paroles édifiantes: les Éloges d'Antoine-Léonard Thomas," *Cromohs* 13, 1–19.

Finocchiaro, Maurice A. 2002. "Philosophy versus Religion and Science versus Religion: The Trials of Bruno and Galilei," in *Giordano Bruno: Philosopher of the Renaissance*, edited by H. Gatti, Aldershot: Ashgate, 51–96.

Fischer, Kuno. 1878–93. *Geschichte der neuern Philosophie*, 8 vols., Munich: Vassermann.

Foucault, Michel. 1969. *L'Archéologie du savoir*, Paris: Gallimard, 1969.

——. 1996. "What Is Critique?" in *What Is Enlightenment? Eighteenth Century Answers and Twentieth Century Questions*, edited by J. Schmidt, Los Angeles: University of California Press, 382–98.

——. 1990. "Qu'est-ce que la critique [Critique et *Aufklärung*]," *Bulletin de la société française de philosophie* 84, 35–63.

Fraenkel, Carlos. 2006. "Maimonides' God and Spinoza's *Deus sive Natura*," *Journal of the History of Philosophy* 44:2, 169–215.

Frankfurt, Harry. 1970. *Demons, Dreamers, and Madmen: The Defense of Reason in Descartes's* Meditations, Indianapolis: Bobbs-Merrill.

Frede, Michael. 1987. *Essays in Ancient Philosophy*, Oxford: Clarendon.

——. 1988. "History of Philosophy as a Discipline," *Journal of Philosophy* 85, 666–72.

French, Steven. 2003. "Scribbling on the Blank Sheet: Eddington's Structuralist Conception of Objects," *Studies in History and Philosophy of Modern Physics* 34, 227–59.

French, Steven and James Ladyman. 2003. "Remodeling Structural Realism: Quantum Physics and the Metaphysics of Structure," *Synthese* 136, 31–56.

Frey, J.-C. 1648 [1628]. *Cribrum Philosophorum qui Aristotelem superiore et hac aetate oppugnarunt*, Paris.

Friedman, Michael. 1992. *Kant and the Exact Sciences*, Cambridge, MA: Harvard University Press.

——. 1998. "On the Sociology of Scientific Knowledge and Its Philosophical Agenda," in *Studies in History and Philosophy of Science* 29, 239–71.

——. 2001. *The Dynamics of Reason*, Chicago: University of Chicago Press.

——. 2010. "A Post-Kuhnian Approach to the History and Philosophy of Science," *The Monist* 93:4, 497–517.

Fülleborn, Georg Gustav. 1799. "Verzeichniss einiger philosophischen Modethematum," in *Beyträge zur Geschichte der Philosophie*, 12 vols., edited by G. G. Fülleborn, Züllichau: F. Frommann 1791–1799, vol. 10 (1799), pp. 143–61, and vols 11–12 (1799), 209–25.

Gadamer, Hans-Georg. 1924. "Zur Systemidee in der Philosophie," in *Festchrift für Paul Natorp zum siebzigsten Geburtstage von Schülern und Freunden gewidmet*, Berlin: Walter de Gruyter, 55–75.

——. 1998. "Die Philosophie und ihre Geschichte," in F. Ueberweg, *Grundriss der Geschichte der Philosophie*, 13th ed., edited by H. Flashar, J.-P. Schobinger, and H. Holzhey, vol. 1, Basel, 1983; off-print from vol. 1 (Basel, 1998), iii–xxvi.

Galilei, Galileo. 1953. "A Madama Cristina di Lorena granduchessa di Toscana" [1615], in id., *Opere*, edited by F. Flora, Milan: Riccardo Ricciardi, 1007–45.

——. 1957. "The Assayer," in *Discoveries and Opinions of Galileo*, edited and translated by S. Drake, New York: Anchor Books.

Galison, Peter. 2008. "Ten Problems in History and Philosophy of Science," *Isis* 99, 111–24.

Garber, Daniel. 1988a. "Does History Have a Future?" in *Doing Philosophy Historically*, edited by P. Hare, Buffalo, NY: Prometheus Books, 27–43.

——. 1988b. "Descartes, the Aristotelians and the Revolution that Did not Happen in 1637," *The Monist* 71, 471–86.

——. 1992. *Descartes' Metaphysical Physics*, Chicago: University of Chicago Press.

——. 2001. "Au-delà des arguments des philosophes," in *Comment écrire l'histoire de la philosophie?* edited by Y.-C. Zarka, Paris: Presses Universitaires de France, 231–45.

——. 2002. "Defending Aristotle/Defending Society in Early 17th C Paris," in *Wissensideale und Wissenskulturen in der frühen Neuzeit*, edited by C. Zittel and W. Detel, Berlin: Akademie-Verlag.

——. 2005. "What's Philosophical about the History of Philosophy," in *Analytic Philosophy and History of Philosophy*, edited by T. Sorell and G. A. J. Rogers, Oxford: Clarendon Press, 129–46.

——. 2008 "Should Spinoza Have Published His Philosophy?" in *Interpreting Spinoza: Critical Essays*, edited by Charlie Huenemann, Cambridge: Cambridge University Press.

——. 2009. *Leibniz: Body, Substance, Monad*, Oxford: Oxford University Press.

Garber, Daniel and Michael Ayers. 1998. "Introduction," in *Cambridge History of Seventeenth Century Philosophy*, edited by D. Garber and M. Ayers, Cambridge: Cambridge University Press.

Garnier, Adolphe. 1835. *Oeuvres philosophiques de Descartes*, edited by A. Garnier, Paris: L. Hachette.

Gassendi, Pierre. 1624. *Exercitationes paradoxicae adversus aristoteleos*. Grenoble.

——. 1630a. *Epistolica exercitatio, in qua principia philosophiae Roberti Flvddi medici reteguntur*, Paris.

——. 1630b. *Parhelia, sive soles quatuor, qui circa verum apparuerunt Romæ, die xx. mensis Martij, anno 1629 ...*, Paris.

——. 1632. *Mercvrivs in sole visvs, et Venvs invisa Parisiis, anno 1631 …*, Paris.

——. 1641. *Viri illvstris Nicolai Clavdii Fabricii de Peiresc, senatoris aqvisextiensis vita*, Paris.

——. 1649. *Animadversiones in decimum librum Diogenis Laertii*, Lyon.

——. 1658. *Adversus aristoteleos libri duo priores*, Lyon.

——. 1658. *Opera Omnia … haetenus edita auctor ante obitum recensuit … posthuma vero, totius naturae explicationem complectentia, in lucem nunc primum prodeunt ex bibliotheca …* , 6 vols., Lyon.

Geertz, Clifford. 1974. "From the Native's Point of View: On the Nature of Anthropological Understanding," *Bulletin of the American Academy of Arts and Sciences* 28:1, 26–45.

——. 1983. *Local Knowledge*, New York: Basic Books.

Geldsetzer, Lutz. 1989. "Problemgeschichte," in *Historisches Wörterbuch der Philosophie*, 13 vols., general editor J. Ritter, Basel: Schwabe, 1971–2007, vol. 7 (1989), cols. 1410–17.

Gerdmar, Anders. 2009. *Roots of Theological Anti-Semitism: German Interpretations and the Jews from Herder and Semler to Kittel and Bultmann*, Leiden: Brill.

Gettier, Edmund. 1966. "Is Justified True Belief Knowledge?" *Analysis* 23, 121–23.

Giancotti-Boscherini, Emilia. 1978. "Man as Part of Nature" in *Spinoza's Philosophy of Man*, edited by Jon Wetlesen, Oslo: Universitetsforlaget, 85–96.

Giere, Ronald N. 1973. "History and Philosophy of Science: Intimate Relationship or Marriage of Convenience?" *British Journal for the Philosophy of Science* 24, 282–97.

Gierke, Otto Friedrich von, 1966. *The Development of Political Theory*, translated by Bernard Freyd, New York: H. Fertig.

Gillespie, Charles. 1960. *The Edge of Objectivity*, Princeton, NJ: Princeton University Press.

Glassie, Henry. 1977. "Archaeology and Folklore: Common Anxieties, Common Hopes," in *Historical Archaeology and the Importance of Material Things*, edited by Leland Ferguson, Columbia, SC: Society for Historical Archaeology, 22–35.

Glock, Hans-Johann. 2008a. "Analytic Philosophy and History: A Mismatch?" *Mind* 117, 867–97.

——. 2008b. *What Is Analytic Philosophy?* Cambridge: Cambridge University Press.

Goldenbaum, Ursula. 1999. "Die *Commentatiuncula de judice* als Leibnizens erste philosophische Auseinandersetzung mit Spinoza nebst der Mitteilung über ein neuaufgefundenes Leibnizstück. Beilage: Leibniz' Marginalien zu Spinozas *Tractatus theologico-politicus* im Exemplar der Bibliotheca Boineburgica in Erfurt, also zu datieren auf 1670–71," in *Labora diligenter*, edited by Hartmut Rudolph et al., *Studia Leibnitiana* Sonderheft 29, Wiesbaden: Steiner, 61–127.

——, ed. 2004. *Appell an das Publikum. Die öffentliche Debatte in der deutschen Aufklärung 1687–1796. Mit Beiträgen von Frank Grunert, Peter Weber, Gerda Heinrich, Brigitte Erker und Winfried Siebers*, 2 vols., Berlin: Akademie Verlag.

——. 2008a. "Leibniz' Marginalia on the Back of the Title of Spinoza's *Tractatus Theologico-Politicus*," *Leibniz Review* 18, 269–72.

——. 2008b. "*Vera Indivisibilia* in Leibniz's Early Philosophy of Mind," in *Infinitesimal Differences: Controversies between Leibniz and His Contemporaries*, edited by U. Goldenbaum and D. Jesseph, Berlin: De Gruyter, 53–94.

——. 2011a. "Sovereignty and Obedience," in *The Oxford Handbook of Philosophy in Early Modern Europe*, edited by D. Clarke and C. Wilson, Oxford: Oxford University Press, 500–21.

——. 2011b. "Mendelssohn's Spinozistic Alternative to Baumgarten's Pietist Project of Aesthetics," in *Moses Mendelssohn's Metaphysics and Aesthetics*, edited by R. Munk, Dordrecht: Springer, 299–327.

——. 2012. "Universal oder plural? Zum scheinbaren Gegensatz von Lessing und Mendelssohn über die 'Erziehung des Menschengeschlechts,'" in *Lessing Yearbook*, Special Issue edited by Monika Fick and Stephan Braese, 241–260.

——. 2013. "Moses Mendelssohn's *Causa Dei*—eine jüdische Theodizee oder reine Metaphysik?" in *Die Rezeption der Theodizee*, edited by W. Li, Studia leibnitiana Sonderheft, Wiesbaden: Steiner, 115–136.

——. Forthcoming. "How Kant Was Never a Wolffian or Estimating Forces to Enforce *Influxus Physicus*," in *Leibniz and Kant*, edited by B. Look, New York: Oxford University Press.

Goldstein, Rebecca. 2006. *Betraying Spinoza*, New York: Schocken.

Goodenough, Ward H. 1970. *Description and Comparison in Cultural Anthropology*, Chicago: Aldine.

Goodman, Nelson. 1983. *Fact, Fiction, and Forecast*, 4th ed., Cambridge, MA: Harvard University Press.

Goody, Jack. 1986. *The Logic of Writing and the Organization of Society*, Cambridge: Cambridge University Press.

Grafton, Anthony. 2005. "The History of Ideas: Precepts and Practice 1950–2000 and Beyond," *Journal of the History of Ideas* 67:1, 1–32.

Graham, Gordon. 1982. "Can There Be History of Philosophy?" *History and Theory* 21:1, 37–52.

Grant, Edward. 2007. *A History of Natural Philosophy: From the Ancient World to the Nineteenth Century*, Cambridge: Cambridge University Press.

Grattan-Guinness, Ivor. 1990. "Does History of Science Treat of the History of Science? The Case of Mathematics," *History of Science* 28: 149–73.

Grene, Marjorie. 1985. *Descartes*, Minneapolis: University of Minnesota Press.

Grunberg, E. and F. Modigliani. 1954. "The Predictability of Social Events," *Journal of Political Economy* 62, 465–78.

Gueroult, Martial. 1953. *Descartes selon l'ordre des raisons*. Paris: Montaigne.

——. 1962. "De la méthode prescrite par Descartes pour comprendre sa philosophie," *Archiv für Geschichte der Philosophie* 44, 172–84.

——. 1968. *Spinoza, I: Dieu*. Paris: Aubier.

——.1974. *Spinoza II: L'âme*, Paris: Aubier.

——. 1979. *Dianoématique. Livre II. Philosophie de l'histoire de la philosophie*. Paris: Aubier-Montaigne.

Haakonssen, Knud. 1996. *Natural Law and Moral Philosophy from Grotius to the Scottish Enlightenment*, Cambridge: Cambridge University Press.

——. 2004. "The Idea of Early Modern Philosophy," in *Teaching New Histories of Philosophy*, edited by J. B. Schneewind. Princeton, NJ: University Center for Human Values, Princeton University, 99–121.

Hacking, Ian. 1984. "Five Parables," in *Philosophy in History*, edited by Richard Rorty, J. B. Schneewind, and Quentin Skinner, Cambridge: Cambridge University Press, 103–24.

Hadot, Pierre. 1995. *Philosophy as a Way of Life. Spiritual Exercises from Socrates to Foucault*, translated by M. Chase, introduction by Arnold I. Davidson. Oxford: Blackwell.

Hamann, Johann Georg. 1825. "Golgatha und Scheblimini," in *Hamann's Schriften*, edited by F. Roth, Part 7, Leipzig: Reimer.

——. 1959. *Briefwechsel*, vol. 4, edited by A. Henkel, Frankfurt: Insel.

——. 1993. *Londoner Schriften*, edited by O. Bayer and B. Weißenborn, München: Beck.

Hands, Wade. 1990. "Grunberg and Modigliani, Public Predictions and the New Classical Macroeconomics," *Research in the History of Economic Thought and Methodology* 7, 207–23.

Hanson, Norwood Russell. 1958. *Patterns of Discovery*, Cambridge: Cambridge University Press.

Hare, Richard M. 1973. "Rawls' Theory of Justice–I," *Philosophical Quarterly* 23, 144–55.

Harkin, Michael. 1988. "History, Narrative and Temporality: Examples from the Northwest Coast," *Ethnohistory* 35, 99–130.

Harrison, Peter. 2007. *The Fall of Man and the Foundations of Science*, Cambridge: Cambridge University Press.

Harvey, Warren Zev. 1981. "A Portrait of Spinoza as a Maimonidean," *Journal of the History of Philosophy* 19:2, 151–72.

Hatfield, Gary. 1996a. "Review Essay: The Importance of the History of Science for Philosophy in General," *Synthese* 106, 113–38.

——. 1996b. "Was the Scientific Revolution a Revolution in Science?" in *Tradition, Transmission, Transformation*, edited by F. J. Ragep and S. P. Ragep, Leiden: E. J. Brill, 489–525.

——. 2005. "The History of Philosophy as Philosophy," in *Analytic Philosophy and History of Philosophy*, edited by T. Sorell and A. J. Rogers, Oxford: Clarendon Press, 83–128.

Havelock, Eric. 1981. *The Literate Revolution and Its Consequences*, Princeton, NJ: Princeton University Press.

Hazony, Yoram. 2012. *The Philosophy of Hebrew Scripture: An Introduction*, Cambridge: Cambridge University Press.

Heilbron, John L. 1999. *The Sun in the Church: Cathedrals as Solar Observatories*, Cambridge, MA: Harvard University Press.

Heinrich, Gerda. 2004. "'Man sollte itzt beständig das Publikum über diese Materie en haleine halten.' Die Debatte um 'bürgerliche Verbesserung der Juden' 1781–1786," in *Appell an das Publikum. Die öffentliche Debatte in der deutschen Aufklärung 1687–1796. Mit Beiträgen von Frank Grunert, Peter Weber, Gerda Heinrich, Brigitte Erker und Winfried Siebers*, edited by U. Goldenbaum, Berlin: Akademie Verlag, 813–95.

Hendricks, Vincent F. and John Symons. 2005. *Formal Philosophy: Aim, Scope, Direction*, Copenhagen: Automatic Press.

Henkes, Barbara. 1993. "De a-historische sensatie van Tollebeek en Verschaffel," *Leidschrift* 9:3, 137–43.

Herder, Johann Gottfried. 1774. *Auch eine Philosophie der Geschichte zur Bildung der Menschheit: Beytrag zu vielen Beyträgen des Jahrhunderts*, Riga: Hartknoch.

Hill, Nicholas. 1619. *Philosophia Epicurea, Democritiana, Theophrastica proposita simpliciter, non edocta*, Geneva.

Hinske, Norbert. 1977. "Nachwort zur zweiten Auflage," in *Was ist Aufklärung? Beiträge aus der Berlinischen Monatsschrift*, edited by N. Hinske and M. Albrecht, Darmstadt: Wissenschaftliche Buchgesellschaft.

Hobbes, Thomas. 1651. *Section Three, Concerning Government and Society*, London.

——. 1656. *De corpore as The First Section, Concerning Body*, London.

——. 1994. *Leviathan*, edited by E. Curley, Indianapolis: Hackett.

Holt, Edwin and Walter T. Marvin, W. P. Montague, Ralph Barton Perry, Walter B. Pitkin, and Edward Gleason Spaulding. 1910. "The Program and First Platform of Six Realists," *Journal of Philosophy, Psychology and Scientific Methods* 7:15, 393–401.

Holzhey, Helmut. 1989. "Problem," in *Historisches Wörterbuch der Philosophie*, 13 vols., general editor J. Ritter, Basel: Schwabe, 1971–2007, vol. 7 (1989), cols. 1397–408.

Hook, Sidney. 1930. "A Personal Impression of Contemporary German Philosophy," *Journal of Philosophy* 27:6, 141–60.

Hooker, Brad and Margaret Little, eds. 2000. *Moral Particularism*, Oxford: Clarendon Press.

Hornig, Gottfried. 1996. *Johann Salomo Semler: Studien zu Leben und Werk des Hallenser Aufklärungstheologen*, Tübingen: Niemeyer.

Hueglin, Thomas O. 1999. *Early Modern Concepts for a Late Modern World: Althusius on Community and Federalism*, Waterloo, Ontario: Wilfrid Laurier University Press.

Hume, David. 2000. *A Treatise of Human Nature*, edited by D. F. Norton and M. J. Norton, Oxford: Oxford University Press.

Hunter, Graeme. 2005. *Radical Protestantism in Spinoza's Thought*, Aldershot: Ashgate.

Hylton, Peter. 1990. *Russell, Idealism, and the Emergence of Analytic Philosophy*, Oxford: Clarendon Press.

Israel, Jonathan. 1986. *European Jewry in the Age of Mercantilism, 1550–1750*, Oxford: Oxford University Press.

——. 2001. *Radical Enlightenment. Philosophy and the Making of Modernity 1650–1750*, Oxford: Oxford University Press.

——. 2006. *Enlightenment Contested: Philosophy, Modernity, and the Emancipation of Man 1670–1752*, Oxford: Oxford University Press.

——. 2010. *A Revolution of the Mind: Radical Enlightenment and the Intellectual Origins of Modern Democracy*, Princeton, NJ: Princeton University Press, 2010.

——. 2011. *Democratic Enlightenment: Philosophy, Revolution, and Human Rights 1750–1790*, Oxford: Oxford University Press.

Jacobi, Friedrich Heinrich. 2003. *Briefwechsel*, edited by M. Brüggen and S. and H. Gockel, Stuttgart-Bad Cannstatt, vol. I.4.

Janiak, Andrew. 2008. *Newton as Philosopher*, Cambridge: Cambridge University Press.

Jardine, Nicholas. 2000. *The Scenes of Inquiry*, Oxford: Clarendon Press.

Jeffrey, Richard. 1995. "Carnap's Voluntarism," *Studies in Logic and the Foundations of Mathematics* 134, 847–66.

Jolley, Nicolas. 2003. "Reason's Dim Candle. Locke's Critique of Enthusiasm," in *The Philosophy of Locke. New Perspectives*, edited by P. Anstey, London: Routledge, 179–91.

Jones, Andrew. 2007. *Memory and Material Culture*, Cambridge: Cambridge University Press.

Jones, Keith. 1986. "Is Kuhn a Sociologist?" *British Journal for the Philosophy of Science* 37, 443–52.

Kane, Robert Hillary. 1976. "Nature, plenitude and sufficient reason." *American Philosophical Quarterly*, 13(1), 23–31

Kant, Immanuel. 1910–(?). *Gesammelte Schriften*, edited by Academy of Prussia, Berlin: Reimer.

——. 1963. "Idea for a Universal History from a Cosmopolitan Point of View," in *On History*, translated by Lewis White Beck, Indianapolis: Bobbs-Merrill.

——. 1996a. *Critique of Practical Reason*, in Kant, *Practical Philosophy*, translated by M. Gregor, Cambridge: Cambridge University Press.

——. 1996b. "Answer to the Question: What Is Enlightenment?" in Kant, *Practical Philosophy*, translation by M. Gregor, Cambridge: Cambridge University Press.

——. 1998a. *Kritik der reinen Vernunft*, edited by J. Timmermann. Hamburg: Felix Meiner.

——. 1998b. *Critique of Pure Reason*, edited and translated by P. Guyer and A. Wood, Cambridge: Cambridge University Press.

——. 2009. *Religion within the Boundaries of Mere Reason, and Other Writings*, translated and edited by A. Wood and G. di Giovanni, Cambridge: Cambridge University Press.

Kagan, Shelly. 2001. "Thinking about Cases," *Social Philosophy and Policy* 18, 44–63.

Keevak, Michael. 1992. "Descartes's Dreams and Their Address for Philosophy," *Journal of the History of Ideas* 53:3, 373–96.

Kelley, Donald R. 1998. *Faces of History*. New Haven, CT: Yale University Press.

Kenny, Anthony. 1968. *Descartes*, New York: Random House.

——. 2005. "The Philosopher's History and the History of Philosophy," in *Analytic Philosophy and History of Philosophy*, edited by T. Sorell and A. J. Rogers, Oxford: Clarendon Press, 13–24.

Keynes, J. M. 1936. *The General Theory of Employment, Interest and Money*, London: Macmillan.

Kitcher, Philip. 1998. "A Plea for Science Studies," in *A House Built on Sand: Exposing Postmodern Myths about Science*, edited by N. Koertge, Oxford: Oxford University Press, 32–56.

Klein, Julie R. 2003. "Spinoza's Debt to Gersonides," *Graduate Faculty Philosophy Journal* 24:1, 19–43.

Knappett, Carl. 2005. *Thinking through Material Culture: An Interdisciplinary Perspective*, Philadelphia: University of Pennsylvania Press.

Kolesnik-Antoine, Delphine, 2011. "Comment rendre l'âme 'comme' matérielle ? Le cas de Malebranche," *Corpus* 61, 205–19.

——. 2012 . "La structure passionnelle de l'âme malebranchiste: entre Descartes et Regius ?" in *Emotional Minds*, edited by Sabrina Ebbersmeyer, Berlin: De Gruyter Verlag, 51–68.

——. 2013a. "La référence à Malebranche dans *L'Âme matérielle*: décontextualisation et transplantation," in *Les Malebranchismes des Lumières*, edited by D. Kolesnik-Antoine, Paris: Honoré Champion.

——. 2013b. "Préface" in *Les Malebranchismes des Lumières*, edited by D. Kolesnik-Antoine, Paris: Honoré Champion.

Koselleck, Reinhart. 1997. "Histoire sociale et histoire des concepts," in idem, *L'Expérience de l'histoire*, Paris: Gallimard/Le Seuil, 101–19.

Koyré, Alexandre. 1939. *Etudes galiléennes*, Paris: Hermann.

Kranz, Margarita, et al. 1989, "Philosophie," in *Historisches Wörterbuch der Philosophie*, 13 vols., general editor J. Ritter, Basel: Schwabe, 1971–2007, vol. 7 (1989), cols. 572–879.

Kremer, Michael. Forthcoming. "What Is the Good of Philosophical History?" in *The Historical Turn in Analytic Philosophy*, edited by E. Reck, Hampshire: Palgrave Macmillan.

Krieger, W. H. 2006. *Can There Be a Philosophy of Archaeology?* Lanham, MD: Lexington Books.

Kristeller, Paul Oskar. 1964. "History of Philosophy and History of Ideas," *Journal of the History of Philosophy*, 2, 1–14.

Kröger, Wolfgang. 1979. *Das Publikum als Richter. Lessing und die "kleineren Respondenten" im Fragmentenstreit*, Wolfenbütteler Forschungen 5, Nendeln/Liechtenstein: KTO-Press.

Krüger, Lorenz. 1984. "Why Do We Study the History of Philosophy?" in *Philosophy in History: Essays in the Historiography of Philosophy*, edited by R. Rorty, J. B. Schneewind, and Q. Skinner, Cambridge: Cambridge University Press, 77–101.

Kuhn, Thomas. [1962] 1970. *The Structure of Scientific Revolutions*, 2nd ed., Chicago: University of Chicago Press.

——. 1977. *The Essential Tension: Selected Studies in Scientific Tradition and Change*, Chicago: University of Chicago Press.

——. 2000. *The Road since Structure: Philosophical Essays, 1970–1993, with an Autobiographical Interview*, edited by J. Conant and J. Haugeland, Chicago: University of Chicago Press.

Ladyman, James. 1998. "What Is Structural Realism?" *Studies in History and Philosophy of Science* 29:3, 409–24.

——. 2009. "Structural Realism," in *The Stanford Encyclopedia of Philosophy (Summer 2009 Edition)*, edited by E. N. Zalta, http://plato.stanford.edu/archives/sum2009/entries/structural-realism.

Laudan, Larry. 1981. "A Confutation of Convergent Realism," *Philosophy of Science*, 48, 19–49.

——1990. "The History of Science and the Philosophy of Science," in *Companion to the History of Modern Science*, edited by R. C. Olby, G. N. Cantor, J. R. R. Christie, and M. J. S. Hodge, London: Routledge, 47–59.

Launoy, Jean de. 1653. *De varia Aristotelis in Academia parisiensi fortuna*, Paris.

Leibniz, G. W. 1875–1890. *Die philosophischen Schriften*, edited by C. I. Gerhardt, Berlin.

——. 1923–. *Sämtliche Schriften und Briefe*, edited by Deutsche (before 1945, Preussische) Akademie der Wissenschaften. Berlin: Akademie Verlag.

——. 1969. *Philosophical Papers and Letters*, edited and translated by L. E. Loemker, Dordrecht: Reidel.

——. 1989. *Philosophical Essays*, edited and translated by R. Ariew and D. Garber, Indianapolis: Hackett.

Lennon, Thomas M. 1993. *The Battle of the Gods and Giants. The Legacies of Descartes and Gassendi, 1615–1755*, Princeton, NJ: Princeton University Press.

——. 2008. *The Plain Truth. Descartes, Huet, and Skepticism*, Leiden: Brill.

Lepenies, Wolf. 1984. "'Interesting Questions' in the History of Philosophy and Elsewhere," in *Philosophy in History. Essays on the Historiography of Philosophy*, edited by R. Rorty, J.B. Schneewind, and Q. Skinner, Cambridge: Cambridge University Press, 141–72.

LePore, E., ed. 1986. *Truth and Interpretation*. London: Blackwell.

Lessing, Gotthold Ephraim. 1968. *Sämtliche Schriften*, edited by K. Lachmann and F. Muncker, Berlin: De Gruyter (1st ed. Leipzig: Goeschen, 1897).

——. 2005. "The Education of the Human Race (1780)," in *Philosophical and Theological Writings*, translated by H. B. Nisbet, Cambridge: Cambridge University Press.

Lewis, David. 1983. "Introduction," in *Philosophical Papers*, vol. 1, New York: Oxford University Press, ix–xii.

——. 1999. "Psychophysical and Theoretical Identifications," in *Papers in Metaphysics and Epistemology*, 2, Cambridge: Cambridge University Press.

Livingston, Donald W. 1998. *Philosophical Melancholy and Delirium,* Chicago: University of Chicago Press.

Locke, John. 1706. *Examen de la vision en Dieu de Malebranche* (reprint: Paris: Vrin, 1978).

——. 1975. *An Essay Concerning Human Understanding,* edited by P. Nidditch, Oxford: Oxford University Press.

Longo, Mario. 2011. "A 'Critical' History of Philosophy and the Early Enlightenment: Johann Jacob Brucker," in *Models of the History of Philosophy. Volume II: From the Cartesian Age to Brucker*, edited by G. Piaia and G. Santinello, translated by H. Siddons and G. Weston, Dordrecht: Springer, 477–577.

Look, Brandon. 2006. "Some Remarks on the Ontological Arguments of Leibniz and Gödel," in *Einheit in der Vielheit. Proceedings of the VIII. International Leibniz Congress*, Hanover, 510–17.

Lord Smail, Daniel. 2008. *On Deep History and the Brain*, Berkeley: University of California Press.

Lötzsch, Frieder. 1973. "Zur Genealogie der Frage 'Was ist Aufklärung?': Mendelssohn, Kant und die Neologie," *Theokratia. Jahrbuch des Institutum Judaicum Delitzschianum* 2, 307–22.

Lovejoy, Arthur Oncken. 1936. *The Great Chain of Being. A Study of the History of an Idea*, Cambridge, MA: Harvard University Press.

Löwenbrück, Anna-Ruth. 1994. "Johann David Michaelis und Moses Mendelssohn. Judenfeindschaft im Zeitalter der Aufklärung," in *Moses Mendelssohn im Kreise seiner Wirksamkeit*, edited by M. Albrecht, E. J. Engel, and N. Hinske, Tübingen: Niemeyer, 315–32.

Luhrmann, Tanya M. 1989. *Persuasions of the Witch's Craft*, Cambridge, MA: Harvard University Press.

Macherey, Pierre. 2011. *Hegel or Spinoza*, translated by S. Ruddick, Minneapolis: University of Minnesota Press.

——. 1998. "Spinoza's Philosophical Actuality (Heidegger, Adorno, Foucault)" in idem, *In a Materialist Way; Selected Essays*, edited by W. Montag, translated by T. Stolze, New York: Verso, 125–35.

——. 1979. *Hegel ou Spinoza*, Paris: Maspero.

MacIntyre, Alasdair. 1984. "The Relationship of Philosophy to Its Past," in *Philosophy in History: Essays on the Historiography of Philosophy*, edited by R. Rorty, J. B. Schneewind, and Q. Skinner, Cambridge: Cambridge University Press, 31–48.

Maggi, Armando. 2001. *Satan's Rhetoric. A Study of Renaissance Demonology*, Chicago: Chicago University Press.

Mäki U. 2011. "Scientific Realism as a Challenge to Economics (and vice versa)," *Journal of Economic Methodology*, 18:1, 1–12.

Maimonides, Moses. 1963. *The Guide of the Perplexed*, translated by Shlomo Pines, Chicago: University of Chicago Press.

——. 1982. *Mishne Torah*, Jerusalem: Vagshal.

Malusa, Luciano. 1993. "The First General Histories of Philosophy in England and the Low Countries," in *Models of the History of Philosophy: From Its Origins in the Renaissance to the "Historia philosophica,"* edited by G. Santinello et al., Dordrecht: Kluwer, 161–370.

Malinowski, Bronislaw. 1922. *Argonauts of the Western Pacific*, London: Routledge and Kegan Paul.

Mann, Wolfgang-Rainer. 1996. "The Origins of the Modern Historiography of Ancient Philosophy," *History and Theory* 35:2, 165–95.

Manzini, Frédéric, ed. 2011. *Spinoza et ses scolastiques. Retour aux sources et nouveaux enjeux*, Paris: Presses universitaires de France.

——. 2009. *Spinoza: une lecture d'Aristote*, Paris: Presses universitaires de France.

Marx, Karl. 1845. *La Sainte famille*, Paris: Editions Sociales.

Mates, Benson. 1986. *The Philosophy of Leibniz: Metaphysics and Language*, Oxford: Oxford University Press.

Matheron, Alexandre. 2011. *Études sur Spinoza et les philosophies de l'âge classique*, Lyon: ENS Editions.

——. 1991. "Essence, Existence and Power in *Ethics* I: The Foundations of Proposition 16," in *God and Nature: Spinoza's Metaphysics* (Spinoza by 2000,vol. 1), edited by Y. Yovel, Leiden: Brill.

Mauskopf, Seymour, and Tad Schmaltz, eds. 2012. *Integrating History and Philosophy of Science: Problems and Prospects*, Dordrecht: Springer.

McMahan, Jeff. 2000. "Moral Intuition," in *Blackwell Guide to Ethical Theory*, edited by H. LaFollette, Malden, MA: Blackwell, 92–110.

Melamed, Yitzhak Y. 2009. "Spinoza's Metaphysics of Substance: The Substance-Mode Relation as a Relation of Inherence and Predication," *Philosophy and Phenomenological Research* 78:1, 17–82.

——. 2010a. "Spinoza's Anti-Humanism: An Outline," in *The Rationalists*, edited by C. Fraenkel, D. Perinetti, and J. E. H. Smith, Dordrecht: Springer Press, 147–66.

——. 2010b. "The Metaphysics of the *Theological Political Treatise*," in *Spinoza's* Theological Political Treatise: *A Critical Guide*, edited by Y. Y. Melamed and M. A. Rosenthal, Cambridge: Cambridge University Press, 128–42.

——. 2012a. "*Christus secundum spiritum*: Spinoza, Jesus, and the Infinite Intellect," in *The Jewish Jesus*, edited by N. Stahl, New York: Routledge, 140–51.

——. 2012b. "Why Is Spinoza not an Eleatic Monist (Or Why Diversity Exists)," in *Spinoza on Monism*, edited by Philipp Goff, London: Palgrave Macmillan, 206–22.

——. 2013. *Spinoza's Metaphysics: Substance and Thought*, Oxford: Oxford University Press.

——. "Spinoza's Mereology," unpublished manuscript.

Meli, Domenico Bertoloni. 2006. *Thinking with Objects: The Transformation of Mechanics in the Seventeenth Century*, Baltimore: Johns Hopkins University Press.

Mendelssohn, Moses (1971– ongoing), *Gesammelte Schriften. Jubiläumsausgabe*, edited by Fritz Bamberger et al., Stuttgart-Bad Cannstatt: Frommann-Holzboog.

Mersenne, Marin. 1624. *L'impiété des Déistes, Athées, et Libertins de ce temps, combattue, et renversée de point en point par raisons tirée de la Philosophie, et de la Théologie*, Paris.

——. 1625. *La verité des sciences*, Paris.

Merton, Robert K. [1996, reprint]. *On Social Structure and Science*, Chicago: University of Chicago Press.

Monconys, Balthasar. 1665–66. *Journal des voyages de Monsieur de Monconys*. 3 vols. Lyon: Boissat and Remeus.

Monk, Ray. 1996. *Bertrand Russell: The Spirit of Solitude 1872–1921*, New York: Free Press.

Moore, G. E. 1953. *Some Main Problems of Philosophy*, London: G. Allen and Unwin.

——. 1993a. "A Defence of Common Sense," in *Selected Writings*, edited by T. Baldwin, London: Routledge, 106–33.

——. 1993b. "External and Internal Relations," in *Selected Writings*, edited by T. Baldwin, London: Routledge, 79–105.

——. 1993c. "The Nature of Judgement," in *Selected Writings*, edited by T. Baldwin, London: Routledge, 1–19.

——. 1993d. "A Proof of an External World," in *Selected Writings*, edited by T. Baldwin, London: Routledge, 147–70.

Moreau, Pierre-François. 1978. "Spinoza et Victor Cousin," in *Archivio di Filosofia*, 327–32.

——. 1979. "Spinozisme et matérialisme au XIXe siècle," *Raison présente* 52, 85–94.

——. 1983. "Trois polémiques contre Victor Cousin," *Revue de Métaphysique et de Morale* 4, 542–48.

——. 2007. "Spinoza est-il Spinoziste?" in *Qu'est-ce que les Lumières "radicales"?* edited by C. Secrétan, T. Dagron and L. Bove, Paris: Éditions Amsterdam, 289–97.

——. 2013. "Aourner l'ontologie," in *Qu'est-ce qu'être cartésien?* edited by D. Kolesnik-Antoine, Lyon: ENS Editions, 521–30.

—— Forthcoming. "*In naturalismo.*" Leibniz, Spinoza et les spiritualistes français," in *Spinoza/Leibniz. Rencontres, controverses, réceptions*, edited by R. Andrault, M. Lærke and P.-F. Moreau, Paris: Paris: Presses Universitaires de Paris Sorbonne.

Mulligan, Lotte, Judith Richards, and John Graham. 1979. "Intentions and Conventions: A Critique of Quentin Skinner's Method for the Study of Ideas," *Political Studies* 27, 84–98.

Muth, J. F. 1961. "Rational Expectations and the Theory of Price Movements," *Econometrica*, 29, 315–35.

Nadler, Steven. 2005. "Hope, Fear and the Politics of Immortality," in *Analytic Philosophy and History of Philosophy*, edited by T. Sorrell and G. A. J. Rogers, Oxford: Oxford/ Clarendon.

——. 2012. “Spinoza’s Vision of Freedom, and Ours,” in *New York Times: Opinionator Blog*, February 5, 2012.

Nagel, Ernest. 1936a. “Impressions and Appraisals of Analytical Philosophy in Europe. I,” *Journal of Philosophy* 33:1, 5–24.

——. 1936b. “Impressions and Appraisals of Analytical Philosophy in Europe. II,” *Journal of Philosophy* 33:2, 29–53.

—— 2011. *Gödel’s Proof*, New York: NYU Press.

Nelson, Alan. Forthcoming 2013. “Logic and Knowledge,” in *Companion to Early Modern Philosophy*, edited by Dan Kaufman, New York: Routledge.

Nelson, Alan and David Landy. 2011. “Qualities and Simple Ideas: Hume and His Debt to Berkeley,” in *Primary and Secondary Qualities*, edited by Lawrence Nolan, Oxford: Oxford University Press.

Newen, Albert. 1998. “Logische Analyse und der philosophische Begriff der Aufklärung. Programmatische Bemerkungen,” in *Philosophiegeschichte und logische Analyse/ Logical Analysis and History of Philosophy*, 1, Paderborn: Schöningh, 23–29.

Newman, William. 2006. *Atoms and Alchemy: Chymistry and the Experimental Origins of the Scientific Revolution*, Chicago: University of Chicago Press.

Newman, William and Laurence Principe. 2002. *Alchemy Tried in the Fire: Starkey, Boyle, and the Fate of Helmontian Chymistry*, Chicago: University of Chicago Press.

Newton, Isaac. 2004. *Newton: Philosophical Writings*, edited by Andrew Janiak, Cambridge: Cambridge University Press.

Nietzsche, Friedrich. 1983. “On the Uses and Disadvantage of History for Life,” in *Untimely Meditations*, translated by R. J. Hollingdame, New York: Cambridge University Press.

——. 2011. *Dawn*, translated by B. Smith, Stanford, CA: Stanford University Press.

Olivier de Sardan, Jean-Pierre. 1998. “Émique,” *L’Homme* 14, 151–66.

Nolan, Lawrence. 2008. “Malebranche’s Theory of Ideas and Vision in God,” in *Stanford Encyclopedia of Philosophy*, edited by E. N. Zalta, <http://www.science.uva.nl/~seop/archives/sum2010/entries/malebranche-ideas/>.

Osler, Margaret. 2002. “Pierre Gassendi,” in *A Companion to Early Modern Philosophy*, edited by S. Nadler, London: Blackwell.

Pap, Arthur. 1949. *Elements of Analytical Philosophy*, London: Macmillan.

Park, Katharine, and Lorraine Daston. 1981. “Unnatural Conceptions: The Study of Monsters in Sixteenth- and Seventeenth-Century France and England,” *Past and Present* 92, 20–54.

Parry, Milman. 1971. *The Making of Homeric Verse*, edited by A. Parry, Oxford: Clarendon.

Passmore, John. 1967. “Philosophy, Historiography,” in *The Encyclopaedia of Philosophy*, 8 vols., edited by P. Edwards, New York: Macmillan, vol. 6, 226–30.

Picavet, François. 1891. *Les idéologues, Essai sur l’histoire des idées et des théories scientifiques, philosophiques et religieuses, etc., en France depuis 1789*, Paris: Félix Alcan.

Pico della Mirandola, Giovanni. 2004. *De hominis dignitate*, in *Opere*, 3 vols., edited by E. Garin, Florence, 1942–1952, reprinted in Milan: Aragno 2004, vol. 1, 101–64.

Pietsch, Wolfgang. 2012. "The Underdetermination Debate: How Lack of History Leads to Bad Philosophy," in *Integrating History and Philosophy of Science: Problems and Prospects*, edited by S. Mauskopf and T. Schmaltz, Dordrecht: Springer, 83–106.

Pike, Kenneth L. 1954. *Language in Relation to a Unified Theory of Human Behavior*, Glendale: Summer Institute of Linguistics.

Poincaré, Henri. 1952. *Science and Hypothesis*, New York: Dover.

Poser, Hans. 1978. "Leibniz' Parisaufenthalt in seiner Bedeutung für die Monadenlehre," *Studia Leibnitiana Supplementa* 18, 131–44.

Priselac, M. 2012. *Locke's Naturalized Epistemology*. Ph.D. dissertation, University of North Carolina, Chapel Hill.

Principe, Lawrence M. 2000. "Apparatus and Reproducibility in Alchemy," in *Instruments and Experimentation in the History of Chemistry*, edited by Frederic L. Holmes and Trevor H. Levere, Cambridge, MA: MIT Press, 55–74.

Pryor, James. 2000. "The Skeptic and the Dogmatist," *Nous* 34, 517–49.

Quine, Willard Van Orman. 1961. "Two Dogmas of Empiricism," in *From a Logical Point of View*, Cambridge: Harvard University Press 1961 [original edition in *The Philosophical Review* 60 (1951), 20–43]

——1969. "Epistemology Naturalized," in *Ontological Relativity and Other Essays*. New York: Columbia University Press.

—— 1976a. "Carnap and Logical Truth," in *The Ways of Paradox and Other Essays*, revised and enlarged edition, Cambridge, MA: Harvard University Press, 107–32.

——. 1976b. "Truth by Convention," in *The Ways of Paradox and Other Essays*, revised and enlarged edition, Cambridge, MA: Harvard University Press, 77–106.

——. 1980. "Two Dogmas of Empiricism," in *From a Logical Point of View*, 2nd ed., rev., Cambridge, MA: Harvard University Press, 20–46.

Ransmayr, Christoph. 1990. *The Last World*, translated by John E. Woods, New York: Grove Press.

Rawls, John. 1951. "Outline of a Decision Procedure for Ethics," *Philosophical Review* 60, 177–97.

——. 1971. *A Theory of Justice*. Cambridge, MA: Harvard University Press.

——. 1974–75. "The Independence of Moral Theory," in *Proceedings and Address of the American Philosophical Association* 48, 5–22.

——. 2001. *Justice as Fairness: A Restatement*, Cambridge, MA: Harvard University Press.

Reichenbach, Hans. 1938. "On Probability and Induction," *Philosophy of Science* 5, 21–45.

——. 1951. *The Rise of Scientific Philosophy*, Los Angeles: University of California Press.

Reinhold, Karl Leonhard. 1791. "Über den Begrif der Geschichte der Philosophie. Eine akademische Vorlesung," in *Beiträge zur Geschichte der Philosophie*, edited by G. G. Fülleborn, vol. 1, 5–35.

Renfrew, Colin. 2008. *Prehistory: The Making of the Human Mind*, New York: Modern Library.

Renouvier, Charles. 1842. *Manuel de philosophie moderne*, Paris: Paulin.

Richardson, Alan W. 2002. "Engineering Philosophy of Science: American Pragmatism and Logical Empiricism in the 1930s," *Philosophy of Science* 69:3, 36–47.

——. 2003. "Logical Empiricism, American Pragmatism, and the Fate of Scientific Philosophy in America," in *Logical Empiricism in North America*, edited by A. Richardson and G. Hardcastle, Minneapolis: University of Minnesota Press.

Ritschl, Otto. 1906. *System und systematische Methode in der Geschichte des wissenschaftlichen Sprachgebrauchs und der philosophischen Methodologie*, Bonn: C. G. Universitäts-Buchdruckerei.

Rogers, Brian, and Alan Nelson. Forthcoming 2013. "Descartes' Logic and the Paradox of Deduction," in *Gods and Giants in Early Modern Philosophy*, edited by P. Easton, Toronto: University of Toronto Press.

Rorty, Richard. 1984. "The Historiography of Philosophy: Four Genres," in *Philosophy in History. Essays on the Historiography of Philosophy*, edited by R. Rorty, J. B. Schneewind, and Q. Skinner, Cambridge: Cambridge University Press, 49–76.

Rorty, Richard, J. B. Schneewind, and Quentin Skinner, eds. 1984. *Philosophy in History: Essays on the Historiography of Philosophy*, Cambridge: Cambridge University Press.

——. 1984. "Introduction," in *Philosophy in History. Essays on the Historiography of Philosophy*, Cambridge: Cambridge University Press, 1–14.

Roux, Sophie. Forthcoming. "Malebranche chez Locke. Les idées avec ou sans la vision en Dieu," in *Les Malebranchismes des Lumières*, edited by D. Kolesnik-Antoine, Paris: Honoré Champion.

Russell, Bertrand. 1910a. "The Monistic Theory of Truth," in *Philosophical Essays*, London: Longmans, Green, 150–69.

——. 1910b. "Some Explanations in Reply to Mr. Bradley," *Mind* 19, 373–78.

——. 1912. "The Philosophy of Bergson," *The Monist*, 22, 321–47.

——. 1914. "On Scientific Method in Philosophy," republished in electronic form, www.readbookonline.net/readOnLine/22894/.

——. 1918. "Mathematics and the Metaphysicians" in *Mysticism and Logic and Other Essays*, London: Longmans.

——. 1927. *An Outline of Philosophy*, London: George Allen and Unwin.

——. 1956a. "Logical Atomism," in *Logic and Knowledge*, edited by Robert C. Marsh, New York: George Allen and Unwin, 321–43.

——. 1956b. *My Philosophical Development*. London: George Allen and Unwin.

——. 1956c. "The Philosophy of Logical Atomism," in *Logic and Knowledge*, edited by Robert C. Marsh, New York: George Allen and Unwin, 175–281.

——. 1967. *The Problems of Philosophy* (1st ed. 1911). Oxford: Oxford University Press.

——1985. "The Philosophy of Logical Atomism," in *The Philosophy of Logical Atomism*, David Pears (ed.), La Salle: Open Court, pp. 35–155.

Ryle, Gilbert. 1949. *The Concept of Mind*, New York: Barnes and Noble.

Said, Edward W. 1978. *Orientalism*. New York: Vintage Books.

Salmon, Merrilee. 1982. *Philosophy and Archaeology*, New York: Academic Press.

Santinello Giovanni, ed. 1993. *Models of the History of Philosophy: From Its Origins in the Renaissance to the "historia philosophica,"* vol. 1, translated by C. Blackwell and P. Weller, Dordrecht: Kluwer.

Savan, David. 1986. "Spinoza: Scientist and Theorist of Scientific Method," in *Spinoza and the Sciences*, edited by M. Grene and D. Nails, Boston: D. Reidel, 95–123.

Schaffer, Jonathan. 2008. "Monism," in *Stanford Encyclopedia of Philosophy (Fall 2008 Edition)*, edited by E. Zalta, http://plato.stanford.edu/archives/fall2008/entries/monism.

——. 2010. "Monism: The Priority of the Whole," *Philosophical Review* 119, 31–76.

Schlick, Moritz. 1910. "Die Grenze der naturwissenschaftlichen und philosophischen Begriffsbildung," translated and reprinted in *Philosophical Papers*, vol. 1, edited by H. L. Mulder and B. F. B. van de Velde-Schlick, Dordrecht: Reidel, 1978, 25–40.

——. 1931. "The Future of Philosophy," reprinted in *Philosophical Papers*, vol. 2, edited by H. L. Mulder and B. F. B. van de Velde-Schlick, Dordrecht: Reidel, 1979, 210–24.

—— 1932. "Positivismus und Realismus," *Erkenntnis* 3, 1–31.

——. 1935. "Facts and Propositions," *Analysis* 2:5, 65–70.

——. 1936. "Meaning and Verification," *Philosophical Review* 45:4, 339–69.

—— 1959. "The Turning Point in Philosophy," translated by D. Rynin, in *Logical Positivism*, edited by A. J. Ayer, New York: Free Press, 82–107.

Schliesser, Eric. 2006. "Articulating Practices as Reasons: Adam Smith on the Social Conditions of Possibility of Property," *Adam Smith Review* 2, 69–97.

——. 2011a. "Newton's Challenge to Philosophy: A Programmatic Essay," *HOPOS: The Journal of the International Society for the History of Philosophy of Science*, 1:1, 101–28.

——. 2011b. "Four Species of Reflexivity and History of Economics in Economic Policy Science," *Journal of the Philosophy of History* 5, 425–44.

——. 2012a. "The Newtonian Refutation of Spinoza: Newton's Challenge and the Socratic Problem," in *Interpreting Newton*, edited by Andrew Janiak and Eric Schliesser, Cambridge: Cambridge University Press, 299–319.

——. 2012b. "Newton and Spinoza: On Motion and Matter (and God, of course)," *Southern Journal of Philosophy* 53, 436–58.

Schmidt, James. 1996. *What Is Enlightenment?* Berkeley: University of California Press.

Schönfeld, Martin. 2012. "Kant's Development." (March 30, 2012); <http://plato.stanford.edu/entries/kant-development/>.

Secada, J. E. K. 1986. "Review of *Philosophy in History*, edited by Richard Rorty, J. B. Schneewind, and Quentin Skinner," *Philosophy* 61, 409–14.

Schaffer, Simon. 2009. "Newton on the Beach: The Information Order of *Principia Mathematica*," *History of Science* 47:3, 243–76.

Schneider, Ulrich Johannes. 1992. "A Bibliography of Nineteenth-Century Histories of Philosophy in German, English, and French (1810–1899)," *Storia della storiografia* 21, 141–69.

——. 1993. "The Teaching of Philosophy at German Universities in the Nineteenth Century," in *History of Universities*, edited by L. Brockliss, Oxford: Oxford University Press, 197–338.

——. 2003. "'Historical Contributions to Philosophy' in the Nineteenth Century and the Shaping of a Discipline," *Rivista di storia della filosofia* 2, 231–46.

——. 2004. "Teaching the History of Philosophy in 19th-century Germany," in *Teaching New Histories of Philosophy*, edited by J. B. Schneewind, Princeton, NJ: University Center for Human Values, 275–95.

Semler, Johann Salomo. 1771–75. *Abhandlung von freier Untersuchung des Canon*, 4 parts, Halle: Hemmerde.

——. 1777. *Versuch einer freiern theologischen Lehrart*, Halle: Hemmerde.

——1779. *Beantwortung der Fragmente eines Ungenannten insbesondere vom Zweck Jesu und seiner Jünger*, Halle: Hemmerde.

Shank, Michael H. 1994. "Essay Review: Galileo's Day in Court," review of Mario Biagioli's *Galileo, Courtier: The Practice of Science in the Culture of Absolutism*, *Journal of the History of Astronomy* 25, 236–42.

——. 1996. "Shall We Practice History? The Case of Mario Biagioli's 'Galileo, Courtier,'" *Early Science and Medicine* 1, 106–50.

Shapin, Steven and Simon Schaffer. 1985. *Leviathan and the Air-Pump: Hobbes, Boyle, and the Experimental Life*, Princeton, NJ: Princeton University Press.

Shea, William. 1978. "Descartes as a Critic of Galileo," in *New Perspectives on Galileo*, edited by R. E. Butts and J. C. Pitt, Dordrecht: Reidel, 139–59.

Shein, Noa. 2009. "The False Dichotomy between Objective and Subjective Interpretations of Spinoza's Theory of Attributes," *British Journal for the History of Philosophy* 17:3, 505–32.

Sibum, Heinz Otto. 1995. "Reworking the Mechanical Value of Heat: Instruments of Precision and Gestures of Accuracy in Early Victorian England," *Studies in History and Philosophy of Science* 26:1, 73–106.

Sider, Theodore. 2001. *Four-Dimensionalism: An Ontology of Persistence and Time*, Oxford: Clarendon Press.

Silver, D. J. 1965. *Maimonides Criticism and the Maimonidean Controversy, 1180–1240*, Leiden: Brill.

Simon, Herbert A. 1954. "Bandwagon and Underdog Effects and the Possibility of Election Predictions," *Public Opinion Quarterly* 18, 245–53.

Singer, Isaac B. 1961. *The Spinoza of Market Street*, New York: Farrar, Straus and Cudahy.

Singer, Peter. 1974. "Sidgwick and Reflective Equilibrium," *The Monist* 58, 490–517.

Sinnot-Armstrong, Walter. 2007. "Overcoming Christianity," in *Philosophers without God*, edited by Louise M. Anthony, Oxford: Oxford University Press, 69–79.

Skinner, Quentin. 1969. "Meaning and Understanding in the History of Ideas," *History and Theory* 8:1, 3–53.

——. 1972. "Intentions and Interpretations of Texts," *New Literary History* 3:2, 393–408.

——. 1990. "Machiavelli's *Discorsi* and the Pre-Humanist Origins of Republican Ideas," in *Machiavelli and Republicanism*, edited by G. Bock, Q. Skinner, and M. Viroli, Cambridge: Cambridge University Press.

——2002. "Meaning and Understanding in the History of Ideas," in *Visions of Politics*, 3 vols., Cambridge: Cambridge University Press, 2002, vol. 1, 57–89.

——. 2011. "Quentin Skinner on Meaning and Method," in *The Art of Theory*, www .artoftheory.com/quentin-skinner-on-meaning-and-method.

Sleigh, Robert. 1990. *Leibniz and Arnauld*, New Haven. CT: Yale University Press.

Smith, Adam. (1976 [1981]). *An Inquiry into the Nature and Causes of the Wealth of Nations*, edited by R. H. Campbell and A. S. Skinner, Indianapolis: Liberty Fund.

Smith, Kurt and Alan Nelson. 2011. "Divisibility and Cartesian Extension," in *Oxford Studies in Early Modern Philosophy*, vol. 5, edited by D. Garber and S. Nadler, 1–24.

Smith, Norman Kemp. 1952. *New Studies in the Philosophy of Descartes: Descartes as Pioneer*, London: Macmillan.

Soames, Scott. 2003. *Philosophical Analysis in the Twentieth Century*, vol. 1: *The Dawn of Analysis:* vol. 2: *The Age of Meaning*, Princeton, NJ: Princeton University Press.

Sober, Elliott. 1991. *Reconstructing the Past: Parsimony, Evolution, and Inference*, Bradford.

——2009. *Core Questions in Philosophy*, 5th ed., New York: Prentice Hall.

Sorell, Tom. 2005a. "Introduction," in *Analytic Philosophy and History of Philosophy*, edited by T. Sorell, and G. A. J. Rogers, Oxford: Oxford University Press, 1–11.

——. 2005b. "On Saying No to History of Philosophy," in *Analytic Philosophy and History of Philosophy*, edited by T. Sorell and G. A. J. Rogers, Oxford: Oxford University Press, 43–59.

Sorensen, Roy. 2006. "Epistemic Paradoxes," in *Stanford Encyclopedia of Philosophy*, at, accessed July 23, 2011.

Spalding, Johann Joachim. 1764. *Berliner Antrittspredigt*, Berlin: Lange.

Spinoza, Benedictus. 1925. *Opera*. 4 vols., edited by C. Gebhardt, Heidelberg: Carl Winter.

——. 1895. *Opera*, 3 vols., edited by J. van Vloten and J. P. N. Land, Hague: Martinum Nijhoff.

——. 1985. *The Collected Works of Spinoza*, vol. 1, edited and translated by E. Curley, Princeton, NJ: Princeton University Press.

——. 1994. *Ethics*, in *A Spinoza Reader*, edited and translated by E. Curley, Princeton, NJ: Princeton University Press.

——. 1995. *The Letters*, translated by Samuel Shirley, Indianapolis: Hackett.

——. 1999. *Traité théologico-politique*, edited by F. Akkerman, translated by J. Lagrée and P.-F. Moreau, Paris: Presses universitaire de France.

——. 2002. *Complete Works*, translated by S. Shirley and edited by M. Morgan, Indianapolis: Hackett.

—— 2007. *Theological-Political Treatise*, translated by M. Silverthrone and J. Israel, Cambridge: Cambridge University Press.

Soros, George. 2009. *The Crash of 2008 and What It Means: The New Paradigm for Financial Markets*, rev. ed., New York: Public Affairs.

Sowaal, Alice. 2004. "Cartesian Bodies," *Canadian Journal of Philosophy*, 34, 217–40.

Sprat, Thomas. 1667. *The History of the Royal Society of London, for the Improving of Natural Knowledge*, London: J. Martyn.

Stone, Abraham. 2006. "Heidegger and Carnap on the Overcoming of Metaphysics," in *Martin Heidegger, International Library of Essays in the History of Social and Political Thought*, edited by S. Mulhall, London: Ashgate, 217–44.

Strauss, Leo. 1965. *Spinoza's Critique of Religion*, New York: Schocken Books (original German edition, 1930).

——. 1989. "Persecution and the Art of Writing," in *Persecution and the Art of Writing*, Chicago: University of Chicago Press, 22–37.

Strawson, Peter. 1966. *Bounds of Sense: An Essay on Kant's* Critique of Pure Reason, London: Metheun.

Stewart, Dugald. 1816. *Philosophical Essays*, Edinburgh: George Ramsay.

Stuever, Roger, ed. 1970. *Historical and Philosophical Perspectives of Science*, Minneapolis: University of Minnesota Press.

Suárez, Francisco. 1998. *Disputationes Metaphysicae*, 2 vols., Hildesheim: Olms Verlag.

Taube, Mortimer. 1937. "Positivism, Science, and History," *Journal of Philosophy* 34:8, 205–10.

Tarlton, Charles. 1973. "Historicity, Meaning, and Revisionism in the Study of Political Thought," *History and Theory* 12:3, 307–28.

Taylor, Charles. 1984. "Philosophy and Its History," in *Philosophy in History. Essays on the Historiography of Philosophy*, edited by R. Rorty, J. B. Schneewind, and Q. Skinner, Cambridge: Cambridge University Press, 17–30.

Thomas, Antoine Léonard. 1765. *Éloge de Descartes*, Paris: Regnard.

——.1802. *Œuvres complètes*, Paris: Desessarts.

Till, Dietmar. 2006. "Fröhlicher Positivismus. Ursula Goldenbaum über die Streitkultur in der deutschen Aufklärung." <http://www.literaturkritik.de/public/rezension.php?rez_id=9701&ausgabe=200608>.

Tollebeek, Jo and Tom Verschaffel. 1992. *De vreugden van Houssaye. Apologie van de historische interesse*, Amsterdam: Wereldbibliotheek.

Toulmin, Stephen. 1961. *Foresight and Understanding: An Enquiry into the Aims of Science*, Bloomington: Indiana University Press.

Tremblay, Marc-Adélard. 1991. "The Key Informant Technique: A Non-Ethnographic Application," in *Field Research: A Sourcebook and Field Manual*, edited by R. G. Burgess, New York: Routledge, 98–106.

Tully, James, ed. 1988. *Meaning and Context: Quentin Skinner and His Critics*, Cambridge: Polity Press.

Van Inwagen, Peter. 1995. *Material Beings*, Ithaca, NY: Cornell University Press.

——. 2009. *Metaphysics*, 3rd ed., Boulder, CO: Westview Press.

Vartanian, Aram. 1975. *Diderot and Descartes: A Study of Scientific Naturalism in the Enlightenment*, Westport, CT: Greenwood Press.

Vermeir, Koen. 2005. "The Magic of the Magic Lantern (1660–1700): On Analogical Demonstration and the Visualization of the Invisible," *British Journal for the History of Science* 38:2, 127–59.

Watkins, Eric. 1995. "The Development of Physicus-influxus in 18th Century Germany. Gottsched, Crusius, and Knutzen," *Review of Metaphysics* 49, 295–339.

——. 1998. "From Pre-established Harmony to Physical Influx: Leibniz's Reception in Eighteenth Century Germany," *Perspectives on Science* 6:1–2, 136–203.

Waugh, Joanne. 1991. "Heraclitus: The Postmodern Presocratic?" *The Monist* 74, 605–23.

Whipple, John. 2010. "The Structure of Leibnizian Simple Substances," *British Journal for the History of Philosophy* 18, 379–410.

White, Hayden. 1973. *Metahistory*, Baltimore: Johns Hopkins University Press.

——. 1978. *Tropics of Discourse. Essays in Cultural Criticism*, Baltimore: Johns Hopkins University Press.

Willey, Gordon R. and Philip Phillips. 1958. *Method and Theory in American Archaeology*, Chicago: University of Chicago Press.

Williams, Bernard. 2002. *Truth and Truthfulness. An Essay in Genealogy*. Princeton, NJ: Princeton University Press.

—— 2006, "Descartes and the Historiography of Philosophy," in *The Sense of the Past. Essays in the History of Philosophy*, edited by M. Burnyeat, Princeton, NJ: Princeton University Press, 257–64.

Williams, Thomas. 2008. "Some Reflections on Method in the History of Philosophy," http://shell.cas.usf.edu/~thomasw/Some%20reflections%20on%20method%20II.pdf.

Williamson, Timothy. 2007. *The Philosophy of Philosophy*. Oxford: Blackwell.

Wilson, Catherine. 1995. *The Invisible World: Early Modern Philosophy and the Invention of the Microscope*, Princeton, NJ: Princeton University Press.

—— 2005. "Is the History of Philosophy Good for Philosophy?" in *Analytic Philosophy and History of Philosophy*, edited by T. Sorell and G. A. J. Rogers, Oxford: Clarendon Press, 61–82.

Wilson, Margaret. 1992. "History of Philosophy in Philosophy Today; and the Case of the Sensible Qualities," *Philosophical Review* 101:1, 191–243.

—— 1999. "History of Philosophy in Philosophy Today; and the Case of the Sensible Qualities," in idem, *Ideas and Mechanism: Essays on Early Modern Philosophy*, Princeton, NJ: Princeton University Press, 455–512.

Wittgenstein, Ludwig. 1974. *Tractatus Logico-Philosophicus*, translated by B. McGuinness and D. Pears, London: Routledge.

Wolf, Friedrich August. 1807. *Darstellung der Alterthums-Wissenschaft*, Berlin.

Wolfson, Harry Austryn. 1934. *The Philosophy of Spinoza*, 2 vols., Cambridge. MA: Harvard University Press.

Woodward, James. 2008. "Causation and Manipulability," in *Stanford Encyclopedia of Philosophy* edited by E. Zalta, http://plato.stanford.edu/entries/causation-mani.

Worrall, John. 1989. "Structural Realism: The Best of Both Worlds?" in *The Philosophy of Science*, edited by D. Papineau, Oxford: Oxford University Press, 139–65.

Wylie, Alison. 2002. *Thinking from Things: Essays in the Philosophy of Archaeology*, Berkeley: University of California Press.

Young, Robert M. 1990. "Marxism and the History of Science," in *Companion to the History of Modern Science*, edited by R. C. Olby, G. N. Cantor, J. R. R. Christie, and M. J. S. Hodge, London: Routledge, 77–86.

Zammito, John H. 2004. *A Nice Derangement of Epistemes: Post-Positivism in the Study of Science from Quine to Latour*, Chicago: University of Chicago Press.

Zarka, Yves Charles. 2005. "The Ideology of Context: Uses and Abuses of Context in the Historiography of Philosophy," in *Analytic Philosophy and History of Philosophy*, edited by T. Sorell and G. A. J. Rogers, Oxford: Clarendon Press, 147–59.

Zumthor, Paul. 1990. *Oral Poetry*, translated by K. Murphy-Judy, Minneapolis: University of Minnesota Press.

Index Nominum

Index Rerum